Data Modeling

Theory and Practice

Graeme Simsion

Technics Publications, LLC
New Jersey

Published by:

Technics Publications, LLC

Post Office Box 161

Bradley Beach, NJ 07720 U.S.A.

Orders@technicspub.com

www.technicspub.com

Edited by G.C. Simsion & Associates

Cover design by Mark Brye

Layout by Owen Genat

The publisher offers discounts on this book when ordered in quantity for special sales. For more information, please contact:

Technics Publications Corporate Sales Division

Post Office Box 161

Bradley Beach, NJ 07720 U.S.A.

CorporateSales@technicspub.com

This book is printed on acid-free paper.

ISBN, print ed.   978-0-9771400-1-5

First Printing 2007

Printed in the United States of America

Library of Congress Control Number: 2007900370

Forget your perfect offering
There is a crack in everything
That's how the light gets in.

Leonard Cohen, *Anthem*

Table of Contents

PREFACE

"... there are indeed wide differences between the academic and practitioner focus in conceptual data modeling"

– Batra and Marakas (1995)

First, a warning: this is not an introductory text. Readers looking for an explanation of data modeling conventions, basic principles of data structure, and the data modeling process will be better served by one of the many "how to" books on the market, including my own *Data Modeling Essentials*, or by the overviews of data modeling in most database texts.

My goal here is to move beyond a bland statement of the rules to address some of the most important issues about employing them in practice. I have two audiences in mind:

1. The academic community, who are accustomed to studying the subject from the outside, but often at *too* great a remove from practice

2. Practitioners who require a deeper understanding of their discipline and a theoretical framework to organize and make sense of their knowledge and experience.

It should be apparent from my characterization of the two audiences that each should be well-placed to address the other's needs. Unfortunately in the three decades since Ted Codd's academic work provided the basic principles for data organization in practice, and Bill Kent's practice-inspired *Data and Reality* was required reading for researchers, the two communities have diverged to the extent that they now operate virtually independently.

Even a cursory comparison of current academic and practitioner publications[1] shows that the two communities are occupied with different issues, and refer only occasionally to work outside their own group. Conferences also reflect the culture of one group or the other, despite some attempts at inclusiveness. The occasional practitioner who visits an academic conference out of curiosity seldom repeats the

---

[1] Academic directions are evident in refereed journal articles and published research agendas (e.g. Wand and Weber 2002). Practitioner interests can be identified from publications such as *The Data Administration Newsletter* - www.tdan.com - as well as discussion groups such as DM-Discuss - http://tech.groups.yahoo.com/group/dm-discuss/.

mistake, and academics may struggle to find financial support and recognition for attendance at practitioner conferences.

Even when the academic and practitioner communities have addressed the same topics, the lack of communication and influence is apparent:

Academics have given a great deal of attention to inventing and testing data modeling languages, to the extent that the derisory acronym YAMA ("yet another modeling approach") was coined. Yet for many years the practitioner community stuck with a simple notation that owed more to the data structure diagrams of the late 1960s than to Chen's Entity-Relationship approach (despite their appropriation of the label) or to any of the later innovations. When change finally came, it was to the Unified Modeling Language (UML), an assemblage of techniques with no real theoretical foundation.

Researchers have conducted numerous studies of human factors in data modeling, but have overwhelmingly taken the easy option of using students as their research subjects. As a result we know a great deal about the behavior of *novice* data modelers – and just enough about experts (who, we might assume, are the people who lead real-world data modeling efforts) to know that they behave differently from novices.

Both communities have proposed data modeling methods and associated terminology. Predictably the academic methods suffer from lack of validation in practice, and the practitioner methods sometimes lack the consistency and insights that a more formal foundation could provide. Serious differences in the use of common terms bear witness to the insularity of the communities – and will need to be overcome if any real communication is to take place.

As the title *Theory and Practice* implies, this book aims to present a picture of data modeling that combines academic rigor with practical relevance, and to place that picture in the context of the literature from both communities. It reports the results of a four-year research project in the Department of Information Systems at the University of Melbourne, conducted with the level of rigor appropriate to academic research. The object of the study, however, was practice and practitioners. I was interested in the views and behavior of experienced data modelers and their impact on the quality of databases developed for real-world applications.

The academic role was not entirely new to me, as I had been involved with universities since the 1980s, teaching data modeling at undergraduate and postgraduate level, and publishing a few journal articles and academic conference papers, but my background is primarily as a practitioner and teacher of practitioners. That background drove both the direction and the design of my research.

Academic research generally explores a single specialized topic in depth. In the interests of illuminating a wider area, I deliberately framed a research question that touched on most of the important issues in the discipline. The research covered *inter alia* the definition of data modeling, its philosophical underpinnings, inputs and deliverables, the necessary behaviors and skills, the opportunity for creativity, product diversity, quality measures, personal styles, and the differences between experts and novices.

The value to the academic reader should be apparent. By accessing nearly five hundred practitioners through interviews, surveys and laboratory studies, the results provide a picture of practice that has heretofore been missing, or at least unsubstantiated by convincing evidence. The work includes many results of direct relevance to current research work in data modeling, and challenges a number of widely-held assumptions.

For practitioners, the book offers a window into the great body of academic research, focusing on that of most relevance to current practice. I have deliberately included extensive references, Harvard style, recognizing that they may be at first an annoyance to readers unused to academic literature, in the interests of encouraging familiarity with the style and with relevant research. I have also described my methods in more detail than would be usual in a journal article, making explicit some practices that would be assumed by academic readers. In more immediate practical terms, I found that the research has delivered insights that have been directly relevant to answering many of the most difficult questions that arise in practice.

The book does not need to read in sequence, although it makes sense to start with the Introduction in Part I. Part II is essentially a review of the academic literature plus a series of interviews with practitioner thought-leaders. Either makes a suitable starting point for understanding the key issues and the different positions. Part III can be seen as six separate papers within a common framework (described in the Research Design chapter). They can be read independently. Part IV summarizes the findings, with references to the relevant discussions in the body of the book. Readers may like to start here and follow up the results of most interest.

ACKNOWLEDGMENTS

This book began as a PhD dissertation[2], and my greatest debt is thus to my principal supervisor, Dr. Simon Milton of the University of Melbourne, and associate supervisor Professor Graeme Shanks of Monash University. The research question was seeded by an insightful observation by my colleague Hu Schroor in the 1980s, and the desire to earn a PhD by a casual comment from my father in the 1960s.

Professor Anne Buist, Dr. Jennie Carroll, Associate Professor Peter Seddon, and Professor Liz Sonenberg also offered valuable input and support, and I appreciated the insightful and detailed comments provided by the two thesis examiners[3] Professor Michael Rosemann of Queensland University of Technology in Australia, and Professor Bernhard Thalheim of Christian-Albrechts University, Kiel, Germany. Paul Gruba, Terry Halpin, Rod Miller, and Rens Scheepers might be surprised at the impact of their wise words and encouragement at crucial junctures.

Enes Drinjak, Cathie Lange, and (in particular) Jasmina Nuredini helped to code, organize and present the large volume of data that this project generated. Owen Genat assisted with layout of the original thesis, and of the final manuscript.

Publishers are traditionally wary of academic dissertations. Steve Hoberman, an expert in data modeling, but relatively new to the publishing business, stepped forward and managed a no-fuss process that many more-established publishers could learn from.

The practitioner thought-leaders, whose names appear in Chapter 6 and the expert data model reviewers (John Alexander, Glen Bell, Glenn Cogar, Eva Gardyn, Dagna Gaythorpe, John Giles, Michael Gorman, Dave Hay, Steve Hoberman, Corine Jansonius, Mark Kortink, Karen Lopez, Colin Reilly, Hu Schroor, Alec Sharp, Len Silverston, Anne Tillig, Chris Waddell, and David Wiebe), whose role is described in Chapter 11, not only made a valuable direct contribution, but continued to correspond, contribute, and challenge. Their sometimes passionate engagement reassured me that the work was worth pursuing.

---

[2] Readers may be relieved to know that I have removed 24 appendices and a large chunk of the Research Design chapter, as well as some detailed demographics in Part III.

[3] The examiners made their identity known to me after the examination process was complete.

The officers of the Data Management Association (DAMA), Tony Shaw of Wilshire Conferences, and Eskil Swende and Jeremy Hall of IRM provided me with the access to practitioners that was central to the research.

Finally, I would like to acknowledge the many practitioners who participated in the interviews, surveys, and laboratory studies, and in piloting and seminar discussions. This book rests on their contribution.

PART I – INTRODUCTION

CHAPTER 1
INTRODUCTION

Begin anywhere.

– John Cage

1.1. THE STARTING POINT

This book looks at some of the most fundamental issues in data modeling and logical database design, from both theoretical and practical perspectives. It takes as its starting point and theme a specific question about the nature of data modeling: Is data modeling better characterized as:

(a)   a *descriptive* activity, the objective of which is to document some aspect of the real world *or*

(b)   a *design* activity, the objective of which is to create data structures to meet a set of requirements?[4]

To address what might appear at first to be a quite narrow (and even obscure) question, it transpires that we need to explore a substantial part of the data modeling and database design landscape including questions likely to be of interest to any researcher or practitioner in these fields. We ask, for example:

---

[4] The question is presented as a choice of mutually exclusive characterizations. At this early point, it might appear that "neither" and "both" would also be possible answers. We develop the argument that the two characterizations are opposed (hence disposing of the "both" option), and that the dichotomy is relevant to data modeling (disposing of the "neither" option) in this chapter and in Chapter 2. In using the term *better characterized*, we recognize that data modeling may not conform exactly to either extreme position.

How do practitioners and researchers define data modeling and its stages?

What are the boundaries between data modeling and other activities in database design?

Will different modelers produce different models in response to a common specification?

Will expert data modelers agree on the relative quality of different solutions to a common modeling problem?

Is there a role for creativity in data modeling?

Do data modelers work from "first principles" or draw on past models?

Do experienced data modelers perceive the data modeling process in a different way to novice data modelers?

What formalisms do data modeling practitioners choose to use?

Do data modelers exhibit personal styles?

In tackling these and other questions, we draw on the substantial body of academic and practitioner literature in the field, as well as purpose-designed interviews, surveys and laboratory tasks involving some 489 participants, predominantly data modeling practitioners[5] from North America, the United Kingdom, Scandinavia, and Australia. This number compares with a total of 26 practitioner[6] participants across the 27 studies listed in the most recently-published and comprehensive survey of empirical research in data modeling (Topi and Ramesh 2002), and the 147 practitioner participants in the 59 studies covered by the more inclusive review in Chapter 5.

The result is a revealing picture of how data modeling practitioners behave and think, set in the context of theory as espoused by both the academic community and practitioner thought-leaders. The findings challenge a number of established beliefs and assumptions about data modeling, and provide a strong case for reconsidering important aspects of research, teaching, and practice.

---

[5] The term embraces a range of roles involving data modeling. A summary of the principal occupations provided by the participants appears in Chapter 7, Section 7.6.

[6] A rule of 12 months industry experience was used as the qualification for "practitioner".

1.2. CONFLICTING VIEWS

The description / design issue that provides the unifying theme for this book pervades the data modeling literature. A small amount of research directly addresses the distinction, or some aspect of it. A much larger body of work embodies an explicit or implicit alignment with one or other position.

Direct examination of alternative views of modeling has largely been within a philosophical framework, focusing on the impact of different philosophical positions. Wand and Weber (2002) note the longstanding debate between *positivists* and *interpretivists*, with the latter group arguing that the phenomena to be modeled are created rather than discovered. Klein and Hirscheim (1987) contrast *objectivist* and *subjectivist* positions: "The difference is whether one believes that a data model 'reflects' reality or consists of subjective meanings and thereby constructs reality." Lyytinen (1987) draws a distinction between *reality mapping* in which "all entities … are assumed to exist in the sense of naive realism" and *formal language development* in which "rules are formulated, developed, and adopted" and notes that "the literature in information modeling does not discuss much these beliefs and they have not been exposed clearly".

In the broader data modeling literature, Veryard (1984, p1) points out that even if the existence of an objective reality is accepted, *semantic absolutists* will argue there is only one correct or ideal way of modeling it, whereas *semantic relativists* believe that most things in the real world can be modeled in many different ways. Atkins (1997) classifies data modeling definitions according the objectivist / subjectivist dichotomy, whether the focus is on modeling *reality* or *data*, and whether the purpose is *infological* (stakeholder communication) or *datalogical* (database specification), and also notes that data modeling may be characterized as either *analysis* or *design*.

Explicit comparisons of the kind described above are the exception rather than the rule. Some authors acknowledge alternative characterizations of modeling and declare a position that aligns more closely with either description or design, usually without providing reasons for their choice. For example, Olle *et al.* (1991) distinguish between *analysis*[7] activities (which they characterize as descriptive) and *design* activities. Within this framework, they classify data modeling as

---

[7] A number of publications in this area have used the word *analysis* rather than *description* as the opposite of *design*; the reasons for preferring *description* are discussed in Section 2.1.

analysis. Chaiyasut and Shanks (1994) recognize the same distinction but take the opposite view: "The process of conceptual data modeling is sometimes seen as an analytical, descriptive task", but it "is better viewed as a design activity where the data modeler is an active participant in the modeling process and adds value to the quality of the model." Some writers frame the distinction as one of *art* versus *science*, usually in the context of asserting that data modeling is more art than science (Storey, Thompson et al. 1995; Avison and Fitzgerald 2003 p177).

Other authors simply state a position without acknowledging any alternative. The descriptive characterization is most common:

> *[a data model is]* "*a precise and unambiguous representation of organizational information requirements.*"
>
> (Kim and March 1995)

> "*Conceptual modeling (or semantic modeling) focuses on capturing and representing certain aspects of human perceptions of the real world.*"
>
> (Wand, Storey et al. 1999)

> "*The main challenge is to describe the UoD [universe of discourse] clearly and precisely*"
>
> (Halpin 2001 p6)

> "*The objective ... is an accurate representation of reality*"
>
> (Teorey, Lightstone et al. 2006)

Conversely, De Carteret and Vidgen (1995 p334) present data modeling as a creative activity in which a modeler "often needs to dream up several different possibilities". In describing an expert system for supporting data modeling, Parent (1997) says "it is hoped that the results of this study may generalize to other *design* applications…" (emphasis added). Bubenko (1986), writing about data modeling says: "We should realize that design will always have an artistic component and that not everything can be prescribed."

The practitioner literature exhibits a similar diversity of views. Fowler (1999 pp40-41) writes:

> "*We try to abstract… yet such abstractions are constructed… Can we, should we be passive describers when we analyze? And if we are not, are we really doing design rather than analysis?*"

Hay (2003 pp xxxii-xxxiii) cites this passage and defends the descriptive view:

"In my view this is wrong... The [data] analyst will indeed construct artifacts, but the purpose of the artifacts is to describe the fundamental structures and concepts behind the world that the business sees."

In introducing his book with a challenge to the design position, Hay makes it clear that he perceives the design / description issue as being of some importance to practice[8].

Finally, much of the data modeling literature, including most empirical work[9], assumes either the design or (more often) the description characterization, without explicitly declaring it. As discussed in the following section, such undeclared assumptions, if not valid, may compromise the conclusions drawn from the research.

1.3. IMPORTANCE OF THE DISTINCTION

A characterization of data modeling that properly reflects the nature of the task is fundamental to performing it well in practice, teaching it effectively, and designing research (Simsion 1991).

Description and design differ in important ways (Lawson 1997 pp113-127). For example, design disciplines involve different processes from those appropriate for description, require different skills and teaching strategies, and acknowledge multiple solutions to the same problem. Each of these differences, in particular the last, is relevant in the context of data modeling, as outlined below.

1.3.1. Different processes

Description and design require different methods, techniques, tools, and behavior. Unlike designers, analysts need to behave as if there is an objective reality awaiting their discovery and their task is to uncover this pre-existing information (Atkins 1997). Data modeling tools generally support "uncovering information" and would require different facilities to fully support a design process (Shanks and Simsion 1992; Crerar, Barclay et al. 1996). Similarly, the development of heuristics for data modeling (Batra and Zanakis 1994) and expert systems for

---

[8] Hay also challenges the design argument in Hay (1996b).

[9] Chapter 5 includes a summary of empirical data modeling research, identifying work that reflects the descriptive characterization – in particular the assumption of a single correct model.

database design (Tauzovich 1990; Bouzeghoub 1992; Storey, Dey et al. 1998) requires an understanding of the nature of the data modeling task.

1.3.2. Skills and learning

Design activities require distinct skills – and arguably certain personal characteristics. In particular, creativity has a central role in design. This has implications for the selection and training of data modelers, a subject that has received some attention in the literature (Glass and Vessey 1994; Storey, Thompson et al. 1995; Yang 2003). Wand and Weber's (2002) research agenda includes "predicting which cognitive and personality variables bear on a user's ability to undertake conceptual modeling work".

Data modeling is notoriously difficult to learn and teach (Mantha 1987; Pletch 1989; Goldstein and Storey 1990; Hitchman 1995; Atkins 1996; Tansley 2003; Batra and Wishart 2004). A possible explanation is that data modeling is a design discipline that is being taught as description. Data modeling texts almost invariably support a descriptive view by limiting any discussion of choice in data modeling to choice of construct (e.g. whether to represent a real-word concept as an attribute or an entity), and providing only one solution to data modeling problems. Despite its importance, anecdotal and research evidence is that data modeling is not done well, and there have been calls to develop better training and education (Wand and Weber 2002). Understanding the nature of the subject being taught would appear fundamental to achieving this.

1.3.3. Multiple solutions

In design, there is no "single right answer", nor an algorithm for producing the best answer. Parsons and Wand (2000), comment that "an interesting consequence [of classification theory as applied to data modeling] (is that) … different class structures can be used to model precisely the same domain of instances and properties." The word *interesting* highlights the fact that this view is not universally accepted, and leaves open the question as to whether different models might be produced in practice. Reproducibility of results in systems development is a highly contentious area, and difficult to test (Avison and Fitzgerald 2003 pp534-535).

The possibility of there being multiple valid data models for the same real-world problem has important consequences:

(a) Where more than one solution is possible, quality criteria are required to enable alternative designs to be evaluated and compared. The growing body of work on data model quality demonstrates the impact of the two different characterizations of data modeling. Approaches that reflect the descriptive characterization focus on measures of syntactic "correctness" and semantic "completeness" (e.g. Kim and March 1995). Approaches that reflect the design characterization include relative measures instead of or as well as absolute measures, acknowledge subjectivity in assessment, and discuss the possibility of trade-offs amongst the criteria (e.g. Moody and Shanks 2003; Simsion 2005a).

(b) Most research in which subjects are required to develop data models relies on comparison with a *gold standard* or benchmark solution – a single correct solution produced in advance by the researcher (Atkins and Patrick 1996; Topi and Ramesh 2002). This approach strongly suggests an underlying belief that data modeling is descriptive. If this characterization is incorrect, the research results need to be reconsidered in that light.

(c) Data modeling has been advocated as a technique for software package selection. In one approach, a model of the organization's data requirements is developed, then compared with the model used by candidate packages (Hay 2003 p17); in another, a common model is synthesized from the different vendor models (Gorman 2000). If the vendors' models represent different *designs*, then the first approach could result in the rejection of packages that meet business requirements but in an unanticipated way, and the second might not be feasible if the designs are too different to be reconciled.

The above examples are framed largely as problems that might arise if data modeling was generally considered to be description, but was better characterized as design. It should be evident that mis-characterization at such a fundamental level would affect many aspects of the discipline beyond these.

1.3.4. Are these problems real?

This book, and the research that it describes, was motivated by my observations of data modeling practice and discussions with practitioners, teachers, and researchers over a period of twenty-five years, leading to a view that articulation and resolution of the description / design question was of fundamental importance to data modeling research, teaching, and practice.

Specific observations included:

(a)   Explicit arguments, amongst both academics and practitioners, as to whether the description or design paradigm was correct. Interviews undertaken in the early stages of this research (Chapter 4) established that the differences in beliefs were substantial and perceived as important.

(b)   Clashes[10] between data modeling practitioners who subscribed to the descriptive paradigm, but had produced different models that were difficult to reconcile.

(c)   Disagreement over the appropriateness of data modelers introducing new concepts and terminology rather than simply documenting an established view of business entities.

(d)   Difficulty in teaching data modeling using texts and teaching materials which treated it as a descriptive process.

(e)   Experienced data modeling practitioners struggling to develop models, and observing that data modeling in practice was much more difficult than it should be, if it was essentially concerned with describing data requirements.

(f)   Antipathy towards data modelers, who were frequently seen as pursuing an ideal description of reality rather than contributing in the most productive way to an information systems design.

(g)   A developing personal view that data modeling was a design discipline, based on reflections on the mental processes involved in producing data models.

Some time ago, I suggested in a conference paper that data modeling was a creative discipline (Simsion 1991), and that there was value in deliberately encouraging the development of innovative and novel data models. That paper, and subsequent publications and presentations in both academic and practitioner

---

[10] The word "clashes" is used deliberately. Arguments about which of two or more models was correct frequently became passionate and political in the absence of an objective basis for resolution.

10

forums (in particular, Simsion 1996; 2005c), have stimulated much debate, but have also highlighted a lack of empirical data beyond the anecdotal.

1.3.5. How much does it matter?

The issues discussed above need to be seen in the context of the importance of data modeling in information systems development. It has a major impact on the ultimate quality of the system because:

(a) It is performed relatively early in the development process, at least prior to construction (Avison and Fitzgerald 2003 pp73-75). It has long been accepted that effort devoted to producing high quality requirements and designs will pay off many times over in lower construction costs – in particular the costs of correcting errors (Boehm 1981; Deming 1986)

(b) The structure of a database, as specified by a data model, has a profound effect on the structure of the application(s) that it supports. In "data centric" applications at least, program structure reflects data structure (Jackson 1975; Simsion and Witt 2005 pp8-9). Strategic breakthroughs in systems design may more often come from redesigning the data rather than through innovative programming (Brooks 1995)

Data structures are expensive to change (even during program development) because of the impact on the programs that use them (Marche 1993; Wedemeijer 2002). In short, effort devoted to producing a high-quality data model – and understanding what is required to do so – is likely to be well spent.

1.4. CLARIFYING THE QUESTION

In this section we discuss the framing of the description / design question, including terminology and scope, and introduce a framework for addressing it.

1.4.1. Framing the question

As noted earlier, contrasting views of data modeling can be framed in terms of several different dichotomies (objectivism-subjectivism, absolutism-relativism, analysis-design, art-science, etc). Although each offers a different perspective, they have some common practical implications, such as whether there is a "single correct model".

The decision to look at data modeling in terms of *design* versus *description* was the result of three key considerations:

1. The explicit or implicit appearance of the distinction across the academic and practitioner literature.

2. Connection to practice. The concepts of description and design are familiar to information systems practitioners. A formulation in terms of philosophical concepts would have built on some more-considered work in the data modeling literature, but the issues and results would have been less accessible to practitioners and academics without a background in philosophy.

3. The availability of cross-disciplinary literature on design, much of it drawing on examples from architecture and engineering. These two disciplines are frequently used as metaphors for data modeling (Section 1.4.3).

Given the level of disagreement (and in many cases lack of clarity) in both the academic and practitioner literature, it was not expected that a simple, one-dimensional answer would emerge – rather that there might be differences between theory, espoused practice, actual practice, and perceptions, and amongst individual practitioners, and for different stages of the data modeling process. I have sought to describe such differences, to contribute not only to the understanding of what data modeling is or should be, but of problems that may originate from a lack of a common view.

1.4.2. Terminology and scope

The following usages and definitions are relevant to the description / design question. Their provenance and reasons for their choice are discussed in Chapter 2 and Chapter 3.

1. In the data modeling literature, the term *data model* is used in two quite different ways, sometimes within the same publication[11] (Marcos and Marcos 2001). The first use refers to a data modeling formalism (language, set of conventions): e.g. the Relational Data Model, the

---

[11] For example, Connolly and Begg (2005 p43) provides a formal definition using the first sense, but uses the second sense in the sentences immediately preceding and following the definition.

Entity-Relationship Model, or the Object-Role Model. This use is common in the academic literature, but not in practitioner publications. The second use refers to a model applicable to a particular *universe of discourse* (UoD) (e.g. "the data model for the finance application", "a conceptual data model"). This book uses the convention suggested by Loosely & Gane (1990): the first meaning is indicated by the use of capitals (upper case), hence *Data Model*, the second by lower case (*data model*). The terms *(data) modeling language, (data) modeling formalism* and *(data) modeling conventions* are used as synonyms for *Data Model*.

2.   We use *data modeling* to refer to the set of activities required to specify a conceptual schema prior to any modifications made to achieve performance goals. The term *specify* acknowledges that the resulting data model need not be in the form of a final DBMS-specific conceptual schema, *provided it can be mechanically*[12] *translated into a conceptual schema.* The definition embraces many (but not all) definitions of *conceptual data modeling.*[13] The caveat on performance tuning reflects the common practice of deferring such changes to a later stage and regarding them as compromises from the data model rather than as changes to it. This definition is shown to be consistent with practitioner perceptions in Chapter 8.

We note here that *conceptual schema* and *conceptual (data) model* have different meanings and that the distinction is important in this book. The former term is little used by practitioners[14], but has the advantage of a standard definition (ISO/TR9007:1987(E) 1987). It refers to a component of the completed database. In a relational database context, it is broadly equivalent to *database (base*[15]*) tables* In contrast, a conceptual data model is an input to the conceptual schema specification,

---

[12] "Mechanically" implies an algorithm that may contain knowledge of the target DBMS.

[13] As we discuss in Chapter 2, Sections 3.4 and 3.6, the key issue is whether the conceptual model can be transformed mechanically into a conceptual schema. Descriptions of data modeling frequently divide it into *conceptual data modeling*, *logical data modeling* and (sometimes) *physical data modeling*. The latter two phases *may* be characterized as mechanical and / or purely performance-oriented – and that characterization may or may not be justified.

[14] A practitioner using a relational DBMS would capture the broad idea with the term *base tables*.

[15] *Base* as distinct from the derived tables – views – of the external schema.

and is (at least in the academic literature) usually documented using a different formalism from that used for the conceptual schema (Palvia, Liao et al. 1992).

Alternative definitions of *data modeling (*and the distinctions between *conceptual, logical, and physical data modeling)* are central to the description / design question, and are explored Chapter 3 and Chapter 8.

The words *entity, attribute*, and *relationship* are treated as synonymous with *entity type, attribute type,* and *relationship type* respectively, in keeping with common practice (Teorey, Lightstone et al. 2006 p13). If it is necessary to refer to a single instance, the word *instance* is added e.g. *entity instance*.

When referring to relational data models (or the Relational Model itself), the SQL terms *table, row* and *column* (ISO/IEC9075-1:2003 2003) are preferred to *relation* or *relvar*, *tuple,* and *attribute* (Codd 1970; Date 1998), both to reflect practice and to avoid confusion with the use of *attribute* in the Entity-Relationship Model (Chen 1976).

In direct quotations from the literature that do not follow these conventions, the quotation has not been changed, but a note has been added where necessary to avoid ambiguity.

Definitions of *design* and the use of *description* as its antithesis are discussed in Section 2.2. Broadly:

> *Design* is the key concept (*ideal type*) against which data modeling is measured in this research, and in Chapter 2 (Section 2.2) we look at descriptions from the specialist literature on design. These generally accord with non-specialist usage. Buchanan's (1990) definition of design as *the conception and planning of the artificial* is representative. This is the sense in which the term is used throughout this book, and in the description / design question in particular. By contrast, in the information systems field, *design* is frequently used to denote a broad stage in information systems development, regardless of its nature.

> *Description* is used largely in a negative role – it answers the question "if data modeling is not design, what is it?" The term is common in definitions of data modeling and the resulting dichotomy is consistent with those in the design literature (Section 2.2).

By defining the ultimate outcome of data modeling as a conceptual schema, we have also excluded from direct consideration the use of data models for purposes other than designing databases, in particular to support information systems strategy and planning (Zachman 1987; Lederer and Sethi 1988; Sager 1988; Martin 1989; Olle, Hagelstein et al. 1991; Goodhue, Kirsch et al. 1992; Adelman, Moss et al. 2005), information resource management (Kahn 1983; Friedlander 1985; Goodhue, Quillard et al. 1988; March 1992; Moody and Simsion 1995; DAMA-International 2002), data integration (Brancheau and Wetherbe 1986; Scheer and Hars 1992; Kim and Everest 1994; Shanks and Darke 1999; Persson and Stirna 2001), package selection (Hay 2003 p47; Shanks, Tansley et al. 2003; Hoberman 2005 p12), understanding organizations and business areas (Rob and Coronel 2002 p110; Avison and Fitzgerald 2003 p76; Hoberman 2005 p11), project estimation (Bhagwat 2003), and reverse engineering to document existing databases (Kalman 1991; Hall 1992; Aiken, Muntz et al. 1994; Premerlani and Blaha 1994; Wedemeijer 2002). Each of these represents a different use of data modeling, with significantly different objectives, and (in the cases of systems planning, information resource management, integration, and reverse engineering) its own literature. Reverse engineering clearly falls within the "descriptive" paradigm (Chikofsky and Cross 1990; Andersson 1994; Aiken 1995; Chiang, Barron et al. 1997)– and indeed serves as a convenient illustration of it.

We also confine our investigation data modeling for conventional, record-based databases, in particular databases to be built using relational or object-relational database management systems (*DBMSs*), which are dominant in industry (Date 1998 p26). Data models intended for implementation using other software, such as object-oriented or cadastral DBMSs are excluded, not because of any belief that the description / design issue should be fundamentally different in these cases, but because reviewing the separate literature and incorporating the additional features, terminology, methods, and beliefs (as well as accessing practitioners to participate in the research) would have added substantially to the complexity of the book with little prospect of commensurate additional insight.

1.4.3. A framework for addressing the description / design question

This section draws on ideas from design theory and the closely-related field of creativity to synthesize a framework for refining and addressing the description / design question. The framework divides the description / design question into five dimensions, facilitating the formulation of sub-questions and identification of relevant literature.

There has been a growing interest in design as a generic discipline since the late 1970s (Archer 1979). Of particular interest is research centered on architecture or engineering, as these have a history of use as reference disciplines for data modeling (Finkelstein and Martin 1981; Zachman 1987; Marche 1991; Martin 1991; Hoberman 2002 p19) and information systems development (Lee 1991a; McDermid 1991 pp83-106; Avison and Fitzgerald 2003 pp83-106, 395-407) of which data modeling is a part.

Lawson (1997 pp121-127) synthesized from the design literature a list of "some of the important characteristics of design problems and solutions, and … the design process itself." (Lawson's characteristics of design are frequently referred to in this book. We provide a reference only for the first mention in each chapter.) These characteristics are intended not only to describe design, but to differentiate it from description: "The designer has a prescriptive rather than descriptive job" (Lawson 1997 p113). Although the characteristics – and the work as a whole – are intended to apply to all design disciplines (Lawson 1997 pp3-12), the reference discipline is architecture, which, as already noted, is widely used as a metaphor for data modeling. Lawson provides a discussion of each of the characteristics, frequently stating how it serves to differentiate design from description. He acknowledges that the list is not exhaustive, and that the characteristics are interrelated. Collectively, however, "they sketch an overall picture of the nature of design as it seems today" (Lawson 1997 p121). The characteristics are divided into three groups or dimensions – *Problem*, *Solution*, and *Process* – and could serve as a high-level framework for investigating the properties of data modeling.

There are alternative frameworks. Research work on the psychology of design and (in particular) creativity is often classified according to whether it addresses the *Person or Group*, the *Process*, the *Product*, or the *Environment* (Rhodes 1961). This grouping is sometimes known as the *4Ps* framework (using the word *Press* instead of *Environment*). The framework has been used for information systems research (Couger and Dengate 1992; Fellers and Bostrom 1993).

The 4Ps framework aligns reasonably well with data modeling research which often focuses on one of the dimensions – for example *Process* (data modeling stages and deliverables) or *People* (comparisons of novice and expert data modelers). The *Environment* and *People* dimensions take us beyond the problem-process-solution focus of Lawson's framework, and suggest examination of the technical, cultural, and human context in which data modeling and data modeling research take place. These could include the place of data modeling in the database design process, languages and tools, and beliefs of practitioners and researchers.

Magyari-Beck (1990) proposes an alternative creativity framework. This is presented as a matrix with columns for *Ability, Process,* and *Product* and rows covering *Organization, Group,* and *Person* – similar to the *Person or Group* dimension in the 4Ps framework. In adapting it for IS research, Couger (1996), renames the first column *Characteristics* (of the problem), resulting in a set of columns very similar to Lawson's framework.

Given Lawson's inclusion of a number of characteristics under *Problem,* and the presence of a similar column in the modified Magyari-Beck matrix, it makes sense to extend the basic 4Ps framework to include *Problem.* The resulting *5Ps* framework (*Environment* [*Press*], *Problem, Process, Product, Person*) thus synthesizes the perspectives of three existing frameworks, and enables us to incorporate all of Lawson's properties, with the minor adjustment of using *Product* in place of *Solution.* While referring to the framework as *5Ps,* we follow common practice in the literature and use the term *Environment* rather than *Press.*

1.4.4. Refining the question

The 5Ps framework introduced in the previous subsection allows us to address the description / design question from five perspectives: *Environment, Problem, Person, Process,* and *Product,* which in turn provide headings for a set of sub-questions. (The derivation of these sub-questions from the description / design question, the literature, and interviews with practitioner thought-leaders is discussed in Sections 4.5 and 7.2). The emphasis on data modeling practice should be apparent.

Environment

Is the description / design question considered important by data modeling practitioners? What are their espoused beliefs on the description / design issue? What do academics and practitioners believe is the scope and role of data modeling within the overall process of database design, and does this role align better with the description or design characterization? These questions have both social (beliefs) and technical (process, method) aspects. Beliefs, even amongst practitioners, will not necessarily reflect the reality of practice (Sayer 1992 p43).

Problem

Are data modeling problems design problems? The reference for this question is Lawson's characteristics of design problems, which include subjectivity and negotiability of requirements.

Process

Are data modeling processes design processes? Lawson's characteristics again provide a set of criteria against which data modeling can be compared, in particular the absence of an "infallibly correct process" for design, and the need for subjective judgment.

Product

Do the products of data modeling have the characteristics of design products? Lawson's characteristics of design solutions include diversity of possible answers, subjectivity in choosing amongst them, and their role as a contribution to knowledge (*patterns*). It is under this heading that Lawson discusses creativity, and we follow his classification when addressing creativity in its own right, but also recognize its role within the other perspectives (recall that our 5Ps framework incorporates creativity frameworks).

Person

Are data modelers designers? This question is implicit in the other four perspectives which imply the need for certain behavior (e.g. seeking a holistic perspective, using patterns, determining when refinement should stop) and associated skills (e.g. judgment, negotiation, creativity) for design disciplines, and is covered within them. We also ask: do data modelers exhibit personal styles that influence the models that they produce?

1.5. OVERVIEW OF RESEARCH DESIGN

A substantial proportion of this book, including all of Part III, is devoted to reporting the results of a research program carried out at the University of Melbourne to address the description / design question. The scope of the basic question, as evidenced by the range of sub-questions above, and the paucity of existing empirical research, suggested an approach that deliberately sacrificed some depth for breadth, in order to establish at least a preliminary answer that incorporated all five perspectives. Research methods and instruments were employed as appropriate to investigate the different perspectives and associated sub-questions, with attention given to triangulation of measures and method. The research design is described in some detail in Chapter 7. It was built around three surveys to ascertain practitioner attitudes, and three "laboratory studies" that required practitioners to complete data modeling tasks under controlled conditions.

The desire to make the most effective and efficient use of participants' time was an important consideration in the research design. One outcome was that research components frequently addressed more than one aspect of the description / design question, and therefore did not map to the five perspectives in a simple one-to-one manner.

1.6. ORGANIZATION OF THE BOOK

The book is in four parts.

Part I is this chapter, introducing the questions and the approach.

Part II reviews the theory of data modeling. It begins with a short chapter on definitions of data modeling and design (Chapter 2), then provides an end-to-end review of the database design process (*Environment* - Chapter 3) and an evaluation of published descriptions of data modeling against Lawson's characteristics of design (*Problem, Process, Product* - Chapter 4).

Chapter 5 is a review of research on human factors in data modeling (*Person*), highlighting the most important assumptions and limitations.

Chapter 6 shifts the emphasis from the academic body of knowledge to the practitioner community's beliefs, and reports a series of interviews with practice "thought-leaders". Readers may find this chapter a useful alternative starting point, particularly if they want to understand the problem from a practical viewpoint without exploring the academic background. If they choose to do so, they should also read at least the short review of empirical research in Chapter 5.

Part III presents the results of an examination of data modeling practice and practitioners.

Chapter 7 describes the research design. It shows how the five perspectives, and the sub-questions within them, are addressed by the six research components that follow. It also covers aspects of the research method common to several components – in particular administration and use of statistics – and provides an overview of participant numbers, response rates, and demographics.

The first three chapters in Part III report a survey-based examination of perceptions of data modeling, addressing all five dimensions of the 5Ps framework.

Chapter 8 looks at practitioner perceptions of the overall database design process, and of the place of data modeling within it, complementing the theoretical treatement of the topic in Chapter 3. It examines the assumptions about data modeling embodied in the organization of the process and provides the understanding of practitioner terminology needed to interpret responses to the surveys in the two following chapters.

Chapter 9 analyzes practitioner responses to a forced-choice presentation of the description / design question and to an open question: "what is data modeling?" It can be seen as the practice complement to the review of definitions in Chapter 2.

Chapter 10 reports the results of a survey of practitioners based on Lawson's characteristics of design. The objective was to encourage respondents to move beyond received definitions of data modeling and reflect on their experiences of the specific characteristics. The results complement the review of data modeling theory against the Lawson framework, presented in Chapter 4.

The remaining three chapters in Part III examine diversity in the *products* of data modeling through a series of laboratory tasks. The emphasis given to the *Product* dimension was motivated by discussions with leading academics and practitioners (including those reported in Chapter 6) that indicated that substantial differences in the data models produced by competent modelers in response to a common scenario would provide the most compelling evidence for characterizing data modeling as design.

Consequently, Chapter 11 explores diversity in conceptual data models developed in response to a common business scenario. Chapter 12 explores diversity in logical data models (logical database designs) produced from a common conceptual data model. Chapter 13 incorporates the *Person* perspective by investigating a widely-observed characteristic of design disciplines: designers develop personal styles which influence their approaches to individual problems.

Participants developed models in response to two different scenarios. The models were analyzed to determine whether data modelers showed a bias towards higher or lower levels of generalization, independent of the scenario.

Part IV consists of a single chapter (Chapter 14) that draws the research results back into the 5Ps framework, reflects on these results, and comments on their implications.

Chapter 1 – Introduction

PART II – THEORY

CHAPTER 2
DEFINITIONS OF DESIGN AND DATA MODELING

And why beholdest thou the mote that is in thy brother's eye, but considerest not the beam that is in thine own eye?

– Matthew 7:3-5

This short chapter provides an initial review of the design / description issue by comparing published definitions of data modeling with generic definitions of design. As the opening quote implies, data modelers, who regularly extol the value of common definitions, have failed to establish agreed definitions for some of the key terms used in their own work, including *data model* and *data modeling*, and the differences appear to reflect different perceptions of the nature of modeling.

The final section establishes *description* as an appropriate antonym for design in the context of data modeling.

2.1. DESIGN IN INFORMATION SYSTEMS

Before turning to the generic literature on design, we draw attention to some ambiguity in the use of the word *design* in the context of information systems development. *Design* is frequently used to name or describe a broad stage in systems development whether or not it conforms to a formal – or indeed plain English – definition of design. Typically, but by no means universally (Larman 1998 p14), *design* is used to name the later, more technical, stages in systems development (Hirschheim, Klein et al. 1995; Hay 2003). In contrast, *analysis* is more often used to name the earlier, business-focused stages.

This use is perhaps a legacy of early information systems practice in which the goal was automation of manual processes, and effective use of the new technology was the major creative challenge: the "analysis" stage described existing processes (the "requirements" or "problem"); the "design" stage that followed created computerized systems to perform them (DeMarco 1978; Davis 1993).

This usage carries into the information systems sub-discipline of data modeling. Atkins (1997) provides some examples of the resulting inconsistency and ambiguity, and cites the following textbook extract (Hawryszkiewycz 1997 p182) as a compact illustration of different uses of *design* (and indeed of *analysis*) in the context of data modeling:

> *"Data modeling is part of the development process. In the linear development cycle, it is used during the system requirements phase to construct the data component of the analysis model. This model represents the major data objects and the relationships between them. It should not be confused with data analysis, which takes place in the systems design phase. System design organizes data into good shape. Usually this means removing redundancies, a process often called normalization... Most designers develop only the high-level conceptual model in the system specification phase. The more detailed analysis using normalization is carried out during design."*

Even more compactly (and again in the context of data modeling): "The analysis phase includes the creation of a logical systems design" (Rob and Coronel 2002 p324).

Some authors do try to use the terms *analysis* and *design* to capture much the same distinction as we seek in using the terms *description* and *design*. Olle et al. (1991) characterize the difference as one of *description* (analysis) vs. *prescription* (design) – and classify data modeling as analysis. Veryard (1984 p1) states that "data analysis is a branch of systems analysis and therefore shares its principles. Of particular relevance are [sic] the separation of analysis from design..." His position on data modeling[16] would appear to be implicit in the term *data analysis*. Witt (1997) divides data modelers into *analysis modelers* who see data modeling as determining, understanding, and communicating business information requirements, and *design modelers* who focus on producing a database blueprint. Here, the difference is portrayed as one of personal preference or style rather than as relating to different stages in the data modeling process or different contexts / purposes.

The different uses of *design* and resulting imprecision in meaning created two problems in reviewing the literature and designing the research described in this book:

---

[16] Veryard's later book *Information Modelling* (1992), as the title indicates, opts for the more neutral term *modelling*.

1. Publications on data modeling do not articulate a position on the description / design question as clearly as they would if the term *design* was employed with more precision. The word *design* in a task name, job role, or artifact cannot reliably be interpreted as meaning that it entails design in a strict sense. Similarly, use of the word *analysis* does not preclude it describing a design task, role, or artifact.

2. The description / design question itself may be misunderstood; *design* might be interpreted as locating data modeling in a particular stage of systems development rather than as describing the nature of the task. Preliminary discussions with data modeling researchers and feedback from practitioner-oriented articles (Simsion 1996; 2005c) that presented the question as a choice of *analysis* or *design*, were dogged by confusion of this kind. Substitution of the word *description* for *analysis* to clarify the dichotomy reduced the problem, at least to some extent.

While *design* and *analysis* may be used loosely in information systems work, we could expect them to carry some flavor of their original meanings, particularly for non-specialists involved in the development of information systems. *Data analysis* has historically been used as a synonym for data modeling (Veryard 1984; Howe 2001; Avison and Fitzgerald 2003 pp75 77), and may well carry the implication to business participants that process is one of investigation and description. The term *modeling* is more neutral: one can construct a model of an existing object (description) or of a proposed object (design) (Barker 1996).

2.2. DEFINITIONS OF DESIGN

Despite (or perhaps because of) the substantial body of literature on the subject, there is no single accepted definition of design. The following two, however, are representative of definitions that seek to embrace design across a wide range of disciplines:

"To initiate change in man-made things"

(Jones 1970)

"The conception and planning of the artificial"

(Buchanan 1990)

Gero and Maher's (1993) preface to a book on creative design is consistent with these:

"Design… creates a new, artificial world for us to inhabit…"

The dictionary[17] definition conveys the same flavor of design as a vehicle for creating something new:

"1. A plan or drawing produced to show the look and function or workings of something before it is built or made. 2. The art or action of producing such a plan or drawing."

2.2.1. Lawson's properties of design

Lawson's list of design characteristics, synthesized from the design literature, identifies some of the important characteristics of design problems, processes, and products. The list (Table 2–1) is organized into three groups (corresponding to *Problem, Product and Process*) of numbered items with descriptions. Lawson uses the word *characteristics* for all three levels; for clarity, we will use the words *Dimensions* for the groups, *Properties* for the numbered items, and *Characteristics* for individual statements about the Properties.

---

[17] Compact Oxford Dictionary (Soanes and Hawker 2005)

Design Problems
1. Design problems cannot be comprehensively stated
2. Design problems require subjective interpretation
3. Design problems tend to be organized hierarchically
Design Solutions[18]
1. There are [sic][19] an inexhaustible number of different solutions
2. There are no optimal solutions to design problems
3. Design solutions are often holistic responses
4. Design solutions are a contribution to knowledge
5. Design solutions are parts of other design problems
The Design Process
1. The process is endless
2. There is no infallibly correct process
3. The process involves finding as well as solving problems
4. Design inevitably involves subjective value judgments
5. Design is a prescriptive activity
6. Designers work in the context of a need for action

Table 2–1: Lawson's properties of design

A notable omission from Lawson's synthesis is that creativity is not treated as a Property in its own right[20]. Creativity is widely seen as playing a central role in design (Archer 1965; Jones 1970; Akin 1990; Owen 1992; Kepner 1996 p3). Lawson's framework does recognize creativity under Process Property No. 3: *The process involves finding as well as solving problems* where he states that "we must expect the design process to involve the highest levels of creative thinking." We also note one of Willem's (1991) properties[21] not covered explicitly by Lawson: *Design solutions occur in terms of media (rather than as pure knowledge).*

---

[18] We refer to Lawson's Solutions as Products in the 5Ps framework.

[19] This minor point of grammar is corrected in further references to this Property in this book.

[20] Lawson clearly recognizes the importance of creativity by devoting a chapter of his book to it.

[21] The other three properties in Willem's framework correspond reasonably well to properties covered by Lawson.

We review data modeling against each of Lawson's Properties in Chapter 4 (theory) and Chapter 10 (practitioner perceptions).

2.2.2. The antithesis of design

When the generic design literature seeks to contrast design with other activities, the usual choice of antithesis is *science* or (more precisely) *scientific investigation*. The defining principle of design is a concern with the development of *things*, whereas science is concerned with the development of *knowledge of the world* (Willem 1991). Designers suggest how the world might be; scientists *describe* how it is (Lawson 1997 p113). Gat and Gonen (1981), writing on design in general, suggest an alternative dichotomy of *design* and *planning*, but the same flavor is evident in their use of the terms *pure will* and *pure inquiry* to characterize the two extreme positions.

Unfortunately, the word *science* can simply imply rigor in a process rather than investigation. Thus far we have used the term *description* to denote the antithesis of design, and this would seem to be appropriate in the context of data modeling[22], while retaining the spirit of the design literature dichotomy.

2.3. DEFINITIONS OF DATA MODELING

Representative definitions of data modeling[23] and data models[24] are well-removed from even the very inclusive definitions of design in the previous section; on the contrary they clearly reflect the opposite. A number of examples from the research, teaching, and practitioner literature are listed (in chronological sequence) to illustrate the pervasiveness of the descriptive characterization. Chapter 1 (Section 1.1) provides some further examples.

---

[22] The word *science* has occasionally been used to describe data modeling (Wood-Harper and Fitzgerald 1982) and that characterization is implicit in such statements about data modeling as "a key criterion for any real discipline is replicability" (Warner 1996).

[23] Some of these definitions apply specifically to conceptual data modeling, but, as discussed in Section 3.6, there is usually an assumption that the conceptual model can be mechanically transformed into a conceptual schema.

[24] *Design* is, of course, both a verb and a noun. The definitions need to be matched with *data modeling* or *data model* as appropriate.

"A model[25] is a basic system of constructs used in describing reality. It reflects a person's deepest assumptions regarding the elementary essence of things"

(Kent 1978 p93)

"formalizing and representing the data structures of reality"
(Shoval and Frumermann 1994 p28)

"Conceptual modeling is a process of extracting and representing knowledge."

(Wand, Monarchi et al. 1995 p290)

"a representation of the things of significance to an enterprise and the relationships among those things."

(Hay 1996a)

"an attempt to capture the essence of things both concrete and abstract..."
(Kouffel 1996)

"an abstract representation of the data about entities, events, activities, and their associations within an organization"
(McFadden, Hoffer et al. 1999)

"the activity of discovering and documenting information requirements."
(DeAngelis 2000 p7)

(Conceptual modeling is) "motivated by a single goal – namely to provide an accurate, complete representation of someone's or some group's understanding of a domain."

(Bodart, Patel et al. 2001)

"The core idea underlying all the definitions is the same: a data model is used for describing entities and their relationships within a core domain."
(Topi and Ramesh 2002)

If these definitions of data modeling were universally accepted, then it would seem that data modeling was description, *by definition*. But "almost every company has its own understanding of 'data modeling'" (Maier 1996) and there are alternative descriptions in the research, teaching, and practitioner literature that that convey at least the flavor of design:

---

[25] Kent is using *model* as Model (formalism)

"Data modeling is generally viewed as a design[26] activity"

(Srinivasan and Te'eni 1990)

"an activity that involves the creation of abstractions…"

(Davydov 1994)

"the development of a conceptual data model is a design activity…"

(Shanks 1997b)

"the art and science of arranging the structure and relationship of data…"

(McComb 2004 p293)

"data modeling is a design discipline"

(Simsion and Witt 2005 p7)

Stephens and Plew (2001 pp58-59) cite dictionary definitions of design and use them to characterize data modeling. Also at odds with descriptive characterizations is the use of design disciplines as references for data modeling. Engineering and architecture have long been employed as paradigms for information systems development in general (Lee 1991a; McDermid 1991 pp83-106; Avison and Fitzgerald 2003 pp83-106, 395-407), and data modeling in particular (Finkelstein and Martin 1981; Zachman 1987; Marche 1991; Martin 1991; Hoberman 2002 p19). *Architect* is a common job title for data modelers[27] (Hay 2003 p58).

To summarize: definitions of data modeling commonly characterize it as description, but there are dissenting views and common metaphors which align better with the design characterization.

---

[26] The authors make it clear that they are using design in a strict sense by adding, "however, research on the data modeling process has not drawn from research about design in general".

[27] See also participant occupations in Section 7.6.

CHAPTER 3
BELIEFS ABOUT THE DATABASE
DESIGN PROCESS

Yeah let's do something crazy,
Something absolutely wrong
While we're waiting for the miracle, for the miracle to come

– Leonard Cohen, *Waiting for the Miracle*

This chapter looks at the context or *environment* in which data modeling is performed – the overall database design process of which it is a part, and beliefs about that process and its components. This broader perspective is critical to a proper examination of data modeling. Most research in data modeling examines only part of the total database design process, and embodies assumptions about the excluded parts. Of particular relevance to the description / design question are assumptions that design takes place and diversity arises in activities outside the scope of a particular investigation: "then a miracle occurs[28]".

In the data modeling stages, we ask "is this stage better characterized as description or design?" In those that precede and follow it, the primary question is, "does this stage contribute to the data modeling problem being a design problem?" These questions are addressed in the context of more fundamental (and frequently conflicting) beliefs about each stage.

The next section presents a generic model of the database design process, comprising eight stages. The eight sections which follow discuss the individual stages. At the end of the chapter, we summarize the dominant and alternative beliefs for each stage to produce an end-to-end picture of beliefs – about the database design process.

It bears emphasizing that our source of these beliefs is the academic and practitioner literature. Chapter 8 complements this review of theory with a survey of practitioner perceptions of the process.

---

[28] This is from a well-known cartoon of the design process; "then a miracle occurs" covers a gap between otherwise well-defined activities.

3.1. A MODEL OF THE DATABASE DESIGN PROCESS

Figure 3-1 is a synthesis of methods and frameworks from across the data modeling literature (while many more papers were taken into account, it can be synthesized from Batini, Lenzerini et al. 1986; Klein and Hirschheim 1987; Navathe 1992; Teorey, Lightstone et al. 2006 p4). It shows database design as a process beginning with the Universe of Discourse (*UoD*) – the part of the real world that is to be modeled – and finishing with a complete database specification. It is intended as a reasonably inclusive framework for locating arguments and assumptions rather than a methodology. As such, it includes several stages that are not included in all published frameworks, which typically show five or less stages at this level of granularity. Nor does it show all of the inputs and outputs to the stages.

It is important for readers (particularly practitioner readers) to recognize that practitioner and academic terminology differ, with the same term being used in different ways by the two communities – and within the communities. The generic model used here leans towards representative academic terminology: experience suggests that many practitioners will need to make the translations shown in Table 3–1.

Academic Term	Practitioner Term
Scoping model (not included here)	Conceptual Data Model
Conceptual Data Model	Logical Data Model
Logical Data Model	First-cut Physical Data Model
Physical Data Model	Physical Data Model

Table 3–1: Academic versus practitioner terminology

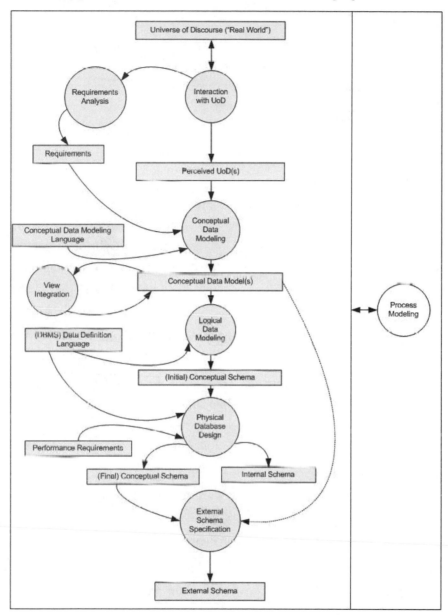

Figure 3-1: Stages in database design – a generic framework

Very broadly:

Interaction with the UoD is usually referred to as *perception,* but we acknowledge the possibility that the modeler may contribute to or alter the UoD – hence the double-headed arrow. The *Perceived UoD* represents the conception or image of the UoD in the modeler's or analyst's mind.

Requirements Analysis is included in some but not all methods. The modeler's direct perceptions of the UoD are replaced or supplemented by a statement of business requirements.

Conceptual Data Modeling covers the production of one or more DBMS-independent data models, represented in a conceptual modeling language e.g. the Entity-Relationship Model (Chen 1976). In some methods, different perspectives (whether descriptions or designs) are progressively synthesized within this stage to produce a single model; in others, a separate model (*view*) is produced for each perspective.

View Integration is required if Conceptual Data Modeling has produced multiple views. This stage consolidates the models into a single conceptual data model.

Logical Data Modeling converts the conceptual data model into a conceptual schema (ISO/TR9007:1987(E) 1987) (often called a *logical data model or logical database design*) in the data definition language (*DDL*) of the implementation DBMS – usually some variant of the Relational Model (Codd 1970).

Physical Database Design specifies the internal schema (ISO/TR9007:1987(E) 1987), and may change the initial conceptual schema in order to improve performance.

External Schema Specification defines the external schema (ISO/TR9007:1987(E) 1987) or *views*, in terms of mappings to the final conceptual schema.

Process Modeling complements database design by specifying the procedural component of an application (programs, manual tasks etc). It is frequently portrayed as a parallel process to database design, and we examine it primarily to compare beliefs about it with beliefs about database design.

The subsections that follow this one cover each of these stages in more detail. Our model cannot incorporate every possible variant, but it does (allowing for differences in terminology and level of detail) include the stages from a wide range of published frameworks and methods. The principal exception is that the role of an enterprise model as an input or constraint (as in McFadden, Hoffer et al. 1999 p47), is not included. The use of an enterprise model has been widely advocated (Zachman 1987; Shanks and Darke 1999; Persson and Stirna 2001) as a means of improving data management across application systems. Three factors contributed to the decision to omit it: (1) the overwhelming majority of the research literature (including *all* of the empirical studies listed in 0) does not acknowledge an enterprise model as an input to database design; (2) actual use of and fidelity to enterprise models in practice is the exception rather than the rule (Lederer and Sethi 1988; Earl 1993; Beynon-Davies 1994; Kim and Everest 1994; Shanks and Swatman 1997); (3) if the role of the enterprise model is to impose a standard data model on the database design process, then we would need to ask "is the development of an *enterprise* model description or design?", adding significant complexity to the research without any real extension to the basic question.

Similarly, large scale "subject area" models (Hoberman 2002 pp157-236; Avison and Fitzgerald 2003 pp400-404) have been excluded. Detailed interaction with process modeling activities is also not shown although there are various techniques for cross-checking process and data models[29] (Rob and Coronel 2002 pp322-325; Avison and Fitzgerald 2003 pp227-238; Hay 2003 pp195-196).

Despite efforts over a long period to establish standard names and definitions for data modeling and database design activities and deliverables (e.g. ISO/TC97/SC/WG3-N695 1982; Jardine 1984; Teorey, Yang et al. 1986; Navathe 1992; Olle 1993), the terminology is not settled (Date 1998 pp410-416; Thalheim 2000 pp3-4). Hirschheim *et al.* (1995, pxi) refer to the "terminological diversity and confusion that abounds in the data modeling community". The stage that we have called *logical data modeling* is frequently called *logical database design* (e.g. Storey and Goldstein 1988; Kesh 1995; McFadden, Hoffer et al. 1999; Simsion and Witt 2005). Conceptual data modeling is sometimes included in a broader *requirements* stage (Hawryszkiewycz 1997 p182). In much of the practitioner literature, (e.g. Hoberman 2002 pp112-113) *logical data analysis / modeling* is similar to our *conceptual data modeling* and is preceded by a higher level scoping stage often called *conceptual data modeling*.

---

[29] Indeed, methodologies may be characterized by which of the two models is produced first and used as input to the other ("process-driven", "data-driven", "blended") (Avison and Fitzgerald 2003 pp347-352) and the process model may form part of the requirements input to data modeling. For simplicity, and because they add little to the discussion at this point, these variants are not shown on the diagram.

Many authors recognize a four stage core, as in our process: *requirements analysis, conceptual data modeling, logical data modeling* and *physical database design* (e.g. Navathe 1992; Elmasri and Navathe 1994; Storey, Thompson et al. 1995; D'Orazio and Happel 1996; McFadden, Hoffer et al. 1999; Rob and Coronel 2002; Simsion and Witt 2005). Some variants (e.g. Fleming and von Halle 1989; Barker 1990; DeAngelis 2000) combine the logical and physical modeling stages, referring to the consolidated stage as *physical database design* and to our *conceptual data modeling* as *logical data modeling*.

An older view, dating at least from Smith and Smith (1978) but still widely seen in teaching material (Atkins 1997) focuses on user views and their integration: *requirements analysis* identifies the views, *conceptual data modeling* integrates them, *physical database design* creates the physical structures, and (optionally) *view definition* re-creates the views as external schemas (Yao, Navathe et al. 1978; Navathe and Gadgil 1982; Storey and Goldstein 1988). View integration is recognized as a key stage, if not the focus of the approach, in many current texts (George, Batra et al. 2004 p236; Teorey, Lightstone et al. 2006 pp66-74).

Figure 3-1 accommodates the above variants in structure, if not nomenclature, and has generally employed an equal or finer granularity.

Before proceeding with the stage by stage review, we note some points that cover more than one stage:

(a)   Database design as a whole is almost invariably called *design;* the terms *analysis* and *modeling* are used only for individual stages. It has been described as more art than science (Bouzeghoub 1992; Storey, Thompson et al. 1995; Date 1998 p401) or both art and science (Halpin 2001 p5; Rob and Coronel 2002 p110).

(b)   A frequently-stated view (arguably in conflict with (a) above) is that a database's structure should mirror the UoD or real-world system (Durding, Becker et al. 1977; Hammer and McLeod 1981 p 73; Everest 1986 p199; Crockett, Guynes et al. 1991; Wand and Weber 1993; Ramesh and Browne 1999; Halpin 2001 pp22-23; Wand and Weber 2002; Hay 2003)[30]. In this *reality mapping* (Lyytinen 1987) view, the basic goal of database design is to map the structure of the UoD accurately onto the conceptual schema: "A database whose organization

---

[30] Everest cites Boulding (1956) as the source of this idea.

is based on naturally occurring structures will be easier for a database designer to construct and modify than one that forces him to translate the primitives of his problem domain into artificial specification constructs" (Hammer and McLeod 1981). (Note the pejorative use of the word *artificial*, a term that frequently appears in definitions of design – Section 2.2. The term *naturally occurring* is also interesting as it seems to preclude concepts created by humans – a topic discussed in the section on interaction with the UoD that follows.) While this ideal has been challenged on both theoretical and pragmatic grounds (Kent 1978 p1; Lyytinen 1987; Lewis 1993; Agerfalk and Eriksson 2004), it is a common assumption at all stages of database design. Kroenke (2005 p285) puts an alternative view concisely: "systems and organizations do not just influence each other – they create each other".

(c)　　The use of two different languages / formalisms, one for conceptual modeling and one for implementation (Palvia, Liao et al. 1992), is a feature of virtually all modern frameworks, although the 3-schema architecture standard (ISO/TC97/SC/WG3-N695 1982) envisaged only a single "conceptual schema" language. The driving factor has been the dominance of the Relational Model as the language of commercial DBMSs, and a widespread view, supported by empirical research (summarized in Batra and Srinivasan 1992) that this formalism is not appropriate for developing and presenting conceptual data models. There was a time when researchers proposed alternative languages intended to serve both purposes (Hammer and McLeod 1981; Brodie, Mylopoulos et al. 1984; Hull and King 1987; Peckham and Maryanski 1988), but such languages were not widely adopted by DBMS vendors. The transformation from one language to another at the logical data modeling stage is of critical importance to the nature of the database design process. Jackson (1995 p3), firmly in the "reality mapping" camp, foreshadows some of the issues of language translation (and the underlying goal of translating a representation of the real world into a database specification) in arguing that in principle three models (*descriptions*) are required: the application domain description, the machine description, and a common description as "there's always more to say about the application domain and more to say about the machine too."

3.2. INTERACTION WITH THE UoD

The part of the real world of relevance to a data modeling exercise is referred to as the *Universe of Discourse* or UoD (ISO/TR9007:1987(E) 1987 p10). Database design begins with an interaction with the UoD.

Two issues are of relevance to the description / design question:

1. Does the UoD exist independent of observers, or is it a human (mental or social) construction? In data modeling terms, is our problem to model an objective reality, or to model – and perhaps even help to *design* – a reality that may differ from person to person or group to group?

2. Do different observers perceive the UoD differently, to the extent that descriptive data models would differ as a result? If so, we may not need to invoke design as an explanation for differences in data models.

These questions have received some attention in the data modeling literature, and researchers have drawn on two branches of philosophy – ontology and epistemology – to address them. Ontology deals with the order and structure of reality, whilst epistemology is concerned with the nature of knowledge and how it is acquired (Angeles 1981).

Wand and Weber (2002) mention the *positivist-interpretivist* debates that occurred in the IS field throughout the 80s and 90s, in which interpretivists argued that the phenomena to be modeled were "created" not "discovered". Their wording positions the interpretivists as challengers of conventional wisdom, and indeed most data modeling research, including seminal papers and standards, is based on the *realist*[31] assumption of an objective UoD independent of observers (Klein and Hirschheim 1987; Lewis 1993).

The alternative *nominalist* position holds that reality is a construction of the mind. Something of a nominalist position, or at least the view that social reality is a human construction (Berger and Luckmann 1967; Toumin 1972; Searle 1997; Thomasson 2003) can be seen in Kent's (1978 p22)[32] argument that we are not

---

[31] Terminology (*realism* and *nominalism*) follows Klein and Hirschheim who in turn cite Burrell and Morgan (1979). This usage may not reflect the broader philosophical literature (*naturalism* and *idealism* might have been closer terms for these concepts) but it captures the distinction of interest here.

[32] Page references are to the 1998 reprint by 1st Books Library.

modeling reality when developing information systems, but the way information about reality is processed by people. He argues that most things are in the database because they exist in people's minds without having any "objective" existence. *Rule based* perspectives of data modeling, which see it as formalizing the meaning of data (or *messages*) to be exchanged within a community, embody a view of reality as socially constructed (Klein and Hirschheim 1987; Lyytinen 1987). Lyytinen provides examples of socially-constructed entities such as *legal person, loan, customer,* and *order.* Such "soft" entities usually form the majority of entities populating data models (Kent 1978 p20; Lyytinen 1987; Sampson 2002).

The two positions – realist and nominalist – have different implications for the characterization of data modeling. If we accept the (dominant) realist assumption, we cannot attribute diversity in data models developed by different data modelers to the lack of an objective UoD. A nominalist could argue that such diversity was a result of the modelers faithfully describing the different realities that they or others have constructed.

Conversely, if we accept that some or all of the UoD is socially constructed, then we need to ask whether any part of the construction falls within the data modeling process. There is some evidence that data modelers may create new business concepts (Simsion 1991; Gjersvik 1993; Barker 1996, see also Chapter 4). Krogstie, Lindland et al (1995) state directly that conceptual modeling can be looked upon as a process of social construction. Creation of new concepts would seem to be better characterized as design than description.

Research on the philosophical foundations of data modeling also covers the issue of perception. It generally asserts that the literature and practice are dominated by a *positivist*[33] belief that the UoD can be seen impartially, rather than a *subjectivist* belief, in which knowledge depends on the modeler's frame of reference and conceptual abilities (Klein and Hirschheim 1987; Lyytinen 1987). On the contrary, acknowledgement that there may be multiple views of a UoD (albeit generally an *objective* UoD) is common in both the academic and practitioner literature in which *reality* frequently becomes *perceptions of reality* (Oxborrow 1986 p20; Zeleny 1987; Navathe 1992; Parsons 1996; Wand, Storey et al. 1999; Pascal 2000 p150; Shanks, Tansley et al. 2003).

---

[33] Terminology is again from Klein and Hirschheim.

Avison and Cuthbertson (2002 p10) put this position concisely:

> *"We can never fully know reality; our view of the real world is distorted by our perceptive process."*

Stamper, Althans et al. (1988) take an even stronger position, arguing that "the social realities of a business are infinitely rich and complex and totally beyond our powers of analysis…"

The acknowledgement of differences in perception is often qualified by a contention or assumption that such differences can be resolved to produce a common view, as in the view integration approaches discussed in Section 3.5. Even an objective reality (UoD) is not essential; it can be replaced by an agreed and workable *inter-subjective* reality (Kent 1978 p203; Wand, Monarchi et al. 1995; Atkins 1997; Avison and Fitzgerald 2003 p77). Carlis & Maguire (2001 pp22-23) state that although different users will disagree about their information needs and how to describe them, as a result of "provincial" views, there is nevertheless a "global integrated perspective".

Empirical evidence of differences in perception in the context of data modeling, even at an anecdotal level, is lacking. More common is the attribution of any differences that might arise in models of the same scenario to differences in modelers' or users' perceptions (Navathe, Elmasri et al. 1986; Hawryszkiewycz 1991 p119; Teorey, Lightstone et al. 2006 p66). In terms of the description / design question, an alternative explanation for difference in models is that they are design products in which difference is to be expected. Different architects *might* see their clients' requirements differently, but this factor alone is not seen as the reason for them producing different designs.

3.3. REQUIREMENTS ANALYSIS

A *Requirements Analysis*[34] stage appears in some descriptions of the data modeling process (e.g. Teorey, Lightstone et al. 2006 pp3-4) but not in all (e.g. Barker 1990; McFadden, Hoffer et al. 1999 p46) and is implicit as a preliminary step in laboratory experiments that require data modelers to develop a model from a documented set of "business requirements" (Chapter 5).

---

[34] Names for the activity vary. This is the term used in Teorey, Lightstone et al (2006 p3). Sometimes the term is used to embrace conceptual data modeling (e.g. Wand and Weber 2002)

Requirements analysis – sometimes referred to as requirements *engineering* or requirements *elicitation* (Goguen and Linde 1993; Sommerville and Sawyer 1997) – is a well-recognized activity in information systems development with an associated body of literature. Work on requirements analysis falls into two camps (Stamper, Althans et al. 1988). One camp builds high-level formal "languages", and the other focuses on the business problem and looks to produce broad statements of requirements. Requirements in the data modeling literature generally fall into the second camp, insofar as no language or format is specified, nor any process to exploit such formality[35]. Frequently, the format and contents of the requirements document are not specified at all (e.g. Navathe 1992).

In terms of the description / design question, the requirements stage is interesting because (a) its inclusion undermines the simple descriptive characterization in which the data modeler directly describes the UoD; (b) its output could be viewed as a statement of a design problem, and (c) it may itself embody or be characterized as design. We look briefly at each of these now, and return to (b) in the discussion of data modeling problems (Section 4.2).

If conceptual data modeling is a matter of mapping the UoD onto corresponding Data Model structures, as implied by descriptive characterizations, (Section 2.3 and 3.4), then it is difficult to see the value of interposing a requirements statement – in particular an informal one – except when direct access to the UoD is not possible, as in laboratory tasks. The omission of a requirements statement from some methods would support that view.

Alternatively, the requirements stage could be seen as articulating a problem to be solved by data modeling. This view is consistent with the term *requirements* – and with the design characterization. Witt's use of an *object class hierarchy* (Witt 2002b; Simsion and Witt 2005 pp261-270) to document business data requirements is explicitly intended to separate the statement of the problem from its solution; similarly natural language can support this separation by preventing "too early a resolution of conflicts" (Darke and Shanks 1995). More subtly, the "concepts" and "natural relationships" that appear in Teorey, Lightstone, et al's (2006 p3) requirements could be recorded directly in a data model, rendering the requirements stage superfluous, *if* there was not some (undeclared) intermediate

---

[35] The initial deliverables in the NIAM / ORM approach (Halpin 2001) are more structured but are probably better seen as an early representation of the model itself rather than requirements – see Terry Halpin's comments in Chapter 4 (Section 6.4.1).

work to be done. The inclusion of information beyond a passive description of the UoD (e.g. Thalheim 2000 p15; Teorey, Lightstone et al. 2006 p2), presumably to guide or constrain the modeler, would also support this characterization of the requirements as a problem statement.

Finally, requirements analysis may overlap with high-level design (e.g. Yourdon 1989; Sutcliffe and Maiden 1992; Lubars, Potts et al. 1993), and the term *design* may be used to describe part or all of the requirements process (Bubenko 1995; Catledge and Potts 1996; Gasson 1998). Maiden and Gizikis (2001) argue that requirements engineering is a highly creative design process, but note that current research does not recognize the "critical role" of creative thinking. Smith and Smith (1978), in an early paper on data modeling outlining a view integration approach, described requirements analysis as the *design* of interfaces – views – to suit the "idiosyncrasies" of individual end-users. Whether the (possible) characterization of requirements analysis as design is directly relevant to the present question depends on whether it is perceived as distinct from data modeling. Characterizing data modeling as a component of requirements definition (e.g. Batra, Hoffer et al. 1990; Hawryszkiewycz 1997 p182; Hay 2003) at least leaves open the possibility that it is a design activity.

In summary, requirements specifications may serve as descriptions of the UoD to supplement or replace direct access. Alternatively, they may be seen as problem statements to be addressed by conceptual modeling. Finally, they may themselves embody design decisions. Most of these roles contrast strongly with the picture of a conceptual data model as "out there", waiting to be documented.

3.4. CONCEPTUAL DATA MODELING

Conceptual data modeling is recognized in the academic literature as the most crucial stage in database design (Pletch 1989; Batini, Ceri et al. 1992; Dey, Storey et al. 1999; Ramesh and Browne 1999; Rob and Coronel 2002), and has been the focus of data modeling research. In this section, we examine beliefs about its nature and its role within the database design process. We begin with some direct statements of position on the description / design question. We then review conceptual modeling languages and their two widely-declared purposes – describing reality and specifying databases.

3.4.1. Positions: Description or design?

In Section 2.3, we noted that most definitions of data modeling characterized it as descriptive. Statements supporting or assuming this characterization are common in the literature, for example:

> *"a one to one correspondence between the entities in the real world and the objects in the model must exist..."*
>
> (Mattos 1989) – stated as an "axiom".

> *"By using a conceptual model, one can describe a reality"*
>
> (Lee and Choi 1998)

> *"The main challenge is to describe the UoD clearly and precisely"*
>
> (Halpin 2001 p6)

> *"The conceptual model helps designers accurately capture the real data requirements"*
>
> (Teorcy, Lightstone et al. 2006 p55)

Work on the philosophical foundations of modeling, discussed in Section 3.2, acknowledges that the dominant view is one of describing, mapping, or reflecting reality (Klein and Hirschheim 1987; Lyytinen 1987; Tolis 1996; Agerfalk and Eriksson 2004), and argues that alternative perspectives have received insufficient attention. In essence, "The difference is whether one believes that a data model 'reflects' reality or consists of subjective meanings and thereby constructs reality" (Klein and Hirschheim 1987). In the Formal Language Definition view (Lyytinen 1987), the purpose of data modeling[36] is to translate meaning in users' professional languages into a formal language (the conceptual data model), and is a "creative, interpretive task". Similarly speech act theory suggests that data modeling could be seen as representing the "communication acts" that are to be supported by the system (Agerfalk and Eriksson 2004).

Outside these philosophical treatments, the characterization of conceptual data modeling as other than description is much less common and even less often supported by argument. Chaiyasut and Shanks (1994), like Olle et al (1991), acknowledge conflicting "analysis" and "design" positions, but where Olle et al

---

[36] Lyytinen uses the term "information modeling" for conceptual schema development and uses "data modeling" to describe specification of access and storage structures. The terminology has been changed here to accord with more common practice as used elsewhere in this book.

take the analysis position, Chaiyasut and Shanks take the design position. Under the heading *Conceptual Data Modeling as a Design Process*, they state: "The process of conceptual data modeling is sometimes seen as an analytical, descriptive task", but it "is better viewed as a design activity where the data modeler is an active participant in the modeling process and adds value to the quality of the model." In describing an expert system for supporting data modeling Parent (1997) says "it is hoped that the results of this study may generalize to other *design* applications…" (emphasis added).

3.4.2. Conceptual data modeling languages

The call for research to address alternatives to the descriptive (objectivist, reality mapping) view of conceptual data modeling appears to have gone unheeded. A longstanding focus on improving data modeling languages, firmly aligned with the reality mapping paradigm, has been given new impetus with the introduction of naturalist[37] ontology as a reference.

Early work on languages (Codd 1970; CODASYL 1971) focused on the organization of the database itself. Chen's seminal paper (1976) added another dimension to research and practice by describing a conceptual modeling language that was distinct from implementation languages. It was at least in part motivated by a desire to more faithfully describe the real world:

> *"The entity-relationship model adopts the more natural view that the real world consists of entities and relationships"*

> (Chen 1976).

In another paper, Chen (1977) refers to an entity-relationship (E-R) model as a "pure representation of reality". Chen's work marks an early point in a continuing and substantial thread of research that aims to develop conceptual data modeling languages or *Semantic Data Models* (Hull and King 1987; Peckham and Maryanski 1988) that "provide richer, more expressive concepts with which to capture more meaning than was possible when using classical data models[38]"

---

[37] The characterization of Bunge's ontology, as used in data modeling work, as *naturalist* is from Milton (2004). In Klein and Hirschheim's (1987) classification, it would be referred to as *realist*.

[38] Note that *data model* is being used in the sense of language or Data Model here. *Classical* refers to implementation Models, in particular the Network, Hierarchical and Relational Models.

(Brodie, Mylopoulos et al. 1984 p11). Examples[39] include Bachman's (1977) addition of the "role" construct to Logical Data Structure diagrams (Bachman 1969), extensions to the Relational Model (Codd 1979; 1990), the Semantic Data Model (Hammer and McLeod 1981), NIAM (Verheijen and van Bekkum 1982), fact-based modeling (Kent 1984), the Extended Entity Relationship Model (Teorey, Yang et al. 1986), the Object Role Model (Halpin 2001), and (as a more recent example) property precedence extensions to UML (Parsons and Cole 2004). The coining of the derisory term *YAMA* – Yet Another Modeling Approach (Oei, van Hemen et al. 1992) – did not stem the flow. Thalheim (2000) estimates the number of proposed extensions to the E-R Model at 80, and Halpin's (2001 pp106-107) short history of the ORM language mentions fourteen named variants.

The goal of reducing the *semantic distance* (Hutchins, Hollan et al. 1985) between the real world and the data model or (equivalently) improving *modeling efficiency* (Peckham and Maryanski 1988) has been regularly restated (Batra, Hoffer et al. 1990; Coad and Yourdon 1990; Martin and Odell 1992; Hirschheim, Klein et al. 1995; Bodart and Weber 1996; Weber 1996; Rumbaugh, Jacobson et al. 1999; Liao and Palvia 2000). There are echoes of Hammer and McLeod's (1981) claim that a database based on naturally occurring structures will be easier to construct in Wand and Weber's (2002) statement that if the modeling language reflects the structure of reality, it should allow users with minimum resources to map the UoD onto the grammar's constructs.

Klein and Hirschheim (1987) saw the proliferation of proposals for alternative modeling formalisms as evidence *against* the realist assumption: "If there is a unique and objectively given reality, there should be a unique way of modeling it." Recent work would seem to be taking up that challenge.

The major innovation has been the use of established ontologies[40] as theoretical bases for developing, comparing and improving data modeling languages (Weber and Zhang 1991; Wimmer and Wimmer 1992; Wand and Weber 1993). The selected ontology provides a description of real-world structures that can then be compared with the structures supported by a particular modeling language. The

---

[39] The list here focuses on those suggested by the academic community rather than the practitioner community, whose goals have not so often been stated in terms of capturing more meaning. Nor have we included approaches motivated primarily by goals other than better mirroring reality.

[40] The interest is in high-level, generic ontologies, sourced from philosophy, rather than the detailed ontologies that have been developed to organize concepts and terminology within specific communities (Gruber 1993; Kim 2002; McComb 2004 pp56-57).

concept of semantic distance is reframed as *ontological clarity* (Burton-Jones and Weber 1999).

Bunge's ontology (Bunge 1977) has been the most widely used for this purpose (Wand and Weber 1989; Wand and Weber 1990; Weber and Zhang 1991; Wand and Weber 1993; Wand, Monarchi et al. 1995; Weber 1997c; Weber 1997b; Weber 1997a; Burton-Jones and Weber 1999; Wand, Storey et al. 1999; Parsons and Wand 2000; Bodart, Patel et al. 2001; Shanks, Nuredini et al. 2002a; Shanks, Nuredini et al. 2002b; Shanks, Nuredini et al. 2002c; Shanks, Tansley et al. 2002; Wand and Weber 2002; Shanks, Tansley et al. 2003; Shanks, Tansley et al. 2004). Milton and others (Milton and Kazmierczak 2004) have used Chisholm's ontology (Chisholm 1996). Both ontologies postulate an objective reality independent of human perceptions. Bunge's ontology, at least as used by data modeling researchers, may favor a more "naturalist" view, with less acknowledgment of social construction (Milton 2004).

This substantial body of research embodies an *ideal* of data modeling as description – of a simple mapping from real-world structures to conceptual model structures. However, there is no serious belief – certainly no demonstration – that any current or proposed data modeling language achieves this. To draw an analogy with architecture or engineering: while we seek to improve materials towards an ideal of strength, weight, durability, etc, perfect materials do not exist, and the nature of our task is affected by the constraints thereby imposed (Portillo and Dohr 1994). Recall also Willem's (1991) property of design, noted in Section 2.3: *Design solutions occur in terms of media (rather than as pure knowledge).* Data modeling languages could readily be seen as the media here.

The descriptive paradigm that appears to drive (academic) data modeling language research is not the only possible motivation for improving languages. If language developers or evaluators subscribed to the design paradigm, we could expect formalisms to be advocated on the basis that they provided the modeler with better tools to shape conceptions of reality (Beynon-Davies 1992) or to create innovative solutions. In the next section we look at modeling languages in practice, where the provision of a design "toolkit" appears to have been at least as much of a goal as reality mapping.

3.4.3. Conceptual data modeling languages – in practice

The Entity-Relationship (E-R) Model (Chen 1976), is not the dominant formalism in data modeling practice (Hitchman 1995; D'Orazio and Happel 1996; Chan, Siau et al. 1998; Kroenke 2005 p127; Frost, Day et al. 2006 p17), despite regular statements to that effect (Reiner 1992; Batra and Kirs 1993; Bock and Ryan 1993; Batra and Antony 1994b; Batra and Zanakis 1994; Shoval and Frumermann 1994; Hardgrave and Dalal 1995; Kesh 1995; Crerar, Barclay et al. 1996; Shoval and Shiran 1997; Gemino 1998; Burton-Jones and Weber 1999).

A simpler formalism, often referred to as the *crow's foot notation* (Teorey, Lightstone et al. 2006 p20) is widely used in practice (Hitchman 1995), practitioner-oriented texts (Martin 1987; Veryard 1992; Carlis and Maguire 2001; Silverston 2001; Hoberman 2002; Hay 2003; Simsion and Witt 2005), increasingly in teaching texts (Atkins 1996; Rob and Coronel 2002 p109; Kroenke 2005 p130), and supported by popular data modeling and Computer Aided Software Engineering (CASE) and documentation tools (e.g. Barker 1990; DeAngelis 2000).

In its basic form, the crow's foot notation is little more[41] than a diagrammatic representation of a (normalized) relational schema (Cerpa 1995; Atkins 1997; Benyon 1997; Simsion and Witt 2005 pp65-72), though it is often described as an E-R variant[42] (e.g. Halpin 2001 p7) or *the* E-R Model (Barker 1990 pp115-129; Henderson 2002; Avison and Fitzgerald 2003 p 177)[43]. It lacks many of the features of even the original E-R Model, which has long since been enhanced to produce, *inter alia*, the Extended Entity Relationship (EER) Model (Teorey, Yang et al. 1986). For example, it does not support relationships of degree higher than two, role names, or the distinction between weak and regular entities. If the E-R Model is "a thin layer on top of the relational model" (Date 1998 p426), the basic crow's foot notation is an even thinner one.

---

[41] The two are not exactly isomorphic (Simsion and Witt 2005 pp350-354) but the differences would seem to be accidental rather than deliberate.

[42] Atkins (1997) calls it an E-R/Relational Hybrid, a term that seems appropriate for some of the extended variants, if not the Model in its most basic form.

[43] The regular use of "E-R" to describe the crows' foot notation in practice probably accounts for the belief that practitioners use the (Chen) Entity-Relationship Model. The notation has more in common with Bachman's (1969) data structure diagrams.

The basic crow's foot notation has evolved into several semantically richer forms (Halpin 2001 pp347-348; Hay 2003 pp343-378), including the *Information Engineering* notation (Finkelstein 1989), *Barker* notation (Barker 1990), IDEF1X (Bruce 1992), the Merise notation (Flynn and Diaz 1996; Avison and Fitzgerald 2003 pp387-395) and dozens of variants (Halpin, ibid). By virtue of these additions that do not directly reflect the Relational Model, it has become a conceptual modeling language in its own right, or, more correctly, several languages or dialects. Their development does not appear to have been driven by fidelity to any particular Model or ontology, nor by the substantial work on developing a more rigorous theoretical basis for conceptual modeling and the E-R Model in particular (Thalheim 2000).

Two other languages deserve mention in this brief review of practice.

Object-Role Modeling (Halpin 2001), its ancestors NIAM (Verheijen and van Bekkum 1982) and fact-based modeling (Kent 1984; Halpin and Orlowska 1992), and variants (Atkins 1997) are well-developed conceptual modeling languages with an extensive literature, much of which predicts or seeks to encourage greater practitioner acceptance (ISO/TC97/SC/WG3-N695 1982; Everest 1988; Nijssen and Halpin 1989; Weber and Zhang 1991), and some support from modeling tools (Halpin, Evans et al. 2003). Advocates of NIAM in particular have stressed its ability to more faithfully capture real-world concepts and reduce – but not eliminate – the need for creativity on the part of the modeler (Nijssen and Halpin 1989 p30; Atkins 1996). Empirical research has not been convincing in supporting claims of greater usability (Shoval and Even-Chaime 1987; Kim and March 1995), at least by novices.

The only effective challenge to the dominance of the crow's foot variants has come from the Unified Modeling Language (UML) (Rumbaugh, Jacobson et al. 1999). *Class diagrams* are intended to represent data structures which might be directly implemented using an object-oriented DBMS. Given the failure of OODBMSs to become established in the marketplace (Kroenke 2005 p21), the UML modeler will usually need to translate the class diagram and associated documentation into a relational schema. In this scenario, the UML model (class diagram) plays the role of conceptual data model (George, Batra et al. 2004 p206).

UML class diagrams offer a richer set of constructs than those offered by the crow's foot notations, but the underlying concepts are similar (George, Batra et al. 2004 p206). UML grew from a synthesis and rationalization of existing formalisms rather any underpinning ontology, and the authors of the language seem to have been at least as focused on providing tools for designers (they use the analogy of programming languages) as on mirroring the UoD (Rumbaugh, Jacobson et al. 1999 pp 5-7).

3.4.4. The conceptual model as a basis for database design

So far in this section, we have focused on the role of a conceptual model as a representation of the UoD (or, in terms of the design paradigm, a *response* to the UoD). Tsichritzis and Lochovsky (1982) refer to this as the *infological* role[44] and contrast it with the *datalogical* ("machine-oriented") role of serving as a basis for database design (Kung and Solvberg 1986 pp206-207; Ross 2003; Kroenke 2005 p120).

There is a tension between the infological and datalogical roles (Atkins 1996), seldom acknowledged in the literature that addresses the former. Atkins cites Campbell (1992): "there is a conflict between the desire to address design issues and the need to create a form of data model with which the business user is comfortable".

The issue is essentially one of *implementation independence* – the goal (or assumption) that the conceptual data model be independent of the implementation language. This view dates at least from Chen (1976), is the basis of the *conceptualization principle* in the ANSI/SPARC framework (ISO/TR9007:1987(E) 1987 p46), and has been frequently re-stated (e.g. Shave 1981; Hull and King 1987; Storey and Goldstein 1988; Jarvenpaa and Machesky 1989; Barker 1990; Navathe 1992; Bock and Ryan 1993; Schenck and Wilson 1994; Shoval and Frumermann 1994; Siau, Wand et al. 1996; Dey, Storey et al 1999; McFadden, Hoffer et al. 1999 p86; Avison and Fitzgerald 2003 pp75-76; George, Batra et al. 2004 p205).

This ideal does not appear to be achieved in practice. In the previous subsection we noted the tight connection between the crow's foot notation and the Relational Model. Many texts suggest that the conceptual model should be normalized (e.g. Cerpa 1995; Benyon 1997; Hay 2003 p109), a requirement not consistent with implementation independence (Jarvenpaa and Machesky 1989). There is also

---

[44] The concepts of infological and datalogical models date from Langefors (1963)

evidence that modelers work with one eye on the implementation environment. Data modeling instructors observe that students learn conceptual modeling more easily if they have an understanding of how the models might be implemented (de Carteret and Vidgen 1995 p xi; Simsion and Witt 2005 p33). A concern with using expert tools rather than humans to perform modeling is that the conceptual models that they produce will not translate to normalized relations (Batra and Antony 2001). Atkins (1996) comments: "If the implicit target for most conceptual models is relational, it is highly likely that the most useful categories in a conceptual model will be seen to be normalized, candidate relations".

We look further at the relationship between conceptual and implementation models in Section 3.6 which covers the logical data modeling stage, and find that if we are to automate the translation of the conceptual data model to a logical data model, we may have to further compromise data independence. For now, we note that proposing and evaluating conceptual modeling languages only in terms of their ability to describe reality addresses only half of their purpose. Taking the datalogical role into account may challenge the view of conceptual modeling as purely descriptive.

3.5. VIEW INTEGRATION

Views and view integration were fundamental to the ANSI/X3/SPARC (1975) framework, which implicitly specified a four step method (Atkins 1997):

1. seek to ascertain each user's view of the data, i.e. analyze each user's data requirements,

2. integrate these views, i.e. design the conceptual schema [this view of conceptual schema design as being a process of view resolution is articulated by Smith and Smith (1978)]

3. create physical structures in which to store the relevant data, i.e. create the physical database design or internal schema, and

4. reproduce the original views for each individual user; i.e. create the external schema

As noted in Section 3.1, this approach continues to influence published methods. In this version of the method, it is different conceptual *schemas* that are the subject of integration; in our framework is the precursor conceptual *models* that are integrated[45] as in Batini, Lenzerini, et al (1986).

The view integration stage is interesting for two reasons:

1. The requirement for such a stage is predicated on the belief that conceptual modeling may produce several different models (views) that will then need to be consolidated to produce a common model. "Different" implies more than simple overlap that would be trivial to resolve, suggesting some support for the design paradigm, although the differences are generally attributed to differences in perceptions.

2. Many methods do not include a view integration stage, on the basis that the conceptual modeling stage is expected to deliver only one model (Batini, Lenzerini et al. 1986), consistent with the description paradigm.

Batini, Lenzerini, et al (1986) identify three reasons for model diversity:

1. Different perspectives (on a common reality): the examples provided are different names for the same concept, and an intermediate level in a hierarchy.

2. Equivalence among constructs in the model: the examples are the choice as to whether to model a concept as an attribute or as a relationship to an entity, and whether to use a generalization hierarchy or an attribute value to distinguish different subsets of an entity.

3. Incompatible design specifications: errors in one or more of the models.

Different but "equivalent" representations are presented as a matter for algorithmic resolution, rather than as representing different semantics. The example described is of a single "Person" entity with a "Sex" attribute being equivalent to a "Person" entity with subtype entities "Man" and "Woman". In fact, these two representations are semantically different in important ways: for example the subtyped version can directly support the constraint that particular attributes or relationships only apply to persons of a particular gender (Simsion 1991; Simsion and Witt 2005 pp111-116).

---

[45] The language used by Batini et al is confusing, as they refer to the 'high level view of requirements' produced by conceptual design as the *conceptual schema*, which is then and transformed by logical database design into the *logical schema* of a DBMS. Their conceptual schema is our conceptual model.

On the one hand such research undermines the idea of a "single right answer" and hence might seem to support the design paradigm, but on the other it conveys a belief that the differences are due to error, simple differences in choice of construct, or viewing different subsets of a common reality. The authors note the absence of reported experience with any of the twelve schema integration methodologies reviewed.

View integration is considered (at least theoretically) extremely difficult to automate with the key issue being the detection and resolution of conflicts (Bouzeghoub 1992; Storey, Thompson et al. 1995). It is not supported by popular modeling tools and associated methods (e.g. Barker 1990; DeAngelis 2000).

3.6. LOGICAL DATA MODELING

The logical data modeling phase as defined here covers the production of an initial conceptual schema (*logical data model*), using the target DBMS language[46], prior to performance tuning. This phase is widely characterized as mechanical or near-mechanical (Jajodia and Ng 1984; Roman 1985; Batra and Zanakis 1994; Wand, Monarchi et al. 1995; Muller 1999; Teorey, Lightstone et al. 2006 pp83-106). Shoval and Shiran's (1997) statement is typical:

> *"Once approved by users (as a proper representation of reality), the conceptual schema[47] is converted into a specific database schema, depending on the data model and DBMS that is used for implementation. (This conversion is usually a simple matter, being an algorithmic, automatic process.)"*

The exemplar for this "algorithmic, automatic process" is the mapping of the original Entity-Relationship Model (Chen 1976) onto the original Relational Model (Codd 1970), the Network Model (CODASYL 1971), or the Entity Set Model (Senko, Altman et al. 1973). This scenario, clearly stated in the original description of the E-R Model (Chen 1976) does not describe current practice.

---

[46] Some methods address DBMS-specific variations at the physical database design stage; addressing this variant would merely involve deferring some of the discussion in this section to the discussion of physical design.

[47] Context shows that their *conceptual schema* is our *conceptual model* ("a data model of reality"); their *database model* is our *conceptual schema.*

As noted in Section 3.4, variants of the crow's foot notation dominate conceptual modeling practice. On the other side of the transformation, commercial DBMSs based on the Relational Model[48] now offer a range of extended semantic facilities, including but not limited to subsets of the current relational standard (ISO/IEC9075-1:2003 2003). Object Relational DBMSs (ORDBMSs) lack a standard: essentially they are relational DBMSs with some object-oriented extensions (George, Batra et al. 2004 p242). There are several hundred "relational" DBMSs in the marketplace (Connolly and Begg 2005 p71).

Creating a transformation for every possible combination of conceptual modeling language and DBMS platform would be a formidable task. Of course an individual organization will only need to develop transformations for those combinations that it actually uses, but even this may not be feasible. The E-R Model was richer semantically than the implementation Models that it supported, and a functional mapping of conceptual onto logical constructs was therefore possible. But if the implementation language supports constructs without equivalents in the conceptual model, a functional mapping will not be logically possible unless some facilities of the implementation language are ignored.

One of the best-developed expositions of the task of "transforming" a conceptual data model to a database schema is Halpin's (2001 pp403-456) mapping of the Object-Role Modeling (ORM) language to the Relational Model. While Halpin provides default transformations for most situations, he acknowledges room for some intervention on the part of the modeler, often looking at the implications for programming against the resulting database, and limits the target database to one implementing the original Relational Model. An earlier version of the method (Nijssen and Halpin 1989 pp245-279) also acknowledges that the default transformation may not be optimum. Other authors similarly provide choices and guidelines, and acknowledge the need for judgment, even when a functional mapping is possible (Fleming and von Halle 1989 p206; Blaha and Premerlani 1998 pp276-309; Simsion and Witt 2005 pp321-357). Use of default mappings is often discouraged by practitioner authorities (Borrie 2004 p210; Barkin-Goodwin 2005).

To appreciate the extent to which mapping from a conceptual to a logical data model is not a "simple matter" it is worth looking at one transformation in detail.

---

[48] XML and Object Oriented databases are also becoming more prevalent; their inclusion in this discussion would simply reinforce the argument that target DBMSs support diverse semantics.

We deliberately choose one that *could* be mechanized. Subtypes and supertypes (Teorey, Yang et al. 1986) are a common and longstanding extension to the conceptual modeling techniques used by practitioners (Winter 1986; Simsion 1989; Barker 1990; Hay 1996a; Silverston, Inmon et al. 1997; DeAngelis 2000), but are not included in the original Relational Model (Codd 1970) and historically have not been directly supported by popular DBMSs.

There are three basic options[49] for mapping a subtype hierarchy[50] onto tables in a conventional RDBMS, *with different semantics* and implications for programming and performance (Barker 1990; Hawryszkiewycz 1991 p225; Halpin 2001 p428; Connolly and Begg 2005 p468 ; Simsion and Witt 2005 pp328-334). The options are: (a) a table for the supertype, (b) a table for each subtype, and (c) a table for each entity.

Halpin's (2001 p428) procedure, the *Powerdesigner*[51] modeling tool, and the *Visio for Enterprise Architects*[52] modeling tool (Halpin, Evans et al. 2003) use Option (a); Connolly & Begg (2005 p468) recommend Option (b); Date[53] (1998 pp423-424), Fleming and von Halle (1989 pp306-307), McFadden, Hoffer et al (1999 pp231-232), Teorey, Lightstone et al (2006 p101), and the *ERwin*[54] and *ER/Studio*[55] modeling tools recommend or default to Option (c). Simsion and Witt (2005 pp328-334) discuss the three options and leave the decision to the modeler. Barker (1990 ppF5-F9) considers only Options (a) and (c) and leaves the choice to the modeler. Blaha and Premerlani (1998) consider all three options and note that they "usually implement" Option (c). Post (1999 p96) considers only Options (a) and (c) and recommends (c) as a better approach "in most cases". D'Orazio and Happel (1996 p142) advise leaving the decision to the physical database designer.

---

[49] Hybrid solutions are also possible; there are also alternative treatments for the primary keys (Simsion and Witt, 2005, p328-334).

[50] The solutions listed here address only true hierarchies of non-overlapping subtypes as recommended by Barker (1990), and others. Different rules for subtypes at the conceptual level add another layer of complexity to the problem.

[51] Product of Sybase

[52] Product of Microsoft

[53] This is consistent with Date's objection to the use of nulls (ibid, pp575-577), including "not applicable" values, which would arise if Option b was used.

[54] Allfusion ™ ERWin ™ Data Modeler - Product of Computer Associates

[55] Product of Embarcadero Technologies

Most texts present their transformation as a "default" or "recommended" option only, and tools may support manual intervention, but Pascal (2000 pp152-157) insists on Option (c). Some modeling tools allow the modeler to override the defaults (Ambler 2003; Teorey, Lightstone et al. 2006 p102) and some instructors specifically advise modelers using the tools to review each case individually (Barkin-Goodwin 2005).

The problem is more difficult when the implementation language is richer (or *potentially* richer) than the conceptual modeling language (Atkins 1996). Witt (1997) provides a simple example of the problem: how does the modeler decide on the best method of recording the location of a vehicle for a hire car company – street address or geographic coordinates? The availability of a spatial data type in the DBMS may affect that choice. Even if this data type is available in the conceptual modeling language, the modeler will need to "look ahead" to see if the implementation language supports it.

In summary, the assumption of a mechanical translation from conceptual data model to logical data model described by Chen (1976) does not remain valid when the formalisms used for these models are changed. Batra and Marakas (1995) state "The [academic] community has failed to show how a conceptual data model can map to an accurate logical data model," and the "translation" from conceptual model to implementation model has been described as "a main issue in systems development" (Wand, Monarchi et al. 1995, p292). In Gero and Maher's (1993) classification of design as *routine* and *non-routine* (the latter involving a higher level of creativity), logical data modeling appears in practice to be closer to a non-routine design task than theory would suggest. With current tools, data modelers are forced to either consider the semantics of the DBMS during conceptual data modeling or intervene in logical data modeling if they are to retain control of what is implemented. Making one stage "pure" description or automation just moves the need for judgment (and arguably design) to the other.

3.7. PHYSICAL DATABASE DESIGN

Physical database design addresses database performance rather than semantics, and is normally treated as a separate activity from data modeling (Goldfine 1986; Elmasri and Navathe 1994; Rob and Coronel 2002; Connolly and Begg 2005 p494; Teorey, Lightstone et al. 2006 pp3-8). Writers on physical database design generally assume that an initial conceptual schema is already in place (Prietula and March 1991; Shasha and Bonnet 2003); in the absence of a third discipline responsible for filling the gap between earlier deliverables and the conceptual schema, this provides some confirmation that the responsibility for specification of the conceptual schema lies with the data modeler.

In order to achieve performance goals, it may be necessary to make changes ("performance compromises") to the conceptual schema: denormalization (Shasha and Bonnet 2003 p136), introducing redundant data (Fleming and von Halle 1989 pp435-473), or other changes (Fleming and von Halle 1989 pp475-515). In Prietula and March's (1991) empirical study of physical database design, three of five practitioners (though none of the eight novices) made changes to the conceptual schema to achieve performance. If the data modeler has ultimate responsibility for semantic content, which may be affected by such changes, there is an argument that they should be a party to any change made to the conceptual schema, for whatever reason (Moody 1995; Simsion and Witt 2005 p359). In this scenario, data modeling continues as a component of the physical design stage.

The physical database design stage is almost invariably called "design". Prietula and March (1991) go further and explicitly characterize it strictly as such: "Because database design is, in fact, a *design* task, the forms of reasoning brought to bear should be similar to those evidenced in studies of design in other domains".

3.8. EXTERNAL SCHEMA SPECIFICATION

External schema (view) specification was traditionally seen as a means of re-creating the individual user views that had been integrated at the View Integration stage. As such it formed part of an overall approach that acknowledged different models of the same UoD, albeit models that could readily be mapped to and from a common conceptual schema. We discussed this approach in Sections 3.1 and 3.5, and noted that it had been largely superseded by approaches that directly produced a common conceptual model.

In the absence of individual "user view" models, external schemas are usually developed at a late stage of database design, based on application programming, security, and data independence considerations rather than on views identified during the conceptual modeling process (Fleming and von Halle 1989; McFadden, Hoffer et al. 1999 p363; Stephens and Plew 2001 pp322-323; Connolly and Begg 2005 p84). The relevance to the description / design question is that the application programmers' (or other direct users') interests may be met through the construction of views rather than directly by the conceptual schema. A conceptual schema that was not acceptable as a model of reality (or indeed as a model of database structures) might be rendered more acceptable through manipulation and presentation as a view.

3.9. PROCESS MODELING

Process modeling is seldom included as a task in database design frameworks, but systems development methodologies recognize close relationships between data and process modeling (Avison and Fitzgerald 2003 pp227-238). Methodologies may be characterized as "data-driven", "process-driven" or "blended" (Avison and Fitzgerald 2003 pp347-352), according to the sequence in which models are developed, and generally include techniques for verifying that the data and process models support each other, i.e. that the data model includes the data required to support each process and that the process model provides for maintenance of all data. Given the complementary roles of data and process models, it is worth looking briefly at whether process modeling is characterized as description or design.

Early computerized systems were typically automated versions of the manual systems that they replaced. But since at least the late 1970s, writers on information systems development have advocated the redesign of business processes to better exploit information technology. Process modelers are warned to beware of simply reproducing the current way of doing things. "Structured analysis" approaches (DeMarco 1978; Gane and Sarson 1979; Yourdon 1989) made a distinction between the "old logical" and "new logical" process models and encouraged consideration of alternatives (Avison and Fitzgerald 2003 p357). But there was only one data model – derived relatively mechanically from data used by the (new) processes (DeMarco 1978; Gane and Sarson 1979; Shoval and Even-Chaime 1987). Process modeling continues to be characterized as design with opportunities for creativity (Sharp and McDermott 2001), most prominently in the context of business process re-engineering (Hammer 1990) in which "radical re-design" plays a central role (Hammer and Champy 1993 p36).

Perhaps the key difference in how process modeling and data modeling are perceived is embodied in the oft-repeated claim that data structures are intrinsically more stable than processes, a view strongly promoted by Martin (1985 pp159-60), and frequently restated (Elmasri and Navathe 1994; Kim and Everest 1994; Hay 2003 p73). The "data is stable" belief is a part of information systems folklore that has not been supported by theoretical argument (Marche 1993;

Avison and Fitzgerald 2003 pp76-77).   The reason for the belief may be that *databases* once implemented are only changed infrequently because of the cost of dealing with the impact on the programs that use them (Everest 1986 pp416-417; Marche 1993).   Simsion (1989; 1993) and Ross (2003 pp209-215) argue that stability is not intrinsic to data models, but depends upon generalization decisions made by the modeler.   From the perspective of the description / design question, the "data is stable" belief suggests that data is "out there" to be described, in contrast to processes, which are designed.

Empirical work on schema evolution (Marche 1993; Wedemeijer 2002) has shown that data structures, as modeled, *do* change over time in line with business changes.   We may at least speculate that business *process* changes (which, as we have noted, are encouraged) could lead to such data changes.   Hammer's (1990) seminal paper on business process reengineering cited the case of an organization eliminating the invoicing of suppliers and it would be reasonable to expect that the *supplier invoice* entity (if it existed[56]) might have disappeared from the conceptual data model.

3.10. BELIEFS FROM END-TO-END

Table 3–2 is a summary of the dominant and alternative beliefs about stages of the overall database design process, as discussed in the preceding eight sections.

---

[56] It could be argued that the data model would hold the relevant data in a more fundamental form than an invoice entity; such an approach, however, would surely involve a more sophisticated (design?) approach than reflecting or describing "things of interest to the business".

Stage	Dominant Belief	Alternative Belief
Interaction with the UoD	One view of reality (intrinsically or by consensus)	Reality as socially constructed, multiple views
Requirements Analysis	An aid to perception of the UoD	Formulation and negotiation of the modeling problem / high-level design
Conceptual Data Modeling	Description independent of implementation environment	Design taking into account implementation environment
View Integration	Not required / straightforward discrete task	Complex, requires judgment, progressive
Logical Data Modeling	Mechanical transformation	Requires decisions by the modeler
Physical Database Design	Design (outside scope of data modeling)	Design (conceptual schema changes are within scope of data modeling)
External Schema Specification	Reflects user views	Serves applications programmers*
Process Modeling	Design independent of the data model	Design that may impact the data model

*This is probably the *dominant* belief amongst practitioners

Table 3–2: Perspectives on stages in the database design process

If the dominant beliefs about the nature of each component are aggregated, they provide an end-to-end picture of the database design process as descriptive, in line with the "reality mapping" objective described in Section 3.1, with the exception of compromises made for performance reasons. Conversely, the alternative beliefs allow for choice, judgment, and possibly creativity at each stage, and the characterization of the (central) conceptual and logical data modeling stages as design.

This completes the end-to-end review of the database design process – the *environment* in which data modeling takes place – addressing the first of the five perspectives in the 5Ps research framework.

Chapter 3 – Beliefs about the database design process

CHAPTER 4
COMPARISON WITH LAWSON'S MODEL

If it looks like a duck, and quacks like a duck, we have at least to consider the possibility that we have a small aquatic bird of the family Anatidae on our hands.

— Douglas Adams, *Dirk Gently's Holistic Detective Agency*

We now look at data modeling from each of the three perspectives provided by the Lawson Framework: *Problem*, *Process*, and *Product*. The focus is on characterizing the stages that we have called *conceptual data modeling* and *logical data modeling*, but we will frequently need to refer to the other stages, particularly in discussing inputs and outputs.

4.1. LAWSON'S CHARACTERISTICS OF DESIGN

Lawson's list of design characteristics, synthesized from the design literature, appears in Section 2.2.1. The list is organized into three groups of Properties, covering *Problem, Process* and *Product*.

The *Problem, Process,* and *Product* sections follow a consistent format of presenting each Property then examining whether the literature characterizes data modeling as having that Property.

4.2. PROBLEM

In this section, we review descriptions of data modeling *problems*, using Lawson's Properties of design (Section 2.2.1) as a reference. This is the shortest of the three sections covering the different dimensions of the Lawson framework, because the literature has relatively little to say about data modeling problems. The dominant descriptive characterization does not require a *problem* as such, beyond using the term for the UoD itself and therefore characterizing the conceptual model as a problem description (Kung and Solvberg 1986; Srinivasan and Te'eni 1995; Ramesh and Browne 1999).

Lawson describes design problems as having three Properties: they cannot be comprehensively stated; they require subjective interpretation; and they tend to be organized hierarchically. We assess data modeling against each of these Properties in turn.

4.2.1. Problem property 1: Design problems cannot be comprehensively stated

Lawson states that it is never possible to be sure when all aspects of a design problem have emerged, and that design problems are often full of uncertainties about both the objectives and their relative priorities. Some requirements will emerge only after an attempt has been made at a solution. The term *ill-structured* has been used to describe design problems (Simon 1973; Willem 1991).

Data modeling problems have also been described as ill-structured (Vitalari and Dickson 1983; Ryan, Bordoloi et al. 2000) and ill-defined (Parent 1997), as well as informal, incomplete, and ambiguous (Chaiyasut and Shanks 1994; George, Batra et al. 2004 p209). As noted in Section 3.3, the "requirements" shown as input to conceptual modeling in data modeling frameworks generally lack formality, and indeed there may not be any requirements document as such; the data modeler may work directly from interviews and observations. The use of informal and incomplete "fuzzy pictures" (Sommerville and Sawyer 1997) rather than more formal languages for the requirements specification resonates with the observation that designers prefer to start with a short and incomplete brief rather than a comprehensive statement of requirements (Lawson 1994 p23).

The Unified Modeling Language (UML) (Rumbaugh, Jacobson et al. 1999) provides an example of approaches recommended in practice[57] in its use of *use cases* as the principal tool for representing business requirements. Their limitations are apparent in advice that use cases may only cover about a third of the user requirements needed to develop a conceptual data model and that unspecified "other requirements" should also be studied (George, Batra et al. 2004 p209). Attempts at a more complete specification might better be characterized as at least partial solutions. Witt's (2002b) *object class hierarchy* could easily be characterized as an early version of a conceptual data model, as could Teorey et al's (2006 pp3-4) description of requirements elicitation that shows "the concepts

---

[57] The associated Rational Unified Process is owned and marketed by IBM.

of products, customers, salespersons and orders being formed in the mind of the end user *during the interview process*." (Italics added to highlight that the example suggests joint design or discovery rather than the user knowing *in advance* the set of classes to be modeled (Marche 1991; Parsons and Wand 1992)).

Lawson's observation under this Property that some requirements only become apparent as solutions are attempted is consistent with Roozenburg and Cross's (1991) characterization of the (architectural) design process as *conjecture-analysis* in which requirements emerge through client feedback on proposed designs. Elicitation of data modeling requirements has been described as a social process, wherein analyst and user knowledge is combined, with systems requirements being "emergent" from that process Darke & Shanks (1995). De Carteret and Vidgen (1995 p368) state that a good data model is one which *creates* a shared understanding and that the way to develop such a model is through participation and facilitation. Iteration is also apparent in Steinberg, Faley, et al's (1994) conceptual modeling tool that supplements its parsing of plain language requirements by eliciting further information from the user.

Conversely, much empirical work has assumed that requirements *can* be comprehensively stated, as participants are presented with a problem description (e.g. Shoval and Even-Chaime 1987; Batra, Hoffer et al. 1990; Shanks, Simsion et al. 1993; Batra and Antony 1994a; Hitchman 1995; Srinivasan and Te'eni 1995; Antony and Batra 1999; Howard, Bodnovich et al. 1999; Liao and Palvia 2000; Moody, Sindre et al. 2003; Yang 2003). These "business requirements" are generally plain language descriptions of the UoD and goals of the proposed application, although some researchers have used examples of input forms and / or reports (Mantha 1987; Batra and Antony 1994b), data flow diagrams (Shoval and Even-Chaime 1987) or functional dependencies amongst data items (Yang 2003)[58]. Batra, Hoffer et al (1990) highlight the implication: "One may question the relevance of this [conceptual modeling] phase, and argue that some kind of conceptual model is already available at the end of the elicitation process, albeit in a natural language".

The question is whether such "requirements" are representative of real-world data modeling problems. In many cases the problem description appears to have been reverse engineered from a solution, or at least "loaded" with the semantics

---

[58] These last two studies were the only examples of descriptions intended to support a "bottom up" approach found in the survey of empirical studies described in Chapter 5.

required to produce a complete solution. This approach is apparent when problems are described in terms of the number of entities and relationships that they specify, e.g. "the task included two supertype / subtype clusters, four binary compositions, one ternary composition, and a composite chain involving five different entities at different levels of abstraction... Subjects had to build an appropriate data model..." (Batra and Davis 1992). This is not to criticize the design of such experiments *per se*; rather to note that they do not add to our understanding of data modeling problems in the real world.

4.2.2. Problem property 2: Design problems require subjective interpretation

Lawson states that designers bring their own skills, perceptions and ideas to a problem; not only are they likely to design different solutions, they also perceive the problem differently. "What seems important to one client or user or designer may not seem so to others."

We have previously seen (Section 3.2) some acknowledgment that different people may perceive the UoD differently. The context there was of directly perceiving concepts (entities, relationships, attributes or their counterparts in other formalisms) that would then be *described* in a data model. Differences in perception would lead directly to different models. In this section, our concern is with different perceptions of data modeling *problems* in the form of requirements a distinction that is probably meaningless if one subscribes to the descriptive paradigm wherein the UoD *is* the requirement.

In a data modeling literature that focuses on notations and methods, there is little about the "interpretation of meaning" in requirements (Beynon-Davies 1992), but there are indications that different categories of stakeholders generically see different aspects as being important. Business users, systems analysts, (enterprise) information architects, project managers and application developers will bring different perspectives and priorities to a data modeling problem (Moody, Simsion et al. 1995). Arguments between data modelers and physical database designers over the importance of performance compared with other goals (such as normalization) are common in industry (Pascal 2000 pp143-145; Stephens and Plew 2001 pp199-200; O'Rourke, Fishman et al. 2003 p374; Simsion and Witt 2005 pp58-59).

The issue of relative importance of different aspects of data modeling *problems* overlaps with the evaluation of solutions (if, for example, stakeholders see performance as an important requirement, they will presumably favor solutions which offer high performance). We look at quality of data models in Section 4.4.2, where we note that different authors have proposed different quality measures, reflecting different views about the requirements for a good data model.

4.2.3. Problem property 3: Design problems tend to be organized hierarchically

"Hierarchical organization" means essentially that a design problem can be broken into (or give rise to) sub-problems that are also design problems, and itself can be seen as subordinate to higher level design problems.

Theoretical work and instructional texts on data modeling do break down data modeling problems into sub-problems. The task may be partitioned into stages (as discussed in Section3.1) subject areas (Finkelstein 1989; Hoberman 2002 pp118-123, 157-206) or generic problems such as modeling ternary relationships (Ferg 1991; Hawryszkiewycz 1991; Jones and Song 1996; Hitchman 1999; Halpin 2001 pp125-126; Simsion and Witt 2005 pp96-98; Teorey, Lightstone et al. 2006 pp60-61)[59]. Data modelers also decompose data modeling problems into sub-problems (Jarvenpaa and Machesky 1989; Srinivasan and Te'eni 1995). There is nothing surprising here: breaking down large problems into smaller problems is a ubiquitous technique. What is generally missing in terms of Lawson's definition is an explicit characterization of the smaller problems as *design* problems, although choices requiring judgment are frequently presented.

The idea that data modeling problems are components of higher level design problems is more interesting. Data modeling is part of the overall task of database design, which, as previously noted (Section3.1) is generally acknowledged as being a true design task. In turn, databases are built to support applications, business processes and organizations, all of which are generally seen as *designed*. Explicit recognition of this context (which casts data modeling problems as at least components of design problems) is uncommon in the data modeling literature. Exceptions include Moody's (1995) advice to "keep your eye on the big picture",

---

[59] The varying advice provided by these authors is some evidence of the choices available to data modelers and the consequent need for judgment.

and Hoberman's (2005 p14) use of a "scope cube" to encourage looking at data modeling projects in the context of business functions, processes, and applications.

4.3. PROCESS

In this section, we review descriptions of data modeling *processes*, the third dimension of the Lawson framework. The data modeling literature addresses *process* at two levels: methods for data model development and the behavior of data modelers.

In Chapter 3, we reviewed the overall database design process and noted different approaches and conflicting beliefs. Uncertainty and conflict persist as we look in more detail at conceptual and logical data modeling methods: "the principles for building a data model as set out in the literature are contradictory, unclear, unspecific and / or incomplete" (Marche 1993).

Until relatively recently the processes and expertise employed by data modelers had received little research attention (Batra and Davis 1992). A number of studies have since observed novice and expert data modelers performing laboratory tasks, typically the development of a conceptual data model from a plain language description and / or sample forms and reports. Direct observation, videotaping, and protocol analysis have been used. The last of these involves participants speaking aloud as they solve a problem (Newell and Simon 1972). While the technique has been used in other disciplines (e.g. Lloyd and Scott (1994) studied electrical engineers), its ability to reveal cognitive processes has been questioned (Nisbett and Wilson 1977; Goguen and Linde 1993). Some researchers have used models of *design* as a reference for analyzing modeler behavior (Srinivasan and Te'eni 1990; Chaiyasut and Shanks 1994).

Lawson lists six properties of design processes.

1. The process is endless (knowing where to stop requires judgment)

2. There is no infallibly correct process (that will reliably lead to sound solutions)

3. The process involves finding as well as solving problems. Lawson includes creativity under this property.

4. Design inevitably involves subjective value judgments.

5. Design is a prescriptive activity.

6.   Designers work in the context of a need for action.

We assess data modeling against each of these properties in turn, with particular attention to Property 2, which covers method, and Property 3 which covers the role of creativity.

4.3.1. Process property 1: The process is endless

There is some recognition in the literature that the search for a perfect data model is potentially endless and that modeling should stop when the cost of further modeling is higher than the costs of applying the model in its current state (Lindland, Sindre et al. 1994). This is a pragmatic decision, requiring judgment, and designers can put too much effort into model development (Avison and Fitzgerald 2003 p180). One of Moody's (1995) seven guidelines for data modelers, based on observations of practice, is "know when to stop". Apparently even experienced practitioners may find it difficult to determine the end-point, and we might expect this to be particularly problematic if they were performing an "endless" design process whilst under the impression that the work was descriptive. Perhaps they would explain the apparent slowness as "care for accuracy" (Avison and Fitzgerald 2003 p188). After implementation, the schema may continue to evolve, apparently not only as a result of changes to the UoD: Wedemeijer (2002) found that only half of the changes in the four schemas that he studied over five to ten years were due to contemporary change in the UoD.

4.3.2. Process property 2: There is no infallibly correct process

If there is an infallibly correct process for data modeling, it seems we have yet to find it, given the diversity of methods discussed in Chapter 3, and evidence from research and practice that it is not done well (Wand and Weber 2002; Pascal 2004). Some approaches *have* claimed to be able to reliably produce high-quality models. Teorey, Yang and Fry's (1986) method was presented as leading to "nearly reproducible *designs* from a given requirements specification" (emphasis added), and similar statements have been made about NIAM in particular (e.g.Yunker 1993). No empirical evidence appears to have been published in support of such claims. Atkins (1997) argues that the search for a perfect data modeling process is "inappropriate, wasteful and dangerous"

Published methods give far more attention to the rules of the modeling language than to how to use it (Batra and Zanakis 1994), with the implicit message that the actual modeling is relatively straightforward (Lewis 1993). In contrast, Simsion and Witt (2005 p231) liken the modeler who knows only the language to an architect who has learned only the drawing conventions.

A feature common to many methods is a detailed, step-by-step prescription (or at least heuristics) for every stage *except the selection of the initial abstractions* (e.g. Nijssen and Halpin 1989; Teorey, Lightstone et al. 2006), and it is on this critical phase that we now focus our attention. Some authors have discounted this phase as trivial: "designers do not spend their time in academic discussions of methods to find the objects: in the physical or abstract reality being modeled, the objects are just there for the picking!" (Meyer 1988)[60]. Others do provide more specific guidance on the selection of the initial abstractions, most commonly one of the following:

1. *Underline the nouns.* Data modelers are advised to start by identifying the nouns in a description of the UoD (Chen 1983; Veryard 1984 p15-18; Eden 1996; Mannino 2001 p231). These become candidate entities and a framework for adding relationships and attributes – and perhaps entities identified from verb phrases and "hidden classes" (Song, Yano et al. 2005)[61]. Some attempts have been made to automate data modeling using the technique (Steinberg, Faley et al. 1994). This (clearly descriptive) approach has been criticized as simplistic (Simsion 1991; Crerar, Barclay et al. 1996; Simsion and Witt 2005 p276) and more appropriate to student exercises than to the complexity of real-life situations.

2. *Identify attributes and normalize.* This bottom-up style of data modeling, using *synthesis* (Bernstein 1976) to build relations from functional dependencies amongst data items, is described in some texts (e.g. Hawryszkiewycz 1991) and sometimes acknowledged as an alternative to a top-down approach, but does not appear much in more recent practitioner literature (an exception is Mannino 2001 pp273-276).

---

[60] The reference here is to the first edition – the claim does not appear in later editions.

[61] These authors are writing from an object-oriented perspective, but the goals and approach are similar.

It is associated particularly with earlier process-driven approaches (DeMarco 1978; Gane and Sarson 1979). As generally described, it is a descriptive process, relying on data items already in place or otherwise nominated by the process modeler or user (Avison and Fitzgerald 2003 p358). Such an approach can perpetuate existing views of data by relying on historical identifiers as a source of entities (Simsion 1991).

3. *Work from examples.* NIAM (Verheijen and van Bekkum 1982; Nijssen and Halpin 1989) and the related ORM (Halpin 2001) approach begin with business statements that may be at the instance or type level. The method is much more structured than the "find the nouns" approaches, and recognizes the role of the modeler in choosing abstractions. Interestingly for an approach that is frequently characterized as more prescriptive than entity-based approaches (Atkins 1996), there is an acknowledgment, albeit indirect, of the role of creativity, when it is noted that the method removes the need for it from *all but this first step* (Nijssen and Halpin 1989 p30).

4. *Use patterns.* A few practitioner-oriented texts (Hay 1996a; Fowler 1997; Silverston 2001; Simsion and Witt 2005 p277) recommend that modelers adapt generic patterns. The use of patterns is discussed further in Section 4.4.4, in the context of pattern use being a property of design.

5. *Propose abstractions based on a holistic understanding.* This approach, consistent with the design paradigm, is proposed by a few authors (Langefors and Sundgren 1975; McFadden, Hoffer et al. 1999 p47; Simsion and Witt 2005 p252) and is discussed under Product property 3: *Design products are often holistic responses* (Section 4.4.3).

We have little evidence as to which of these approaches are used in practice, but laboratory studies have noted some differences in the approaches used by experts and novices. Literal translation of nouns to entities seems to be a practice more common in novices than experts (Shanks, Simsion et al. 1993; Shanks 1997b). Pattern use has been observed in experts, but (unsurprisingly, given their likely lack of knowledge of patterns) not in novices (Batra and Davis 1992; Chaiyasut and Shanks 1994).

Finally, work on automating aspects of the database design process (Tauzovich 1990; Reiner 1991; Bouzeghoub 1992; Storey, Dey et al. 1998; Storey, Goldstein et al. 2002) can provide some indication as to how well it can be formalized.

Batini, Ceri, et al (1992) state that conceptual database design is a difficult problem and cannot be fully automated. Conversely, Storey, Thompson, et al, (1995) comment that expert systems are a response to the difficulty of obtaining consistent and reliable results and suggest that conceptual design can be automated to the level of an intermediate performer. Convincing evidence is lacking (as indeed is a good description of "intermediate performer").

In summary, the lack of an agreed infallibly correct process for data modeling is evidenced by continuing controversy as to the most appropriate approach, criticism of widely-advocated methods as simplistic, difficulty in automating the process, and indications that it is not well done in practice.

4.3.3. Process property 3: The process involves finding as well as solving problems (creativity)

Two ideas are covered by this Property: the concurrent development of problem and solution, and the central role of creativity. The connection between the two is not obvious, and we treat them as separate topics within this subsection.

Lawson describes problems and solutions progressively emerging and becoming clearer together, leading to a design process that is more "argumentative" than linear. This is consistent with some generic design models (Maher, Poon et al. 1996) and protocol analysis of industrial designers (Cross and Dorst 1999).

Observations of experienced data modelers have shown that formalisms alone are not enough to evoke the appropriate types of questions (Ridjanovic 1986). Experienced modelers move iteratively back and forth between requirements elicitation and solution development (Srinivasan and Te'eni 1990; Chaiyasut and Shanks 1994; Srinivasan and Te'eni 1995; Milton 2005). Keuffel (1996) recognizes an "exploration mode" in modeling, and suggests that the rigor of languages such as NIAM may be counterproductive during that phase.

Creativity is generally considered a fundamental property of design, although it is not as prominent in Lawson's framework.

In 1988, Couger (1996) found only six papers in the information systems field that devoted more than a page to creativity, yet creativity and innovation in systems development was seen as an important issue by IT managers (Couger 1988). Since then, there has been a substantial amount of research published on the subject, but Couger's later (1996) list did not include any papers on data modeling.

Data modeling is occasionally characterized as creative (Pletch 1989; Simsion 1991; de Carteret and Vidgen 1995 p334) or as having a creative component (Avison and Cuthbertson 2002 p20). Moody (2000) proposes a role for lateral thinking in achieving the quality goal of "simplicity". Two papers have discussed the role of tools in supporting a creative approach to data modeling (Shanks and Simsion 1992; Crerar, Barclay et al. 1996). The need for human creativity is sometimes seen as related to choice of data modeling language and method (Falkenberg 1993; Atkins 1996).

Other (occasional) mentions of creativity in data modeling refer to peripheral aspects, around a core characterization of data modeling as description: Hoberman (2002) encourages the data modeler to "let your imagination soar" and to "be as creative as possible" but his examples focus on tools and techniques (e.g. for communicating concepts) rather than the models themselves. Some examples of "creativity" might be better characterized as judgment: distinguishing whether something should be represented as an entity, a relationship or a "data abstraction" and putting things into familiar categories (Storey, Thompson et al. 1995). (The latter example is interesting in that, even in the context of illustrating creativity, it limits the data modeler to *familiar* categories).

Glass and Vessey (1994) used a list of defining characteristics of creativity (Newell, Shaw et al. 1962) to ask: "Is the work of software predominantly clerical, intellectual or creative?" and solicited experts' judgments of the level of creativity of various information systems tasks. Data modeling was not explicitly addressed but "use of models" (under "requirements representation") was rated as a creative task by two of the four experts[62].

4.3.4. Process property 4: Design inevitably involves subjective value judgments

We have previously noted (Sections 3.6 and 4.3.2) that instructions in the literature are not always fully prescriptive; rather data modelers are provided with guidelines for making choices, with the implication that they will need to exercise judgment.

---

[62] This lack of agreement amongst the experts was not peculiar to data modeling; the authors note the lack of agreement across a range of tasks.

Conceptual modeling has been characterized as a qualitative, subjective, and people-oriented task requiring "soft" skills (Mannino 2001 p202) and complex problem solving skills (Jarvenpaa and Machesky 1989). These properties are not strictly incompatible with "reality mapping", but they do suggest a more subjective process.

Closely related to subjectivity is the concept of *style,* a well-accepted characteristic of design disciplines (Chan 1999; 2001). Do individual data modelers consistently model in certain (valid) ways that differ from other modelers? The academic literature appears to be silent on this issue, but practitioners are aware of it, and discomforted that it does not sit well with the descriptive paradigm: "For many a sense of style in a model is disturbing. After all, how can a quality deliverable come from anything so personal and subjective? Yet every modeler knows the unspoken truth… (Claxton and McDougall 2001)."

Lawson observes under this heading that designers find it difficult to be dispassionate about their work and are often possessive of their designs. Data modelers often have difficulty in remaining objective and can become emotionally attached to their models (Hoberman 2002 p463; Hay 2005).

4.3.5. Process property 5: Design is a prescriptive activity

Lawson identifies this property as "the most important, obvious and fundamental difference" between design and science. Designers focus not on what is, but on what might be, could be, and should be. Olle, Hagelstein et al (1991), reviewing information systems methods, similarly treat *prescription* as the defining property of design activities and characterize the difference between analysis and design as one of *description* vs. *prescription.* As noted earlier, they classify data modeling as analysis – hence description.

Some other authors use the prescription-description dichotomy, but in the context of data modeling *methods*: prescriptive methods presuppose an objective reality to be uncovered whereas a descriptive method acknowledges a subjective reality (Rolland, Souveyet et al. 1995; Atkins 1996; Eden 1996). On this basis, Atkins characterizes the NIAM approach as being more prescriptive than the Entity-Relationship approach. Similarly, the statement that "We should realize that design will always have an artistic component and that not everything can be prescribed" (Bubenko 1986) uses data modeling as the *object* of prescription – and thus associates prescription with method.

In applying the prescription-description dichotomy to the method rather than the design process itself, these authors are in effect referring to Process Property 2 (existence of a correct process), and characterizing the more tightly-defined option as more prescriptive. These alternative uses of the *prescription* and *description* are noted here because they illustrate that authors in the field do not necessarily interpret or use the dichotomy in the same way. The possibility for misinterpretation is worth noting, as both Olle, Hagelstein, et al and Lawson give particular weight to the distinction in describing design.

4.3.6. Process property 6: Designers work in the context of a need for action

This property recognizes the pragmatics of design: designs are required to meet some real-world need, typically within budgets and deadlines.

As data modeling is undertaken in order to build an information system[63], it would seem evident that the modeler works in the context of a "need for action". Yet, as noted in Section 3.4, a substantial portion of the literature pays scant attention to this context. The emphasis is on describing reality rather than contributing in the most effective way to the resulting database – on the infological rather than the datalogical role (Atkins 1996). Fidelity is more often stated as a goal than utility. Even the literature on data model quality (discussed in Section 4.4.2) makes little reference to the well-established characterization of quality as "fitness for purpose" (Juran and Godfrey 1999 pp4.20-4.21).

There is of course an assumption that the best description of reality will result in the best database (Section 3.1), but this is a philosophical rather than an empirically-established position. It is not unreasonable to suggest that sometimes the most effective business solution, even if only in terms of timeliness, will involve some compromise from the descriptive ideal.

If, in the business world, responding to the "need for action" was compromised by another goal, we could expect the perpetrators to be criticized for not "getting with

---

[63] Other uses of data modeling such as reverse engineering and systems planning were excluded from the scope of the present study, as noted in Section 1.4.2.

the program". There is evidence of exactly that. Data modeling practitioners themselves observe that they are perceived as impractical (Duffy 2000), uncompromising (Hay 2005), overly theoretical (Simsion 1996; McQuade 2005), unresponsive to deadlines (Silverston quoted in Pascal 2004), and ultimately expendable (Seiner 2001). Asked to nominate their greatest challenge, data modelers routinely state that it is convincing others of the value of their (real or prospective) contribution (Simsion 2005b) and tensions between data modelers and other development professionals are well-recognized (Ambler 2002 p24; 2003 pp4-5). Many organizations choose not to do data modeling (MacDonell 1994; Hitchman 1995; Maier 1996), despite it being a component of most published methods.

This is not simply a case of antipathy to information systems professionals; these criticisms come from within the information systems profession, are quite specific in character and target, and are entirely consistent with a view that data modelers as a class pay insufficient heed to the "need for action."

4.4. PRODUCT

In this section, we review descriptions of data modeling *products* (i.e. data models), using Lawson's properties of design as a reference. Lawson describes five properties of design products (Lawson's term is *solutions*):

1. There is an inexhaustible number of different solutions

2. There are no optimal solutions to design problems

3. Design solutions are often holistic responses

4. Design solutions are a contribution to knowledge

5. Design solutions are part of other design problems

The first of these properties is particularly interesting because the contrary assumption of a *single* correct answer is widespread in data modeling research and in instructional material. Accordingly we look at this property at some length, taking note of the relatively recent application to data modeling of research on classification and categories from philosophy and cognitive science. We also look in some detail, under Property 2, at the measurement of data model quality, another subject that has received attention over the past decade.

4.4.1. Product property 1: There is an inexhaustible number of different solutions

In Section 3.2, we addressed some philosophical issues in data modeling, in particular whether there was a single objective UoD and whether different observers' perceptions of that UoD could be reconciled. If the answer to either of these questions is "no" then there will be potentially as many models as there are observers, but it would probably be wrong to attribute such diversity to *design*. Differences attributable *only* to perception or the lack of an objective UoD might be better characterized by the description paradigm. We therefore ask: given an agreed UoD, as Wand, Monarchi, et al (1995) suggest as a reasonable starting point, is there more than one workable data model? (If we are not comfortable with the idea of an agreed UoD, we could re-frame the question: could *one modeler* produce more than one workable data model of his/her perceived UoD?).

One right model?

Before turning to the literature, we note that it is difficult to find an *argued* case for there being only one theoretically viable data model for an agreed UoD, at least in the context of popular data modeling languages. An exception is the substantial ("record") level of correspondence (Stodder 1996) prompted by an article in a practitioner magazine arguing that data modeling was design (Simsion 1996). Most of the letters published (Hay 1996b; Schmidt 1996; Warner 1996) contended that data modeling, competently performed, should be deterministic and provide a single answer.

Many papers do in fact take this "one right model" position, explicitly or implicitly, but without offering any justification. In particular, much empirical research has been designed around a *gold standard*[64] or *benchmark solution* in which a single correct solution is established in advance by the researcher (Atkins and Patrick 1996; Topi and Ramesh 2002).

Most explicit examinations of the question acknowledge that different modelers may produce different models (e.g. Hawryszkiewycz 1991 p119; Batra and Davis 1992). The context frequently suggests some discomfort with the possibility of

---

[64] The term "gold standard" seems to originate with (Shoval and Even-Chaime 1987)

multiple solutions – an occasional flaw in the descriptive paradigm rather than evidence that data modeling is design. Rumbaugh (1993) captures something of this flavor: "I frequently receive inquiries from readers asking for guidance in situations that seem to permit more than one way of modeling."

A common position, explicit in some work (Falkenberg 1993; Schouten 1993; Yunker 1993), and implied by authors who confine their discussion of difference to this area, is that data models of the same UoD may differ, but that the differences are the result of shortcomings in the data modeling language. The argument is that data modeling is essentially descriptive, but that current data modeling languages allow some choice in how the description is documented. The point that the modeler has some choice in whether to use an entity, relationship or attribute to represent a given UoD concept has been repeatedly made (Kent 1978 p94; Veryard 1984 p20; Hawryszkiewycz 1991 pp119-120; Storey, Thompson et al. 1995; Wand, Monarchi et al. 1995; Date 1998 pp426-427). Binary or fact-based modeling (Kent 1984) and its relatives NIAM (Nijssen and Halpin 1989) and Object-Role modeling (Halpin 2001) address this issue by reducing the number of options available to the modeler. The Relational Model also reduces such choice through using a smaller number of basic constructs (Date 1998 pp426-427).

In fact, there are some rules and heuristics for deciding whether to represent a concept as a relationship or as an entity (Teorey, Yang et al. 1986) or as an entity or attribute (Teorey, Yang et al. 1986 pp119-120; Hawryszkiewycz 1991; Batra and Davis 1992; Avison and Fitzgerald 2003 p181; Teorey, Lightstone et al. 2006 p56). Empirical evidence (Batra and Davis 1992; Weber 1996) is that even novice data modelers do not have difficulties in deciding whether to classify a concept as an entity or as an attribute.

The classification of real-world concepts as entities, attributes or relationships (or their counterparts in other formalisms) discussed above is the most commonly advanced reason for differences amongst models. But there is an argument that diversity can arise from more fundamental classification decisions, when real-world instances are classified into categories. Atkins (2003) states: "The need to create categories of data, i.e. to identify entities, before the construction of an E-R Model can begin, ensures that an analyst will be forced into making what are essentially design decisions from the beginning..." We look at the question of choice in classification in the next subsection.

Classification theory and data modeling

Classification has long been recognized as intrinsic to data modeling (Smith and Smith 1977). Recently, theoretical and empirical work on classification and categories has been applied to conceptual data modeling (Parsons and Wand 1992; Parsons 1996; Parsons and Wand 1996; Parsons and Wand 2000), and although the links are still "somewhat weakly defined" (Topi and Ramesh 2002) this work offers some insights into the "one right answer" issue.

Research in the 1970s effectively spelt the end of the *classical view* of categories: the idea that categories were characterized solely by the properties shared by their members and that real-world entities could be classified unambiguously according to their common attributes (Murphy 2002, p16). Lakoff (1987 p6) observes that before that time the classical view was not even thought of as a theory; in most disciplines it was taught as "unquestionable, definitional truth" – a case in which an idea from philosophy was believed in spite of overwhelming evidence against it. This view survives in the data modeling literature: "entities in the real world are of one type if they have *all* of their attributes in common" (Pascal 2000 p151, emphasis in original). It is beyond the scope of this book to explore the range of research (Murphy 2002) that addresses the gap left by the classical theory. We simply highlight some findings that emphasize the subjective nature of classification and the possibility of alternative classification schemes for the same UoD.

Wittgenstein (1953) explored the idea that members of a category may be related to one another without all members having any properties in common (his example is *game*). Boundaries of a category may be extended over time (Wittgenstein's example is *number*) and some categories have degrees of membership and no clear boundaries. Empirical work (Hampton 1979) undermined the idea that categories could be differentiated by "defining features". Ad hoc categories are frequently made up as required to serve some specific purpose (Barsalou 1983; 1984). Some attributes only become relevant once an object has been categorized: e.g. "large" for a piano classified as furniture (Rosch 1978), and identification of the attribute then *follows* identification of the category, rather than vice versa. Different cultures classify differently: for example some languages have a single word which covers both "blue" and "green" (Berlin and Kay 1969). (In data modeling practice, the present author noted differences in the number of eye colors recognized by different police forces – and hence in the definition of the corresponding attributes in the data models).

Researchers who have applied these ideas to data modeling explicitly reject the "one right answer" position. Kent (1978 p15) states simply: "there is no natural set of categories" and (p107) quotes Sapir (1931): "Categories such as number, gender, case, tense, mode, voice, aspect and a host of others...are not so much discovered in experience as imposed upon it". In summary, classes are abstractions created by humans in order to describe useful similarities among things, different class structures can be used to model the same domain, and there is no inherent basis or clear rules for deciding that one view is superior (Parsons and Wand 1992; 2000 p239). The last clause is perhaps expressed a little too strongly[65], to the extent that it does not sit easily with the design paradigm. All structurally-sound bridge or building designs are not equally good.

The potential for data to be classified in different ways need not be incompatible with a descriptive view of modeling. A business will normally have established categories in advance of the modeling effort. The question is whether the data modeler needs to add to or modify those categories.

Finally, in the context of choosing classes, it is interesting to look at a comment by Jackson (1995, p24): "Obviously, deciding which classes to recognize is an important early step in *description*" (emphasis added). Classification is a common part of description; the fact that there is more than one way to classify information (and that creating a suitable taxonomy may well be a design process) does not make us re-think all descriptive tasks as design. But in data modeling, the classification task is central: the classification scheme is the greater part of the deliverable, rather than a means of organizing it.

Evidence of diversity in data models

Having established that classification theory allows for different possible models of the same UoD, it remains to be established whether such differences arise in practice – or even whether alternative credible models can be constructed. Marche (1991), reviewing personal experience in data modeling, observes that modelers have a misplaced confidence in the coherence, uniformity and logic of language, and suggests that "the focus on the classification system must be on whether it is useful rather than whether it is true". Carlis and Maguire (2001 p21), writing for practitioners, state that even a culture's basic categories are imprecise and will

---

[65] In fact Parson and Wand (1992) state that any 'world view' which satisfies certain quite basic criteria is as valid as any other.

change, and Moody (1995) advises modelers to reject the "one correct model myth" and to deliberately generate alternatives.

Examples of multiple models for the same scenario are rare in the literature, but this may be a result of blindness induced by an assumption of a single answer, or the simplicity of the examples (Simsion 1994 p7). The exception is in discussions of view integration that include examples of non-trivial differences between models (Batini, Lenzerini et al. 1986; Teorey, Lightstone et al. 2006 pp69-74)[66]. Simsion (1989; 1991; 1994 pp132-135) provides a number of examples of alternative models for the same business scenario which meet basic quality criteria but offer different compromises amongst other quality goals, in particular stability and representation of business rules[67].

Evidence of diversity in models beyond these (largely contrived) examples is sparse. In most laboratory experiments, the combination of pre-defined solutions, "problems" which are effectively descriptions of those solutions and novice modelers (discussed in Chapter 5) could be expected to suppress opportunities for diversity.

The experiment described in Shanks, Simsion, et al (1993), comparing novice and expert performance, is unusual in that the problem presented to nine experienced modelers and eight novices was obtained directly from a user (the problem was presented as a verbatim transcript of the user's verbal description) rather than reverse-engineered from a solution. The modelers produced a variety of models (all 17 were different), which were assessed in terms of meeting the stated business requirements rather than against a "gold standard". All were judged as "to some extent" satisfactory. The models from the experienced group ranged in size from 13 to 21 entities and 12 to 23 relationships; those of the novices ranged from 8 to 14 entities and 8 to19 relationships. A later study (Simsion and Shanks 1993) presented the same case transcript to 51 modelers of varying experience, resulting in 51 different models. Neither of these experiments was conclusive in establishing the nature of and reasons for the variations amongst models, beyond

---

[66] The two references use the same example.

[67] It might be argued that a data model which does not reflect all the business constraints is incomplete. Simsion and Witt (2005 pp427-436) addresses this issue: information systems hold constraints in places other than the database structures: as program logic, data values and non-automated business rules such as user instructions. Nor are popular data modeling languages capable of capturing many types of constraints in any case.

the fact that the variations could not be accounted for solely in terms of syntactic and semantic errors.

Classifying variation amongst models

A classification scheme for variability among data models of the same UoD has been proposed by Verelst (2004a). Three classes, not intended to be exhaustive, are proposed:

1. *Construct variability* – use of different modeling constructs (e.g. attribute vs. entity) to represent the same real-world concept

2. *Vertical variability* – use of different levels of generalization

3. *Horizontal variability* – different categorizations at the same level of generalization.

In terms of our earlier discussion, construct variability is the most commonly cited reason for diversity, vertical variability appears in a few view reconciliation examples (e.g. the subtyping example cited in Section 3.5), and horizontal variability would seem to best characterize alternative classification schemes as discussed in the preceding section. Examples of the last are rare in the data modeling literature (Simsion and Witt 2005 p108, p127, pp285-288, provide a few).

There is a sense in work of this kind (and in earlier work in view reconciliation – Section 3.5) of reducing differences in models to a set of well-defined mappings, a goal that would seem strange and impractical in an archetypal design discipline such as architecture. Even while recognizing diversity, the deeper paradigm appears to be one of description.

4.4.2. Product property 2: There are no optimal solutions to design problems

Design, says Lawson, always involves compromise. Rarely can a designer optimize one requirement without sacrificing another. The evaluation of the tradeoffs is a matter for skilled judgment, and the ultimate test of a design is its utility in practice.

Some authors state that compromise is intrinsic to data modeling (Veryard 1984 p28; Moody, Simsion et al. 1995; Mannino 2001 p202). The literature does not offer much in the way of individual examples but work on data model quality provides some information on the (quality) factors that modelers might seek to optimize.

Early work on data model quality[68] focused on normalization (Codd 1970; Kent 1983) and the associated issues of non-redundancy and update anomalies. Although this work claimed to address absolute criteria of correctness, rather than tradeoffs, normalization potentially conflicts with performance. It has been frequently observed (Date 1998 pp393-395; Pascal 2000 pp143-145; Stephens and Plew 2001 pp199-200; Moody and Shanks 2003; O'Rourke, Fishman et al. 2003 p374; Simsion and Witt 2005 pp58-59) that finding an acceptable compromise is a question of judgment and the subject of dispute – an "attempt to impose an art on a science" (Hoberman 2002 p346).

Early quality frameworks were developed to evaluate data models produced in laboratory experiments (Ridjanovic 1986; Batra, Hoffer et al. 1990; Bock and Ryan 1993; Kim and March 1995; Shanks, Tansley et al. 2003). As most subjects were novices, measures were simple, focusing on whether the language had been used correctly and whether the semantics in the problem description had been represented in the model (Atkins and Patrick 1996). Parsons and Wand (1992; 1996) proposed principles derived from cognitive psychology and linguistics for evaluating entity classes, but these were not significantly more stringent than the basic completeness and non-redundancy criteria already noted.

Drawing on concepts from linguistics, Lindland, Sindre & Sølvberg (1994) extended these ideas and proposed a framework built around syntactic quality (correct use of language), semantic quality (validity and completeness), and pragmatic quality (comprehension). Here we see the beginning of some recognition of choice in modeling and subjectivity in evaluation: the authors accept that there may be several syntactically and semantically sound models that differ in the ease with which they can be understood.

Simsion (1991) having argued that data modeling is design, suggested *completeness, non-redundancy, simplicity and elegance, stability, representation of constraints* and *comprehensibility* as criteria for comparing alternative designs,

---

[68] Although such work was often published under the topic of database design, it relates to the conceptual schema, and accordingly is treated here as a data modeling issue.

later adding *data re-usability, performance* (Simsion 1994), *integration* (Simsion and Witt 2005) and *ease of programming / inquiry* (Simsion 2005a).

Moody & Shanks (1994) also assert that data modeling is design, and note that "one of the major practical *problems* encountered in design generally is the large number of alternative designs that can be produced for a particular problem" (emphasis added). They proposed a six element framework (*completeness, simplicity, flexibility, understandability, integration, implementability*). This framework has since been refined, operationalized and empirically tested (Shanks and Darke 1997; Moody and Shanks 1998; 2003). Other lists with varying emphases[69] have been proposed in the practitioner literature (von Halle 1991; English 1999 pp87-89; Claxton and McDougall 2001; Piscione 2003; Hay 2005; Hoberman 2005 pp113-125).

The apparent simplicity of these varied lists may hide the fact that most of the criteria are:

(a) *Problem-specific*. The relative importance of the criteria will vary from problem to problem (Moody and Shanks 1994; Kesh 1995; Simsion and Witt 2005 p 252).

(b) *Interdependent*. For example, enforcement of business rules (or semantic completeness) may result in a loss of flexibility or simplicity (Simsion 1993; Hoberman 2002 p367). Experts' models are more complete than those of novices, but as a result are more complex (Moody and Shanks 2003).

(c) *Difficult to measure objectively*. Moody and Shanks (2003) relied on evaluators' (subjective) judgments to assess two of their five dimensions. Of the remaining three, *completeness* was measured by reference to written requirements, *simplicity* by a count of entities and relationships, and *correctness* as correct use of syntax (this last perhaps being more of a test of modeler competence and of limited applicability to models developed by experts). Shanks (1997b) refers to "transcendental properties of data models" which are not included in individual quality factors (Kaposi and Kitchenham 1987) and to "the quality without a name" (Alexander 1979).

---

[69] e.g. Hay gives particular attention to the quality of the graphical presentation and Claxton and McDougall emphasize effectiveness of communication with other stakeholders.

In terms of Lawson's Property and of the description / design question in general, this more recent work on data model quality embodies an acceptance that there may be differences in data models of the same UoD that cannot be resolved by simple measures of "right" and "wrong", tradeoffs amongst quality criteria, and the need for judgment in making those tradeoffs.

4.4.3. Product property 3: Design solutions are often holistic responses

Lawson states that designers seek an understanding of a problem as a whole. Solutions that embody that understanding cannot be reduced to a simple mapping of problem components to solution components.

A few authors (Langefors and Sundgren 1975; McFadden, Hoffer et al. 1999 p47; Simsion and Witt 2005 p252) encourage data modelers to gain a holistic understanding of the relevant business area as a precursor to modeling. Batra and Davis (1992) state that conceptual modeling requires the modeler to engage in broader conceptual thinking as well as focused problem solving activities.

Empirical research has shown differences between experts and novices. Novices given a data modeling problems translate literally from elements of the case descriptions (Batra and Antony 1994b; Chaiyasut and Shanks 1994) and make errors as a result whereas experts attempt to gain a holistic understanding (Batra and Davis 1992; Chaiyasut and Shanks 1994; Milton 2005).

4.4.4. Product property 4: Design solutions are a contribution to knowledge

Lawson's description of this Property is primarily about *patterns* that become part of a discipline's body of knowledge. Designers both produce and use patterns rather than solving problems from "first principles". Patterns may be published or remain part of the designer's personal repertoire. The recognition of the critical role of patterns in design is generally attributed to Alexander's (1977) book on architecture and urban planning. Patterns now have a well-established place in software design (Coplien and Schmidt 1995; Hanscome 1998; Larman 1998; Schmidt, Stal et al. 2000; Galambos, Vasudeva et al. 2001; Berczuk and Appleton 2002; Douglass 2002; Duyne, Landay et al. 2002; Marinescu 2002; Alur, Malks et al. 2003; Crawford and Kaplan 2003; Hohpe and Woolf 2003) and, to a lesser extent, systems analysis (Coad 1997; Penker, Penker et al. 2000; Schmidt, Stal et al. 2000; Rueping 2003; Yacoub and Ammar 2003).

The recognition of patterns in the context of data modeling is more recent (Simsion 1991; Batra 2005). Simsion (1994 pp124-131) states that "Experienced data modelers rarely develop their models from first principles. Like architects, they draw on a library of proven structures and structural components", and goes on to provide some examples of adapting generic models to suit particular requirements. Barker's (1990 pp8-1 - 8-27) text includes a chapter of "Classical Structures and Generic Patterns" and more comprehensive compilations have since been published (Hay 1996a; Coad 1997; Fowler 1997; Silverston, Inmon et al. 1997; Silverston 2001)[70]. Silverston's (2001) two-volume collection runs to 1,118 pages with additional material on CDROM, and, along with Hay's, has remained popular in the practitioner community[71]. In reviewing and synthesizing some of these patterns, Batra (2005) describes them as solutions to *design* problems. Empirical research has found evidence that experts re-use patterns, but novices do not (Batra and Davis 1992; Chaiyasut and Shanks 1994) and evaluated patterns as an alternative to rules as a basis for teaching data modeling (Batra and Wishart 2004). Thalheim's (2000 pp11-12) extensions to the Entity-Relationship Model include support for "pattern-based" modeling.

The above examples are exceptions, and largely from outside the academic community. In most of the academic and practitioner literature on data modeling, patterns are not mentioned at all.

4.4.5. Product property 5: Design solutions are parts of other design problems

Lawson argues that the products of design create, in aggregate, new design problems. Whilst little argument is offered in support of this assertion, it seems that the "other design problems" arise from the need to accommodate the new and unpredicted – particularly as designs "inevitably involve compromise" (Product Property 2). Automobiles create traffic management and safety problems, buildings create urban planning problems, even a new design for a chair can create

---

[70] Coad's and Fowler's books use the object-oriented approach.

[71] Lopez's list of "IRM Classics" at www.infoadvisors.com includes both books.

a problem for the decorator. These could well be characterized as *integration* problems, a class of problems well known to the information system profession.

Different data models (or at least the resultant databases) within the same organization will often represent the same business concepts in different ways (Sheth and Larson 1990; Simsion 1994; Kim, Choi et al. 1995 p280; Silverston 2001 pp3-5), creating, in aggregate, an unintegrated "disparate" data resource that is difficult to understand, access, coordinate, and manage (Brackett 2000 pp1-12). It is worth noting that if there were "one right answer" or if differences amongst models were easily reconciled (as proponents of the descriptive paradigm might argue), these integration problems would not arise. They seem to be an outcome of different *designs*.

Insofar as it creates problems in sharing data amongst applications and drawing data together for reporting purposes, this situation is the raison d'être for enterprise data management (Martin 1982; Zachman 1987; Moody and Simsion 1995) and (at least to some extent) data warehousing (Inmon 1992; Witt 1998; Kimball and Caserta 2004).

4.5. SUMMARY AND REVIEW

This chapter explored the description / design question from three different perspectives.

The *Problem* perspective, combined with observations about the Requirements Analysis stage (Section 3.3), provides contrasting views. In the first view, there is barely a "problem" at all – data structures are "out there" to be documented. The second view sees data modeling problems as ambiguous, multidimensional, context-dependent, and negotiable, in line with the design characterization. We have little knowledge of how data modeling problems are manifested in practice.

The *Process* perspective similarly reveals two positions. Simple recipes for data model construction contrast with observations from the laboratory and practice which see data modelers showing at least some of the characteristics of designers. Creativity, a key characteristic of design processes, is generally seen as peripheral to the main modeling task, but a few researchers have argued that it has a central role. In terms of evidence from practice (or at least from laboratory tasks involving practitioners), the process perspective is perhaps the best addressed of the five perspectives, but empirical studies have used small numbers of subjects and have not addressed creativity.

The *Product* perspective is dominated by the "one right answer" issue. Are differences in valid data models for the same UoD trivial, attributable to language limitations and easily resolved, or is data modeling an exercise in classification and intrinsically nondeterministic? Is the translation from conceptual data model to logical data model deterministic? There are theoretical positions on either side of the question. The "multiple *possible* answers" view from the literature on classification is theoretically compelling – but there is little evidence as to whether such differences arise in practice or whether classification is the responsibility of the modeler. If they do, it is not clear whether published quality criteria would support selection of the "best" model amongst alternatives. Generic patterns are seen by some authors as an important resource for data modeling, but we have no information about how prevalent their use is in practice.

Our review of the description / design question in this chapter and the two which precede it has been able to draw on a substantial cross-section of the data modeling literature, suggesting that the issue is pervasive, and arguably fundamental to data modeling research and practice. The net result is a contrast between the "conventional wisdom" of data modeling as description, and a tantalizing array of observations, opinions, and empirical results that would support the design characterization.

CHAPTER 5
STUDIES OF HUMAN FACTORS IN DATA MODELING

Drunk: I've lost my keys.
Passer-by: Where did you lose them?
Drunk: Over there.
Passer-by: So why are you looking here?
Drunk: The light's better.

— Old joke

This chapter is a short review of research – specifically empirical research – on human factors in data modeling. We have already referred to such research in earlier sections. Here, following Topi and Ramesh (2002), we examine it as a whole – as a body of work – to assess its limitations in answering the description / design question, and, in a complementary manner, to identify issues that need to be addressed in designing the present research.

There have been a number of empirical studies of human factors in data modeling, and several reviews of such studies (Batra, Hoffer et al. 1990; Batra and Srinivasan 1992; Palvia, Liao et al. 1992; Kim and March 1995; Shanks 1997b; Lee and Choi 1998; Topi and Ramesh 2002). Only the last of these reviews discusses the basis on which papers were selected for inclusion[72], and all omit some journal and conference papers of interest to the present research.

To obtain a more comprehensive picture of relevant research, an extensive search for relevant publications was undertaken, using a combination of methods, and covering *inter alia* 24 of the top 25 IS journals as listed by Schwartz and Russo (2004), and all publications covered by the aforementioned seven reviews.

Inclusion criteria were:

1.   Empirical investigation of data modeling *and*

2.   Observation or measurement of *individuals* developing or interpreting data models *and*

---

[72] Publication in academic journal or Proceedings of the ICIS conference since 1978.

3.   Publication in a refereed journal or as a refereed conference paper.

Comparisons of query / manipulation languages (which appeared in the broader Batra and Srinivasan (1992) survey, but not in the others), were not included, as they were considered peripheral to the description / design question. No study found to meet the above inclusion criteria was otherwise excluded. In cases where studies were reported in more than one place, only one paper was selected.

The search yielded 59 journal and conference papers, summarized in the Appendix. This compares with the most comprehensive previous review (Topi and Ramesh 2002), which covered 27 studies. The preceding chapters in this book have referred to many of these studies.

When considered together as a body of work, some important limitations are apparent. These are discussed below.

5.1. THE GOLD STANDARD

As noted in Section 4.4.1, much research in which subjects are required to develop models is built around a *gold standard* – a single correct solution devised in advance by the researcher (Atkins and Patrick 1996; Topi and Ramesh 2002). For example: "the goal of the subject was to create a complete model containing 16 entities, 20 relationships, 40 attributes, 40 links and 80 cardinalities" (Parent 1997). Of the 28 studies listed in the appendix in which the research task involved developing a data model, 21 measured results against a pre-defined solution.

The gold standard approach implies an underlying belief in the descriptive characterization, at least for the part of the data modeling process under investigation. Many studies relieve the subject of the task of selecting suitable abstractions by embedding entity and relationship names in the problem / task descriptions. The "business requirements" amount to a plain language description of the gold standard model and the subject's task is essentially to translate the description back to the original diagram. For example, "An employee can report to only one department. Each department has a phone number" (this example from Batra, Hoffer et al. 1990).

Exercises of this kind can do little more than test participants' facility with the modeling formalisms. If data modeling is akin to architecture, these research tasks are akin to drafting. Yet it is common to encounter conclusions such as "empirical studies have indicated that novices designers do not run into much trouble modeling entities and attributes" (Batra and Antony 2001). In the context of the simple task descriptions given to subjects, "modeling entities" may mean little more than "identifying nouns".

5.2. INDUSTRY PARTICIPATION

The papers reviewed listed a total of 3210 participants across the 59 studies. Of these, only 147 participants (5% of the total) across nine studies had material industry experience involving data modeling (a nominal criterion of one year was used). Sixty-five of these were accounted for by one mailed-out survey (Hitchman 1995), and only two other studies involved more than ten such participants. What initially might appear to be an extensive body of research on data modelers therefore consists largely of studies of students.

It requires at least 100 hours of learning and practice to acquire any significant cognitive skill to a reasonable degree of proficiency (Anderson 1982) and behavior and performance change in important ways as expertise is acquired (Fitts and Posner 1967). Barker (1990 p1-3), writing on data modeling, states simply: "there is no substitute for experience", a view echoed by Wade (1991) and Mannino (2001 p211). Data modeling research supports these views. Novices are only able to tackle simple or "low level" modeling tasks (Jarvenpaa and Machesky 1989) and even then are likely to struggle to produce workable models (Hoffer 1982; Batra and Antony 1994a; Batra and Sein 1994; Batra 1996). Comparisons of novice and expert data modelers (Batra and Davis 1992; Chaiyasut and Shanks 1994) have identified behaviors characteristic of designers (attempting to gain a holistic understanding, categorization of problems, pattern re-use) in the experts but not in the novices. This would strongly suggest that our understanding of novice data modelers who are unable to correctly perform simple (and deliberately simplified) tasks cannot be used to make predictions about (real) experts' behavior (Batra and Marakas 1995; Moody and Shanks 1998; Hitchman 1999). Despite these established differences in expert and novice behavior, the word "expert" is often used loosely and sometimes even applied to students. Siau, Wand, et al (1995) classify students as experts and draw conclusions about expert modelers. In Lee and Choi's (1998) comparison of novices and experts, the experts are graduate students (the novices are undergraduates).

It may be that the use of novices simply reflects the relative ease of access to students compared with professional modelers. Research using students is better than no research at all (Berkowitz and Donnerstein 1982; Fenton, Pfleeger et al. 1994), but it is of limited use in investigating the description / design question.

5.3. PROBLEM COMPLEXITY

In the studies reviewed (refer Appendix), the median number of entities across 59 models used in the various research tasks was seven[73]. This compares with an industry study (Maier 1996) that found only 9% of models had less than 20 entities and only 8% had less than 100 attributes.

Norbotten and Crosby (1999) noted (unsurprisingly) that comprehension fell as graphic complexity rose[74] and this factor creates real problems in designing laboratory tasks with reasonable face validity. Jarvenpaa and Machesky (1989) provide a frank discussion of the need to simplify in order to obtain usable results from student modelers. Even with a highly prescriptive flowcharted method, examples had to be restricted to five entities after piloting showed that more complex tasks were too time consuming. The observation that textbooks "use simple applications, ignore the complexity of domain, and provide a false sense of security to their readers regarding their ability to model applications" (Batra and Zanakis 1994) could readily be applied to much empirical research.

Simple models and prescriptive instructions could be expected to limit any scope for choice and design behavior. The issue of "semantic relativism" becomes more important as complexity increases (Hammer and McLeod 1981).

5.4. FOCUS OF THE STUDIES

In keeping with the longstanding interest in data modeling formalisms, empirical work has focused on comparing the ease of use and interpretation of different formalisms (different Data Models or constructs within an established Data Model). Thirty-three of the 59 empirical studies listed in were experiments with data modeling formalism or use of alternative constructs as the independent variable. By contrast, only six compared the performance of novices and "experts[75]". A few studies have looked at tools or consultancy to support the

---

[73] Where information about size was provided.

[74] Language and student training may have been confounding factors here (Venable 1999).

[75] In only four cases did the "experts" meet a criterion of one year's industry experience.

modeling process (Barclay, Crerar et al. 1994; Batra and Sein 1994; Crerar, Barclay et al. 1996; Antony, Batra et al. 1997; Antony and Batra 1999; Batra and Antony 2001).

Few studies have looked at the characteristics of the modelers themselves and differences amongst modelers. Yang (2003) used a cognitive styles instrument, described as similar to the Myers Briggs Type Indicator (Myers, McCaulley et al. 1998) and hypothesized that Thinking styles would outperform Feeling styles. No simple correlation emerged, but Feeling styles did better on the experiment requiring interpretation of a text description. Unfortunately, although the research collected data in the Intuitive (N) / Sensing (S) dimension, differences between these groups were not reported. This measure has been reported as being associated with creativity (Myers and McCaulley 1985 pp214-221).

Hoffer (1982) administered the Kolb Learning Style Inventory (LSI) to student modelers but noted no correlations with performance. The very poor overall performance may well have obscured differences that would have arisen with more competent subjects.

5.5. GENERALIZING THE FINDINGS

Many of the studies were designed as experiments or quasi-experiments, and presented inferential statistics, but the representativeness of samples was seldom discussed. In all cases, participants were from a single country, most commonly from a single institution. Replicability was an implicit goal, but there were very few examples of attempts to validate results in this way.

Student participants were frequently described as surrogate users or surrogate novice modelers, with an implication that findings could be generalized to those groups. This expectation seems optimistic. End users might (for example) have far deeper domain knowledge than students. *Prima facie*, working from strong internalized knowledge would seem to be different from using information recently acquired from a written description. (Students' understanding of the "familiar" domains sometimes used, such as student-teacher-course scenarios, may well be of a different kind to that of a manager or professional involved in the *management* of such domains). More broadly, despite the contention that with the growth of end-user computing, inexperienced users will need to create data models (e.g. Batra and Srinivasan 1992), there is no evidence that end-users who build information systems create formal data models at all.

In all cases, recruitment of practitioner participants was opportunistic – from a single organization (Shanks, Simsion et al. 1993; Parent 1997), faculty (Batra and Davis 1992), or referrals that may have been dominated by a single organization (Mantha 1987; Chaiyasut and Shanks 1994; Moody and Shanks 2003).

5.6. SUMMARY

The substantial body of empirical work on data modeling has some serious limitations when applied to the description / design question. Many studies assume the descriptive characterization of data modeling or so constrain the tasks that only a descriptive approach is possible. Few practitioners have been studied, and then largely through small convenience samples. The student participants who dominate the samples are not representative of expert practitioners, and possibly not even of end-users. Laboratory tasks are generally simple, and most commonly have been designed to compare languages rather than investigate the modeling process and products.

The "bottom line" is that there is very little published information about how experienced or expert data modelers approach their work and about the models that they produce – hence about how models for real business applications are built.

CHAPTER 6
WHAT THE THOUGHT-LEADERS THINK

6.1. INTRODUCTION

Data modeling is a science based on mathematics.

– Eskil Swende[76]

It's currently more of an art than a science.

– Terry Halpin

I believe it's half science and half art.

– Alec Sharp

This chapter presents the results of interviews with seventeen "thought-leaders" in data modeling practice. It serves three purposes:

1. It complements the review of the literature presented in the preceding chapters by reporting ideas and positions that are disseminated in the practitioner community through training courses, presentations, internet discussion groups and consulting rather than publication[77]. Practitioner views and goals in data modeling are not the same as those of academics (Batra and Marakas 1995; Hitchman 1995; 1997; Wand and Weber 2002).

2. It contributes to the formulation of the research questions and research design described in Chapter 7 by identifying key differences in practitioner views.

3. It begins the empirical component of the research by addressing a component of the *Environment* dimension of the description / design question: viz, the beliefs about data modeling held and promulgated by influential "elites."

---

[76] All quotes in this chapter are from the interview transcripts, unless otherwise attributed (references to the literature are identifiable by the inclusion of dates).

[77] The majority of the interviewees had in fact published books, several of which are cited in the Literature Review (Chapter 2), but these generally focused on method and techniques rather than conceptual underpinnings.

This chapter can thus be seen as a bridge between the review of theory (Part II) and the examination of practice in Part II.

The central question is *do the thought-leaders in data modeling practice characterize data modeling as description or design?* The term *thought-leaders* conveys the author's judgment that the interviewees are shapers of the culture in which data modelers work and learn[78]. They also work in the culture and inevitably are shaped by it themselves.

We begin with a description of the research design, followed by a brief profile of each of the participants. The main body of the chapter uses the 5Ps framework – *Environment[79], Problem, Process, Product,* and *People* – to organize the themes that emerged from the interviews. The chapter concludes with a discussion of the key themes, their relevance to the description / design question, and their impact on the design of later research components.

6.2. DESIGN AND METHOD

Thought-leaders arguably fall into the category of *white collar elites* (Neuman 1999 pp273-274). It is recommended that interviews with elites be conducted personally by the researcher, and that the interviews be built around open-ended questions (Dexter 1970). I[80] followed that recommendation and used semi-structured interviews, recorded on videotape[81]. Interviews were conducted at locations convenient to the interviewee, ranging from quiet rooms to cafes. The format took into account the fact that interviewees were senior professionals, accustomed to presenting and debating data modeling topics, and that I could assume that they would see me as a peer. I initially took a neutral role on each topic, but then presented challenges and alternative views to encourage interviewees to expand on and justify their positions.

---

[78] From Section 7.6, the dominant methods of learning are experience, industry education and books, all of which we could expect to be influenced by practitioner thought-leaders.

[79] As noted in Section 1.4.3, the first *P* is from using *Press* as a synonym for *Environment.*

[80] In this chapter I have departed from the style used elsewhere in the book and use the first person on occasion, as the more appropriate way of reporting conversations in which I was a participant.

[81] One interview (Hoberman) was not recorded due to equipment being unavailable; notes were taken instead.

Confidentiality is usually a crucial issue when interviewing "white collar elites" (Neuman 1999 p274). An alternative perspective is that the interviewees are not "subjects" but contributors of ideas who deserve the acknowledgment that would be due if they had published the ideas themselves. I therefore gave interviewees the choice of anonymity or acknowledgment. All chose the latter, and, in this spirit, many of the quotes that appear in the text have been attributed. An obvious advantage of this arrangement is that the status of the interviewees as thought-leaders can be verified.

I first presented the description / design question directly and asked for their views, then asked them (if they had not raised the topics unprompted) to comment on three issues identified by the literature review as central to the characterization of data modeling as description or design:

1. Whether the data modeler should challenge business requirements (*Problem*),

2. Whether data modeling problems had a single right answer (*Product*),

3. Whether data modeling was a creative activity (*Process*).

Analysis was based broadly on the phenomenological methodology described by Colaizzi (1978):

1. I transcribed all videotapes personally, omitting only the material clearly outside the topic area.

2. I separated the conversations into individual statements and organized the statements according to common meanings (e.g. "some data modelers tend to over-generalize").

3. I organized the meanings (retaining the original statements) into themes (e.g. "views on generalization") that I then placed within the research framework (*Context and Environment, Problem, Process, Product, Person*).

4. I synthesized the results into a description of views and positions on the description / design question, making frequent use of direct quotes for illustration.

5.   I returned the draft chapter to all interviewees, with an invitation to submit corrections. This step is included in Colaizzi's methodology, and was part of the compact with the interviewees. In the draft document, prior to validation, names were changed; interviewees were given the code only for their own name.

6.3.   PARTICIPANTS

I selected participants based solely on my perceptions of their influence in the *practitioner* data modeling community at that time (early 2002). In turn, these perceptions reflected some 20 years involvement in that community, primarily in Australasia, North America, and the United Kingdom. Some validation of the selection lay in the responses to the question *where did you learn data modeling?* included in the demographics questionnaire given to participants in other research components of this project, and analyzed after thought-leader interviews had been completed. The authors of three of the five books most frequently cited by respondents[82] had been included in the selection of thought-leaders. Gaining access to professionals and "elites" can be difficult (Ostrander 1993; Lofland and Lofland 1995 p12), but all but one of those selected was interviewed.

The participants, and their positions or roles at the time of interview were:

Peter Aiken, data management consultant, Associate Professor at Virginia Commonwealth University, author of five books including *Data Reverse Engineering* (Aiken 1995) and *Building Corporate Portals with XML* (Finkelstein and Aiken 1999).

Richard Barker, company director, architect of the Oracle CASE tool, author of *CASE Method Entity-Relationship Modelling* (Barker 1990) which popularized the Barker Notation.

Michael Brackett, President of the International Data Management Association (DAMA), served as Data Resource Coordinator for the State of Washington, author of five books on data management topics including *Data Resource Quality* (Brackett 2000).

---

[82] Barker, Hay, Silverston. The present author's book was excluded from this assessment.

Harry Ellis, data modeling consultant to the British Department of Defence, architect of the original ICL CASE product, author of the CBML data modeling language.

Larry English, leading proponent of data quality techniques, founder of Information Impact International, author of Improving Data Warehouse and Business Information Quality (English 1999).

Terry Halpin, Professor at Northface[83] University Utah, responsible for formalizing the Object Role Modeling (ORM/NIAM) approach to data modeling. Formerly head of database research for Visio Corporation (later with Microsoft). Author of five books including *Information Modeling and Relational Databases* (Halpin 2001).

David Hay, independent data modeling consultant and educator. Author of the first book of data model patterns (Hay 1996a) and books on requirements analysis (Hay 2003) and metadata (Hay 2006).

Steve Hoberman, global reference data manager with Mars, Inc, industry educator, convener of Data Modeling Challenges[84], author of two books on data modeling (Hoberman 2002; 2005).

Karen Lopez, data modeling consultant and commentator, moderator of Infoadvisors[85] discussion groups on data modeling topics, frequent conference speaker, and convener of data modeling "contentious issues" forums

Dawn Michels, data modeling specialist, Vice President of Chapter Services for DAMA International (see Brackett, above), responsible for establishing and supporting DAMA Chapters worldwide.

Terry Moriarty, president of Inastrol data modeling consultancy, co-chair of International Business Rules Forum, regular presenter, author and columnist.

Ronald Ross, editor of the *Database Newsletter* for 22 years, editor of the Business Rules Manifesto, books include *Principles of the Business Rules Approach* (Ross 2003).

---

[83] Now Neumont University

[84] www.stevehoberman.com

[85] www.infoadvisors.com

Robert Seiner, data management consultant, editor of *The Data Administration* Newsletter86, frequent presenter at industry forums.

Alec Sharp, independent data and process modeling consultant, industry educator in data and process modeling worldwide since 1986. Author of *Workflow Modeling* (Sharp and McDermott 2001).

Len Silverston, data modeling consultant, industry educator, compiler of "universal data model" patterns, author of two books of patterns (Silverston, Inmon et al. 1997; Silverston 2001).

Eskil Swende, Chief Executive of the IRM (Information Resource Management) group, a specialist data modeling consultancy which at the time of interview had just delivered its 1000th data model. President of the Scandinavian chapter of the Data Management Association.

John Zachman, industry consultant and educator, originator of the widely-used Zachman Framework (Zachman 1987; Sowa and Zachman 1992).

6.4. RESULTS

> *There isn't a common body of knowledge in data modeling – generally agreed-upon standards of practice. There's a wide range in data modeling styles and what's right and wrong.*
>
> – Karen Lopez

As is usual in qualitative research (Miles and Huberman 1994 pp55-57) the interviews produced a large volume of transcripts for summarization. The relatively narrow focus, assisted by some strong repeated themes, meant that this task was not as difficult as is sometimes the case.

All of the interviewees, as would be expected from their backgrounds, were articulate and able to draw on extensive personal experience in support of their views. Not all had previously considered the description / design question directly, but all clearly understood it and were able to relate it to their views on associated matters, and bring well-practiced arguments to bear. Several made it clear that their beliefs were very strongly-held.

---

[86] www.tdan.com

The summary that follows begins with responses to the description / design question itself, then continues with themes organized according to the research framework.

6.4.1. Description vs. design – explicit positions

I'm sure I could find people who fit both those ends of that spectrum very well and are adamant that they're right about it.

– Karen Lopez

Opinions on the description / design question, presented directly, covered the full spectrum. Table 6–1 summarizes my overall classification of the interviewees' positions, based both on their direct responses and the wider-ranging discussions that followed.

Position	Number of Interviewees
Strongly supports description	5
Somewhat supports description	1
Supports neither position more strongly than the other	3
Position depends on language	1
Somewhat supports design	3
Strongly supports design	4

Table 6–1: Interviewees' overall positions as assessed by the author

The above assessment is included primarily to show that each characterization had support from several interviewees, and that the diversity of views reported in this chapter was not a product of including one or two "outlier" individuals. The "position depends on language" row in the table reflects the view of Harry Ellis who argued that data modeling with Entity-Relationship-based approaches should be strongly characterized as design, but that that his current work using the CBML language[87] is properly characterized as highly descriptive. As such, his comments provided qualified support for both positions.

---

[87] Corporate Business Modelling Language (Department of Defence (UK) 2005; Ellis and Nell 2005).

Interviewees clearly understood this question and their views were largely articulate and unambiguous:

"Data modeling is not a process of creation; it is a process of discovery."

"Data modeling is a certainly a descriptive activity, it's not a design activity."

"I believe rabidly and intensely that it's a design process."

"We're designing (but) some of the people that we work with see us as scribes."

It bears re-emphasizing that the context of the question was development of a new database rather than (for example) enterprise modeling, creating reference data for metadata repository mappings, data warehouse design[88] or reverse engineering. Several interviewees were concerned that their views be reported only in that context.

Proponents of the descriptive characterization as well as those of the design characterization generally contended that the resulting model could be translated relatively mechanically into a conceptual schema (*logical database design* was the common term), or at least a default schema prior to performance tuning. They did not see a descriptive model as merely an input to a design stage. "There is no translation: we model the tables," said one advocate of the descriptive view.

Key themes in the descriptive characterization were:

(a) The view that the system should mirror the real world: "Our goal is to minimize the gap between the real world and the representation of the real world."

(b) A focus on the business rather than the database: "data modeling is an attempt to describe the structure of the organization as exhibited by the structure of its data – that is, the entities are things of significance to the business."

(c) The use of the term *requirements* (in contrast to *solution*) to characterize the data model: "(A) data model is one method of doing a specific

---

[88] The issue with data warehouse design was not the use of different modeling languages (viz star schemas) but the constraining effect of accommodating existing (legacy) data structures.

articulation of a user requirement; I've always considered data models as descriptive of certain types of requirements"

(d)   Discovery rather than mere documentation. The business may not understand its own data or may need help to describe it properly: "there is a set of information requirements that may or may not be known by knowledge workers or management"; "the business may have bad terminology or missing entities."

(e)   A requirement for a high level of skill and even creativity: "It is creative, but it's creative in the scientific sense of discovering things, of figuring things out…"

The concept of a single objective reality was often at least implicit. One interviewee discussed a situation in which he had, on reflection, changed the way that the *product* concept was represented in a data model. Was this a case of coming up with a better design? "No," he said, "we finally figured out the product for this particular organization." *Finally?* "I have no claims of infallibility. It's perfectly reasonable that someone would be smarter … and I'd look at him and say 'yeah you're right…'"

The practical impact of the descriptive position is illustrated by one interviewee's account of his testimony as an expert witness in an intellectual property case. He argued that "the data model is a description of the problem and therefore by definition one data model will look pretty similar to others. It's not a patentable or copyrightable thing… My model is my best description of my understanding of the nature of things and therefore I can't patent that because it's reality".

Proponents of the design position offered less elaboration at this point. Three key themes that they raised – negotiability of requirements, diversity of product and the role of creativity – are discussed later.

The "design" group saw data models as *solutions*. John Zachman used the Zachman Framework (Zachman 1987; Sowa and Zachman 1992) to distinguish the descriptive "business owner's view" (Row 2) from the logical data model of Row 3. In this formulation, the logical data model[89] is a solution to the business owner's well-articulated problem: "Once you've defined what the things are you're trying to manage… someone has to invent the filing system… " John

---

[89] Most interviewees used the term "logical data model" to denote what in academic work would generally be called a conceptual data model.

Zachman was among several of the design proponents who drew an analogy with architecture.

Two interviewees' responses highlighted the role of the modeling language. Terry Halpin, noting that he was "biased" from using ORM,[90] saw data modeling as both description and design. On the one hand, ORM supports a descriptive approach to requirements – "In ORM you verbalize the data requirements and that verbalization itself is the model – essentially" – on the other, there are numerous opportunities to modify the default conceptual schema that results. Harry Ellis echoed some of the earlier proponents of the ORM method when he argued that "if the language was adequately rich, what the domain expert is saying could be precisely and accurately written down … in such a way that the technical applications would be absolutely definitive".

6.4.2. Environment

Sometimes "it's an art" is used as an excuse for not following generally accepted practices or internal standards.

– Karen Lopez

Describing only in terms of data misses the big picture.

– Ron Ross

Two themes fell under the heading of *Environment* – the context in which data modeling takes place. The first was the impact of an model on data modeling at the application level. Here the choice and creativity associated with the design characterization were seen as impediments to the consistency needed to support data integration:

"The crucial problem with creativity is that the more creativity goes into the model – the more idiosyncratic the models – the harder they are to fit together. Even if it's excellent it becomes problematic – and generally it isn't."

By establishing standards for data representation, an enterprise data model or architecture should (and would) render data modeling a more descriptive process. An enterprise model could become a surrogate for the business as an "absolute statement of truth". As one interviewee put it, if you still insist on being a soloist,

---

[90] Object Role Modeling – (Halpin 2001)

you'll be asked to leave the orchestra. Enterprise models were also seen as valuable for encouraging a broader view at the application level: "if you see only one line of business your model is going to be very different than when you're looking at it across the entire enterprise." All but one of the interviewees who raised the role of an enterprise model as a vehicle for enforcing conformity was speaking from the position of enforcer rather than conformer, and the scenario was seen more as a goal than a current reality.

The second *Environment* theme was the need to see data modeling as only one technique amongst many, particularly in the context of understanding or negotiating business requirements. Several interviewees pointed out the danger of over-reliance on data models as a means of understanding the business and its requirements. Other techniques nominated included process and workflow modeling, Critical Success Factor and Key Performance Indicator analysis, Use Cases, and business objectives. These were seen as adjuncts or (often) precursors to data modeling. In the context of the description / design question, they suggested a separate "requirements elicitation" stage rather than direct, descriptive mapping of business concepts onto a model.

6.4.3. Problem

The negotiability of requirements

Data modeling is all about helping a business come up with a better way of doing business

– Alec Sharp

Data modelers should not resolve business problems

– Michael Brackett

If the description position was more comprehensively argued when the description / design question was presented directly, the balance was restored in the discussion of the negotiability of requirements. Consistently, the proponents of the design position argued not only that business requirements were negotiable, but that data modelers should be active in exposing new ways of doing business. The preferred method was to inform business stakeholders of the (negative) consequences of existing perspectives (to "expose the business to itself"), using the data models to facilitate discussion. Business rules may reflect the limitations of past technologies or systems, and need to be challenged rather than blindly accepted.

Peter Aiken stated that "if the users aren't by a third to a half way through the session jumping up to the board and saying 'this is wrong' then … I don't consider the modeling session a success". Alec Sharp expressed the view even more strongly: "it's criminal not to do something to help people see the consequences of having chosen a particular reality."

Implicit (or indeed explicit in some cases) is the view that the business does not know what it wants – or at least what is best for it. Modelers were seen as being able to make suggestions ("Have you thought about doing it this way?"), and to bring in their own general or industry-specific business knowledge to provide new perspectives. One interviewee cited a case in which the business had specified some 500 attributes to be included in a database for reporting; after the data modeler reviewed how they would be used in practice, the number was reduced to 150.

More broadly, Alec Sharp talked of the "myth of requirements," arguing that the view that the business knows them already and that the job of the analyst is to extract them is "patently false" and a legacy of the early days of computerized systems. Data modelers who buy into the myth "may end up with a better data model but not with a better business." Architecture was invoked as a very close analogy ("don't tell me how to do it, tell me what you need to do") including recognition of the right of the client to say "thanks for your idea but no thanks."

Some of the aims and claims for business change were ambitious, even grandiose: "a skilled data modeler might help a business transform itself"; "the client said 'this has been a revelation'"; "the real benefit of data modeling … is in synthesis of new ways of looking at things"; "I can help companies see themselves differently"; "help them define where they want their business to go – and model that"; "(changing) the management practices of the organization itself." Alec Sharp, addressing the apparent "scope creep" in the definition of data modeling commented: "I'm perfectly happy to do this from my role as data modeler, because I don't choose to limit that role…"

Richard Barker offered an opposing view: "I used to play around in that area but until I became a main board director of a company and learned the essence of running a business, I didn't really understand. That was a massive change". Interviewees from the description camp also supported the primacy of the business in determining its data model: "What we're modeling is what the domain expert says is right. You have to presume that the domain expert knows exactly the way the business is or wants to be – every little bit of it. The modeler is only articulating that…"

On the subject of challenging business requirements, one interviewee simply stated, "I never have that conversation." Another said that the business's view of its data should be questioned only in rare cases. And the final decision definitely lay with the business: "when there is a discrepancy it is the business which answers the discrepancy, not the data modeler". This extended to changing data names in the interests of precision: "Right up front you put your own spin on the business rather than letting the business have its say."

6.4.4. Process

We should de-skill the modeling, we should automate the design, and we should become full-time analysts and concentrate on understanding what the business needs.

– Harry Ellis

Most interviewees talked in terms of a core three-stage process of requirements identification / negotiation, logical data modeling, and physical database design, and indicated that as data modelers they performed or were involved in at least the first two stages. The term *conceptual data modeling* was used by some as a synonym for logical data modeling and by others to reflect a preliminary "high level" stage.

I initiated discussion on the transition from data model to conceptual schema and on the role of creativity. No other common themes emerged, but one comment is worth noting as relating to one of Lawson's Properties of design (Chapter 4):

"You reach the point of diminishing returns – it will never be perfect" (Lawson's Property: the design process is endless*).*

From data model to conceptual schema

You can push a button and from that generate your E-R model, logical models, your DDL

– Terry Halpin

The transition from data model to pre-performance-tuning conceptual schema was generally presented as mechanical: (the database design is) "automatic if you have a good model of the business."

Harry Ellis offered a perspective on the ready "translatability" of data models that is consistent with observations from some teachers of data modeling (de Carteret and Vidgen 1995 p xi; Simsion and Witt 2005 p33) and with Atkins' (1996) observation (noted in Section 3.4) that if the target is a relational database, the most useful categories in a conceptual model will be seen to be normalized, candidate relations:

> *"I was actually visualizing a working data structure. People ask 'what is an entity?' I came to realize that ... the bottom line was an entity is something you could have a table for. A bit of a con; deep down in my subconscious I was creating an effective data structure, although openly, publicly, I was actually modeling the business. I wasn't really. I thought I was, and everybody else thought I was, and it worked. People who had no notion of what a good data structure was couldn't do it – they would use the notation beautifully, but it was completely useless – they'd have an entity for something you couldn't have a table for."*

Tuning for performance was seen as involving important choices and even an "artistic component" (this comment from an interviewee who was a firm supporter of the descriptive position on modeling).

Creativity

> *It's a creative activity when I do the model, a documentation activity when I write the definitions (laughs).*
>
> – Len Silverston

> *Presentation has much more creative content than coming up with the categories.*
>
> – David Hay

Views on creativity were in line with positions on the description / design question. Those who supported the design characterization assigned it a central role. Several recounted personal "eureka" moments from their data modeling experience: "Sometimes you can just get an insight and say 'hey, gee, if I do it this way, it's going to work better.'" Some supporters of the description characterization recognized a place for creativity, but in peripheral areas such as the layout and presentation of the model, or the approach to understanding the business: "There's nothing creative about it from the standpoint of 'I make it up';

it has to be a discovery of what the business must know in order to operate effectively."

Adjectives were used liberally by some in the design school: "Managed properly, it is a *highly* creative activity – or should be"; "Anything we do when we are developing information systems is an *extremely* creative process"; I prided myself on my …*great* creativity".

Karen Lopez voiced a concern that creativity should not be interpreted as license: "I'd say it's a creative endeavor but constrained by what I believe are standards of practice about what's right, what's appropriate, what's practical…there is creativity but I don't believe that data modeling is an art."

Some saw creativity as intrinsic to "creating" the objects in the model: "The people you interview don't dictate the entities you have; perhaps 10-15% of entities are obvious and everyone agrees with them, but (beyond that) the actual choice of entities requires a lot of imagination and creativity." Creativity was not seen as being the sole preserve of the professional modeler. Ron Ross observed that bringing people together with different points of view to obtain a consensus often results in new ideas that might not have been anticipated at the outset and Alec Sharp prefers to "set up situations where the business people can be the ones who are creative." Conversely "IT people" (a group that most of the interviewees clearly did not see themselves as belonging to) were seen as impediments not only to creativity but to data modeling itself.

6.4.5. Product

Three key themes emerged in the *product* dimension: product diversity, the role of patterns, and product quality. Product diversity and quality drew a range of conflicting views, broadly – but not entirely - in alignment with positions on the description / design question. In contrast, there was general agreement on the value of patterns[91], if not their exact role. Some interviewees also commented on data model quality. We look at each of these themes in turn.

---

[91] Use of patterns might seem better placed under *process*; in Lawson's framework they are discussed under the *Product* property *design solutions are a contribution to knowledge*.

Diversity of Product – one right answer?

If we are both experts we should come up with the same solution

– Eskil Swende

Every little bit of the (CBML) model down to the most minute detail is a precise expression of something that is either right or wrong. And that's not a matter of choice.

– Harry Ellis

Given the same set of business rules, two very very good modelers will come up with completely different models.

– Terry Moriarty

Why should all houses be the same, why should all cars be the same, why are there competitive businesses around?

– Richard Barker

The "one right answer" question – will different (competent) data modelers, faced with the same set of business requirements produce different data models? – generated strongly conflicting responses, but not exactly in line in with positions on the description / design question. Some interviewees who believed that requirements were negotiable were less sure that the models would vary once requirements were settled.

Several interviewees in fact contended that there should, and would, be a single right model, allowing for variation only in notation and (perhaps) the naming of objects: "They should come up with the same answer which is the correct description of the business; we may have different notations but the underlying names and definitions should be identical; the relationships should be identical" or as another put it "not the same words but the same number of entities". The situation was seen as different from process modeling because (a) data was intrinsically stable and / or (b) data modeling was mathematically based.

There should be, said one interviewee, borrowing a common statement about data and applying it to data structure, "only one version of the truth about the data that the business needs." Asked "are you chasing truth rather than coming up with something?", David Hay responded "Absolutely, these are inherent categories: I'm very platonic in that regard."

The primacy of the business view of data was a common theme here. "I try to start hearing the categories they have in their heads" said one practicing modeler.

Differences could and should be resolved by "going back to the business." These included differences in naming and in levels of abstraction.

A second group contended that different modelers would produce different models, but attributed the differences to perception. "It's all in the eye of the beholder" said Bob Seiner. Richard Barker, citing his own definition of an entity as "something of business significance", said "we will see different significances."

Those who saw differences in models as a natural consequence of the design paradigm spoke in terms of utility rather than truth: "Models are more or less useful – there is no absolute right or wrong." Ron Ross used an example of a model in the natural sciences: "Benzene is modeled as having a circular structure and that is a useful description whether or not that circle truly exists in nature... let's assume it and move on. But if we assume it and it's not the best description, we're going to have some limitations downstream."

Two interviewees with strong process modeling experience offered comparisons. Karen Lopez saw more variation in abstracted process models, but observed that they came together at the primitive level. Conversely (workable) data models "start out being wildly different and stay wildly different."

A few interviewees proffered the basic theoretical position of choice in classification ("when you're trying to conquer and divide the world conceptually... I don't think there can be a single correct answer"), but most who argued against the "one right answer" position drew primarily on personal experience. Instructors noted that students produced different workable models in response to case study scenarios. The difficulties of integrating data within and across organizations (the case of mergers was cited) was also seen as evidence that different workable models could be implemented for the same data.

The trade-off between level of generalization and enforcement of business rules was a central theme amongst those who believed in choice, and was seen as an area for expert decision making. It was also seen as a key source of difference as different modelers made different decisions. It was apparent that there were disagreements between groups that might be described as the *literalists* (concepts should be modeled as per common business use); the *moderate abstractors* (introducing some generalizations within traditional applications) and the *rule removers* (deliberately removing business rules for representation elsewhere).

Ron Ross, as an advocate of the business rules approach, clearly subscribed to the last group, and argued that stability was not innate, but required deliberate design:

"I had to unlearn a lot of data modeling practice and experience… when it comes to using a full rule-based approach in addition to a data approach, because the central opportunity you have is that you can generalize to an extent that is reasonable and productive (emphasizing those words, because you don't want to generalize beyond that), and then let rules handle current business practices within that more generalized database structure. That gives you a much higher degree of flexibility than has been possible in the past because rules, however implemented, are going to be far easier to change than the underlying data or knowledge structure."

One interviewee attributed her view to learning from a prominent authority who believed that there was "an absolute statement of truth" and then finding her experiences inconsistent with that belief. Others simply discovered alternative models that they could not refute: "I can think of lots of cases where I've built models and someone else has come up with a different model and I look at it and say 'hey that would work.'" Len Silverston described the result of having another expert review his models:

"A lot of lunches he'd say 'Len, I feel so bad because you've spent all this time, done all this research … and now I'm giving you a completely different idea.'"

Some modelers found alternative and better solutions themselves, without feeling that they could discard the earlier solutions as wrong: "Every time I look back, I think, I wouldn't do it like that again." Nevertheless, few modelers said that they deliberately generated alternatives.

The possibility of different models arising from subtly different names or definitions of data model objects was raised by two interviewees. Terry Moriarty said "When you allow your data analyst [a different person from the data modeler] to write definitions for the terms that are being used in the data model, and use those definitions as a way of validation, you know that there's more than one way of doing the same thing". Len Silverston provided a detailed example of changing the name of *Order Line* to *Order Item*, prompting a change to the way order adjustments were represented: "the name change showed me a lot of semantics."

Finally, Steve Hoberman offered some experience beyond the personal. Through his website[92] and email list, he convenes a series of "data modeling challenges",

---

[92] www.stevehoberman.com

each presenting a problem to which modelers are invited to submit solutions. He observed that he receives a variety of diverse solutions to each problem. Some are unsound or unworkable, a large group comprises variants of the solution that he envisaged in setting the problem, and a few are "out of left field" innovative solutions. He noted that there were some modelers who regularly contributed such innovative solutions.

Patterns

If you look at my model, Len Silverston's, David Hay's, the IAA IBM insurance industry model – all of these are very good workable solutions to the business problem – we've just had different biases...I just think mine's better (laughs)

– Terry Moriarty

Interviewees from both the descriptive and design camps considered patterns as important input to data modeling. Predictably, the former group saw patterns as representing general "truth" ("there's a certain basic set of generic entity classes").

David Hay, author of two books of data modeling patterns (Hay 1996a; 2006), said:

If you're going after things that are of fundamental importance to the business, you'll come up with things that are common across all businesses – people, organizations, products, contracts are pretty standard in the world of commerce. If you use these as the basis of your organizing, you'll come up with a model which is concrete enough that people will recognize and understand it, but robust enough..."

He added that sometimes his clients asked that he start with a "blank slate" rather than use patterns, but "lo and behold – it ends up being close to the pattern after all."

Terry Moriarty agreed that "there are things that businesses have to do and have to know just to be in business", but argued that the patterns were design products, departing from the familiar architect metaphor to liken the pattern developer to a musical composer. She also pointed out that commonality across business did not equate to obviousness: "Some of these things are very obscure."

Len Silverston, also the author of two books of patterns (Silverston, Inmon et al. 1997; Silverston 2001), described his "universal models" as tools to support exploration ("patterns and alternatives that you might well not have thought of"), and described deliberately generating multiple models: "In my course I give five different variations – any one could be used in any situation and I point out the pros and cons."

Product quality

Larry English nominated three critical characteristics of a quality data model: (1) *stability* (no destructive change when adding new applications); (2) *flexibility* (databases able to adapt with minimal destructive change in the face of business change) and (3) *reuse* (the models and resulting databases are reused with only additive change as opposed to destructive change. A few examples of poor models ("groaners") were cited: "Person was a subtype of Agreement".

Several interviewees criticized the quality of models that they encountered in industry and the quality of work done by some professional modelers. But they generally acknowledged that assessment was subjective. Len Silverston said: "Recently I asked a very confident data modeling consultant about choosing between two and he said 'I'd lean towards the way you did it recently by about a 55% margin'". Describing why he preferred one model over another, he said "I thought that there was a sense of truth to the latter that just felt better." Those from the descriptive school were more likely to see the assessment decisions as simpler: "with experience these are 'binary' choices – one or other configuration – nothing terribly complicated. I don't find it challenging."

6.4.6. Person –modelers and business stakeholders

You have to factor in the modeler bias: just a way a person thinks, a way they want to construct things

– Terry Moriarty

The people who accept the rules would not be the people with good creativity and the creative people are too big-headed to follow the rules

– Harry Ellis

I see very very few good logical data modelers

– Michael Brackett

Three themes were classified under the *Person* perspective in the research framework: data modeler competence, including learning; data modeler bias or "style"; and communication between data modelers and business stakeholders.

Data modeler competence

Data modeling is not learned solely from formal education and books, according to interviewees, most of whom present courses in data modeling and several of whom have written books on the subject. Barker (1990 p1-3) writes "there is no substitute for experience". Dawn Michels agreed that "we need to take on apprentices or students who can follow around someone who's good at it – you can't learn from a course. It takes quite a few years of experience to recognize when to compromise and when to accept somebody else's solution."

Karen Lopez observed that "there are rules that help keep you on the right path but not rules that you could hand off to an apprentice and have them produce a good quality data model". Eskil Swende, whose consultancy conducts its data modeling through facilitated workshops with business experts, stated that it takes at least twenty modeling seminars working alongside a more experienced person to make a good practitioner.

The most common criticism of data modelers was a focus on data models to the detriment of business understanding, communication, and empathy with programmers. Excess generalization was regularly noted. "(Data modelers should) experience the consequences of their model, see what it would be like to put stuff into that structure and get stuff out... They would see that what *seems* elegant would not be a good way to do business" and "Some people who don't have to live with the data structure are really big on excess generalization."

Style

Four interviewees used the word *style* to describe consistencies (or biases) across data models developed by an individual modeler, and others referred to the concept in other terms. In most cases, level of generalization was cited as an example: "There is a level of concreteness that I'm comfortable with (but) I've come across some [modelers] who are way more abstract; some who are way more concrete" and "they might come up with radically different models from exactly the same set of scenarios...but they would reflect different personal styles on things like generalization". David Hay observed that models reflected an overall level of generalization rather than independent entity-by-entity decisions: "it's not as if one goes up and one goes down".

Alec Sharp caught the emotional content of this issue: "I'm really down on excessive generalization – it drives me crazy – it's just as bad as under-generalization."

Communication

Data models were regularly characterized as being important communication tools ("The purpose of data modeling is communication") but as much for reflecting the business back to itself as for communicating its requirements to information system professionals.

Larry English emphasized that data models need to be understandable and readable by the business. "The business should be able to say 'this is not correct'". Some modelers indicated that they gave considerable attention to the aesthetics of the model diagrams, beyond the basic choice of conventions. In the context of data model presentation, one interviewee stated: "There is a very strong aesthetic component to doing a data model … it is ultimately a work of art." Comments from others suggested that communication remains problematic, at least in some cases: "You may have precision and rigor, but your model's incorrect because people can't comprehend it" and "I make a lot of money simplifying other peoples' models for presentation." These observations are consistent with those of Barker[93] (1990), Moody (1996) and with Hoberman's (2002 pp427-453) provision of "beauty tips" for data models.

Some interviewees suggested that data models had intrinsic limitations as vehicles for communication with non-specialists. John Zachman stated: "the (business) owner doesn't deal with data models – they deal with the things that they're trying to manage." Others agreed: "People in a business don't think in (entity) terms at all" and "never use those terms with business people".

An alternative perspective was that different models were needed for different audiences (as indeed is implicit in John Zachman's statement). "Unlike every other discipline (aircraft, railroad, building) we try to put everything in one model – other disciplines have different models for different audiences" and "the construction drawing isn't what the architect shows the client."

---

[93] The preceding quotations were not from Barker or Hoberman in their capacity as interviewees.

6.5.   DISCUSSION

The value of this component of the research lay in being able to focus on the description / design question, and to explore and challenge positions. As noted in the literature review, academic researchers (and practitioner authors) have given the subject little direct attention. Positions are typically assumed or simply declared and not supported by detailed argument. Even establishing the existence of different positions relies on some degree of interpretation.

Here we have quite clear positions, strongly and sometimes passionately argued. If there was any doubt that different perspectives existed, it was erased by four of the interviewees who had changed their positions. Two had moved from *description* to *design,* two from *design* to *description,* and all four saw the change as of fundamental importance to their professional practice.

The question of business requirements negotiability was as much about roles as the nature of data modelling, although there was a flavor of the conjecture-analysis design paradigm (Roozenburg and Cross 1991) in the desire to have "users jumping up to the board and saying 'this is wrong'" and in "playing the business back to itself." The discussion centered on whether data modelers should be (at one extreme) key players in the design of the business or (at the other) passive documenters of the business's view of its data. In between was the option of showing the business the consequences of its view of data and thus pushing them towards designing better structures – perhaps with further facilitation from the modeler. But characterizing the difference as one of roles does not render it trivial. The architect's role would certainly be a different one if clients already had the detailed plans of their buildings in their minds – and we would no longer regard architecture as design, even if some design process was taking place on the client's part.

The strength of the "one right answer" positions is particularly interesting. We noted in the literature review that it is difficult to find an argued case for this view in the academic literature, although it is frequently implied. The practitioner thought-leaders filled this gap and made it clear that the view is widely held and taught.

One goal of this component of the research was to describe something of the environment within which data modelers work and learn. It seems clear from the preceding discussion that there is no consensus on the description / design question. On the contrary, different views are held and promulgated, and have important impacts on the behavior of the thought-leaders, and, presumably the practitioners who are influenced by them.

The second goal of this component was to guide the design of the research, and some findings were incorporated in the approach presented in Chapter 3. The first, and most significant, contribution was confirmation that the description / design question, as framed, was worth investigating as a practical issue: the dissent in evidence in the literature appears to exist also amongst the thought-leaders in practice. An immediate direction suggested by this finding was to investigate which views were dominant amongst practitioners in general, beyond this elite group.

The discussion of creativity made it clear that investigating creativity alone – or characterizing the description / design question in terms of the importance of creativity, as I originally considered – would provide only limited insights as to the nature of data modeling. With a few exceptions, interviewees generally valued creativity, but saw it applied in different ways. The design camp viewed creativity as important to the choice of categories themselves, whereas the description camp focused on its role in investigation, communication, and model aesthetics.

In a similar vein, although use of patterns is one of Lawson's properties of design, interviewees also saw them as relevant to descriptive modeling as a means of sharing correct results. Evidence that data modelers use patterns is thus not necessarily evidence that they are performing design.

In contrast, the dominance of *product* issues in the interviews suggested that this dimension should form at least one focus of the research. Differences in opinion, particularly around the "one right answer" issue, are clear, and it seemed likely that research could be designed to determine whether practitioners' answers to common problems were similar or divergent.

The discussion of differences in preferred level of generalization amongst modelers suggested this as a potential indicator of data modeler *style*, and was the key input to the design of that research component.

Finally, the research needed to clarify the terminology and scope of data modeling. Some modelers included business change in their role, if not in the definition of data modeling, while others took a more constrained view. Use of the terms *conceptual*, *logical* and *physical logical data modeling* were not always consistent with definitions in the literature.

The impact of these findings can be seen in the framing of the description / design question, the attention given to practitioner perceptions (including terminology and scope), comparison of the products of data modeling, and the investigation of style based around level of generalization.

Chapter 6 – What the thought-leaders think

PART III – PRACTICE

CHAPTER 7
RESEARCH DESIGN

Here is my lens. You know my methods.
   – Sherlock Holmes in Conan Doyle: *The Adventure of the Blue Carbuncle*

7.1. INTRODUCTION

This chapter describes the design of the research project that addressed the description / design question:

Is data modeling better characterized as description or design?

The project comprised three phases, with a total of seven components (including the interviews with thought-leaders, presented in the preceding chapter). Each component is described in a dedicated chapter. This chapter covers the purpose and broad design of the research, and shows how the components relate and contribute to answering the description / design question and sub-questions. It also covers some aspects of design and method common to all components, including data collection and administration and statistical techniques. The chapter concludes with a consolidated description of participants and their demographics across the various research components. Detailed designs, measures, materials, methods, analysis techniques, and samples for individual components are covered in their specific chapters.

7.2. RESEARCH QUESTION AND SUB-QUESTIONS

The research question – *Is data modeling better characterized as description or design?* – was introduced in Chapter 1, where we noted some advantages over alternative (though not equivalent) formulations. Briefly, the description / design dichotomy is likely to be comprehensible to practitioners, captures important differences of relevance to practice, and is supported by an extensive (and accessible) body of generic design literature. Scope and definitions were also summarized in Chapter 1 (Section 1.4.2) and elaborated upon in Chapter 2.

As discussed in Section 1.4.3, the description / design question can usefully be viewed from five different perspectives: *Environment ("Press"), Problem, Product, Process, and People* (the *5Ps* framework used throughout this book). Because there was little previous research directly addressing the question, it was decided to address all five perspectives, sacrificing some depth in the interests of establishing at least a preliminary answer that covered different aspects of the question. The focus was on data modeling practice and practitioners. The dearth of data from industry, and the limitations of research using students were discussed in Chapter 5.

The research sub-questions came from two sources – primarily the literature review and the resulting identification of gaps to be addressed, but also from interviews with thought-leaders (Chapter 6)[94]. The interviews provided confirmation of the importance of the description / design question, contributed to refining the sub-questions, and helped to establish what type of evidence would be most useful in differentiating between the two characterizations. The emphasis given to the *product* dimension in the research design reflects disagreement amongst thought-leaders as to whether data modeling problems had a single correct answer, and their frequent reference to that issue as encapsulating the description / design question.

The final set of research sub-questions is listed in Table 7–1. They are organized according to the primary dimension in the 5Ps framework that they address. Those that involve perceptions obviously include an element of the *Person* dimension. The *Style* question addresses the relationship between *Person* and *Product*.

---

[94] As noted in Section 1.6, these interviews served two purposes: to inform the research design (as discussed here) and as direct input to the investigation of *environment*. Because of the latter role, the results are presented after the research design, even though they provided input to it.

Primary (5Ps) Dimension	Question Name	Research Sub-question
Environment (beliefs)	Importance	Is the description / design question considered important by data modeling practitioners?
	Espoused Beliefs	What are the (espoused) beliefs of data modeling practitioners on the description / design question?
Environment (database design)	Scope	What do data modeling practitioners believe is the scope and role of data modeling within the database design process?
Problem	Perception of Problems	Are data modeling problems perceived as design problems by data modeling practitioners?
Process	Methods	Do database design methods used in practice support a descriptive or design characterization of data modeling?
	Perception of Processes	Are data modeling processes perceived as design processes by data modeling practitioners?
Product	Perception of Products	Are data modeling products perceived as design products by data modeling practitioners?
	Diversity in Conceptual Modeling	Will different data modeling practitioners produce different conceptual data models for the same scenario?
	Diversity in Logical Modeling	Will different data modeling practitioners produce different logical data models from the same conceptual model?
	Patterns	Do data modeling practitioners use patterns[95] when developing models?
Person	Style	Do data modeling practitioners exhibit personal styles that influence the data models that they create?

Table 7–1: Research sub-questions

7.3. RESEARCH DESIGN – OVERVIEW

The sub-questions listed in the preceding section were investigated using a combination of surveys, laboratory studies, and semi-structured interviews. Approaches were chosen to suit the individual sub-questions, and also to provide triangulation through use of multiple methods (Alford 1998 pp3-4). In this section we describe the approach to the design of the present research as a whole, show how the research components address the sub-questions, discuss the recruitment of

---

[95] The classification of pattern use under *product* rather than *process* follows Lawson's Property: *Design products are a contribution to knowledge.*

participants, and summarize how the design was refined through piloting and experience.

7.3.1. Design dimensions

Research in information systems, and the social sciences in general, can be classified according to a number of different dimensions (Shanks, Rouse et al. 1993; Neuman 1999 pp20-62):

Purpose

The purpose of research can be exploratory, descriptive and / or explanatory (Saunders, Lewis et al. 2000; Gray 2004 p32). The present research was *primarily* descriptive, in that it attempted to describe a phenomenon (data modeling) as it naturally occurs (Hedrick, Bickman et al. 1993) rather than establish an explanation. The goal was a better description of data modeling within the framework of the description / design dichotomy. A great deal of social research is descriptive, and most data gathering techniques can be used, although true experimental research is less often appropriate (Neuman 1999 pp21-22). There was also an exploratory aspect to the research, particularly in addressing beliefs about the characterization and scope of data modeling.

Type of question

Research questions can be classified as descriptive, normative, correlative, or impact-oriented (Hedrick, Bickman et al. 1993; Gray 2004 p71). Within this scheme, the research question addressed by this book was normative in that it compared data modeling with a norm of design (as noted in Section 2.3, *description* serves as the antithesis of *design* – the absence of design). Max Weber used the term *Ideal Type* (Neuman 1999 p431) to describe a pure standard (e.g. an ideal of democracy or of bureaucracy) against which data or reality can be compared. The concept nicely captures the role of *design* as used here.

Research paradigm

The paradigm for the research project as a whole was positivist. In terms of Lee's (1991b) framework, which integrates positivist and interpretive approaches, our interest was in gaining an understanding of aspects of data modeling *using our own constructs* – specifically, the design paradigm. We tested the proposition that data modeling has the characteristics of a design discipline; in the light of the literature review in Chapter 2, this proposition would appear to meet the spirit of Popper's positivist-paradigm tests of falsifiability, logical consistency, and relative explanatory power (Lee 1991b). Popper includes a fourth test of *survival*. The characterization of data modeling as design has survived to date within the academic and practitioner communities, but only as a minority view, alongside the dominant descriptive characterization. The survival of two conflicting views may reflect a lack of articulation or challenge – goals of the present research.

Methods

The principal methods were interviews (one research component only), surveys, and laboratory tasks. The interviews used a phenomenological framework based on Colaizzi (1978)[96]. Three questionnaires were designed to collect data on perceptions of data modeling.

The laboratory studies were designed to explore diversity and style in data models. These focused on description of variation rather than on causality – hence the use of the term *studies* or *tasks* rather than *experiments*[97]. They are characterized as *laboratory* studies because they were performed under supervision which included provision of standard materials, time limits, and control of interaction with other participants (Singleton and Straits 1999 pp179-206). This was consistent with goals and standards for other laboratory studies of data modeling (Batra, Hoffer et al. 1990).

Data collection

Both qualitative and quantitative data were collected. The principal qualitative data were videotaped interviews, data models, and responses to open-ended survey questions. The last of these were used in the initial exploration of beliefs about data modeling and the database design process. Quantitative data included responses to closed-ended survey questions and demographic data.

---

[96] Use of the framework as a well-established approach to interview analysis did not imply adopting a phenomenological paradigm for the research as a whole.

[97] The term *experiments* is sometimes used to cover studies such as these (e.g. Srinivasan and Te'eni 1990). We have been strict in our usage here, as the design of the tasks and use of statistics may give a false impression that they are true experiments, intended to establish causality.

Data analysis

The analysis of interviews with thought-leaders used qualitative techniques, with identification and analysis of themes following the method described by Colaizzi (1978).

Analysis of the data from surveys and laboratory tasks was quantitative, requiring the coding of the predominantly qualitative data that they delivered. The data models provided a particular challenge, as they included complex combinations of construct names, symbols and text, all of which required interpretation in context. Coding was guided by an overall conceptual framework – 'the best defense against overload" (Miles and Huberman 1994 p55) – in the form of a set of categories of data model diversity.

Although surveys are "quantitative beasts" (Groves 1996), two open questions ("What is data modeling?" and "What are the stages in data modeling?") required some sophistication in coding and, for the latter question, recognition of patterns.

7.3.2. How the research components addressed the sub-questions

Table 7–2 shows the seven research components, numbered according to the chapter in which they are reported, mapped to the research sub-questions.

Component (Chapter)	Research Component	Method	Sub-questions addressed
Chapter 6	Interviews with Thought-leaders	Interviews	Importance, Espoused Beliefs, Perception of Problems, Perception of Processes, Perception of Products, Methods[98]
Chapter 8	Scope and Stages	Survey	Scope, Methods
Chapter 9	Espoused Positions on Data Modeling	Survey	Importance, Espoused Beliefs
Chapter 10	Characteristics of Data Modeling	Survey	Perception of Problems, Perception of Processes, Perception of Products[98]
Chapter 11	Diversity in Conceptual Modeling	Laboratory Study	Diversity in Conceptual Modeling, Patterns
Chapter 12	Diversity in Logical Modeling	Laboratory Study	Diversity in Logical Modeling, Patterns
Chapter 13	Style in Data Modeling	Laboratory Study	Style, Diversity in Conceptual Modeling, Diversity in Logical Modeling, Patterns

Table 7–2: Mapping of research tasks to the sub-questions that they address

As is apparent from the table, the sub-questions do not map to the research components in a simple way. This is a consequence of four factors:

1. Addressing the questions using multiple approaches to provide a richer description.

2. Providing for replication (Yin 1994 p31) at the sub-question level.

3. Designing some tasks and surveys to address multiple questions in order to make most efficient use of limited participant time

4. Taking advantage of data necessarily generated as a result of addressing other questions e.g. the *Style in Data Modeling* task required modelers to develop models – these were also examined for diversity.

The net effect is that all but two of the sub-questions (*Scope* and *Style*) were addressed by more than one research component. A common set of demographic data about participants in the surveys and laboratory studies was collected, and

---

[98] In examining perceptions of data modeling products, these components also noted *perceptions* of the subordinate issues of diversity and use of patterns.

correlations between these the key measures arising from the surveys and tasks were noted. This had the effect of overlaying the *Person* dimension on each of these research components[99].

As can be seen from Table 7–2, the research fell conceptually into three phases, reflected in the organization of the chapters:

1. Phase 1 (described in Chapter 6, which concludes Part I of this book) comprised a single component – *Interviews with Thought-leaders*, exploring the views held by practitioner authorities. The additional role of the interviews in contributing to the research design has been noted earlier.

2. Phase 2 (described in Chapter 8 to Chapter 10) was a survey-based examination of practitioners' beliefs about data modeling.

3. Phase 3 (described in Chapter 11 to Chapter 13) addressed diversity in data modeling products through three laboratory studies.

7.3.3. Recruitment of participants

The major practical challenge in investigating the description / design question in the context of *practice* was gaining access to data modeling practitioners. As noted in Section 5.2, most empirical research has used students. With the exception of Hitchman's (1995) use of a mailing list of magazine subscribers, recruitment of practitioners has been largely through personal contacts in one or two organizations and samples have been small. Gaining access to numbers sufficient to support statistical analysis – a minimum sample size of 30 for metric data and an average cell size of 10 for cross-tabulation of categorical data are typical recommendations (Blaikie 2003 pp166-167) – was significantly more difficult. Ideally, the participants would include specialist and non-specialist data modelers with varying levels of experience from different locations to support generalizability of results.

The approach chosen was to incorporate the research into data modeling seminars and workshops presented by the author and targeting experienced practitioners. Surveys were administered at shorter seminars; the more complex laboratory tasks

---

[99] In treating person as an orthogonal dimension here, the research framework follows that of Magyari-Beck (1990) discussed in Section 1.4.3.

were designed into longer workshops. The author actively sought opportunities to present the seminars to audiences with experience in data modeling on a commercial or non-commercial basis, with due regard for ethical considerations (Section 7.4.1).

A summary of the seminars and participant demographics appears in Section 7.6. Throughout this book we use the term *data modeling practitioners* for this group, while recognizing that it included some novices, many who were not specialist data modelers (as indicated by responses to the *primary occupation* question) and potentially some who were not currently working in industry.

Three other groups of participants were involved in the research. Practitioner thought-leaders (for interviews) and expert model evaluators (*Conceptual Data Modeling* component) were purposive samples. The author selected candidates based on their credentials, and invited them directly to participate. Architects and accountants (surveyed to provide a benchmark for *Characteristics of Data Modeling*) were snowball-recruited from the author's personal and professional contact lists.

7.3.4. Testing and refining the research design

The initial research design was refined by piloting the tasks and questionnaires and by learning from the results of research components as they progressed.

All surveys and tasks were piloted with novice and experienced data modelers to test the instructions and establish completion times. The principal outcomes were changes to the wording of instructions, deletion of a question from the *Characteristics of Data Modeling* questionnaire after no effective wording could be found[100], and a recognition that any time limits would need to be a compromise amongst (a) the time desired by the slowest participants, (b) the time that faster performers could be asked to wait while others finished, and (c) the time that could reasonably be devoted to a research exercise in the context of a seminar. These problems with time would be familiar to any teacher or instructor running class exercises, and are avoided in some research by allowing students unlimited time outside class in combination with academic credit as motivation (e.g. Ramesh and Browne 1999; Sinha and Vessey 1999). In the absence of such external

---

[100] Discussed in Section 10.4. The question tested Lawson's Property: ***Design solutions are parts of other design problems.***

motivation, response rates were likely to fall if participants left the class. There was also a risk in a conference / seminar setting that participants would collaborate. Accordingly judgment was exercised in setting time limits, and a question included as to whether the model would be different if more time had been available.

7.4. DATA COLLECTION AND MANAGEMENT

The research project employed a number of widely-recommended practices for data collection and management. This section summarizes those common to several research components, covering ethical issues, administration of surveys and tasks, and storage, collection of common demographic data, and coding and analysis of data.

7.4.1. Ethical issues

All participants were provided with a project description and ethics statement (posted on the author's website) and advised that participation was voluntary and anonymous. Where the task involved the production of a data model, the associated questionnaire forms were numbered in advance, and models (on a separate sheet) were linked to the questionnaire by that number (rather than names).

Most participants in the study were attendees at seminars for which they had paid (either directly or through membership dues) and invested time. There was an ethical and commercial requirement that the study activities did not detract from the value of the seminar. Several strategies were employed to achieve this:

1. The study tasks were incorporated into the seminars as learning activities: survey results were discussed and compared and modeling tasks were used as examples for later discussion. The author continued to use these activities in seminars for their educational value alone after data collection for the present project was complete.

2. Participants at most seminars were asked (by the organizers) to complete evaluation / feedback forms, all of which allowed for comments or complaints about content and presentation. Participants were also in a position to complain directly to the organizers or the author. Over the entire project, no complaints were received about the research tasks.

3.	Participants could choose to be advised of results by submitting a business card or otherwise providing details. Results were posted on the author's website.

4.	Early results were included in practitioner-oriented articles (Simsion 2005c; 2005a; 2005b)[101], referenced on the author's website.

Most of the above strategies benefited the research by encouraging feedback and discussion.

7.4.2. Administration of questionnaires and tasks

Saunders, Lewis, et al (2000) suggest that when conducting research in an organization, response rates can be dramatically improved by calling all respondents to a meeting and getting the questionnaire completed before people leave the meeting. The approach used here in effect implemented that model.

All research activities at seminars were undertaken before any other activities or presentation (other than administrative tasks) to avoid pollution of data. In one case, some participants had attended a seminar presented by the author the previous day, in which the description / design question was discussed in some detail. They were asked to mark their questionnaires accordingly and their results were reviewed for differences with the other participants[102].

Where laboratory tasks and questionnaires were administered at the same seminar, the tasks always preceded the questionnaires; this was a deliberate tactic to provide recent experience for participants to reflect upon when answering the questionnaires.

7.4.3. Demographics and process data

All participants in the surveys and tasks (except accountants and architects who benchmarked the *Characteristics of Data Modeling* questionnaire and the expert

---

[101] These three articles were also published in the emailed newsletter of IRM UK, the organization that hosted three of the seminars.

[102] The results for this group proved not to be significantly different from those who had not attended the seminar, and they were included in the analysis (Section 10.7.2).

panel who assessed models for the *Diversity in Conceptual Modeling* component) were asked to complete a common demographics questionnaire. All participants who were asked to develop a data model (or two in the case of the *Style in Data Modeling* component) were also asked to complete a set of *Process* questions for each model.

The demographics questions had three purposes. First, they provided an overall profile of the samples, to support a qualitative assessment of whether participants were indeed "data modeling practitioners", and to what extent results might be generalized. Second, they supported a (statistical) analysis of whether differences in survey responses and models were associated with differences in experience, occupation, and method of learning. Third, they allowed comparison with studies that have captured demographic information and noted associated differences in performance or attitudes.

The demographics questions covered three dimensions: experience, principal occupation, and method of learning.

Experience is well established as an independent variable in data modeling studies. Four measures have been used (Hitchman 1995; Shanks 1997b, see also Appendix): classification of participants by the researcher as "novices" or "experts", self-assessment as novice or expert, number of models developed, and years of experience. Given the importance of the experience dimension (Section 5.2), we used two measures – years of experience and number of models developed – chosen because of their relative objectiveness.

Principal Occupation was included to (a) assess what percentage of the samples were specialist data modelers (hence inform generalization) and (b) explore whether perceptions of data modeling varied amongst the different job roles. Hitchman's (1995) survey (notable for the largest sample of data modeling practitioners) collected job category information and noted some differences in perceptions across the groups as did Simsion (1996).

Method of Learning was included because of acknowledged differences in practitioner and academic views of data modeling (Batra and Marakas 1995). We were interested in whether those who had learned primarily from academic sources (tertiary education, publications) would characterize data modeling differently from those who had learned from industry courses or "on the job".

Demographic information was collected as discrete values and post-coded. Experience levels were coded into eight intervals for both years and number of models developed in each case and occupations into seven categories. Despite being asked to nominate "principal method of learning" many respondents nominated multiple methods and it was decided to code each method of learning separately (e.g. "learned on the job" was treated as a separate category – 'yes' or 'no'). Section 7.6 in this chapter shows the schemes applied across all responses to the demographic questionnaires.

Sample sizes were generally not large enough to support comparisons at the finest level of granularity, and the five (binary) *standard demographic splits* shown in Table 7–3 were used for most research components in addition to the *method of learning* splits.

Demographic Split	Categories	Range
Experience (1)	Novice (Years)	0-1 years
	Experienced (Years)	>1 years
Experience (2)	Novice (Models)	0-1 models
	Experienced (Models)	>1 models
Experience (3)	Less Experienced (Years)	0-5 years
	More Experienced (Years)	>5 years
Experience (4)	Less Experienced (Models)	0-10 models
	More Experienced (Models)	> 10 models
Occupation	Data Modeler	Data Modeler
	Other	All other categories

Table 7–3: Standard demographic splits

These splits supported investigation of differences in responses and models across the potentially most interesting demographic categories.

The *process* questions asked participants to report on aspects of the data modeling task(s). Four questions asked about the understanding of the requirements as presented, the difficulty of the problem, whether the participant had made guesses, and whether the model would be different if more time had been available. These were to assess whether diversity might be a result of the problem being ambiguous or too difficult or insufficient time being available for completion, rather than a result of different designs.

Two questions addressed *patterns*, asking whether the participant had added structures that could not be deduced from the problem description, and whether they had drawn upon structures that they had seen or used in the past.

7.4.4. Data coding and analysis

Coding of qualitative data in particular was a critical task in this project. The author was assisted by (at various times and for various tasks) three research assistants, one with some theoretical knowledge of data modeling principles, and two with no background in the field. The four coders (including the author) were deployed in different ways, depending on the nature of the task, as described in the individual research component results. All coding of qualitative data, except some very straightforward demographic data, involved two coders, and inter-rater reliability was measured as appropriate.

Survey responses and coded data were stored in spreadsheets (with the exception of responses to the *Scope and Stages* questionnaire, which were stored in a relational database), and analyzed using the SPSS statistics package. Interviews were recorded on digital videotape, and transcribed by the author.

7.5.   USE OF STATISTICS

This section summarizes the statistics used in the research. Before discussing individual measures, we comment on the use of inferential statistics throughout the book, and note the broader issue of generalizability of results, which is taken up in more detail in the concluding chapter (Section 14.4).

7.5.1. Inferential statistics and generalization

The use of inferential statistics (to estimate the probability that a property of a sample exists in the population), is a controversial area, with some arguing that without strictly random sampling and very high response rates, such statistics have "absolutely no meaning" (Blaikie 2003 p7, 159). Conversely, the use of inferential statistics (as evidenced by the citation of p [statistical significance] values) in less than ideal circumstances is widespread in social research.

Empirical studies of data modeling (Chapter 5) frequently cite p values, despite almost invariably using "convenience" (commonly students from classes), "volunteer" (e.g. Moody 2002), or "snowball" (e.g. Shanks, Nuredini et al. 2002a) sampling. Practitioner and expert participants have generally been recruited through personal contacts, and samples are frequently dominated by individuals from a single organization. Student participants are frequently from a single class.

Sampling in the present research was as follows:

1. Participants had chosen (or been selected by their employers) to attend seminars on data modeling. The author had no involvement in the selection of participants, but participants' decisions to attend may have been influenced by their knowledge of the author and his views[103].

2. All locations were in "Western" countries[104] – North America, Europe, and Australia.

3. Participants were predominantly employed in data management positions.

4. Results across samples were compared. There were very few significant differences in the results obtained when surveys or tasks were administered to more than one group. These are reported in the relevant chapters, but we note in particular that the *Characteristics of Data Modeling* survey, administered to seven of the twelve groups (minimum size 20) covering all settings (conferences, DAMA presentations, and a commercial class) and geographic areas (UK, USA, Scandinavia, Australia) did not produce significantly different results (ANOVA) across the samples (Section 10.7.2).

This approach to sampling compares favorably with other empirical work in data modeling where inferential statistics have been used, and would appear to support cautious generalization to data modeling practitioners in Western countries.

We emphasize here that generalization of results need not rely on statistical inference (Yin 1994 pp30-32). The research design also supports *analytic* generalization, particularly through addressing the description / design question and sub-questions with a variety of surveys and laboratory studies, to establish replication[105] of results. Robson (1993) states that the argument for generalization

---

[103] This issue is taken up in Section 14.4. At one extreme was a commercial class run solely by the author and advertised as such, and at the other the author's presentation at a plenary (no choice of alternatives) session at a larger conference.

[104] Note that not all participants were native speakers of English. English was not the first language for most or all members of the two Scandinavian groups, although the surveys and exercises were conducted in English.

[105] The word *replication* is used carefully to indicate support for a finding using a different survey or task, rather than *reliability* derived from repeating the same survey or task.

of findings can be made by either direct demonstration or making a case (reasoned argument). The present research design is intended to support a "reasoned argument" for generalizing findings to data modeling practitioners working in Western countries at least – noting Myrdal's (1973) warning that "a Western approach is a biased approach".

7.5.2. Statistical tests

This section lists all statistical tests used in this book, and, where necessary, comments on their choice and interpretation.

Univariate statistics

The presentation and analysis of single-variable data was straightforward. Nominal and ordinal data was presented as raw counts and percentages. Summary statistics for metric data included means and standard deviation.

Demographic experience categories were treated as ordinal rather than metric, as intervals were not equal.

Likert scales were generally treated as ordinal, but in the analysis of the *Characteristics of Data Modeling* survey were treated as metric and used in deriving indexes, as is common practice in survey research (Pervan and Klass 1992).

Differences from the "neutral" value in Likert scales (for responses to *Characteristics of Data Modeling* Surveys) were analyzed using one-sample t-tests.

Generalization Scores, calculated by counting different decisions of the same generic kind in a data model, and used in analysis of all of the laboratory tasks, were treated as ordinal.

Reliability measures

Scale reliability was measured using Cronbach's Alpha which produces a value between 0 and 1.

Inter-coder / inter-rater reliability was measured using Cronbach's Alpha (above) for ordinal coding (Likert scale used for coding data modeling definitions, experts' evaluation of data models) and Cohen's Kappa for coding into categories (stages in database design). The Kuder-Richardson 20 (KR20) coefficient was used for the (dichotomous) choices in coding of themes in data modeling definitions. A value of 0.7 is generally considered satisfactory for these measures (Nunally 1978), although values as low as 0.5 are accepted by some (Caplan, Naidu et al. 1984; Moody and Shanks 2003).

Comparison of groups

Comparisons of (metric) values between groups used independent group t-tests (two groups) and ANOVA (three or more groups). These tests were used in analyzing scores from the *Characteristics of Data Modeling* surveys. Levene's test was used to verify normality.

Measures of strength of association

It bears re-emphasizing that the present research was *descriptive* and association between variables is not intended to imply causality.

Table 7–4 summarizes the measures used to quantify association between variables of different kinds. Their selection and use is described below.

	Nominal (dichotomous)	Nominal (non-dichotomous)	Ordinal	Metric
Nominal (dichotomous)	Phi	Cramer's V	Gamma, Kendall's tau-b	Not required
Nominal (non-dichotomous)	-	Cramer's V	Not required	Not required
Ordinal	-	-	Gamma, Kendall's tau-b	Not required
Metric	-	-	-	Pearson's r

Table 7–4: Measures of strength of association used in the research

Phi (for 2x2 tables) and Cramer's V are derivations of the chi-square statistic, normalized to produce measures of strength of association between zero and 1. The associated p values are the same as for the chi-square statistic (de Vaus 1995 p293). They are considered conservative measures compared with the alternative standardized Contingency Coefficient (Blaikie 2003 p102). They are used for a variety of comparisons of nominal data (classifications of data modeling, data modeling choices, demographic categories) throughout the book.

The gamma (*ordered categories gamma*) statistic and Kendall's tau-b were used for comparing ordinal variables or ordinal and dichotomous nominal variables. Kendall's tau-b is more conservative (Blaikie 2003 pp102-105) and was used for comparing *generalization scores* (all laboratory tasks) to avoid overstating key results; gamma was used for correlations amongst demographics and answers to process questions (Section 7.4.3).

Pearson's *r* was used only to measure correlation between scores (indexes) within the *Characteristics of Data Modeling* survey.

Table 7–5 shows the conventions used in the book for describing the strength of an association in words for all the above measures of association except Pearson's *r* (Blaikie 2003 p100).

Value / Range	Description
0.00	None
0.01-0.09	Negligible
0.01-0.29	Weak
0.30-0.59	Moderate
0.60-0.74	Strong
0.75-0.99	Very Strong
1.00	Perfect

Table 7–5: Descriptions of strength of association

For Pearson's r, we follow Cohen (1988), who suggests interpreting values as follows: 0.1 – small, 0.3 – medium, 0.5 or more – large.

Regression analysis (linear, multiple) was used only in assessing the contribution of quality factors to an overall quality assessment of models – a peripheral aspect of the *Diversity in Conceptual Modeling* component.

Covariance

Covariance of (binary) generalization decisions within and across models was assessed using the Kuder-Richardson 20 (KR20) coefficient, which is appropriate for dichotomous values.

7.6. PARTICIPANTS

Four types of participants were involved in the research. Thought-leaders were interviewed for the research component reported in Chapter 6. Data modeling practitioners (the largest group) responded to surveys and undertook laboratory tasks, and provided demographic information.   Architects and accountants completed *Characteristics of Design* surveys for comparison with data modeling versions. A panel of expert data modelers reviewed data models produced in the *Diversity in Conceptual Modeling* component. This section provides a consolidated view of the data modeling practitioner participants, and the components in which they participated.

Participants in surveys and laboratory tasks were attendees at twelve data modeling seminars conducted by the author at ten different locations between May 2002 and November 2004. The laboratory tasks were performed by attendees of classes targeted at experienced data modeling practitioners. Surveys were administered at similar advanced classes as well as data management conferences and four presentations at chapter meetings of the Data Managers' Association (DAMA)[106]. DAMA chapter meetings have previously been used by researchers to gain access to data modeling practitioners (Shanks 1996a; Moody 2001).

Locations, participant numbers, and the research components to which they contributed are summarized in Table 7–6.

---

[106] Formerly the Data Administration Managers' Association. Details at www.dama.org

Location	Date	Research Component	No. of Participants	Response Rate[107]
DAMA / Metadata Conference, San Antonio, TX, USA	May 2002	Diversity in Conceptual Modeling Espoused Positions on Data Modeling	112	66%
DAMA Conference, London, UK	Nov 2002	Diversity in Logical Modeling	17	85%
Enterprise Data Forum, Pittsburgh, PA, USA	Nov 2002	Diversity in Logical Modeling	23	80%
DAMA / Metadata Conference, Orlando, FL, USA	Apr 2003	Data Modeling Style	41	77%
DAMA Chapter Presentation, Portland, OR, USA	Mar 2004	Characteristics of Data Modeling	54	90%**
DAMA Chapter Presentation, Phoenix, AZ, USA	Mar 2004	Characteristics of Data Modeling	28	90%**
DAMA Chapter Presentation, Des Moines, IA, USA	Mar 2004	Characteristics of Data Modeling	39	90%**
IRM Data Modeling Workshop Stockholm, Sweden	Mar 2004	Data Modeling Style Diversity in Logical Modeling*	28	70%**
IRM / DAMA Conference, Stockholm, Sweden	Mar 2004	Characteristics of Data Modeling	70***	90%**
DAMA Chapter Presentation, Sydney, Australia	Jun 2004	Characteristics of Data Modeling	20	90%**

* The *Diversity in Logical Modeling* task was incorporated in the *Data Modeling Style* task in these two locations.

** Estimate – exact attendee numbers not available

*** This group included 28 who attended the Data Modeling Workshop in Stockholm (previous item in table).

Table 7–6: Research samples and research components

---

[107] Incomplete responses are included here. A more detailed breakdown appears in the chapters describing the relevant research components.

Location	Date	Research Component	No. of Participants	Response Rate108
DAMA / Data Quality Conference, London, UK	Nov 2004	Characteristics of Data Modeling Scope and Stages	25	83%
Wilshire Conferences Data Modeling Master class, Los Angeles, CA, USA	Nov 2004	Characteristics of Data Modeling Scope and Stages Data Modeling Style Diversity in Logical Modeling*	30	86%
			459	75%

* The *Diversity in Logical Modeling* task was incorporated in the *Data Modeling Style* task in these two locations

Table 7-6: (cont.)

Figure 7-1 through to Figure 7-4 summarize the responses to the demographic questions, across all surveys and tasks. Note that thought-leader interviewees, architects and accountants, and expert evaluators are not included. Thirty-five participants in laboratory tasks submitted models but did not complete the demographics, and are hence excluded from this analysis. "Not Reported" categories refer to individual questions not answered on submitted demographics questionnaires. Multiple responses were allowed for the "How participants learned" question.

---

[108] Incomplete responses are included here. A more detailed breakdown appears in the chapters describing the relevant research components.

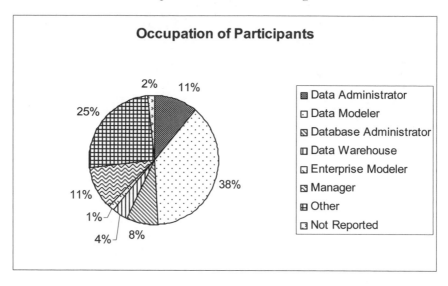

Figure 7-1: Occupation of participants

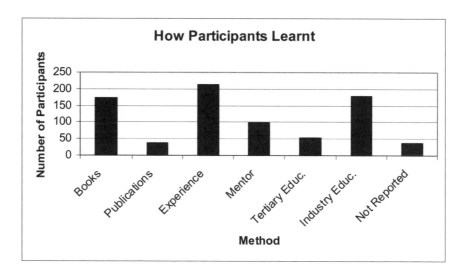

Figure 7-2: How participants learned

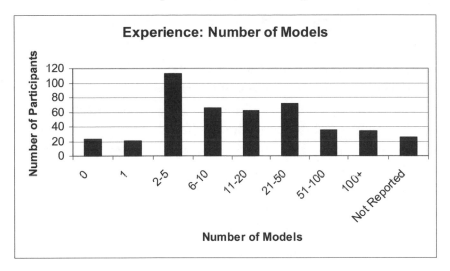

Figure 7-3: Experience: Number of models

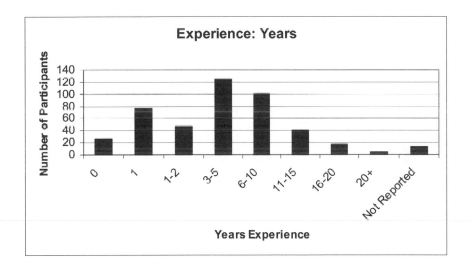

Figure 7-4: Experience: Years

Coding of primary occupations was performed by the author. The *Other* category includes 34 (8% of the total) participants who gave their job position only as *Consultant*. Of the valid responses to the *Primary Occupation* question, 127 (29%) included the word *architect*.

Coding of method of learning and experience into categories was performed by a research assistant with reference to the author as needed.

145

There was a strong correlation between the two experience measures (Gamma = 0.65, p<0.0005).

The number of experienced data modelers, both in total and for each study component, bears noting. The total of 381 participants who claimed at least one year of data modeling experience (there were also 48 participants who did not answer this question) substantially exceeds the *total* number with this level of experience reported across all 59 human factor studies listed in 0. Similarly, only 23 respondents stated that they had not developed a data model in practice (26 participants did not answer this question). On this basis, although a few individuals might not meet a strict definition of the term, we occasionally refer to the participants collectively as *practitioners*[109] particularly when we wish to distinguish them from the students used in other studies.

The minimum number of practitioners to complete any survey or task was 55, in the case of the *Scope and Stages* survey: this exceeds the number in all but one of the studies listed in the appendix.

---

[109] As noted in the literature review, it is common for the term *expert* to be used in empirical work to characterize practitioners in general and even more capable students. The term *practitioner* is less strong – and reflects Hitchman's (1995) observation that many practitioners are not experts.

CHAPTER 8
SCOPE AND STAGES

One man's ceiling is another man's floor.

> – Paul Simon, song title.

8.1. INTRODUCTION

The research described in this chapter investigated practitioner perceptions of the database design process and terminology. It had three objectives:

Firstly, as discussed in Chapter 3, the organization of the database design process reflects beliefs relevant to the characterization of data modeling as either description or design. By examining practitioners' perceptions of the process, we can develop a better understanding of which of the two beliefs is embodied in database design methods used in industry.

The second goal was to establish a working definition of data modeling. The two chapters that follow this one examine practitioners' perceptions of data modeling, using survey-based research methods. In order to properly interpret results (and indeed in order to frame questions appropriately), it was necessary to establish what practitioners mean by *data modeling*. Neither the academic nor the practitioner literature provides a single generally-accepted definition, and many of the definitions that do exist embody a position on the description / design issue. We established a tentative definition in Section 1.4.2 ("the activities required to specify a conceptual schema prior to any modifications required to meet performance goals") but it requires validation.

Finally, and more broadly, this component of the research sought a general description of the database design process and stages, *as perceived by practitioners*, to complement the literature-based framework of Section 3.1. In the same way that the theoretical framework provided a foundation for the review of the literature, a practice-based framework supports interpretation of the empirical work.

These questions address the *Environment* and *Process* perspectives of the 5Ps research framework introduced in Section 1.4.3, and, more specifically, the *Scope* and *Methods* sub-questions (Section 7.2):

What do data modeling practitioners believe is the scope and role of data modeling within the database design process? and

Do database design methods used in practice support a descriptive or design characterization of data modeling?

8.2. RESEARCH DESIGN

The research design recognized that two questions – practitioner perceptions of the database design process and practitioner definitions of data modeling – presented similar challenges that could be addressed with a common approach. The challenges lay primarily in the ambiguity of language. In Section 1.4.2, we noted the "terminological diversity and confusion that abounds in the data modeling community" (Hirschheim, Klein et al. 1995 p xi). A database design process described only in terms of the names of stages would be too ambiguous to be useful, and asking respondents to provide plain-language definitions could simply compound the problem by introducing further terminology. A similar problem arises with definitions of data modeling. Describing the scope of data modeling in terms of inputs and output replaces one definitional problem with another. The terms used for inputs and deliverables, such as *business requirements* and *data models,* are potentially as ambiguous as *data modeling* itself.

The solution was to allow participants to nominate their own set of stages, and then to map a given set of more elementary, better defined activities, such as normalization and definition of indexes, against those stages. The activities, sourced from practitioner and teaching literature, served as common reference points for comparing the higher-level stages nominated by different participants. Participants were also asked to define *data modeling* in terms of the stages that it was perceived to cover. The result was a set of database design processes and definitions of data modeling that could be compared based on the activities that they included.

8.3. MEASURES

Table 8–1 shows six aspects of the database design process that could be expected to vary according to whether the designer(s) of that process perceived data modeling as description or design.

Aspect of the Database Design Process	Response	Implications of Response
1. Business Requirements stage (not including entity, relationship, attribute identification) included?	Yes No	Supports design Supports either
2. Separate stages for DBMS-independent (conceptual) modeling and DBMS-specific (logical) modeling	Yes No	Supports either Supports design
3. Location of entity / relationship / attribute identification	Outside data modeling Within data modeling	Supports description Supports either
4. Location of view integration	Not required After data modeling Within data modeling	Supports description Supports description Supports design
5. Responsibility for and location of external schema specification	Modeler, business analyst (before conceptual schema definition) DBA (after conceptual schema definition)	Supports description Supports either
6. Location of performance-oriented decisions (conceptual schema compromises)	Within data modeling Outside data modeling	Supports design Supports either

Table 8–1: Six aspects of the database design process

The measures were drawn from the analysis of the database design process in Chapter 3, which also provides the basis for the interpretation of the different responses, listed under *Implications of Response* in the table. The word *supports* is used deliberately in describing implications, as none are so strong as to completely preclude an alternative interpretation, and the research design could not completely eliminate the possibility of ambiguity in terminology. The detailed discussion of the database design process in Chapter 3 is the reference for the interpretations and is not repeated here. *Very briefly*, though, the arguments for the interpretations are as below. References to the relevant subsections of Chapter 3 are included.

Question 1: The inclusion of a business requirements stage prior to identification of key model components does not accord with the descriptive view in which the

UoD is mapped directly onto a data model. Requirements may embody design, and / or may be seen a problem statement for which the model provides a solution. (Section 3.3)

Question 2: The well-established (in the literature) separation of conceptual and logical stages, consistent with the descriptive paradigm, may not be workable in practice; the modeler may not be able to undertake a purely descriptive stage followed by algorithmic (mechanical) transformation. In the alternative approach, more consistent with the design paradigm, the data modeler "looks ahead" to the implementation environment, working with the tools that it provides. In such a scenario, we would expect the boundaries between the two stages to blur or for them to be combined into a single stage. (Sections 3.4 and 3.6)

Question 3: If the important concepts to be embodied in the model are established before data modeling starts – e.g. in a requirements phase (Teorey, Lightstone et al. 2006) – then the data modeler does not have the option of "creating" those concepts.

Question 4: In an extreme descriptive characterization, there is one right answer, and view integration is not required, or trivial. If differences are relatively straightforward and can be simply resolved, resolution can be deferred until after the completion of modeling. In a design scenario, models may differ in complex ways, and integration / resolution is an ongoing process of negotiation.

Question 5: One widely-described approach to database design involves the use of external schemas (views) to reproduce the user views identified early in the process. The (descriptive) assumption is that these will be recoverable as mappings from the common conceptual schema that integrated these views in the first place. In this case, the data modeler defines the external schema. If, instead, external schemas are seen as a tool for managing data independence and security rather than reproducing user views (either because this is not possible, or because the alternative role is seen as more important), we might expect them to be defined by the Database Administrator (DBA) – and later in the process.

Question 6: Performance-oriented decisions are generally recognized as design. Inclusion of these within data modeling would add a design component – and perhaps suggest that the data modeler is permitted to deviate from pure description – a view which might extend to other parts of the process. This would be a relatively weak finding as it would rely on that inference.

To provide a basis for representing the database design process (as perceived by practitioners), a three tier framework was constructed (Figure 8-1). The framework allows database design stages to be defined in terms of the common (reference) activities that they contain, and data modeling, in turn, to be defined in terms of stages within the database design process. Survey responses were used to populate the second and third levels of the framework, and to relate them back to the pre-defined set of activities at the bottom level.

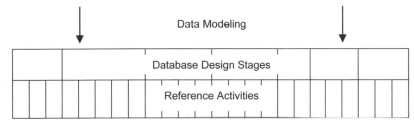

Figure 8-1: Framework for identifying database design stages

Given the variations in the literature, it was not expected that a single database design process and definition of data modeling would emerge; rather the objective was to identify common patterns and describe the nature and amount of the variation.

8.4. THE *SCOPE AND STAGES* QUESTIONNAIRE

The framework described in Section 8.4 provided the basis for a *Scope and Stages* questionnaire.

Several aspects of the questionnaire design should be noted:

1. The questionnaire provided numbered spaces for up to five stages in the database design process (there was room for at least a sixth to be added) and offered two examples, each comprising three stages (two further examples were included in the introduction given to participants – see Section 8.5.1 below). The intent was to encourage a similar level of granularity across the responses, as well as to provide general guidance on what was sought. As noted in Section 3.1, texts and papers which cover end-to-end database design generally provide a high-level view of five stages or less.

2. The questionnaire asked *Is it data modeling?* for each stage in order to identify the (perceived) boundaries of data modeling within the database design process.

3. The questionnaire asked *Who is responsible?* for each stage. This question had three purposes:

    - It provided data necessary to answer Question 5 about responsibility for physical database design (Section 8.3 above).

    - It provided a cross-check on the *Is it data modeling?* question (we could expect data modelers to be responsible for data modeling activities, but note interviewee Alec Sharp's comment (Section 6.4.3) that as a data modeler, he did not choose to limit his activities to data modeling).

    - It supported interpretation of responses to the *primary occupation* question on the demographics questionnaire.

4. The list of activities was not intended to be comprehensive, and their number represented a trade-off between amount of data and the effort required of respondents[110]. Activities were chosen because:

    - They were frequently nominated in teaching and practitioner texts on data modeling and database design (principal sources were Fleming and von Halle 1989; Barker 1990; Date 1998; Teorey 1999; Connolly and Begg 2005; Kroenke 2005; Simsion and Witt 2005), and hence should be familiar to and easily understood by participants in an advanced data modeling seminar.

    - They served to differentiate stages: at least one activity was included from each stage nominated by the reference texts. The emphasis was on activities generally recognized as data modeling. Activities which affect only the internal schema specification are almost invariably grouped into a common stage – hence there seemed little value in including more than two or three of these. Data distribution is occasionally allocated to a separate stage (e.g. Teorey 1999), and accordingly was included as an activity.

---

[110] The concern was to encourage completion within a timeframe consistent with administration and collection during a seminar.

- There appeared to be a reasonable consensus in the academic and practitioner literature as to their definitions (though not necessarily their importance or how and when they should be performed). This was essential to enable them to be used as a common basis for comparing stages.

Two further activities were added: *Changing the database to meet new business requirements* and *Advising programmers on understanding the database.* They were included to ascertain perceived responsibility for the completed database schemas. In turn, this served as a check on the extent to which the conceptual schema[111] was seen as a data modeling deliverable. These two activities were not included in populating the framework of Figure 8-1.

8.5. METHOD

Aspects of method common to several components of the research, including survey piloting, administration, ethical issues, coding of demographics, and use of statistics are covered in Chapter 7. Here we cover specific aspects of questionnaire administration, and the coding, organization, presentation, and analysis of results.

Several steps were required to:

- Reduce the variety of stage names nominated by participants to a set of standard names and categories

- Establish an overall "best fit" sequence of stages and activities.

- Identify the different patterns of stages and sequences

- Determine the composition of stages in terms of activities

- Determine which stages and activities (through their assignment to stages) were classified as data modeling, and what job roles were perceived as responsible.

---

[111] Recall that *conceptual schema* refers to a database component (ISO/TR9007:1987(E) 1987) – broadly base tables in a relational implementation – and should not be confused with *conceptual model*.

8.5.1. Administration of questionnaire

The questionnaire was administered to seminar classes following the general procedure described in Section 7.4. A short explanation with examples was presented.

Participants were allowed ten minutes for completion of the questionnaire, a time established by piloting. Questionnaires were collected at the completion of this period.

8.5.2. Basic coding of completed questionnaires

Initial review and coding of completed questionnaires was performed as follows:

1. Questionnaires with Part 1 (Stages) not completed or not interpretable were eliminated from further analysis.

2. Questionnaires with Part 1 correctly completed but Part 2 (Mapping Activities to Stages) not completed or not interpretable were used only in the analysis of Part 1.

3. Instances in which the respondent had left the "which stage?" box blank were consolidated with the legitimate responses of "?" (*don't know*) and "x" (*not included* in process) into a single *no allocation made* response.

4. Instances in which the respondent had allocated an activity to more than one stage were excluded from further analysis[112].

5. Demographic information was coded according to the procedure and coding schemes described in Section 7.4.3.

6. Responses to the question *Who is responsible?* were classified in the same way as the *primary occupations* demographic data (Section 7.6). The categories *Data Administrator / Manager* and *Enterprise Architect* were then combined, since in this context they were considered to represent similar roles (provision of external guidance and standards).

---

[112] This possibility was overlooked in questionnaire design, and was not detected in piloting.

8.5.3. Coding of stages

Stage names nominated by respondents were rationalized and coded as follows:

1.   The author reviewed all responses and developed a set of *Standard Stage Names,* by grouping reasonably obvious synonyms – primarily variations in spelling and abbreviation (e.g. *Conceptual Data Modeling* became the standard name for *Conceptual Model(l)ing, Conceptual Data Model(l)ing, Conceptual, Conc. DM* etc).   Three further names (classifications) were added: *Preliminary* (stages preceding project-level database development, such as *enterprise modeling*), *Post-Design Activities* (stages following completion of the database specification such as *testing*), and *Other* (stages nominated by only one respondent and not falling into any other classification).

2.   Coding of stages using Standard Stage Names was performed by two independent coders (one experienced in data modeling research, the other with no background in data modeling).   Differences in coding were resolved by the author.

3.   Standard Stage Names that were potential synonyms[113] were examined to determine whether they contained similar activities, did not frequently appear together, and appeared in a similar position in the average sequence of stages.   Where these criteria were met, the stages were combined.

All further analysis used these Standard Stage Names (hereafter referred to simply *stage names* or *stages*).

8.5.4. Stage and activities sequence

Stages and activities were organized into sequence within the database design process:

1.   A *Mean Stage Number* was calculated for each Stage by averaging the Stage Numbers for that stage across all responses (e.g. if a response nominated *Conceptual Data Modeling* as Stage 2, its Stage Number on

---

[113] The single case was Physical Data Modeling and Physical Database Design.

this response would be 2). This number was used to place stages in an overall (mean) sequence.

2. Stage numbers were then used to sort *activities* into an overall sequence, based on the mean of the stage numbers to which they were allocated. This sequence served as a (literal) baseline for graphical representation of activity characteristics – their allocation to stages and (by inheritance from the stage) responsibility, and whether they were classified as data modeling.

8.5.5. Identification of patterns

All responses were inspected to identify common patterns of stages, as a means of classifying and quantifying variation. Pattern identification focused on the most widely-cited stages (nominally set as those which accounted for more than 80% of citations); the resulting set of patterns comprised different combinations and sequences of these widely-cited stages. Responses were classified as following a particular pattern if they matched the pattern exactly (ignoring Preliminary and Post-Design Activities, which were treated as outside the scope of the investigation), or if any additional stages which they contained were (a) not present in any pattern and (b) judged as not materially affecting the conformity to the pattern (e.g. the addition of a Review stage).

8.5.6. Composition of stages

The most widely-cited stages (see previous subsection) were analyzed in terms of the activities that they contained.

For each activity, the frequency of allocation to each stage was calculated. Results were presented graphically and examined for evidence of consensus in definition of stages. The analysis was repeated for the most common patterns (nominally defined as patterns which accounted for more than 15% of responses) to determine whether there might be a higher level of consensus amongst respondents who agreed on the stages and their sequence.

8.5.7. Classification and responsibility for stages and activities

The following statistics were calculated first across all responses, and then for the responses falling into each of the common patterns.

1. The data modeling score for each stage – the percentage of respondents who answered *yes* to the question *Is it data modeling?* for that stage.

2. The data modeling score for each activity – derived from the data modeling scores for the stages to which it was allocated.

3. The frequency distribution of primary occupations nominated as responsible for each stage.

4. The frequency distribution of primary occupations for each activity, derived from the stages to which the activity was allocated.

The above results were presented graphically and inspected to assess whether there was a consensus (across all responses or within individual patterns) as to which stages and activities were data modeling, and which stages and activities were the responsibility of (in particular) data modelers.

The data modeling scores for stages and activities were calculated for each of the demographic groups (as defined in Section 7.4.3) to provide an indication of the level of agreement on the definition of data modeling.

8.5.8. Answering the questions

The six questions listed in Section 8.3 were addressed progressively as relevant results emerged. Findings are summarized in Section 8.8.

8.6. SAMPLE

Respondents to the questionnaire were attendees of two data modeling seminars targeted at experienced practitioners (refer Section 7.6) – a half-day workshop in London, UK and a two-day data modeling class in Los Angeles, USA, both conducted by the author in November, 2004.

Participant numbers and response rates[114] are shown in Table 8–2.

Location	Number of Attendees	Number of Responses Received	Response Rate
London	30 (approximately)	25	83%
Los Angeles	35	30	86%
Totals	65	55	85%

Table 8–2: Response statistics for Scope and Stages questionnaire

8.7. RESULTS

8.7.1. Initial review and coding of the stages

All 55 responses to Part 1 of the questionnaire were valid. There was one invalid response to Part 2 of the questionnaire[115], which was excluded from further analysis.

Allocations of activities to stages were left blank on 25 occasions (1.7% of the 54x28 = 1512 allocations). The "not included" response was given 33 times and the "don't know" response 40 times. Table 8–3 shows the activities that were unallocated to a stage on more than five occasions, accounting for 50% of the total.

---

[114] Administration of surveys and factors affecting the response rates and their measurement are discussed in Section 7.4.2.

[115] The respondent had allocated sequence numbers to the activities rather than mapping them to stages.

Activity Name	Blank	X	?	Total
Ensuring that business change can be accommodated	2	1	5	8
Documenting rules about data which cannot be represented in the data model	0	2	4	6
Integrating different views of the data	3	4	0	7
Removing derivable data	4	2	1	7
Specifying data distribution	4	1	8	13
Specifying views	1	3	5	9
Total	14	13	23	50

Table 8–3: Instances of activities unallocated to a stage

There were 194 allocations to multiple stages[116]. An analysis to determine whether the exclusion of the multiple allocations led to significantly different sequences and responsibilities for the activities showed only minor differences. On this basis, multiple allocations were ignored, considerably simplifying the analysis (and consequently any verification).

In 76 cases (of a total of 243 stages), respondents nominated more than one job role (mean of 2.3 job roles in these cases) in response to the "who is responsible?" question. These were included, unweighted, in the analysis. The "other" category for job classification was required in only one case – a respondent who nominated "vendor" as responsible for two stages.

Figure 8-2 summarizes the number of stages nominated by the respondents: a range of two to six (the two respondents who nominated six stages used the un-numbered space on the questionnaire).

---

[116] 25 of these multiple allocations applied to the two activities which are excluded from further analysis (nos 23 and 28).

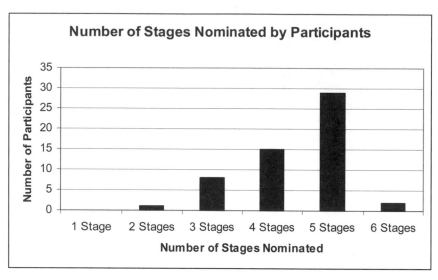

Figure 8-2: Number of stages nominated by participants

Seventeen standard stage names were identified, including Preliminary, Post-design Activities and Other.

Coding of stages was relatively straightforward, as indicated by the inter-coder reliability (Cohen's kappa) of 0.84 (0.7 is considered satisfactory). Thirty-eight percent of the differences were accounted for by different choices between "physical data modeling" and "physical database design".

Five stages were classified as *Preliminary*: Discovery, Data Collection, Scoping/Context Modeling, Inception, and Scoping of Target.

Twenty-seven stages were classified as *Post-Design Activities* (Table 8–4).

Stage	Number of Occurrences
Implementation / Build	21
Testing	3
Change Management	2
Iteration of Previous Stages	1

Table 8–4: Stages classified as post-design activities

Eight stages occurred only once, and were not judged to be Preliminary or Post-Design Activities. They were classified as *Other*.

8.7.2. What are the stages?

Table 8–5 summarizes the responses to Part 1 of the questionnaire (*What are the Stages?*) and shows:

- The 17 standardized stages, sorted in descending order of the number of respondents who nominated them

- The number of respondents who nominated each (standardized) stage name

- The percentage of respondents nominating that stage who classified it as data modeling[117] (the *Data Modeling Score*)

- The number[118] of respondents nominating that stage who allocated it to each of the job classification categories. In some instances, respondents nominated more than one job classification as being responsible for a stage; accordingly the total number of job classification citations for a stage may exceed the number of respondents.

---

[117] This classification data and the job role data is analyzed in more detail in Section 8.7.6, but only the most commonly-cited stages are covered there. Table 8–5 includes all of the standard stages.

[118] Numbers (counts) were used rather than percentages as many of the numbers were small; numbers better communicated the overall picture.

Standard Stage Name	Nominated by (number of respondents)	Data Modeling score	Who is Responsible?					
			Data Modeler	DBA	EM	Analyst	User	Other
Business Requirements	46	44%	21	3	0	30	18	0
Logical Data Modeling	41	100%	38	4	2	7	3	0
Physical Data Modeling	33	70%	25	22	0	1	0	1
Conceptual Data Modeling	32	84%	28	2	2	6	5	0
Post-Design Activities	27	22%	10	16	0	4	3	0
Physical Database Design	22	41%	7	18	0	2	0	1
Data Modeling	9	100%	8	2	0	1	1	0
Other	8	63%	6	0	0	4	3	0
Preliminary	5	60%	2	1	1	2	1	0
Architecture Activities	4	75%	2	0	2	1	0	0
Process Analysis	3	0%	0	0	0	2	1	0
Logical & Physical Data Modeling	3	100%	3	0	0	0	0	0
Validation	3	100%	3	2	0	0	2	0
Analysis	2	50%	1	0	0	1	0	0
Design	2	50%	1	1	0	0	0	0
First Cut Physical	2	100%	2	1	0	0	0	0
Technical Requirements	1	0%	0	0	0	1	0	0

Table 8–5: Summary of nominated stages after standardization of names

All but one respondent nominated at least one (standard) stage that included the words *data modeling*. Every respondent classified at least one stage as data modeling.

A review of the composition and sequence of stages resulted in the Physical Data Modeling and Physical Database Design stages being recognized as synonymous in terms of their place in the database design sequence and the activities that they contain. There was, however, a significant difference in classification and primary responsibility, with the stage more likely to be identified as data modeling (phi=0.29, p=0.03) and the responsibility of data modelers (phi=0.44, p=0.001) if it was called *Physical Data Modeling*. The two names are therefore shown separately in the analysis of classification and responsibility, but are combined in the analysis of sequence and patterns.

In terms of the specific questions that this research component addresses:

1. Forty-four respondents (80%[119]) nominated at least one Business Requirements Analysis stage (Question 1). This was seen as (solely or jointly) the responsibility of the data modeler in 45% of cases (compared with 65% for Analysts and 39% for Users).

2. No respondent nominated a view integration stage (Question 4).

3. No respondent nominated an external schema specification stage (Question 5).

---

[119] Two respondents nominated two separate stages that were classified as Business Requirements

8.7.3. Sequence of stages and activities

Table 8–6 shows the seventeen stages sorted by mean stage number, providing an overall picture of their sequence.

Mean Stage No.	Standard Stage Name	No. of times cited	DM Score
1.00	Preliminary	5	60%
1.15	Business Requirements	46	44%
1.33	Process Analysis	3	0%
1.91	Conceptual Data Modeling	32	84%
2.00	Architecture Activities	4	75%
2.00	Analysis	2	50%
2.00	Technical Requirements	1	0%
2.78	Data Modeling	9	100%
2.80	Logical Data Modeling	41	100%
3.00	Design	2	50%
3.13	Other	8	63%
3.33	Logical & Physical Data Modeling	3	100%
3.50	First Cut Physical	2	100%
3.91	Physical Data Modeling	33	70%
4.00	Validation	3	100%
4.09	Physical Database Design	22	41%
4.52	Post-Design Activities	27	22%

Table 8–6: Stages sorted by mean stage number

Table 8–7 shows the *activities* sorted by the mean of the stage numbers to which they were allocated, providing an overall picture of their sequence. The sequence numbers allocated here are used in the presentation of results later in this chapter. For graphic presentations, the sequence provides the horizontal axis. The two activities which were in the questionnaire primarily to explore responsibility for the database specification following its completion rather than as part of the design process *per se* have not been included and are excluded from the analysis of sequence, patterns and stage composition (they are included in the analysis of responsibility in Section 8.7.6). Mean stage numbers were 3.14 for *Changing the database to meet new business requirements* and 3.78 for *Advising programmers on understanding the database.*

Seq. No.	Activity Name	Mean Stage No.
1	Identifying business (data) requirements	1.17
2	Negotiating compromises with the business stakeholders	2.18
3	Identifying entities and relationships	2.19
4	Documenting rules about data which cannot be represented in the data model	2.32
5	Ensuring that business change can be accommodated	2.35
6	Ensuring (user) data requirements are met	2.37
7	Identifying attributes	2.57
8	Specifying attribute domains	2.76
9	Normalization	2.80
10	Integrating different views of the data	2.85
11	Specifying primary keys	2.89
12	Translating an E-R (or other conceptual) model into a relational model	2.96
13	Disaggregating attributes into atomic data	2.98
14	Including foreign keys	3.00
15	Resolving many-to-many relationships	3.02
16	Removing derivable data	3.09
17	Specifying the data type for each column	3.27
18	Specifying column names	3.40
19	Specifying how subtype hierarchies will be implemented	3.53
20	Specifying views	3.84
21	De-normalization for performance	3.85
22	Specifying data distribution	3.97
23	Adding derivable data to improve performance	4.00
24	Specifying database indexes	4.00
25	Specifying physical placement of data on storage media	4.08
26	Tuning the database for performance	4.26

Table 8–7: Activities sorted by mean stage number.

The sequence of activities can be divided into four groups according to which schema they address[120], with only the placement of Activity no. 3 *Identifying entities and relationships* not fitting the pattern of sequential development of three schemas from business requirements (Table 8–8).

Business interaction, pre modeling	Activities 1-6 excluding 3
Conceptual schema definition	Activities 7-19 plus 3
External schema definition	Activity 20
Performance design (including all internal schema decisions)	Activities 21-26

Table 8–8: Activity sequence mapped against a three-schema development model.

Advising programmers on understanding the database immediately follows the conceptual schema definition activities, as would seem reasonable. *Changing the database to meet new requirements* does not appear near the end of the sequence, but in the middle, suggesting that changes in requirements are perceived as occurring during the process rather than only following implementation.

8.7.4. Identification of patterns

Table 8–6 in the preceding section embodies a sequence of the most commonly used stage names which is included in most of the responses:

1. Business Requirements Analysis

2. Conceptual Data Modeling

3. Logical Data Modeling

4. Physical Data Modeling (incorporating Physical Database Design)

5. Post-design Activities

These stage names account for 201 (83%) of the total of 243 stages cited.

No response presented these stages in a different sequence: for example, whenever Conceptual Data Modeling and Logical Data Modeling were both nominated as stages, Conceptual Data Modeling preceded Logical Data Modeling. In some

---

[120] Strictly, the performance design phase also includes changes to the conceptual schema, but these are generally regarded as compromises rather than part of the main stream of conceptual schma development.

cases one or more of these stages was omitted, and in some cases two stages were explicitly combined (e.g. Conceptual and Logical Data Modeling).

A stage named simply Data Modeling was included on nine occasions and appeared in the same place in the above sequence as Logical Data Modeling. In each of these cases, no other stage that included the words *data modeling* was nominated[121]. This is consistent with the reasonably obvious interpretation that *Data Modeling* is an aggregate term embracing the three more-specific terms.

Forty-one (75%) of the responses fitted this overall pattern (including the variations described above and in the next paragraph). A further nine (16%) of the responses fitted the pattern except for the omission of *Business Requirements*. Thus these two broad patterns accounted for 91% of the responses.

Table 8–9 shows the most common variants of the broad patterns (further references to *patterns* are to these seven or a subset of them). Validation, Architecture Activities, and Process Analysis stages were ignored as being peripheral or supplementary. First Cut Physical immediately preceded Physical Database Design in the two cases in which it was used, and was not treated as giving rise to a separate pattern.

---

[121] The Physical Data Modeling stage that appears for Pattern 5 in Table 8–9 was in all cases named Physical Database Design. As noted earlier, stages with this name were absorbed into Physical Data Modeling.

Pattern No.	LA Count	London Count	Total Count	Stage 1	Stage 2	Stage 3	Stage 4
1	10	9	19	Business Requirements	Conceptual DM	Logical DM	Physical DM
2	7	1	8	Conceptual DM	Logical DM	Physical DM	
3	4	2	6	Business Requirements	Data Modeling	Physical DM	
4	2	1	3	Business Requirements	Conceptual DM	Logical/ Physical	
5	1	0	1	Business Requirements	Conceptual/ Logical DM	Physical DM	
6	4	8	12	Business Requirements	Logical DM	Physical DM	
7	0	1	1	Conceptual/ Logical DM	Physical DM		
Other	2	3	5				
TOTAL	30	25	55				

Table 8–9: Database design process – core patterns

The table illustrates two points of relevance to the questions in Section 8.3 and to our general understanding of practitioner approaches to database design:

1. As previously noted, the absence of view identification, view integration, and view definition / reproduction from any of these high-level patterns places them in opposition to a widely-promulgated academic framework (Question 4 and Question 5)

2. Five of the seven patterns (accounting for 58% of responses) recognized conceptual, logical, and physical data modeling stages (including stages which explicitly combined two of these). Subject to confirming the content of these stages[122], this terminology aligns with the sequence of business description, conceptual modeling, mapping to conceptual schema (logical), and internal schema design / performance design

---

[122] We note now that the perceived division between conceptual and logical data modeling does *not* align with that in the literature – discussed in Section 8.7.5 .

(physical) commonly described in the literature. The remaining two patterns, accounting for 33% of responses, did not recognize separate conceptual and logical data modeling stages (even implicitly as in Pattern 5), though they identified physical data modeling as a distinct stage (Question 2).

8.7.5. What activities are in each stage?

Of the 1220 allocations of an activity to a stage[123], 950 (78%) were to one of the five stages (Business requirements, Conceptual Data Modeling, Logical Data Modeling, Physical Data Modeling, Post-Design Activities) that formed the common (core) stage model described in Section 8.7.4 above. As the goal was to build a representative picture rather than describe the full range of variants, we look only at these allocations. Figure 8-3 summarizes the allocations of activities to these five standard stages.

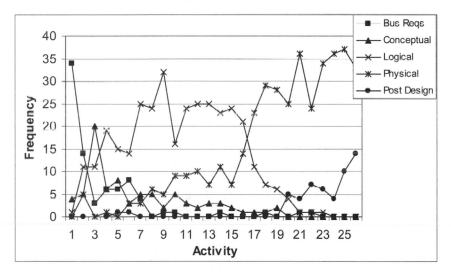

Figure 8-3: Allocation of activities to five core standard stages

There are some broad trends, apparent from the graph. The first two activities, *Identifying business (data) requirements* and *Negotiating compromises with the business stakeholders* are allocated predominantly to the Business Requirements

---

[123] Strictly, the performance design phase also includes changes to the conceptual schema, but these are generally regarded as compromises rather than part of the main stream of development.

stage. The third activity, *Identifying entities and relationships,* is the only activity allocated predominantly to the Conceptual Data Modeling stage.

From that point, activities are predominantly allocated to Logical Data Modeling until there is a distinct cross-over to Physical Data Modeling from *Resolving many-to-many relationships* to *Removing derivable data* and *Specifying the data type for each column.* The Physical Data Modeling stage is the dominant location for all of the later activities with most of the remaining assignments being to Logical Data Modeling (earlier stages) and Post-Design Activities (later stages).

Beyond the consequences of Pattern 2 not including a Business Requirements Analysis stage, and Pattern 6 not including a Conceptual Data Modeling stage (essentially a take-up by adjacent stages of activities generally allocated to these stages), the results for the individual patterns are similar to those for the consolidated responses.

Based on these allocations of sample activities, we can infer some principles (generalizations based on dominant patterns) for allocation of activities to the stages:

Business Requirements Analysis is preliminary to the identification / specification of data model components. Entity, relationship, and attribute definition are clearly seen as being outside this phase (*Question 1*).

Conceptual Data Modeling covers only the identification of entities and relationships. In particular, it excludes identification of attributes. The five cases in which *Identifying attributes* was assigned to this stage were reviewed: the only common demographic factor was that all cited "books" as a source of learning ("books" was cited by 47% of participants in this research component).

Logical Data Modeling is a broad phase embracing many (but not all) of the activities related to conceptual schema specification, as well as several that are included in definitions of conceptual modeling in the literature. Performance-driven decisions are excluded, as are *Specifying the data type for each column, Specifying column names* and *Specifying how subtype hierarchies will be implemented.* These activities are most commonly allocated to Physical Data Modeling.

Physical Data Modeling covers some pre-performance conceptual schema decisions, all internal schema decisions, the specification of the external schema, and all performance-driven changes to the conceptual schema.

The principles for assignment of activities to Business Requirements Analysis are consistent with the framework synthesized from the literature and presented in Chapter 3[124]. *The characterizations of Conceptual, Logical and Physical Data Modeling are not.* Conceptual Data Modeling, as characterized by most respondents, does not deliver a DBMS-independent model for transformation to a DBMS-specific schema (*Question 2*), as it does not include *inter alia* the activities *Identifying attributes, Ensuring (user) data requirements are met,* or *Integrating different views of the data.* Most of the pre-performance conceptual schema definition takes place in the Logical Data Modeling stage. Physical Modeling (or Physical Database Design) covers a broader range of activities than specified in the literature, impinging on the conceptual schema definition even prior to performance compromises.

8.7.6. Is it data modeling? Who is responsible?

Having reviewed the stages and activities in the database design process, we now ask: which of these stages and activities are considered to be *data modeling*? To supplement the answer, we also review the responsibility for the stages: What is the data modeler responsible for? If not the data modeler, who *is* responsible? We focus on the six most commonly nominated stages (treating Physical Data Modeling and Physical Database Design, which contain similar activities, but were allocated different data modeling scores and responsibilities, as distinct stages). Recall that data modeling scores indicated the percentage of respondents who classified a particular stage as data modeling.

Responsibility for stages

The data modeling scores and perceived responsibilities for each stage are summarized below (Figure 8-4) for the full set of responses. The sequence reflects that established in Section 8.5.4. As noted in Section 8.7.4, these stages accounted for 83% of the total number of stages nominated, and no other stage accounted for more than 4% of nominations. We ignore the "Enterprise Modeler", "Data Manager" and "Other" job classifications which accounted for only 3.7% of responses to the "Who is responsible?" question.

---

[124] As noted in the 3.3, some alternative descriptions of the Requirements stage include the development of the conceptual model, a view generally not reflected in the responses.

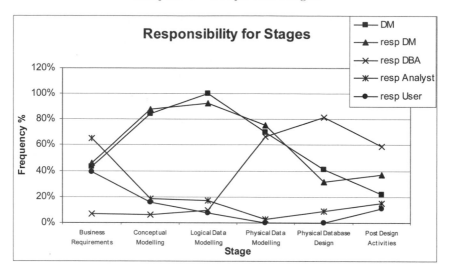

Figure 8-4: Data modeling scores and responsibilities for the most common stages

The graph shows that:

- As noted earlier, there are only four job classifications perceived as having significant responsibility for stages. User and analyst responsibilities relate largely to the earlier stages, the DBA role dominates physical database design and post-design activities, and the data modeler plays a role throughout, dominating the responsibility for the conceptual, logical, and physical data modeling stages.

- The allocation of responsibility to data modelers closely tracks the data modeling score. This can be interpreted fairly simply as data modelers being responsible for data modeling, and in fact categorization of a stage as data modeling and allocation to data modelers were strongly correlated (phi=0.66, $p<0.0005$). Eight percent of tasks nominated as data modeling were allocated (solely or jointly) to a role other than data modeler, and 22% of tasks not nominated as data modeling were seen as the (sole or joint) responsibility of data modelers. This second figure may reflect the fact that the participants were largely data modelers who might see themselves as having broader responsibilities.

The broad allocation of responsibilities was maintained across the different patterns.

shows the data modeling scores and allocations of responsibility for each of the activities. These figures are derived from the stages to which the activities were

172

allocated. The schemas primarily impacted by each sequence of activities are delineated by the vertical lines.

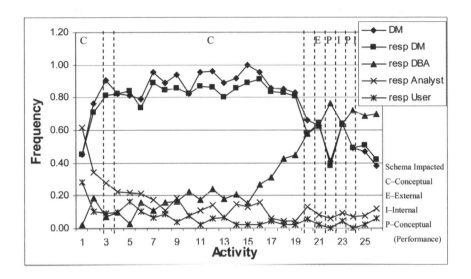

Figure 8-5: Data Modeling scores and responsibilities for activities

Figure 8-5 shows:

1. Analysts, data modelers, and users (in that order) are perceived as having responsibility for the first activity *Identifying business (data) requirements*.

2. After *Identifying business (data) requirements*, the data modeler dominates responsibility for the next set of activities.

3. The data modeler's responsibility falls off progressively as the role of the DBA increases, eventually dominating the final activities. Nevertheless, the (reported) allocation of responsibility to data modelers never falls below 42%. The data modeling score for the activities closely tracks the data modeler responsibility[125].

4. The graph highlights considerable variation in responses in specifying the boundaries of data modeling. At the extremes, 45% of respondents assigned the first activity *Identifying business (data) requirements* to a

---

[125] This is a consequence of the data modeling classification tracking the data modeler responsibility at the stage level.

stage which they classified as data modeling, and 38% assigned the final activity *Tuning the database for performance* to a stage which they classified as data modeling. *Resolving many-to-many relationships* was assigned by 100% of respondents to a stage classified as data modeling.

5. All of the numbered activities from *Identifying entities and relationships* through to (in sequence) *Specifying how subtypes hierarchies will be implemented* have a data modeling score of over 80% with the minor exception of *Ensuring (user) data requirements are met* (79%). There are distinct 'shoulders' in the curve as the data modeling score drops on each side of these activities.

6. In terms of the three-schema architecture, the activities with a data modeling score of 79% or more are all related to the specification of the conceptual schema. The remaining three activities that affect (or may affect) the conceptual schema have lower scores and are more likely than the others be seen as the responsibility of the DBA. These three activities are the performance-driven "compromises" viz *Denormalization for performance*, *Adding derivable data to improve performance,* and (potentially, since the conceptual schema may be affected) *Tuning the database for performance*. All three appear later in the sequence.

7. The activity *Advising programmers on understanding the database* (which was excluded from the detailed analysis) appeared immediately after the pre-performance conceptual schema activities and was seen by 73% as being a (sole or joint) responsibility of the data modeler and 56% as being a DBA responsibility. The scores suggest that the data modeler's ongoing ownership of the conceptual schema – perhaps as performance-related changes are made by the DBA – is less clear than responsibility for its initial development. Similarly, *Changing the database to meet new business requirements* is seen by only 73% as a (sole or joint) responsibility of the data modeler.

On this basis of the above, data modeling (or at least the core of data modeling: viz activities with a data modeling score of over 80%) can be characterized as:

the specification of the initial conceptual schema, to meet agreed business requirements, prior to any performance tuning

This definition, based on the "80% rule" and a distinct drop in data modeling scores at the end of conceptual schema definition activities, holds with only minor perturbations for all of the standard demographic groups[126] (Section 7.4.3). There was, however, a difference between the LA and London groups. The London group showed a sharper drop in data modeling score for internal schema design activities in particular. The overall lower scores would require setting the threshold for "data modeling" at 75% rather than 80% to maintain the same definition.

The definition also needs to be qualified by noting that data modeling was perceived by a significant number of respondents as including most or all of the activities in database design. The lowest data modeling score for an activity was 38% (though the London group scored four activities below 20%). There is a much clearer consensus as to what is included in data modeling than what is not.

Applying this definition to the questions posed in Section 8.3:

1. Entity, relationship, and attribute definition is seen as being within data modeling (Question 3).

2. View integration is included within data modeling, following the activities which would be traditionally be classified as conceptual modeling, and indeed after normalization (Question 4).

3. External schema specification is located outside our (conservative) definition of data modeling and is seen equally as the responsibility of the data modeler and the DBA (Question 5).

4. Performance-related changes to the conceptual schema are located outside data modeling (Question 6).

It bears repeating as a caveat to the above that some respondents defined data modeling more broadly, and located both external schema specification and performance related changes to the schema within it.

---

[126] The novice groups were not tested due to the small numbers in the sample

8.8. DISCUSSION AND CONCLUSIONS

The preceding analysis provides us with a view of the database design process (or, as is evident, *processes*), and the place of data modeling within it, as perceived by data modeling practitioners. No comparable study has been reported in the literature. The consistency of responses obtained from practitioners in two countries in different settings (data management conference, commercially-run advanced data modeling course) adds weight to the findings. The results complement the review of theory in Chapter 3 in providing an understanding of the *environment* in which data modeling is performed, in particular, the assumptions that the database design process embodies about the nature of data modeling.

In this section, we draw on the results to return to the issues set out in Section 8.1: (a) specific questions relevant to the description / design question; (b) the definition of data modeling and (c) other areas in which respondents' views illuminated or differed from those in the literature. The chapter concludes with some observations on the questionnaire and research method.

8.8.1. Answering the questions

Section 8.3 posed six questions about the database design process. Where results were relevant to these questions, they have generally been highlighted. Here we draw them together to provide as complete as possible a response to each question. Again, the interpretation relies on the background analysis in Chapter 2, as noted in Section 8.3.

Question 1: Requirements stage (not including entity, relationship, attribute identification) included?

A Business Requirements Analysis stage was nominated by 84% of respondents, making it the most frequently nominated stage. The activity *Identification of entities and relationships* was allocated[127] to this stage by only 5% of respondents. Business Requirements Analysis was seen as the responsibility of the data modeler (solely or jointly) by 46% of respondents who nominated the stage; 65% saw the analyst as being responsible and 39% nominated the user.

---

[127] Multiple allocations not included

In the majority of cases, then, the data modeler appears to be working from a set of business requirements developed by someone else. These may be negotiable (the activity *Negotiating compromises with the business stakeholders* was perceived by 71% of respondents as a data modeler responsibility), but their existence conflicts with the idea that the data modeler directly describes reality.

Question 2: Separate stages for DBMS-independent (conceptual) modeling and DBMS-specific (logical) modeling?

The most surprising result of this component of the research was the propensity of respondents to group most conceptual schema specification activities into a single stage (typically named Logical Data Modeling) with only entity and relationship identification being treated as part of the Conceptual Data Modeling stage. This suggests a view of a conceptual model as a "sketch plan" rather than a rigorous and complete product amenable to mechanical translation into a conceptual schema.

Question 3. Location of entity / relationship / attribute identification.

Entity, relationship, and attribute definition were clearly seen as data modeling tasks, falling into the Conceptual Data Modeling and Logical Data Modeling stages. This is no real surprise, but some authors (e.g. Batra and Srinivasan 1992; Hawryszkiewycz 1997 p182) locate these tasks within a business requirements stage.

Question 4: Location of view integration.

Integrating different views of the data fell in the middle (it was the median activity in the sequence) of the activities classified as data modeling, supporting the view that it was an ongoing task rather than one that could be deferred until individual models had been constructed. No respondent nominated a separate stage for this activity, again suggesting that it was not a discrete task of the kind that is included in approaches based on view identification and integration.

Question 5: Responsibility for and location of external schema specification.

Specifying views followed all pre-performance conceptual schema specification activities, consistent with the idea, common in the practitioner and some teaching literature (McFadden, Hoffer et al. 1999; Connolly and Begg 2005), that views are primarily for support of database security, data independence and programming. The traditional approach that sees them implementing pre-defined user perspectives (Yao, Navathe et al. 1978; Navathe and Gadgil 1982; Storey and

Goldstein 1988; Mannino 2001), and would accord this activity the status of a stage in its own right, was not supported.

Question 6: Location of performance-oriented decisions (conceptual schema compromises).

The three activities involving changes (or in the case of *Tuning the database for performance*, potential changes) to the conceptual schema for performance reasons were clearly defined as part of Physical Data Modeling / Physical Database Design, and outside the (conservative) definition of data modeling. Responsibility was allocated by the (data modeler dominated) participants equally to data modelers and DBAs.

Table 8–1 (from Section 8.3) is reproduced below as Table 8–10, highlighting the responses supported by the results.

Question	Response	Implications of Response
1. Requirements stage (not including entity, relationship, attribute identification) included?	Yes	Supports design
	No	Supports either
2. Separate stages for DBMS-independent (conceptual) modeling and DBMS-specific (logical) modeling	Yes	Supports either
	No	Supports design
3. Location of entity / relationship / attribute identification	Outside data modeling	Supports description
	Within data modeling	Supports either
4. Location of view integration	Not required	Supports description
	After data modeling	Supports description
	Within data modeling	Supports design
5. Responsibility for and location of external schema specification	Modeler, bus analyst (before conc. schema definition)	Supports description
	DBA (after conc. schema definition)	Supports either
6. Location of performance-oriented decisions (conceptual schema compromises)	Within data modeling	Supports design
	Outside data modeling	Supports either

Table 8–10: Responses to questions about the database design process

178

For all but Question 6, the results support the design characterization or fail to support the description characterization. Question 6 relates to scope and the possibility of data modeling embracing an already-recognized design task rather than to the characterization of data modeling as more generally understood.

8.8.2. Definition of data modeling

The results support a definition of data modeling as embracing conceptual schema specification tasks prior to performance compromises. The definition is conservative, in that many respondents would include a wider range of activities, and that possibility is relevant to the analysis of practitioner perceptions discussed in the following two chapters.

What is clear is that the sample group as a whole, and the demographic subsets, regarded all activities involved in producing a pre-performance conceptual schema from business requirements as data modeling. This is an important result: it is possible that data modeling could have been seen as stopping short of producing a schema or indeed of dealing with the target DBMS architecture as in academic definitions of *conceptual data modeling* (Section 3.4). If we are to discuss and characterize data modeling as perceived by practitioners, these activities are clearly within our scope.

It is worth repeating that the sample was dominated by specialist data modelers (60% of job titles), who might overstate the scope of their authority. There is evidence that DBAs consider data modelers to be responsible, both ideally and in practice, for a smaller range of activities than do data modelers themselves (Simsion 1996). With only three of the respondents in the present sample identifying themselves as DBAs, it was not possible to test this finding – although the comparison of data modelers with other primary occupations did not provide any evidence of a difference.

8.8.3. Comparison with frameworks in the literature

At the stage level, respondents' frameworks reflected either the (requirements)-conceptual-logical-physical frameworks common in the academic and teaching literature, or the (requirements)-logical-physical framework that appears in some practitioner guides and tools. The view definition-integration-reconstruction approach that is also common in the academic literature was completely absent.

The inclusion of a data modeling stage by all participants is in contrast to reports (MacDonell 1994; Hitchman 1995; Maier 1996) that many organizations claim not to do data modeling at all, but hardly surprising given that participants were attending data modeling seminars.

At the activity level, it became clear that the Conceptual Modeling stage nominated by practitioners did not match the academic concept of conceptual modeling (Section 3.4), nor indeed that described in at least some practitioner-oriented texts (e.g. Simsion and Witt 2005). It seems that Conceptual Modeling is seen as a preliminary high-level stage – a "sketch plan[128]" perhaps – rather than as delivering a detailed model that might, even in theory, be mechanically transformed into a complete conceptual schema. It fell well short of specifying a fully normalized set of entities as specified by some authors (e.g. Cerpa 1995). The consolidation of tasks into the logical data modeling phase is in keeping with some practitioner-oriented definitions (e.g. Henderson 2002), with the approach outlined by Avison and Fitzgerald (2003 p187), and with methods and tools (Barker 1990; DeAngelis 2000) which include only a single stage prior to physical data modeling / physical database design. Avison and Cuthbertson (2002 p9) specify an early *coarse grained* model.

Nor did the boundary between Logical Data Modeling and Physical Data Modeling correspond to the three-schema architecture or definitions in the literature, even though the underlying sequence of activities would have supported drawing a clean boundary between pre-performance and performance-related decisions.

8.8.4. Observations on the survey instrument and method

The questionnaire was developed specifically for the present study, in the absence of a suitable existing instrument. Extensive piloting was not possible due to the well-established difficulties of accessing practitioners, and the responses raised some issues which would be worth taking into account if the instrument were to be developed further.

---

[128] The use of sketch plans is a common feature of design disciplines (Goldschmidt 1991).

1. The original design assumed that respondents would provide only one job role in response to the "who is responsible" question (the instructions asked them to nominate who is primarily responsible). Many answered with multiple roles; it was not difficult to adapt the analysis method to deal with these responses, and they provided potentially useful detail. A revised questionnaire could make this option explicit.

2. The original design assumed that respondents would allocate activities to a single stage. A significant number of respondents allocated at least some activities to multiple stages. The problem may have been exacerbated by the inclusion of the two "additional" activities, which are not associated with a single stage in the literature, in particular *Changing the database to meet new business requirements*, which might reasonably be seen to require a re-iteration of all stages. Indeed, this was the activity most frequently allocated to multiple stages. The alternatives are to explicitly allow for allocation to multiple stages (and to plan the analysis accordingly) or to clarify that only one stage (perhaps "the most usual stage" or "the stage in which the largest part of this activity is performed") is nominated. The additional questions should be removed or moved to a separate part of the questionnaire.

3. The dominance of Logical Data Modeling and Physical Data Modeling in the allocation of activities suggests the inclusion of further activities which might be allocated to Conceptual Data Modeling or Business Requirements Analysis, in order to provide more information on the boundaries of those stages.

4. The questionnaire could usefully test for the use of an enterprise model, architecture or standards, as these could be expected to constrain modeling options. Additional activities *Reference to standards* and *Reference to enterprise model / architecture* would address this.

Chapter 8 – Scope and stages

CHAPTER 9
HOW PRACTITIONERS DESCRIBE DATA MODELING

9.1. INTRODUCTION AND OBJECTIVES

In the previous chapter, we looked at data modeling practitioners' perceptions of the overall database design process, and the place of data modeling within it. On that basis, we established a working definition of data modeling as *the specification of the initial conceptual schema, to meet agreed business requirements, prior to any performance tuning,* while noting that some practitioners' definitions would embrace a broader range of activities. With that definition as a reference point, we now look at how practitioners characterize data modeling in terms of the description / design dichotomy that is the focus of this research.

This chapter describes the second of the three research components that examined practitioners' perceptions of data modeling. It had three goals:

1. To establish whether the description / design characterization was included in practitioners' definitions of data modeling. In Section 2.3, we noted that published definitions of data modeling frequently embodied positions on the description / design question. Inclusion in definitions suggests that the characterization is regarded (consciously or otherwise) as important.

2. To establish the declared position (if any) of data modelers on the description / design question.

3. To explore correlations between data modelers' views on the characterization and their experience, job classifications and method of learning about data modeling.

The focus is on declared, *espoused* positions, rather than deeper *theory-in-use* (Argyris and Schön 1974 pp6-7)[129]. As such, this component addresses practitioner beliefs and contributes to the *Culture and Environment* dimension of

---

[129] Theory-in-use is addressed in the third component of this research phase (Chapter 7).

the 5Ps framework introduced in Section 1.4.3 and, specifically, to the *Importance* and *Espoused Beliefs* sub-questions (Section 7.2):

Is the description / design question considered important by data modeling practitioners? and

What are the (espoused) beliefs of data modeling practitioners on the description / design question?

9.2. RESEARCH DESIGN

The research design was built around two survey questions:

1. An open question:

    What is data modeling?

2. A closed (forced choice) question:

    Which better describes data modeling?

    (a) Describing the data requirements of an organization or part of an organization

    or

    (b) Designing data structures to meet the requirements of an organization or part of an organization.

Open and closed questions (or *open-ended* and *closed-ended* questions) are staples of survey research and have a range of well-known advantages and disadvantages (Neuman 1999 pp260-262). In this case, the Open Question was used to discover whether practitioners had a position on the description / design question without presenting them with pre-articulated options, and to expose positions that might not be captured by the description / design dichotomy. The Closed Question was intended to elicit responses that directly addressed the description / design question and could be easily compared.

9.3. METHOD

Aspects of method common to several components of the research, including survey piloting, administration, ethical issues, coding of demographics and use of statistics are covered in Chapter 3. Here we address aspects of administration particular to this component, coding of responses, and the approach to analysis.

9.3.1. Survey administration

Administration of the survey followed the general procedure described in Section 7.4, with the following additions.

1. The respondents had completed a common data modeling task prior to answering the questions. The task involved developing a data model to meet a given set of requirements (described in Chapter 8). The instructions for that task were framed in a way that avoided characterizing it as description or design.

2. The two questions were added to the questionnaire related to the data modeling task ((1) above). They were the first questions on the questionnaire, and were administered before any later questions. The Closed Question itself was not printed. It was shown on a presentation slide after the time for completion of the Open Question had expired to avoid influencing the response to the Open Question. Space was provided for respondents to comment on their answer to the Closed Question.

3. Respondents were told, prior to answering the questions: "we are referring to data modeling to support the development of a relational database; not enterprise data modeling or reverse-engineering".

4. Based on piloting[130], three minutes was allowed for completion of the Open Question and one minute for the Closed Question. Questionnaires were collected during a coffee break following completion of the remainder of the questionnaire (containing questions about the earlier data modeling task).

---

[130] These times were well in excess of times used by pilot subjects (under 1 minute for the Open Question, 20 seconds for the Closed Question) to encourage reflection and careful responses.

5. After collection of the questionnaires, the author asked for a "show of hands" on responses to the Closed Question, and encouraged a plenary discussion of approximately ten minutes.

9.3.2. Review and coding of demographics

Questionnaires that included a response to only one of the questions were included in the analysis for that question. Responses to the Closed Question that nominated both options were included in the analysis (and a separate code created for them).

Demographic information was coded according to the procedure and coding schemes described in Section 7.4.

9.3.3. Coding of responses to open and closed questions

To permit quantitative analysis of the Open Question, responses were coded using a modified Likert scale (values 0 and 3 were consolidated in analysis) as per Table 9–1.

Code	Code Description
0	Does not incorporate a position on the Description vs. Design characterization
1	Strongly supports Description characterization
2	Somewhat supports Description characterization
3	Supports both characterizations (perhaps depending on context)
4	Somewhat supports Design characterization
5	Strongly supports Design characterization

Table 9–1: Coding of Open Question

The reference definitions for the two characterizations were the alternative answers to the Closed Question. The author and an assistant with previous experience in data modeling research independently coded all responses. Disagreements were resolved by discussion between the two coders. All responses were then grouped by code value, reviewed again, and re-coded where agreed by the two coders.

The above codes were used only in the initial presentation (frequency distribution) of results. Further analysis focused on responses that supported one or other characterization: codes 1 and 2 were consolidated, as were 4 and 5.

Responses to the Closed Question were coded as per Table 9–2.

Response	Code
Option a	1
Option b	2
Both options selected	3

Table 9–2: Coding of responses to Closed Question

9.3.4. Analysis

Responses to the Open Question and the Closed Question were assessed for correlation.

The responses to the Open Question and comments attached to responses to the Closed Question were reviewed and coded by the author and an assistant independently to identify common themes, using open coding (Strauss 1987). Results were checked for correlation with responses to the Open Question and Closed Question.

Responses to the Open Question and Closed Question were cross-tabulated against the demographic categories, and correlations noted.

9.4. SAMPLE

The survey sample was the attendees at a one-day advanced data modeling seminar conducted by the author at the Data Management Association International (DAMA-I) Annual Conference in San Antonio, Texas, USA in May, 2002. The conference and seminar attracted a predominantly practitioner audience. Response rates are summarized in Table 9–3.

Number of workshop attendees	170
Both questions and demographics answered	93
Neither question answered	4
Only Open Question answered	1
Only Closed Question answered	4
Demographics not answered (both Open Question and Closed Question answered)	10
Total Questionnaires Returned	112
Response Rate (all questionnaires)	66%
Response Rate (complete questionnaires)	55%

Table 9–3: Response rates for Espoused Positions survey

9.5. RESULTS

9.5.1. Coding and descriptive statistics

Responses to the Open Question were coded and reconciled as described in Section 9.3.3. Inter-coder reliability, as measured by Cronbach's alpha coefficient, was 0.82[131] (0.7 is considered acceptable). The final joint review of codes resulted in a further seven (minor) adjustments.

Figure 9-4 shows representative responses from each category, with emphasis on the most common response, viz "1 – Strongly supports the description characterization".

---

[131] To obtain a continuous scale codes of 0 (no position) and 3 (both positions) were both treated as 3 (neutral-favoring neither description nor design).

Response ID	Response	Coded as
23	The representation of data structure in commonly understood notations / diagrams.	0
68	Description of the things of interest to an enterprise and the relationships of interest between those things.	1
77	The unambiguous expression of business rules in pictorial form.	1
95	It is the process of documenting the data centric business rules of an organization / system.	1
105	Data modeling is a graphical way of representing business requirements.	1
146	Describing in consistent repeatable methods the data requirements of an enterprise, division, project, etc.	1
165	The discipline of representing a business or business area in terms of Entities – the things the business needs to know about; Relationships between entities; Attributes accurately and completely.	1
93	Capturing the structure of the business data in a way that communicates relationships and entities to the business and the developers. If the data is understood correctly the design can be used for many different purposes within the business. REUSE!	2
209	Depiction of relationships between data elements from the business perspective.	2
81	Understanding bus. requirements; providing a design that can be used to implement solutions that support the Bus Rqmts.	3
114	A diagrammatical [sic] representation of where and how data pertaining to a business system or resolution of a business problem is kept. Can be both logical explaining business or physical where it is kept within the database.	3
109	Determining how real life entities (people, places, events etc) can be represented in a physical database to meet business or organizational objectives.	4
67	Creating homes for data to reside…	5
147	Organizing information in a set of buckets with relationships that meets [sic] the information needs now and hopefully some time into the future.	5

Table 9–4: Representative responses to the Open Question

The distribution of coded responses to the Open Question is shown in Figure 9-1. Responses to the Closed Question are shown in Figure 9-2.

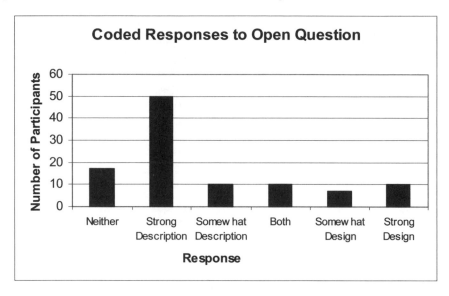

Figure 9-1: Coded responses to open question

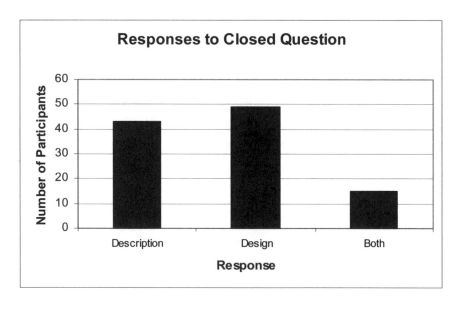

Figure 9-2: Responses to closed question

9.5.2. Comparison of open question and closed question responses

Figure 9-3 compares responses to the Open Question and Closed question: the vertical axis shows the break up of responses to the Closed Question for the participants who gave each of the possible (coded) responses to the Open Question.

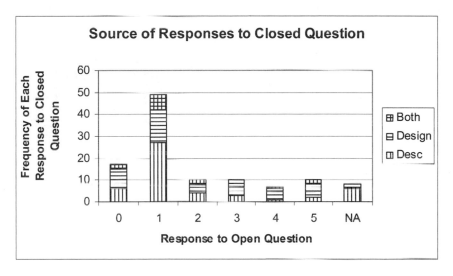

Figure 9-3: Source of responses to closed question

Figure 9-3 shows that participants whose responses to the Open Question supported the design option (codes 4 and 5) largely maintained that view in answering the Closed Question, but that a significant number of participants whose Open Question answers supported the description option provided "design" answers to the Closed Question. This was reflected in a moderate correlation (Phi=0.34, p=0.007) between the responses to the Open Question and Closed Question[132].

---

[132] In calculating the correlation, "neither" and "both" responses were excluded, and remaining responses to the open question were consolidated into two categories (as per Section 9.3.3)

9.5.3. Themes

Open coding of the responses to the Open Question by the author and subsequent revision to incorporate additional concepts identified during post-coding yielded 23 themes. Post-coding was performed independently by the author and an assistant. The mean value of inter-rater reliability measured using the KR20 coefficient for each theme was 0.85. Discrepancies were resolved by discussion. Table 9–5 lists the eleven themes that were identified in ten (9.6%) or more responses.

Theme	No. of responses (from 104 valid)
Pictorial / graphic representation	37
Meeting requirements	36
Business rules	23
Entities, attributes and relationships	20
Database, database design	19
Definition	17
Understanding	16
Documentation, metadata	14
Communication	11
Analysis (specific word)	11
Description (specific word)	10

Table 9–5: Common themes in responses to the Open Question

Figure 9-4 shows the frequency with which each theme was identified, segmenting each bar according to the respondents' answers to the Closed Question (the horizontal axis sequence reflects the percentage who chose "design"; the only significant correlation was between the "description" theme and the "description" response to the question: phi=0.21, p=0.05).

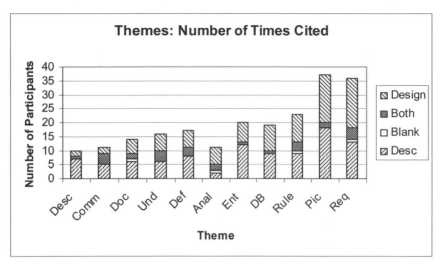

Bars are segmented according to response to the Closed Question.

Figure 9-4: Themes: Number of times cited

In the context of the description / design question, it is interesting to note that the word *design* (as a verb) was used in only six responses.

Thirty-four of the 107 valid responses to the Closed Question used the *Comment* space on the questionnaire to reinforce, qualify, or expand on their response. Table 9–6 summarizes these short additions (none were longer than a single sentence).

Response to Closed Question	Summary / Purpose of Comment	Number of occurrences
Description	Could be either / both	6
	Reinforcing the response	4
	Neither option is complete	2
Design	Reinforcing the response	7
	Description is also required	5
	But often we do description	2
Both	Reinforcing the response	4
	Logical modeling is description, physical modeling is design	3

Table 9–6: Summary of comments supporting responses to Closed Question

9.5.4. Correlation with demographics

Table 9–7 shows the two significant correlations between the responses to the Open Question (description / design) and the demographic groupings. Correlation with the design characterization is shown as positive.

Demographic Factor	phi	p
Method of learning: Books (38 valid responses)	-0.275	.016
Method of Learning: Tertiary Education (7 valid responses)	0.267	.019

Table 9–7: Significant correlations between Open Question characterizations and demographics

There was only one significant (weak) correlation between demographic groups (including the individual *methods of learning*) and responses to the Closed Question: members of the group with less than 6 years of experience were more likely (phi= 0.238, p=0.04) to choose the *description* answer.

9.5.5. Feedback from participants

Two key points emerged from the short discussion that followed collection of the questionnaires.

1. The "show of hands" indicating responses to the Closed Question caused some surprise: discussion confirmed that many participants had expected that their own response would have been clearly dominant.

2. A second "show of hands" indicated a close-to-unanimous view that the distinction between the two Closed Question options was real and important.

9.6. DISCUSSION

9.6.1. Positions on the description / design question

This component of the research was intended to explore the importance of the description / design characterization in the definition of data modeling, and practitioners' positions on the issue.

The results indicated that the characterization was important. Most responses to the Open Question included a characterization of data modeling as description or design (or both). Only 17% of responses did not embody a position. The discussion that followed the completion of the questionnaires reinforced the importance of the characterization.

The inclusion of a position in a definition did not necessarily reflect a strong commitment to that position. Whilst responses to the Open Question strongly favored description (78% of responses with a position), responses to the Closed Question were more evenly balanced: 47% of those who provided a response selected the description option. Forty-three percent of those who selected the design option for the Closed Question had selected the description option for the Open Question. We may speculate that responses to the Open Question reflected received definitions, whereas the Closed Question may have prompted some reflection. Regardless, it seems that the positions embodied in definitions are not so strongly held as to be immune to challenge.

With minor exceptions, there was no correlation observed between responses to the questions and demographics or themes. An experienced practitioner was as likely to classify data modeling as description as an inexperienced one; a data modeler as likely to do so as a practitioner from another occupation.

9.6.2. Themes

The analysis of themes in the open question provides some insights as to how practitioners in the sample perceived data modeling: Of the eleven most common themes, seven would seem to favor the description paradigm (viz Business Rules, Definition, Understanding, Documentation, Communication, Analysis, Description)[133], and one the design paradigm (Meeting Requirements).

The frequency of reference to the graphical or pictorial nature of the data model is perhaps surprising, since there are data modeling formalisms (notably the Relational Model) that do not require diagrams (Sharp 1993; Date 1998; Witt 2002a). The use of diagrams is strongly associated with design disciplines (Porter and Goodman 1988; Lawson 1997 pp241-259). Of course, it is well recognized

---

[133] This is a subjective classification – as a guide, the author used accounting and architecture as paradigms for description and design respectively and considered which discipline each theme would be more likely to be allocated to.

that diagrams are used in data modeling; the reason the result is interesting is because the fact is included in *definitions* of data modeling, suggesting a central role.

9.6.3. Observations on research design and method

The response rate (66%) was the lowest for any of the surveys in this project. Possible reasons are:

- The survey questions were combined with a data modeling task which proved to be difficult for some participants (Section 11.7.1). Despite the anonymity of responses, professional modelers may have been reluctant to hand in a questionnaire containing a model which they were not comfortable with. They may have had similar feelings about their responses to the questions themselves.

- Completed questionnaires were not collected (in sight of others), but handed in.

- The large group may have reduced the intimacy and desire to assist the author's research.

Despite being asked to choose a single option for the Closed Question, some respondents marked both options. It is reasonable to assume that others would have done so if it had not meant violating the instructions, and in fact six respondents who chose the "description" response to the closed question added a comment to that effect.

CHAPTER 10
CHARACTERISTICS OF DATA MODELING

10.1. INTRODUCTION AND OBJECTIVES

This chapter describes the third and final component of the investigation of practitioners' perceptions of data modeling. In Chapter 6, we looked at *espoused* positions as to whether data modeling was better characterized as description or design. Here, we aim for a deeper understanding of *theory-in-use* (Argyris and Schön 1974 pp6-7) by seeking practitioners' perceptions of data modeling *problems, products,* and *processes* (thus directly addressing the corresponding dimensions of the description / design question). Questions were framed in terms of characteristics of data modeling problems, products, and processes, to encourage participants to draw on personal experience rather than received ("textbook") answers.

This component thus addresses three of the research sub-questions (Section 7.2):

1. Are data modeling problems perceived as design problems by data modeling practitioners?

2. Are data modeling processes perceived as design processes by data modeling practitioners?

3. Are data modeling products perceived as design products by data modeling practitioners?

10.2. RESEARCH DESIGN

Lawson's (1997 pp121-127) inventory of design properties (Section 2.2) provided a conceptual basis for this research component. It describes design at three levels[134]:

1. Design *Dimensions – Problem, Solution* (*Product* in our consolidated framework – we use that term here) and *Process*.

2. Design *Properties* for each of the Dimensions – fourteen in all. These provided the subheadings for the review of literature on *Problem, Product,* and *Process* in Chapter 4.

3. *Descriptions* of each Property – a paragraph defining each Property and in some cases introducing subordinate concepts, in particular *creativity*.

In many cases, the meanings of the Properties are not obvious from their names alone; the descriptions add important clarification and content. This was an important issue when using the model as the basis of a questionnaire.

10.3. MEASURES

Lawson's model was used to establish a set of measures at four levels (Table 10–1).

---

[134] The levels are not named in Lawson's description. Names were added as the first stage of operationalizing the model.

Design	Dimension	Property	Characteristic
Overall	A. Design Problems	1. Problems cannot be comprehensively stated	2. Data modeling problems are often full of uncertainties about objectives and relative priorities
			3. Many requirements do not emerge until some attempt has been made at developing a model.
			4. Objectives and priorities are likely to change during the modeling process.
		2. Problems require subjective interpretation	5. In establishing requirements for a data model, something that seems important to one data modeler may not seem important to another data modeler.
			6. In establishing requirements for a data model, something that seems important to one business stakeholder may not seem important to another business stakeholder.
		3. Problems tend to be organized hierarchically	7. Modeling problems are often symptoms of higher level problems.
	B. Design Products	1. There are an inexhaustible number of different solutions	9. Most data modeling problems do not have a single correct solution.
			10. In most practical business situations, there is a wide range of possible (and workable) data models.
		2. There are no optimal solutions to design problems	11. Data modeling almost invariably involves compromise.
			12. Data modelers will almost invariably appear wrong in some ways to some people.
		3. Design solutions are often holistic responses	13. It is not usually possible to dissect a data model and identify which piece of the model supports each piece of the business requirements.
		4. Design solutions are a contribution to knowledge	14. I frequently re-use patterns (structures) from other data models that I have developed myself.
			15. I frequently re-use patterns (structures) that I have seen in models developed by others.

Table 10–1: Lawson's properties of design organized as a set of measures

Design	Dimension	Property	Characteristic
	C. The Design Process	1. The process is endless	17. Identifying the end of the data modeling process (i.e. when to stop modeling) requires experience and judgment.
		2. There is no infallibly correct process	16. There is no infallible correct process that (if properly followed) will always produce a sound data model.
		3. The process involves finding as well as solving problems	21. Data modeling requires a high level of creative thinking.
		4. Design inevitably involves subjective value judgments	23. I find it difficult to remain dispassionate and detached in my data modeling work.
		5. Design is a prescriptive activity	24. Data modeling is prescriptive rather than descriptive.
		6. Designers work in the context of a need for action	25. The final data model is often a result of compromise decisions made on the basis of inadequate information.

Table 10-1: (cont.)

The 19 *Characteristics* at the lowest level were derived from concepts in the descriptions of the Properties, and were operationalized as questions that could be scored on a Likert scale (the numbers, complete with gaps in the sequence, are the numbers of the corresponding questions on the resulting questionnaire). Scores at this level were then aggregated (by taking the mean) to provide a score for the relevant higher level Property. In the same way, Property scores were "rolled up" to provide Problem, Product and Process scores, and ultimately an overall Design score. We use the term *scores* in this chapter: more technically there is an *index*[135] at each level.

There was necessarily some subjectivity in the identification of these concepts and the framing of the questions. There is no question addressing the Property (of design products) *Design solutions are parts of other design problems*. This Property proved difficult to communicate in a simple question or questions, and after pilot testing confirmed this, it was excluded. In all, six questions address *problem*, seven address *product*, and six address *process*.

---

[135] Following Blaikie (2003). We have used the term scale for the instrument as a whole (slightly loosely as unidimensionality had not been verified prior to the research).

Five further questions (Table 10–2) were added based on other differences between description and design discussed elsewhere in the literature, including in Lawson's wider discussion (Lawson 1997). These have been classified under the relevant dimension.

Question	Dimension
8. Business requirements are often negotiable.	Problem
18. When I am developing a data model, I sometimes produce more than one workable solution, and then choose the best one.	Process
19. I often start modeling before I have a thorough understanding of business requirements.	Process
20. Sometimes, even when I understand the business requirements, I find it difficult to produce a data model.	Process
22. I have experienced "eureka" moments (sudden and dramatic insights or solutions to problems) in my data modeling work.	Process

Table 10–2: Questions added to Characteristics of Data Modeling survey

A further question that asked whether "the most difficult part of data modeling is understanding the business requirements" was added. This question served three purposes, the first two exploratory:

1. To pursue the issue, raised in the thought-leader interviews, as to whether requirements are fixed or negotiable. If requirements are negotiable, but perceived as fixed by some modelers (or vice versa), we would expect such modelers to find the task difficult.

2. To determine whether perceived difficulty in understanding the requirements correlated negatively or positively with other indicators of design. On the one hand incompleteness, subjectivity, and negotiability of requirements are cited as properties of design; on the other, if the task is essentially descriptive, then gaining an understanding would seem to be the central (and most difficult) task.

3. In the context of eliciting a deeper understanding of description / design positions, to reduce the possibility that respondents would recognize the dichotomy behind the questions and answer from their espoused position. The question has the same flavor as the other questions, but does not signal the dichotomy. It was placed first on the questionnaire.

The above model was developed specifically for the present research, in the absence of established measures for differentiating description and design activities. There was, therefore, no data for other activities or professions to serve as a basis for comparison. Without comparative data, we would be obliged to rely solely on the soundness of the underlying theory (and on its satisfactory operationalization) in drawing conclusions from the results.

To address this limitation, the questions were adapted, through minor re-wording, to enable them to be used with two other professional groups, viz architects and accountants. The two groups were chosen because:

1. Architecture is generally recognized as a design discipline (Akin 1991; Lloyd and Scott 1994) and is frequently employed as a metaphor for information systems tasks and deliverables (Section 1.4.3).

2. Accounting is a process of "recording, classifying, reporting and communicating…" (Oxford 2005), a definition consistent with the descriptive paradigm. Data modelers have in fact been compared with accountants: "Just as an accountant might use a financial model, the analyst can develop an entity model" (Avison and Fitzgerald 2003 p177).

Architects and accountants perform a variety of roles – for example accountants may offer advice on investments and architects may inspect buildings on behalf of prospective purchasers. To encourage a focus on common tasks, the accountant questions were framed in the context of preparing a set of accounts for a business and the architect questions in the context of designing a building, and guidance to that effect was added to the questionnaires.

10.4. THE *CHARACTERISTICS OF DESIGN* QUESTIONNAIRE

A questionnaire was designed to incorporate the nineteen questions about design Characteristics, the six additional questions, and the standard demographic questions. A 5-point Likert scale was used for all questions, with options *Strongly Agree, Agree, Neutral, Disagree, Strongly Disagree*. Six questions were re-worded in the negative to reduce response set bias (Narayan and Krosnick 1996) with the benefit of improved clarity in some cases.

Variants for accountants and architects were also produced. These did not include the demographics section.

10.5. METHOD

Aspects of method common to several components of the research, including survey piloting, administration, ethical issues, coding of demographics and use of statistics are covered in Chapter 7. Here we cover aspects of administration particular to this survey, and the analysis of responses.

10.5.1. Administration of questionnaires

The questionnaire was administered at seminars and classes for data modeling practitioners, following the general procedure described in Section 7.4, with the following additions:

1. Participants were told, prior to answering the questions: "we are referring to data modeling to support the development of a relational database; not enterprise data modeling or reverse-engineering"

2. Based on piloting, five minutes was allowed for completion of the questionnaire. Questionnaires were collected at the completion of this period.

3. Participants were asked to leave blank the responses to any questions that they did not have sufficient experience to answer.

4. In cases where participants were also asked to complete a data modeling task and / or questionnaire for another component of this research project, the administration of the *Data Modeling Characteristics* questionnaire immediately followed that task and questionnaire (See Section 7.6 for a list of the surveys and tasks administered at each location.)

5. Some members of the Scandinavian group had attended a full-day data modeling seminar run by the author the previous day, in which 90 minutes was specifically devoted to presenting the case for data modeling to be treated as design, and numerous examples discussed in terms of this position. These attendees were asked to mark their survey responses to indicate that they had attended the workshop, and (at their

option) to provide the number of the questionnaire which they had completed at that workshop[136].

10.5.2. Recruitment and administration: Architects and accountants

The "architect" and "accountant" versions of the questionnaires were e-mailed, with internet links to the research description and ethics statement, to the author's professional and personal contact lists, asking them to forward the email to architects and accountants whom they knew. The email solicited responses by fax or email. "Snowball sampling" is a well-established and, in this situation, a low-cost and practical approach to recruiting (Babbie 1998 pp194-196; Neuman 1999 pp199-200) and has been used in previous empirical research in data modeling (e.g. Shanks, Nuredini et al. 2002b).

10.5.3. Analysis of responses

Responses to each question were coded in accordance with a 5-point Likert scale (1=strongly disagree, 5=strongly agree), after reversal of responses to negatively worded questions. Blank, unclear, or invalid responses to individual questions were treated as "no response" for statistical tests, but valid responses on the same questionnaire were not excluded.

Scale reliability for each audience (data modeling practitioners, accountants, architects) was assessed. As this research included the development and testing of a new questionnaire, the assessment of reliability is included under *Results* rather than *Method*. For the application of the survey to the data modeling group, basic descriptive statistics were calculated for the responses to each question, and aggregated to produce scores at the Property, Dimension, and Overall levels as described in Section 10.3. Significant differences from "neutral" (3 on the Likert scale) for scores at the Question, Property, Dimension, and Overall levels were noted.

Results for samples from the different locations were checked for significant differences at the Dimension and Overall levels. Results for the Scandinavian

---

[136] The workshop attendees participated in the research discussed in Chapter 10. The cross-reference supported checking whether there was a correlation between scores on the Design Characteristics questionnaire and decisions taken in a set modeling problem.

group who had attended the data modeling workshop the previous day were compared with those of the other participants in the Scandinavian seminar.

Scores at the Question, Property, Dimension, and Overall levels for the data modeling questionnaires were compared with those of the accountants and architects.

Responses to the data modeling version of the questionnaire were cross-tabulated against the standard demographic categories (as per Section 7.4) and significant differences noted.

Results from the above analysis were summarized under the relevant Properties.

10.6. SAMPLES

This research involved three samples: data modeling practitioners, accountants, and architects. Accountants and architects were surveyed only to provide reference results against which data modeling could be compared, and did not complete a demographics questionnaire.

10.6.1. Data modeling practitioners

Respondents to the data modeling questionnaire were attendees at seven seminars given by the author during 2004 and targeted at experienced data modeling practitioners. Table 10–3 shows the location of the seminars and number of responses received at each.

Event and Location	Questionnaires Submitted
DAMA Chapter Portland, Oregon, USA	54
DAMA Chapter Phoenix, Arizona, USA	28
DAMA Chapter Des Moines, Iowa, USA	39
DAMA Annual Conference, Scandinavia, (Located in Stockholm, Sweden)	70
DAMA Chapter Sydney, Australia	20
Annual European DAMA / Information Quality Conference, London, UK	25
Wilshire Conferences Data Modeling Master class, Los Angeles, USA	30
Total	266

Table 10–3: Summary of responses to Characteristics of Data Modeling survey

Response rates were estimated or measured as between 83% and 90% (see Section 7.6).

Of the 6650 possible responses (266 questionnaires x 25 questions), 298 (4.5%) were left blank (either responding to the instruction to leave answers blank if they had insufficient experience to answer or possibly because the question was not understood[137]). One hundred and ninety three questionnaires contained non-blank responses for every question.

Thirty-three of the Scandinavian participants indicated that they had attended the earlier workshop.

10.6.2. Accountants and architects

Responses were received from 38 accountants and 21 architects. All responses were valid. Of the 1475 responses to questions (59 questionnaires x 25 questions), 30 (2%) were left blank ("insufficient experience to answer" or possibly because the question was not understood). All of the responses were from Australia (the author's country of residence and that of the majority of the email contacts).

Although participants were not asked to provide details of their job positions, it was evident from senders' email and fax addresses and from unsolicited comments accompanying the emailed responses, that the accountants were predominantly employed by (or principals of) accounting practices rather than in corporate roles.

10.7. RESULTS

10.7.1. Scale reliability

Cronbach's alpha values for the questionnaire variants are shown in Table 10–4.

---

[137] The figure for the Scandinavian group (made up largely of non native speakers of English) was slightly higher at 6.3%

Questionnaire Version	Questions Included	Cronbach's Alpha
Data Modeling	Lawson only (19 Questions)	0.73
Data Modeling	All (25 Questions)	0.76
Accounting	Lawson only (19 Questions)	0.65
Accounting	All (25 Questions)	0.73
Architecture	Lawson only (19 Questions)	0.25
Architecture	All (25 Questions)	0.10

Table 10–4: Characteristics of Design scale reliability

A scale is considered reliable if Cronbach's alpha is greater than 0.7. The results are discussed in Section 10.9, but we note here that the low value for the architects group does not affect the validity of the comparisons which follow[138].

The Corrected Item-Total Correlation (CITC) was positive (an indicator that the questions are measuring the same underlying construct in the same direction) for all but one item in the data modeling questionnaire, including those questions added to supplement the Lawson model. In particular, the value for Question 1 ("the most difficult part of data modeling is understanding the business requirements"), which was exploratory rather than based on theoretical properties of design, was +0.23 indicating a positive but weak correlation with the other indicators of design[139]. (Some scale designers recommend as a rule of thumb that items with a value of 0.30 or less should be deleted from the scale (de Vaus 1995 p184).) The single exception to the positive correlations was Question 24: "Data modeling is prescriptive rather than descriptive" which had a CITC value of -0.15.

10.7.2. Overview of results

Individual questions and aggregated scores

Table 10–5 shows the mean scores for the data modeling questionnaire, across the full sample, at the Property, Dimension, and Overall levels. The scores for questions worded in the negative were been recoded so that a higher score always indicates the "design" choice and this convention is followed throughout the

---

[138] The scale was not intended to test variation *within* a professional group; in the case of the data modelers and accountants it appears that there is such variation, but not in the sample of architects.

[139] This was a relatively weak correlation – only four items had lower (positive) values.

presentation and analysis of results. The one-sample t-test results indicate the significance of the difference between the mean and the neutral score of 3.

Design Mean	Dimension	Property	Property Mean
3.75 t(267)=30.78, p<.0005	A. Design Problems Mean=4.11 t(317)=36.97, p<.0005	1. Design problems cannot be comprehensively stated	4.09 t(330)=30.64, p<.0005
		2. Design problems require subjective interpretation	4.08 t(335)=31.08, p<.0005
		3. Design problems tend to be organized hierarchically	4.18 t(342)=23.45 p<.0005
	B. Design Products Mean=3.60 t(302)=22.87, p<.0005	1. There are an inexhaustible number of different solutions	4.04 t(339)=23.13, p<.0005
		2. There are no optimal solutions to design problems	3.90 t(340)=21.30, p<.0005
		3. Design solutions are often holistic responses	2.55 t(334)= -6.44, p<.0005
		4. Design solutions are a contribution to knowledge	3.94 t(320)=19.23, p<.0005
	C. The Design Process Mean=3.49 t(299)=16.29, p<.0005	1. The process is endless	4.00 t(342)=22.73, p<.0005
		2. There is no infallibly correct process	3.34 t(337)=4.93, p<.0005
		3. The process involves finding as well as solving problems	4.00 t(341)=18.00, p<.0005
		4. Design inevitably involves subjective value judgments	3.65 t(331)=10.35, p<.0005
		5. Design is a prescriptive activity	2.66 t(323)=-6.69, p<.0005
		6. Designers work in the context of a need for action	3.35 t(337)=5.10, p<.0005

Table 10–5: Summary of responses to the data modeling questionnaire

Mean scores for 23 of the 25 questions were significantly greater than 3, indicating the "design" option, and this is reflected in means greater than 3 for each of the Dimensions and the Overall Score. Two Properties scored below 3, a consequence of them being derived directly from the two questions that scored below 3.

Figure 10-1 shows the frequency distribution of the Overall score, clearly showing that most values were above the neutral value of 3.

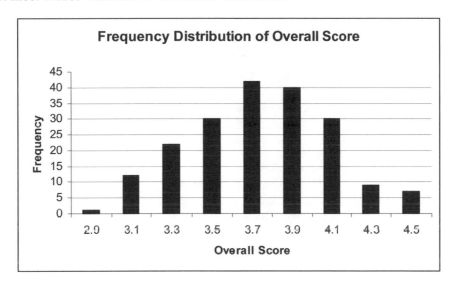

Figure 10-1: Frequency distribution of overall score

Correlation between dimensions

The three Dimensions were moderately positively correlated (Pearson r values lie between 0.33 and 0.40, p<0.001 in all cases), reflecting the overall reliability of the scale as noted earlier.

Differences across sample groups

An ANOVA test[140] showed no significant differences in Overall scores across the seven locations [F(6, 186)= 1.978, p=0.07]. Within the Scandinavian group, there was no significant difference between the Overall scores of those who had attended the workshop on the previous day and those who did not identify themselves as having attended the workshop (t(38) = 0.34, p=0.74).

---

[140] The Kolmogorv-Smirnov statistic for normality was not significant (p= 0.2); therefore the assumption of normality was not violated.

10.7.3. Comparison with accountants and architects

Differences in scores at Dimension and Overall level between data modelers, architects, and accountants were measured using independent group t-tests. Results are summarized in Table 10–6 and Table 10–7.

	Profession	N	Mean	Std. Dev.	t	df	Sig. (1-tailed)
Problem	Data modelers	235	4.11	0.49	3.51	270	<0.01
	Accountants	37	3.81	0.44			
Solution	Data modelers	225	3.60	0.42	4.06	255	<0.01
	Accountants	32	3.29	0.41			
Process	Data modelers	218	3.49	0.41	4.98	253	<0.01
	Accountants	37	3.13	0.44			
Overall	Data modelers	193	3.75	0.35	5.12	223	<0.01
	Accountants	32	3.41	0.32			

Table 10–6: Overall and dimension scores: Accountants vs. data modelers

	Profession	N	Mean	Std. Dev.	t	df	Sig. (2-tailed)
Problem	Data modelers	235	4.11	0.49	2.86	254	<0.01
	Architects	21	3.79	0.42			
Product	Data modelers	225	3.60	0.42	1.28	243	0.20
	Architects	20	3.48	0.35			
Process	Data modelers	218	3.49	0.42	0.65	235	0.51
	Architects	19	3.43	0.45			
Overall	Data modelers	193	3.75	0.35	2.29	209	0.02
	Architects	18	3.55	0.22			

Table 10–7: Overall and dimension scores: Architects vs. data modelers

The two tables show that data modelers scored significantly higher than accountants in all dimensions, and significantly higher than architects in the Problem dimension and overall. Their scores were also higher than architects in the other two dimensions, but the result did not reach significance.

10.7.4. Differences between demographic groups

Results at the Question, Property, Dimension, and Overall levels were compared across the different demographic splits (as defined in Section 7.4.3) using independent group t-tests. Here we summarize the significant results for different primary occupations (data modelers vs. others) and levels of experience. In the next section, results are presented under the relevant Properties, grouped into the *Problem, Process,* and *Product* dimensions. This entails some repetition, but enables the results to be seen from both the demographic and Property perspectives.

Occupation

A comparison of the 92 responses from participants whose primary occupation was classified as "data modeler" with the 149 responses which specified other occupations identified the significant differences shown in Table 10–8:

Item	Mean – Data Modelers	Mean – Others	t	df	p value
Q1: The most difficult part of data modeling is understanding the business requirements	4.20	3.91	2.38	234	0.02
Q14: I frequently re-use patterns (structures) from other data models that I have developed myself	4.18	3.88	2.68	217	0.01
Q15: I frequently re-use patterns (structures) that I have seen in models developed by others.	3.79	4.02	2.06	220	0.04
Q16: There is no infallible correct process that will always produce a sound data model	3.17	3.47	2.18	229	0.03
Q22: I have experienced "eureka" moments (sudden and dramatic insights or solutions to problems) in my data modeling work	4.20	3.91	2.70	230	0.01
B2: There are no optimal solutions to design problems	3.84	4.02	1.99	233	0.05
B4: Design solutions are a contribution to knowledge	4.10	3.84	2.62	217	0.01

Table 10–8: Significant differences between occupation of data modeler and others

As shown in the table, with the exception of Question 16 (infallible process), data modelers' scores for these questions and properties were higher than those of others.

Experience

Four of the demographic groupings are based on data modeling experience in terms of years or number of data models developed.

Table 10–9 shows significant differences between novice modelers and experienced modelers where the former are (a) participants who have developed zero or 1 models or (b) participants who have 1 year or less of data modeling experience.

Item	Basis of comparison	Novices Mean	Exp Mean	t	df	Sig. (2 tailed)
Q1: The most difficult part of data modeling is understanding the business requirements	Years	3.79	4.11	-2.36	231	0.02
Q11: Data modeling almost invariably involves compromise.	No. of Models	3.54	4.03	-2.82	227	0.01
Q14: I frequently re-use patterns (structures) from other data models that I have developed myself	Years	3.73	4.09	-2.71	215	0.01
	No. of Models	3.59	4.04	-2.23	2.11	0.01
Q18: When I am developing a data model, I sometimes produce more than one workable solution, and then choose the best one.	Years	3.28	3.62	2.24	210	0.03
Q19: I do not wait until I have a thorough understanding of business requirements before starting modeling.	Years	2.96	3.33	-2.10	230	0.04
	No. of Models	2.71	3.29	-2.20	225	0.03
Q20: Sometimes, even when I understand the business requirements, I find it difficult to produce a data model	Years	3.61	3.28	2.19	.229	0.03
Q22: I have experienced "eureka" moments (sudden and dramatic insights or solutions to problems) in my data modeling work	Years	3.83	4.11	-2.26	226	0.02
	No of models	3.55	4.09	-3.00	221	<0.01
B4: Design solutions are a contribution to knowledge	Years	3.75	4.01	-2.10	215	0.04

Table 10–9: Significant differences between novice and experienced modelers

Table 10–10 compares less experienced with more experienced modelers based on years of experience (0-5 vs. 6+) and number of models developed (0-10 vs. 11+).

	Basis of comparison	Less Exp	More Exp	t	df	p
Q3. Many requirements do not emerge until some attempt has been made at developing a model.	Years	4.22	4.52	-2.72	232	0.01
Q4. Objectives and priorities are likely to change during the modeling process.	Years	4.04	4.32	-2.47	233	0.01
Q11. Data modeling almost invariably involves compromise.	Years	3.88	4.18	-2.63	232	0.01
Q14. I frequently re-use patterns (structures) from other data models that I have developed myself.	Years	3.93	4.18	-2.21	215	0.03
	No. of Models	3.82	4.21	-3.58	211	<0.01
Q18. When I am developing a data model, I sometimes produce more than one workable solution, and then choose the best one.	Years	3.43	3.75	-2.43	219	0.02
	No. of Models	3.41	3.76	-2.78	214	0.01
Q19: I do not wait until I have a thorough understanding of business requirements before starting modeling.	Years	3.12	3.49	-2.36	230	0.02
Q20 Sometimes, even when I understand the business requirements, I find it difficult to produce a data model	Years	4.48	3.12	2.74	229	0.01
	No. of Models	3.53	3.12	3.19	224	<0.01
Q22: I have experienced "eureka" moments (sudden and dramatic insights or solutions to problems) in my data modeling work	Years	3.97	4.19	-2.05	226	0.04
	No. of Models	3.91	4.21	-2.86	221	<0.01

Table 10–10: Significant differences between less experienced and more experienced modelers

	Basis of comparison	Less Exp	More Exp	t	df	p
Q23: I find it difficult to remain dispassionate and detached in my data modeling work.	No of Models	3.60	3.86	-2.27	215	0.02
A1: Design problems cannot be comprehensively stated	Years	4.03	4.25	-2.67	221	0.01
B2: There are no optimal solutions to design problems	Years	3.85	4.09	-2.62	229	0.01
B4: Design solutions are a contribution to knowledge (patterns)	No of Models	3.81	4.10	-2.88	211	<0.01

Table 10-10: (cont.)

Of the sixteen significant differences recorded across the four demographic splits, all but the three relating to Question 20 ("Sometimes, even when I understand the business requirements, I find it difficult to produce a data model") were the result of the more experienced group preferring the design options.

Two questions elicited significantly different responses from experienced and inexperienced modelers on all four measures:

- Experienced modelers were significantly more likely to report that they re-used patterns from their own models (Q14)

- Experienced modelers were significantly more likely to have experienced "eureka" moments of insight or problem solution (Q22).

10.8. ANALYSIS BY PROPERTY

This section discusses the key results for each of Lawson's Dimensions (*Problem, Process, Product*), and associated Properties. The structure is the same as was used for a major part of the literature review (Sections 4.2 – 4.4), and results can thus be readily compared with the relevant theory. All statistically significant ($p<0.05$) differences between demographic groups (as reported in Section 10.7.4) are cited. All results apply to the data modeling version of the questionnaire unless otherwise stated. Unless otherwise noted all scores from that questionnaire were significantly (one sample t-test, $p<0.01$) greater than 3 (neutral), thus supporting the design characterization.

10.8.1.Design problems

The mean score for the *Problem* dimension was 4.11, the highest of the three dimensions. Accountants also scored highest in this dimension, whereas architects scored highest in the *Process* dimension. This was the only dimension in which the data modeling group scored significantly higher than the architects.

Further support for the relative importance of this dimension came from the score of 4.03 for Question 1 "The most difficult part of data modeling is understanding the business requirements," a perception that was stronger in participants with more than one years' experience and those whose occupation was "data modeler." This score was significantly higher than the architects' and accountants' close-to-neutral responses (2.95 and 3.19 respectively).

Design problems cannot be comprehensively stated

Three questions contributed to this Property.

- Data modeling problems are often full of uncertainties about objectives and relative priorities (Q2). Participants who cited mentorship as a method of learning were more likely to agree, but those who cited industry education were less likely to.

- Many requirements do not emerge until some attempt has been made at developing a model (Q3). This was the second highest-scoring question (4.29), but not significantly higher than the architects' score. Participants with more than 5 years of experience were more likely to agree.

- Objectives and priorities are likely to change during the modeling process (Q4). Again, participants with more than 5 years of experience were more likely to agree.

The only significant difference amongst demographic groups for this Property overall was the greater agreement from participants with more than 5 years of experience.

Design problems require subjective interpretation

Two questions contributed to this Property:

- In establishing requirements for a data model, something that seems important to one data modeler may not seem important to another data modeler (Q5).

- In establishing requirements for a data model, something that seems important to one business stakeholder may not seem important to another business stakeholder (Q6).

There were no significant differences in responses to these questions across the demographic groups. Question 6 produced the highest mean score (4.42).

Design problems tend to be organized hierarchically

This Property was addressed by a single question:

- Modeling problems are often symptoms of higher level problems (Q7).

There were no significant differences in responses across the demographic groups. This was one of four questions in which the data modeling group scored significantly higher than the architects.

Other problem-related questions

Business requirements are often negotiable (Q8) scored 3.35, only marginally significantly above the accountants' score.

10.8.2. The design process

The score for this dimension was significantly higher for those who cited books or publications as a method of learning.

The process is endless

This Property was tested with one question: "Identifying the end of the data modeling process (i.e. when to stop modeling) requires experience and judgment" (Q17).

Respondents who cited tertiary education as a source of learning were more likely to agree. There were no other significant differences across the demographic splits.

There is no infallibly correct process

This property was tested with one question: "There is no infallible correct process that (if properly followed) will always produce a sound data model" (Q16). (The question as it appeared on the questionnaire was less clumsily worded as it was framed in the negative: "There is an infallible correct process…").

Respondents who cited (non-book) publications as a method of learning were more likely to agree that there was no infallible process. Respondents with occupation of data modeler and those who cited tertiary education as a method of learning were less likely to agree (i.e. they had more confidence in an infallible process).

The process involves finding as well as solving problems

This Property was tested by a single question covering the key area of creativity: "Data modeling requires a high level of creative thinking" (Q21). The mean score of 4.00 did not vary significantly across the demographic groups. It was lower, but not significantly so (p=0.63) than that of architects, and significantly higher than that of accountants.

Design inevitably involves subjective value judgments

This Property was tested with a single question: "I find it difficult to remain dispassionate and detached in my data modeling work" (Q23).

Respondents who nominated industry experience as a method of learning or had developed more than 10 models were more likely to agree.

Design is a prescriptive activity

This Property was tested with a single question directly addressing the property itself rather than any subordinate characteristics: "Data modeling is prescriptive rather than descriptive" (Q24).

In strong contrast to its identification in some literature (Olle, Hagelstein et al. 1991; Lawson 1997 p113) as the defining characteristic of design, this property was one of only two to produce a score of below 3, and the only question to return a negative value (-0.15) for the Corrected-Item-Total Correlation i.e. stronger "design" responses on other questions were associated with stronger "description" responses on this question. Accountants scored significantly higher than respondents to the data modeling questionnaire, a situation that occurred for only one other question. This was also the question on the data modeling questionnaire most frequently left blank (26 times in 266 responses: 10% compared with 4.5% overall). Lack of experience would seem less of a reason for leaving the response blank than for other items that required the respondent to draw on experience: here the question could reasonably be answered from theory.

In the literature review we noted some confusion around the use of the terms *prescription* and *description*, specifically their use to characterize the method rather than the task – which would lead to the present question being interpreted in the opposite way to that intended – a *prescriptive* method is appropriate to a *descriptive* task. This would explain the result here.

There were no differences amongst the demographic groups.

Designers work in the context of a need for action

This Property was tested with a single question: "The final data model is often a result of compromise decisions made on the basis of inadequate information" (Q25).

There were no differences amongst the demographic groups.

Other questions relevant to process

The following questions addressed the *Process* dimension, but were not sourced directly from Lawson's Properties and Characteristics.

When I am developing a data model, I sometimes produce more than one workable solution, and then choose the best one (Q 18). Respondents who had developed more than one model or had more than one year experience were more likely to agree than novices, as were respondents who cited books as a source of learning. This was the only question for which architects' scores were significantly higher than those of modelers. The Accountants scored lower on this question than any other (1.92).

I do not wait until I have a thorough understanding of business requirements before starting modeling (Q19). (This question was worded in the negative on the questionnaire and hence less clumsy: "I wait until…"). Respondents who cited books as a source of learning were more likely to agree as were more experienced modelers (three of the four experience groupings). Novices (assessed on both years of experience and number of models developed scored below 3.

Sometimes, even when I understand the business requirements, I find it difficult to produce a data model (Q20). This was the only statement that novices (whether defined by years of experience or number of models developed) were more likely to agree with than experienced modelers. The obvious explanation is that novices are reporting the difficulty that they personally have with producing a model, rather than making a general statement about the nature of the task. Accountants scored 2.69 on this question, compared with 3.37 for data modelers.

I have experienced "eureka" moments (sudden and dramatic insights or solutions to problems) in my data modeling work (Q22). Respondents with occupation of data modeler were more likely to agree as were experienced data modelers (all four groupings).

10.8.3. Design products (solutions)

The *Product* dimension included the critical question of variability in data models (covered by the first two Properties below) and the use of patterns (under the *contribution to knowledge* Property). Respondents to the data modeling questionnaire scored significantly higher than the accountants, but not significantly higher than the architects. The score for the *Product* dimension overall was significantly higher for those who cited books as a method of learning.

There is an inexhaustible number of different solutions

Two questions addressed this Property:

- Most data modeling problems do not have a single correct solution (Q9)

- In most practical business situations, there is a wide range of possible (and workable) data models (Q10).

The only difference in responses from the demographic groups was that those who learned from books were more likely to agree with Question 9. In both questions, the modeling group scored significantly higher than accountants and less than architects, though the latter result did not reach significance (p=0.14 for the difference in Property scores).

In the analysis of questionnaire reliability, Question 10 had the second-highest Corrected Item-Total Correlation value (0.44) – indicating that it was a relatively strong predictor of the overall design score.

There are no optimal solutions to design problems

Two questions contributed to this Property:

- Data modeling almost invariably involves compromise (Q11)

- Data modelers will almost invariably appear wrong in some ways to some people (Q12)

Respondents who had developed more than one model, or had more than five years experience or cited books as a source of learning were more likely to agree that data modeling involves compromise. In the analysis of questionnaire reliability, Question 11 had the highest Corrected Item-Total Correlation value (0.45) – indicating a high correlation with the overall design score.

Respondents who cited tertiary education as a source of learning were less likely to agree with Question 12.

The above results contributed to an overall score for this property that correlated positively with experience in excess of five years, and with occupation of Data Modeler and negatively with tertiary education as a source of learning.

Design solutions are often holistic responses

This Property was tested by Q13 only: "It is not usually possible to dissect a data model and identify which piece of the model supports each piece of the business requirements."

It was one of only two Properties (and questions) whose scores indicated disagreement with the design characterization. The score was 2.55, significantly below the neutral value of 3.0. Accountants scored 2.94 (one of only two cases where they scored significantly higher than modelers), and architects scored 2.75.

Design solutions are a contribution to knowledge

Two questions addressed this property:

- I frequently re-use patterns (structures) from other data models that I have developed myself (Q14).

- I frequently re-use patterns (structures) that I have seen in models developed by others (Q15).

These were two of the four questions on which data modelers significantly outscored architects.

Agreement with Question 14 was more likely from respondents whose occupation was data modeler or who had more experience (there were significant differences across all four of the standard experience splits). Participants with occupation of data modeler were also more likely to agree with question 15.

These results are reflected in significant differences at the Property level with respondents whose occupation was data modeler, respondents who had more than one year experience, and respondents who had developed more than more than ten models more likely to use patterns.

Design solutions are parts of other design problems

As noted in Section 10.3, this property was not addressed by the questionnaire as questions based on it were not effective in communicating the concept.

10.9. DISCUSSION AND CONCLUSIONS

This component of the research concludes the examination of practitioner perceptions of data modeling. It provided considerable detail as to how a substantial number of practitioners perceived individual characteristics of data modeling relevant to the description / design question. The preceding section presented and discussed those results at the Characteristic, Property, and Dimension level, noting differences between professions and the demographic categories within the data modeling samples. In this section, we draw together the most significant overall findings. We conclude with some observations about the research design, in particular generalizability of results, and the questionnaire.

10.9.1. Key findings

The single most important finding from this survey was the consistency with which participants chose the design option in response to questions. Within that overall picture, participants with more experience and / or with the data modeling as their primary occupation scored higher on some questions. These results were in contrast to the results reported in Chapter 6, which reflected more direct views on the description / design issue. There, preferences were strongly for description (analysis of Open Question) or were divided (Closed Question).

These results are consistent with espoused positions being derived directly or indirectly from the literature, which strongly favors the description option, but answers to the present survey being the result of reflections on personal experience. The fact that the literature (as discussed in Chapter 4) does not provide simple, standard answers to the questions posed in this survey lends weight to the argument that the participants were drawing on personal experience rather than received views.

The comparison with architects and accountants produced a surprising result. Given the contention around the description / design question for data modelers, an overall score somewhere between the (descriptive) accountants and (designer) architects might have been expected. In fact, data modelers scored higher than the architects. This was, however, largely due to higher scores in the *Problem* dimension. In Section 6.4.3, we noted that thought-leaders who subscribed to the design view cited the negotiability of data modeling problems more frequently than the variety in solutions. In fact, some regarded the entire "design" aspect of data modeling as being a consequence of problem negotiability; once the problem was agreed, the data model was effectively determined, and the remaining process one of (problem) description.

Another interesting result from the comparison with other professions was the difference in covariance of responses to the individual questions. This was relatively strong for accountants and data modelers, but not for architects. This suggests that data modelers and accountants vary amongst themselves as to their perceived position on a description-design continuum, and answer detailed questions accordingly, whereas architects' perceptions of the properties are not correlated.

The "one right answer" issue was prominent: the two questions with the strongest correlation with the overall design scores related to multiple solutions and subjectivity in deciding amongst them. Part III of the book, which follows this chapter, focuses on this issue.

10.9.2. Review of research design

The development of a new questionnaire was an important part of the design of this research component, and introduced a significant level of complexity insofar as results are subject to the validity of a previously-untested questionnaire. The theory on which it was based reflected one individual's synthesis of design properties and characteristics, which, while it has provided a useful framework for analysis in this book, makes no claim to a deeper theoretical foundation. An encouraging result was that the reliability statistic for the data modeling version of the questionnaire, Cronbach's alpha, exceeded the widely-accepted threshold of 0.7, providing evidence that questions were measuring a common underlying construct (in this case the degree to which data modeling is design). The questions added to those derived from Lawson's framework, but drawn also from the design literature, were also positively correlated with the design scores, and slightly increased the reliability. The prescription / description question (Q24) appeared to be ambiguous. This is supported by different uses of these terms in the literature, and the question would sensibly be deleted if the questionnaire was to be developed further.

The consistency of results across seven groups of data modeling practitioners from locations in four different countries, and across a range of different forums, provides a case for generalizability of results, if not to data modelers as a whole, at least to those who fit the experience profile of the samples and attend data management forums or data modeling classes. It is worth noting that this is the largest and geographically most diverse sample reported in any data modeling empirical study[141] (including studies using students).

The much smaller snowball-recruited samples of accountants and architects are more problematic; however there was no reason to suspect any bias relevant to the description / design question.

---

[141] Based on the survey reported in Chapter 5.

CHAPTER 11
DIVERSITY IN CONCEPTUAL DATA MODELING

And as imagination bodies forth
The forms of things unknown, the poet's pen
Turns them into shapes and gives to airy nothing
A local habitation and a name.

— William Shakespeare, A Midsummer Night's Dream

11.1. OBJECTIVES AND APPROACH

This is the first of three chapters looking at diversity of data models. In this chapter we look at diversity in the *conceptual* data modeling stage, directly addressing the *Product* dimension of the 5Ps framework (Section 1.4.3).

As discussed in Chapter 8, academic and practitioner views of conceptual data modeling differ. In academic work, the conceptual model is seen as a detailed specification of data structures that can be translated more or less mechanically into a database conceptual schema. Practitioners appear to regard a conceptual model more as a "sketch plan" – a preliminary specification at the level of entities and relationships. Both schools, however, see conceptual modeling as proceeding from a set of business requirements[142], and both see the conceptual model as establishing the major concepts for the conceptual schema.

The key question we ask here is: *Will different data modeling practitioners produce different conceptual data models for the same scenario?* (This is the *Diversity in Conceptual Modeling* sub-question from Section 7.2) The question is central to the overall question as to whether data modeling is better characterized as description or design. It was an important theme in thought-leaders' observations (Chapter 6) and was a strong contributor to overall positions on the description / design question (Chapter 10).

---

[142] As discussed in Chapter 3, these requirements may be the outcome of a distinct formal phase or (at the other extreme) exist only in the minds of the business stakeholders.

The review of research on human factors in data modeling (Chapter 5) identified three previous studies of diversity in data models, all focusing on the conceptual modeling stage, all using the same set of requirements as input, and all involving the present author. Lessons from that work have been incorporated here, as has recent work by Verelst (2004a) in providing a theoretical framework for describing data model variability.

We also examine consistency of decision-making within models to provide some initial input to the style sub-question (Section 7.2): *Do data modeling practitioners exhibit personal styles that influence the models that they create?*

11.2. RESEARCH DESIGN

In principle, the research design for this component was simple: provide participants with a data modeling problem and measure the diversity of models produced in response. The challenges lay in establishing measures of diversity, finding a suitable modeling problem, and applying the measures to the resulting models.

Measures of diversity were drawn from previous work (Shanks, Simsion et al. 1993; Simsion and Shanks 1993; Shanks 1997b) and by operationalizing concepts from Verelst's (2004a) working paper.

Designing a task to investigate diversity in conceptual modeling is difficult (Avison and Fitzgerald 2003 pp534-535). Laboratory examples are generally artificial and open to claims of manipulation by the researcher. In the past, these have often been designed with a (single) solution in mind (Section 5.1). Conversely, real-world examples may be too complex to be tackled in the time that can reasonably be made available (Section 5.3). Evaluation might be difficult without the detailed definitions of data model components that would be developed in practice.

Two goals were set for the present task:

1.   The problem needed to be simple enough to allow most participants to complete it in the time that could reasonably be allowed (the author judged this as no more than 45 minutes[143] within the one-day seminar that provided access to experienced modelers).

2.   The problem needed to have face validity; it should be one that could be encountered in practice. Ideally it should be based on a real problem to reduce the possibility and appearance that it was contrived to encourage (or restrict) variability in the models.

Finding a case study was, in fact, not difficult. "Simple" databases are frequently required in industry, and the author was engaged to assist on a pro bono basis with the design of a database to support medical research (described in Duist, Barnett et al. 2002). The clients agreed, in return, to make details of the project available for research purposes. The author gained a detailed understanding of the case through his professional involvement. The research task put the problem in front of participants in order to observe whether they produced the same model as the author – and each other.

As described under Method (Section 11.5), the analysis of the models using the diversity measures required expertise in data modeling, which was provided primarily by the author, with support from an assistant, and (for one measure) a panel of data modeling experts.

11.3. MEASURES

11.3.1. Assessment of diversity

The assessment of diversity employed seven measures, described below. These are not orthogonal, nor is it claimed that they cover every possible difference

---

[143] This represented a significant proportion of a 1 day (6 hour contact time) workshop. The workshop itself was modified to incorporate the case as an integral component and ensure that it did not constitute an imposition on participants.

between models[144]. Rather they provide some different perspectives on overall diversity, and assist in clarifying how and why models differ.

1. The perceived level of difference between models as reported by practitioners reviewing each others' models. Peer assessment (albeit by students) has been previously used in model evaluation (Moody, Sindre et al. 2003). Assessment by researchers and occasionally practitioners is common in empirical studies of data modeling (e.g. Moody and Shanks 2003).

2. The number of entities in each model. This was one of the basic measures used in previous studies (Shanks, Simsion et al. 1993; Simsion and Shanks 1993), and provided an initial quantitative indication of diversity. It is equivalent to Moody's (1998) *simplicity* measure in which a smaller number of entities is a contributor to higher quality.

3. The variety of entity names (i.e. total number of different entity names used across all models) after consolidation of obvious synonyms[145]. This measure provides an aggregate picture of diversity rather than supporting the comparison of individual models.

4. The number and percentage of entity names which corresponded to nouns in the problem description. The percentage measure was used in the earlier studies of diversity, referenced in (2) above, where it was found to be significantly higher for novices than experienced data modelers, and was interpreted as evidence of a more "literal" approach to modeling on the part of the novices. A confounding factor, not discussed in these papers, may have been that the novices' models had less entities in total, a result noted by Moody and Shanks (2003). When the result in Shanks, Simsion et al (1993) is adjusted for number of entities the expert figure falls below that of the novices (applying the adjustment reduces novice percentage from 82% to 49%, compared with the experts' value of 65%). Shanks (1997b) does not report the mean number of entities in novice and expert models.

---

[144] Verelst's framework (Verelst 2004a), which offers the most well-developed classification of data model variability, specifically does not claim to cover all variability.

5. The choice of construct (e.g. entity vs. relationship, entity vs. attribute) used to represent common concepts. This theoretically well-established source of differences amongst models (Kent 1978 p94; Batini, Lenzerini et al. 1986; Date 1998 pp426-427) is referred to as *construct variability* in Verelst's (2004a)framework. Previous empirical work (Batra and Davis 1992) did not find evidence of construct variability in the models produced by student subjects.

6. The level of generalization chosen for common concepts identified in the initial review. The literature recognizes the possibility of different levels of generalization giving rise to different models (Section 4.4.1). Verelst refers to this as *vertical variability*. Generalization scores were calculated for selected constructs as per Table 11–1 (the example is from the actual problem used, which is described in the next section). If a model represented a concept with a subtype structure, the median level of generalization was used. (If the subtype structure represented two levels of generalization, the mean of the scores for each level was assigned e.g. if the concept in the example was represented as a *Health Professional* entity subtyped into *Midwife, Maternal Child Health Nurse* and *Doctor*, a score of -0.5 [mean of 0 and -1] would be allocated). A generalization score was calculated for each model, based on allocating a score as per Table 11–1 below for each of the concepts appearing in the model (the example is from the problem that appears in the next section). This approach is similar to that of Kao and Archer (1997).

7. Holistic difference: The particular combination of entities and relationships used to model a common section of the model identified in the original review. Discussions and examples of models based on different abstractions at the same level of generalization are uncommon in the data modeling literature (but see Simsion and Witt 2005 pp285-288). Verelst's *horizontal variability* captures something of this idea. In order to check whether variants of this kind were acceptable solutions, a selection of the models was evaluated by expert data modelers (see Method).

---

[145] The word *synonym* is used here to mean synonyms in plain English, and refers to spelling and abbreviation variants. There is no implication that they have the same meaning in the context of the models; on the contrary, homonyms were common.

Level of Generalization	Example	Score
More specialized than the most common level of generalization	Midwife	-1
At the most common level	Health Professional	0
Generalized to include other concepts in the problem description, but not beyond it	Survey Participant	1
Generalized to (potentially) include concepts not required by the problem as described	Person or Party	2

Table 11–1: Scoring generalization decisions

Some of the above measures were objective, whilst others involved subjectivity. Table 11–2 summarizes the nature of the measures and highlights the use of evaluators other than the author to improve independence.

Measure	Objective or Subjective?	Assessed by
1. Perceived level of difference	Subjective	Participants
2. Number of Entities	Objective	Research Assistant
3. Number of Matching Nouns	Objective*	Research Assistant
4. Variety of Entity Names	Objective*	Research Assistant
5. Choice of Construct	Objective	Research Assistant
6. Level of Generalization	Objective	Research Assistant with Author
7a. Holistic Difference (selection of models)	Subjective	Author
7b. Holistic Difference (evaluation of models)	Subjective (except complexity measure)	External Experts

* Some subjectivity in identifying synonyms.

Table 11–2: Nature of diversity measurements

11.3.2. Quality measures

The assessment of holistic difference (Measure 7 in the preceding section) required that a sample of models be validated to ensure that they were acceptable solutions. Evaluation was performed by expert modelers and was based on the data model quality framework of Moody and Shanks'(2003). Developed over ten years, and consciously incorporating ideas from other researchers, including the present author (Simsion 1991; 1994), this is almost certainly the most mature of the data model quality frameworks. The authors state that it is unique in being empirically validated, and that it is now a stable and mature approach. The version used in their empirical work contains six criteria: (syntactic) *correctness, completeness, simplicity, understandability, flexibility*, and *overall quality*. Quality criteria used here were:

1. *Complexity* – the total number of entities and relationships. Moody and Shanks use the term *simplicity;* we have preferred *complexity* as a name for a measure which increases with the number of model components. This (objective) measure was calculated by the author.

2. *Flexibility* as used by Moody and Shanks. Assessed by the experts using a five-point Likert scale.

3. *Understandability* as used by Moody and Shanks. Assessed by the experts using a five-point Likert scale.

4. *Overall Quality,* framed in terms of workability, and assessed by the experts using a five-point Likert scale.

Moody and Shanks' *correctness* criterion was not tested, as it relates to correct use of conventions, which was a pre-requisite for selecting models for evaluation (diversity of models as a result of syntax errors was not of interest to the present study). Nor was *completeness* tested as only models that were complete in the relevant area were selected.

To provide a basis for comparison, the experts were also asked to rate a "benchmark" model – an "average" model that they would expect to encounter in their work, developed within the last ten years.

11.4. MATERIALS

This section describes the key materials used for the laboratory task and for the evaluation of models by experts.

11.4.1. Case study

I work in health in the population area – good example

– Participant No. 144

The problem was presented as several components:

1. A videotaped description of the business requirements presented first by the project director and then by the manager responsible for management of the database. The two stakeholders were responding independently to the author's request: "tell me about the project and the data that you need to store."

2. A verbatim transcript of the videotape (Figure 11-1), with a short glossary of terms added by the author in consultation with the project director.

3. A list of questionnaires to be used for data collection, and excerpts from two questionnaires.

CASE STUDY INTERVIEW TRANSCRIPTS

Key Terms (as used in the transcripts):

Post-natal or *post-partum* – after the birth of a baby

Ante-natal – before the birth of a baby (i.e. during pregnancy)

Intervention – action taken by a health professional e.g. counseling, prescription of drugs. Also used by Prof. Buist (final sentence) to mean "actions taken to educate health professionals and the public about Post-Natal Depression."

Screening – administering a questionnaire (to a woman participating in the study)

Professor Anne Buist, Director, National Post-natal Depression Initiative

This project is looking at ante-natal and post-natal depression, and it's going to run over four years, and cover five states of Australia. It's being funded by Beyond Blue, which is the Australian national depression institute, and it's going to cover somewhere between 50,000 and 100,000 women over this time period.

The data collection is in three kind-of-separate bits:

Firstly across all states we're going to be screening women at a minimum of two time points – once through the pregnancy and once post-natally. And the data we're collecting there will be the same in each state.

However there's also going to be state-specific interventions for these women, and that will be evaluated both pre and post intervention with another set of questionnaires that women or / and the research assistants will be completing. And these may be at up to six different time points in covering through pregnancy and post-partum.

The other sort of aspect of the data collection is before we even start the study and at the end of the study we're going to be sending questionnaires to both women who have had babies and health professionals (general practitioners, midwives and maternal child health nurses), and evaluating their understanding of post-natal depression with respect to what it is, with respect to stigma and with respect to treatment. And we'll be evaluating that again after our four-year time period where we're going to be doing some interventions and in particular increasing awareness of post-natal depression.

Dr Justin Biltza, Project Officer, National Post-natal Depression Initiative

So really there are two types of data that we're collecting: the first lot being patient demographic data (name, address, date of birth, contact details), and the other set of data is based on a series of questionnaires which are either "short answer" or the selection of a score based on (say) a range from (say) "good" to "bad". There's approximately forty questionnaires that we're using, five which form a core key component that everyone in the survey is doing, but then each of the states has a number of individual surveys that they're using, none of which cross over, so one of the problems that we have is ensuring that we collect all the data on all the patients.

A couple of the other problems we have are the need for a central identification number that we need to generate: we can't use (for instance) a Medicare number or social security number because of privacy issues. Another one of the problems that we have is that a lot of these surveys are used multiple times – two, sometimes three times. So it's the ability to be able to collect data on the third survey, linking it up with the same patient that we used for the first survey.

So if you were to participate in the study, you would come in to your ante-natal visit and with the help of staff fill out (say) four or five questionnaires asking you about your mood and how you're feeling. You would then answer the same questionnaires again at your post-natal visit, and the reason we have the same questionnaires again is just to see how the mood and the response has changed over a period of time.

Figure 11-1: Postnatal depression interview transcript and glossary

Instructions and a set of "process" questions addressing assumptions, level of difficulty and use of patterns (common to all modeling exercises used in this research project) were added to the standard demographics questionnaire.

11.5. METHOD

Aspects of method common to several components of the research, including survey piloting, administration, ethical issues, coding of demographics and use of statistics are covered in Chapter 7. Here we cover administration and analysis of the task and associated questionnaire, coding and analysis of the results, and the process of expert evaluation of models to support the assessment of holistic variation (Measure No. 7).

11.5.1. Administration of laboratory task

Administration followed the general procedure described in Section 7.4, and comprised the following steps:

1. Participants were advised that they were to develop a data model to support the development of a database for a real-world problem. They viewed and heard the videotape, and were then provided with all materials including a transcript of the videotape.

2. Participants were given 25 minutes to complete this task (based on piloting[146]). They were told verbally and in the written instructions that if time was insufficient, simply to list entities. They were also encouraged to ask the author (who was present throughout) any questions about the procedure or the case itself.

3. At the end of the 25 minutes, participants were invited to discuss their model with another participant to assess the level of similarity. Participants were given the option of watching others or not participating in this stage if they did not want to share their model. Ten minutes was allowed for this stage.

---

[146] The exercise was piloted with four individuals, with levels of data modeling experience ranging from nil (knowledge of theory only) to 16 years industry experience as a specialist data modeler. In all cases, the modelers were able to produce an entity-relationship diagram within 25 minutes, and reported that they had reached a level of "diminishing returns".

4.   Participants were given five minutes to complete the associated questionnaire. Submission of the questionnaires and the models (numbered by the participants to match the questionnaire) at the coffee break that followed was voluntary.

11.5.2. Initial review and coding

Demographic information was coded according to the procedure and coding schemes described in Section 7.4.

All models were reviewed by the author (an experienced data modeling consultant) to establish whether they were workable. The test here was not whether all of the semantics included in the case materials had been represented in the model, but whether a database specified by the model could hold the data needed to support an application that met the basic requirement viz to enable responses to a variety of patient and health-worker questionnaires to be recorded along with respondent demographics. This left open the possibility of some semantics being represented as program logic, data values, or external to the application as discussed in Section 4.4.2.

To support the measurement of diversity as described in Section 11.3.1:

1.   The names of the entities (or alternative abstractions, such as objects) used in each model were recorded. Obvious synonyms (plurals, spelling and abbreviation differences, etc) were consolidated. These were mapped against nouns in the problem description, excluding nouns that referred to a single instance (e.g. "this project" or "postnatal depression"). Entity names that included a qualifier were not mapped (e.g. the entity Possible Response would not be mapped to the noun "response"; the entity Patient Location was not mapped to the noun "patient").

2.   Concepts that had been represented as entities in some models and relationships or attributes in others were noted, and the choices made in each model recorded.

3.   Concepts that were represented at different levels of generalization across models were noted. A coding scheme was established to represent the different levels, and the choices made in each model were recorded.

235

4. A list of reference (standard) entities with names and definitions was created. The object was to (a) provide a basis for assessing (holistic) variability independent of the names used in individual models and (b) support presentation of models to expert evaluators without the confusing factor of different names. In essence, this was a coding exercise. The list of reference entities was synthesized from the models (open coding), using context (other entities and relationships), attributes, definitions, and notes to build an understanding of the modelers' intentions in the absence of detailed definitions. Each model was then coded in terms of the reference entities that it used and the relationships that it implemented between pairs[147] of them. This was a difficult and time consuming exercise, requiring some judgment, and compounded by the problems of interpreting handwriting, notes, and diagramming conventions. It was not practical to involve a second expert modeler to check the reliability of the coding, however, an assistant with theoretical knowledge of modeling delivered consistent results on the less-difficult models.

A log of observations of individual models was kept, noting individual features and variations that fell outside those covered by the above measures.

11.5.3. Expert evaluation of quality

Nineteen expert data modelers evaluated models to support the quality assessment (Section 11.3.2). These experts were known to the author personally or by reputation. All but one had over fifteen years specialist data modeling experience, fifteen were working as consultants, fifteen had published or presented on the subject at conferences, and five were authors of books covering data modeling. They were provided with a copy of the problem transcript, copies of the selected models reproduced using a diagramming tool, definitions for key entities, and instructions including the rating scheme.

---

[147] Because the crows' foot convention does not support relationships of degree higher than two, all relationships were binary.

The models were selected by the author based on:

- Soundness – only models classified as "workable" were included (this was a preliminary classification, and it was possible that more detailed examination by the experts would refute this assessment)

- Clarity – models presented clearly, with correct use of modeling conventions, and supported by explanation and / or attribute lists were less likely to be misinterpreted.

- Difference – clear differences in structure, after standardization of entity names.

The subjective selection of these models by the author should not compromise any finding of diversity: the design paradigm does not require that every person produce a different workable solution, but only that diverse solutions can exist (Lawson 1997 pp122-123). The number of models (ten) was judged as being at the upper limit of what the evaluators would consider a reasonable request.

11.5.4. Analysis of diversity

The measures set out in Section 11.3.1 were calculated and checked for differences across the standard demographic splits (Section 7.4.3).

Choices in use of construct and in generalization decisions were examined to establish whether there was a correlation within models i.e. whether individual modelers showed consistency in choosing one construct over another or in preferring a higher or lower level of generalization. This constituted a preliminary investigation of modeling style.

11.6. SAMPLES

The modeling problem and associated questionnaire were given to attendees at an advanced data modeling seminar conducted by the author at the Data Management Association (DAMA) Annual Conference in San Antonio, Texas, USA in May, 2002. The conference and seminar attracted a predominantly practitioner audience. This was the same group that participated in the research component described in Chapter 9 (the two questions that form the focus of that chapter were included in the questionnaire). The basic demographic information is covered in that chapter (Section 9.5); it includes nineteen respondents who submitted a questionnaire but did not submit a model.

Response rates are summarized in Table 11–3.

Response Type	Rate
Number of workshop attendees	170
Model and questionnaire submitted[148]	91
Model submitted without questionnaire	2
Questionnaire submitted without model	19
Total Questionnaires Returned	112
Response Rate (all questionnaires)	66%
Response Rate (complete questionnaires with models)	54%

Table 11–3: Response rates for Diversity in Conceptual Modeling task and questionnaire

Responses to the questionnaire completed after the administration of the modeling task showed that participants who did not submit a model were on average less experienced (mean 1.8 years[149] vs. 7.0 years experience; $t(99)=3.22$, $p=0.002$), found the problem more difficult (mean[150] 3.4 vs. 2.8; $t(106)= 2.91$, $p=0.004$) and were more likely to think that their model would be substantially different if they had more time (68% vs. 42%; phi= 0.34, $p<0.0005$) than those who submitted models.

---

[148] Some completed questionnaires did not provide responses to all questions.

[149] This figure becomes 1 year if the most experienced modeller is excluded; only three of these respondents claimed more than one year experience.

[150] Treating the difficulty ratings as a Likert scale.

11.7. RESULTS

11.7.1. Perceptions of the task and models

Modestly challenging – mostly because of the unknowns

– Participant No. 126

I like to work in spurts – not to a deadline

– Participant No. 91

The responses to the "Process" questions across all four locations are summarized in Figure 11-2 through to Figure 11-7. Respondents who did not submit a model are not included. Comments added by participants have been noted below the relevant figures.

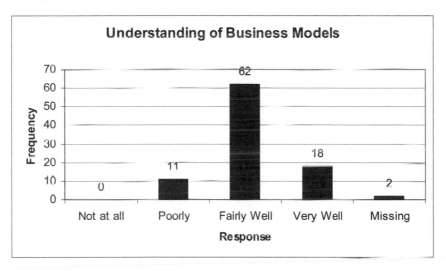

Figure 11-2: How well do you believe you understood the business requirements

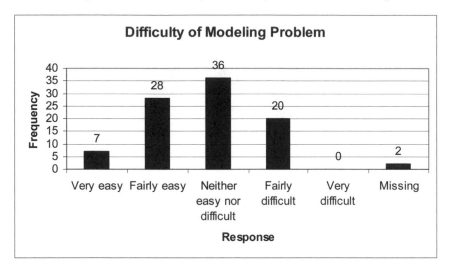

Figure 11-3: How difficult did you find this modeling problem?

Eleven participants added comments to their response to the *understanding* question most to the effect that more detail would be useful. Seventeen participants added comments to the *difficulty* question. Two mentioned experience with similar problems. Most of the remaining comments were to explain that the participant lacked experience (this section preceded the demographics questions, so such participants in an advanced data modeling seminar may have felt the need to explain why they found the problem difficult).

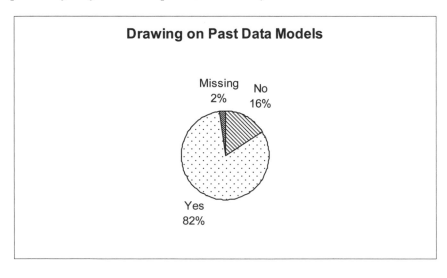

Figure 11-4: Did you draw on data models that you have seen or used in the past?

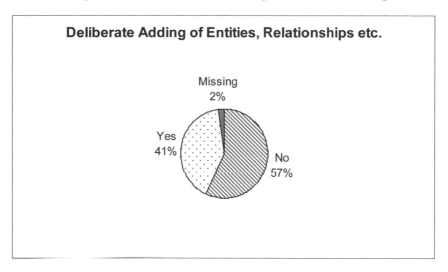

Figure 11-5: Did you deliberately added entities, relationships etc.?

Ten participants added comments to the *re-use* question to nominate the models that they had drawn upon or to cite "general modeling experience". Thirteen participants added comments to the *added concepts* question, two to query the definition of the word *deduced*, the remainder citing specific additions, including generalizations.

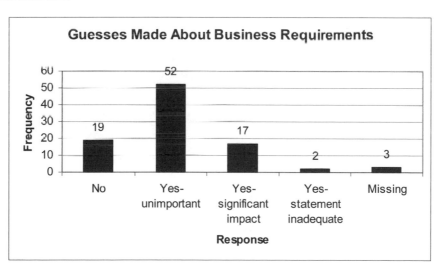

Figure 11-6: Did you make any guesses about the business requirements?

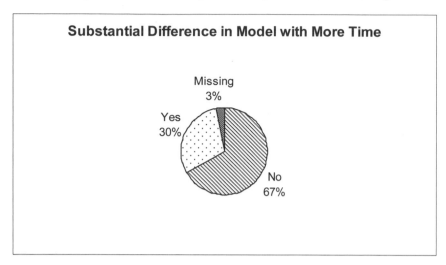

Figure 11-7: Do you think your models would be substantially different with more time?

Fourteen participants added comments to the *guesses* question, noting specific guesses, or that they had documented their assumptions. Of 26 participants who supported their response to the *more time* question with comments, 18 simply noted that more time would have enabled them to add more detail.

Significant correlations amongst the responses and demographic splits are noted below.

Understanding of the requirements was correlated with:

- Difficulty (gamma = -0.67, p<0.001)

- Guesses (gamma = -0.39 p=0.03)

- More time required (gamma = -0.45, p=0.03)

- One year or less experience (gamma = 0.74, p=0.005)

- One model or less developed (gamma = 0.75, p=0.03)

These figures indicate (as might be expected) that the least experienced modelers had the poorest understanding of requirements, and that those with a poorer understanding of requirements made more guesses and found the problem more difficult.

Perceived difficulty was correlated with:

- Understanding (as above)

- Guesses (gamma=0.33 p=.02)

- More time required (gamma==.0.43, p=.01)

- Years experience (gamma=-0.433, p<0.001)[151]

- One year or less experience (gamma=0.67, p=0.004)

- Five years or less experience (gamma=0.43, p=0.005)

- Number of models developed (gamma=-0.421, p<0.001)[152]

- One model or less developed (gamma = 0.88, p=0.003)

These figures indicate (again, as might be expected) that those who found the problem more difficult were less experienced and were more likely to have to make guesses and require more time.

Forty-nine (54%) of the respondents provided responses stating that they understood the problem fairly well or very well, did not find it "very difficult", made no guesses or only unimportant guesses and did not think their models would be substantially different if more time was allowed i.e. they did not provide any reason that their model would be markedly different in a practical setting.

11.7.2. Initial assessment of the models

Of the 93 models submitted, 66 were judged as workable. The participants who submitted workable models were on average more experienced (8.5 years vs. 3.5 years; two tailed $t(87)=4.469$, $p<0.001$), and found the problem less difficult (difficulty rating[153] 2.57 vs. 3.23; two tailed $t(89)=-3.401$, $p=0.001$)

Figure 11-8 shows the modeling conventions used. Eighty-two percent used some variant of the "crow's foot" notation – 88% if the IDEF1/X notation is counted as a crow's foot variant. In these two formalisms, the key constructs are entities, relationships and (optionally) attributes, and these terms have therefore been used

---

[151] Using all eight categories.

[152] Using all eight categories.

[153] Treating the difficulty ratings as a Likert scale.

in discussing the models. None of the models used the original (Chen 1976) E-R notation[154] , which is widely cited as the dominant industry formalism.

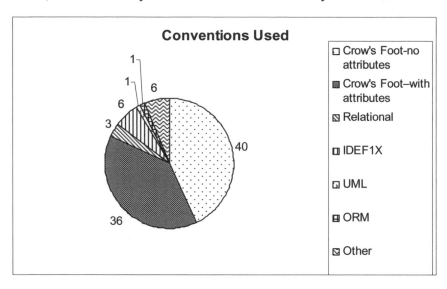

Figure 11-8: Conventions used

Twenty-one of the models (23%) included subtype structures. Five models provided only a list of entities (as was an option if time was insufficient).

A reference set of ten standard entity names, covering entities used frequently to support the core data of survey responses and demographics was developed and supplemented by definitions, as described in Section 11.5.2. They were used to facilitate comparison of models that used different names for what were judged to be the same or very similar entities.

---

[154] In particular, no relationship was represented as a diamond.

11.7.3. Assessment of diversity

This section presents the results for each of the seven measures of diversity. Correlations with the demographics are included under the relevant measures.

Diversity measure no. 1: Participants' perceptions of difference

Differences in 'philosophies' – generic approach vs. capturing the 'real world'

– Participant No. 91

Passionate differences

– Participant No. 146

Figure 11-9 summarizes the responses to the question: "How similar were the two models?" Eleven (9.8%) of the respondents did not answer this question, including three who did not submit models. (The remaining sixteen respondents who did not submit models did answer this question – implying that they had developed a model but chosen not to submit it – and are included in the analysis). Thirty-seven participants added comments, generally to note the differences in the models. The one respondent who considered their model identical to that of their partner noted that "I compared my model with a person from my company".

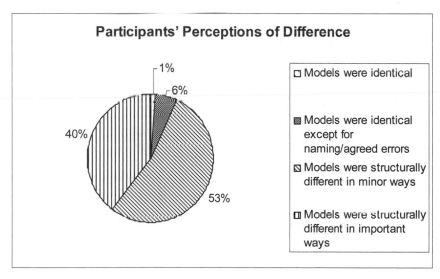

Figure 11-9: Participants' perceptions of difference in partner's model

Diversity measure no. 2: Number of entities

Figure 11-10 is a frequency distribution of the number of entities in the models. Subtypes have been excluded from the count to improve comparability with the 77% of models that did not use subtypes[155].

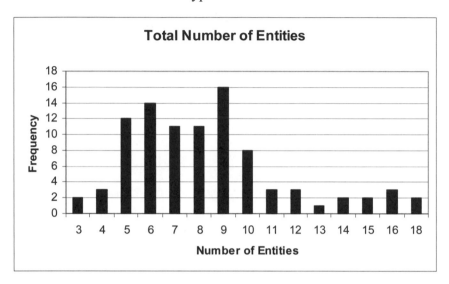

Figure 11-10: Total number of entities in each model

The number of entities in the models was positively correlated with both measures of experience, using the eight experience categories (Section 7.6). (Gamma was 0.29, p=0.001 for the categories based on years of experience below, and 0.26, p=0.006 for the categories based on number of models developed.) There were no significant correlations with occupation or methods of learning.

Diversity measure no. 3: Variety of entity names

The 93 models contained, in total, 291 different entity names after consolidation of reasonably obvious synonyms.

This number provides only a preliminary picture of diversity. In addition to unrecognized synonyms, it includes some homonyms. For example, the entity names *Survey, Response,* and *Questionnaire* were used to represent a range of

---

[155] It is not possible to tell whether these models excluded subtypes because they were not required or because they were not supported by the formalism – subtypes are an extension to the crow's foot notation.

different concepts: this was apparent from the context of relationships to other entities.

Diversity measure no. 4: Use of nouns from the description

The number of entity names that matched nouns in the description (transcripts) varied from zero to seven (Figure 11-11).

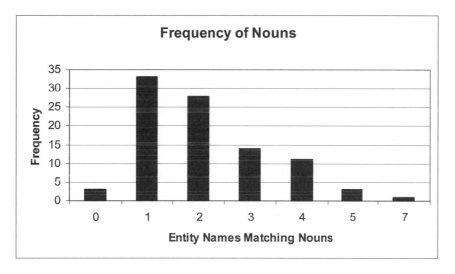

Figure 11-11: Number of entities corresponding to nouns in the problem description

Comparison of novice and expert results was limited by the relatively small number of novices: only 13 of the 84 participants who submitted models and provided demographic information had one year or less experience and only eight had developed one model or less.

Novice participants (one data model or less experience) included a higher *percentage* of nouns in the problem description (mean 33%, std dev 20%) than the more experienced participants (mean 26%, std dev 14%) in their models, but the result did not reach significance ($t(82)=1.26$, $p=0.2$). These figures were, in any case, inflated by the significantly higher total number of entities in the models produced by more experienced participants. The results for raw numbers of matching nouns also did not reach significance (mean for experience less than or equal to one year was 33%, std dev 16%; mean for greater than one year was 26%, std dev 14%, $t(86)=1.61$, $p=0.1$).

Diversity measure no. 5: Construct variability: entity, relationship, or attribute?

Examination of the models identified only one commonly-used concept that was represented in some cases as an entity and in others as a relationship. Table 11–4 shows the frequency of the alternative representations.

Entity Representation		Relationship Representation	
Survey Administration to Person	52	Survey-Person	5

Table 11–4: Alternative representations of same concept – entity and relationship

Three common concepts were represented in some models as entities and in others either explicitly or implicitly as attributes. For example, some models included a Valid Response entity, allowing possible responses to questions to be represented explicitly. Others represented the response only as an attribute in the (Actual) Response entity; if attributes were not explicitly listed on the model, it was assumed that the attribute would be included there.

Concept	Implemented as entity	Entity in which it would appear as attribute	Implemented as attribute
Question	15	Survey Question, Person Survey Question, Response	51
Valid Response	19	Response, Person Survey Question	47
Survey Batch Admin.	7	Survey Admin to Person	45

Table 11–5: Implementation of concepts as entities or attributes

Correlation between the decisions was negligible in two cases and weakly positive but not significant in the third (phi=0.14, p=0.2).

Diversity measure no. 6: Level of entity generalization

Three concepts were identified in the initial review of the models as being subject to different levels of generalization: *respondent, survey (questionnaire),* and *state.*

Table 11–6 through to Table 11–8 show the frequency with which each level of generalization was used. Coding follows the scheme described in Section 11.3.1, with higher scores indicating higher levels of generalization.

Respondent: Level of generalization	Score	Frequency
No Entity	0	2
Separate entities for Health Worker & Patient	-1	6
Respondent subtyped	-0.5	30
Respondent	0	23
Person/Individual/Party	1	32
Total		93

Table 11–6: Frequency of alternative levels of generalization for respondent

Survey (Questionnaire) : Level of generalization	Score	Frequency
No Entity	0	4
Individual Surveys e.g. Beck Depression Indicator	-2	1
Separate Survey groups e.g. health worker/patient or national/state	-1	2
Survey to pre baby /post baby, then by state	-1	1
Survey subtyped into patient/health worker surveys or national/state surveys	-0.5	14
Survey alone	0	71
Total		93

Table 11–7: Frequency of alternative levels of generalization for survey (questionnaire)

State: Level of generalization	Score	Frequency
No Entity	0	38
Entities for individual states	-1	1
State subtyped into individual states	-0.5	6
State	0	38
Location/Region	1	10
Total		93

Table 11–8: Frequency of alternative levels of generalization for state

There were significant correlations between the three generalization decisions (Table 11–9). (Covariance, measured by Cronbach's alpha was 0.37; the low figure reflects the small number of items).

		Gamma	Kendall's tau-b	p
Survey	State	0.77	0.28	0.01
Survey	Person	0.42	0.21	0.02
Person	State	0.49	0.24	0.01

Table 11–9: Correlations between levels of generalization

Figure 11-12 shows the distribution of generalization scores, calculated as per Section 11.3.1.

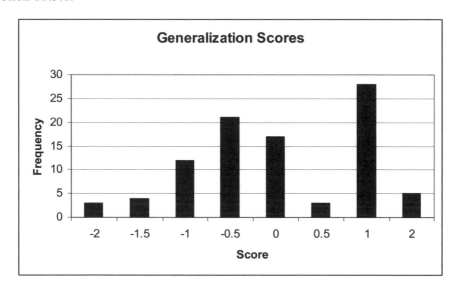

Figure 11-12: Generalization scores

The generalization scores were significantly higher for experienced modelers than for novices. The mean score for modelers with one year or less experience was -0.54 compared with 0.17 for the others (t(86) = -2.5, p= 0.01). The mean score for modelers who had developed zero or one models was -1.06 compared with 0.16 for the others (t(82)= -3.710, p<0.001). As noted earlier, the novices were only a small group in this sample.

There were no significant differences in scores for different occupations or methods of learning, or between the alternative categories of less-experienced and more-experienced.

Diversity measure no. 7: Holistic difference

What a fascinating exercise. Great illustration of the range of models that can come from the same scenario.

– Expert Evaluator

Although there were some differences in the scope of the models, most addressed a core business requirement that could be summarized as "recording the question-by-question responses to a variety of questionnaires given to women being screened for post-natal depression[156]".

As noted earlier (Section 11.5.2) the establishment of reference entities and the mapping of entities in the models to these was difficult and time consuming. Homonyms were common, and both coders remarked on the "slipperiness" of language. Almost certainly, some of the subtler variations were overlooked.

Table 11 10 provides a pictorial summary of some of the variation amongst the 66 models that covered the core business requirement and provided enough information to be mapped. It shows the six most widely used reference entities and the relationships between them (shaded box indicates that the entity or relationship was present in the model). Each row thus represents a model that handled those six entities and associated relationships in a different way. Cardinality and optionality – further potential sources of difference – are not shown.

---

[156] The respondents (women being screened) are specified in this formulation, because the project also surveyed health workers. Some respondents combined the two types of survey, others separated them.

Person	Question	Survey	Response	Allow Resp	Surv Qu.	4-1	1-4	4-2	3-2	3-1	4-3	2-5	5-2	4-5	5-6	5-3	6-3	6-2	4-6	Freq.
1	2	3	4	5	6	7	8	9	10	11	12	13	14	15	16	17	18	19	20	

Table 11–10: Use of six common entities and their inter-relationships in the models

The frequency of 20 against one row is not indicative of a consensus model. That row shows only two direct relationships between the reference entities, a reflection of the fact that those models used additional constructs outside the reference entities. It could be best labeled *other*.

Ten models were selected for expert assessment as described in Section 11.5.3. Recall that the purpose of this assessment was to determine whether these different solutions were viable and if they would be acceptable in practice. Four of these ten models are shown in Figure 11-13 (these were the models rated highest by the experts – discussed below).

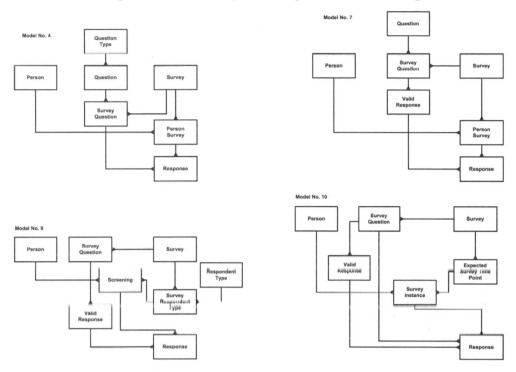

Figure 11-13: Examples of models submitted for expert review

The models were reviewed by nineteen expert data modelers, who gave scores for Overall Quality, Understandability and Flexibility on a 5-point scale as described in Section 11.5.3. Inter-rater reliability, measured by Cronbach's alpha, was 0.92 for the Overall Quality scores, 0.84 for Understandability, and 0.73 for Flexibility. A value of 0.7 is generally considered acceptable. The mean value for Understandability across all evaluators and models was 3.53 (std dev= 0.47), placing it between the values annotated "Neither easy nor difficult to understand" and "Reasonably easy to understand". This rating, combined with the good inter-rater reliability and overall expertise of the evaluators, suggests that evaluation was not seriously impeded by difficulty in understanding the models, a concern that has been noted in relation to past studies where mean understandability was below the midpoint of the Likert scale (Atkins and Patrick 1996).

Figure 11-14 shows, for each of the ten models, the number of experts who scored the Overall Quality as 3 ("application would work with no serious problems") or more (right bar), and the number of experts who scored it equal to or higher than their "benchmark" model – an average model that they would expect to encounter in their work, developed in the last 10 years by someone other than themselves.

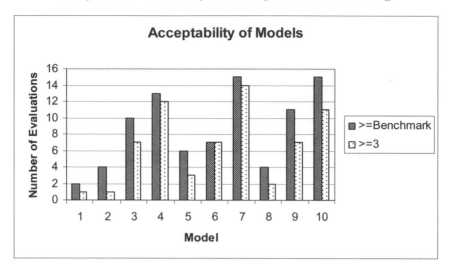

Figure 11-14: Number of times each model rated at or above benchmark and at or above 3[157].

Evaluators were also asked to nominate the best model overall. In total, four different models were selected, each with at least three nominators (Table 11–11)

Model	Nominated by (number)	Overall Quality Rating (mean)	Std Dev
4	3	2.97	0.95
7	9	3.11	0.99
9	3	2.42	0.96
10	4	2.95	1.03

Table 11–11: Models nominated as best overall

Following the approach of Moody and Shanks (2003), a regression analysis was performed with Overall Quality as the dependent variable and Understandability, Flexibility and Complexity[158] (total number of entities and relationships) as predictors. The adjusted R-Square value was 0.46 (p<0.001), indicating that this regression model explains 46% of the variance in Overall Quality. This needs to be qualified by the fact that Complexity was positively correlated with Overall Quality, whereas Moody and Shanks (ibid) argue that it should be negatively correlated (they propose *Simplicity* as a contributor to quality). When this factor is

---

[157] Midpoint of Likert scale.

[158] Moody and Shanks refer to this measure as *simplicity*, in which "less is better". We have preferred clarity to consistency in changing the term.

removed, the adjusted R-Square value falls to 0.33. The adjusted R-Square value in Moody and Shanks' regression model was 0.77; however they included Correctness and Completeness as predictors.

Table 11–12 shows the (standardized) coefficients, representing the relative contribution of the three predictors to explaining the Overall Quality value:

Predictor	Beta (Standardized Coefficient)	T	Sig.
Flexibility	0.50	9.1	<0.0005
Complexity	0.40	6.8	<0.0005
Understandability	0.21	3.6	<0.0005

Table 11–12: Contributions to explaining overall quality – multiple regression analysis.

11.8. CODA: THE REAL-WORLD SOLUTION

The modeling task given to participants was, as noted earlier, drawn from practice, and the author worked with the Project Officer (second interviewee in the transcripts – Figure 11-1) on the model and resulting database design. The work was completed before the administration of the research task, and thus was not influenced by any of the responses from participants or the feedback from experts. The author sought the advice of an expert data modeler[159] specializing in the health sector, and the final model was agreed to by all three parties. The total effort to develop a conceptual model to a level similar to that of those produced by participants in the present study was approximately six person-hours, excluding review with the users (who made no substantial changes). The users have indicated strong satisfaction with the resulting database over a three-year project, which concluded in 2005.

Given the level of expertise employed, the greater time taken, the motivation inherent in a real-life situation, and the practical acceptability of the result, it is interesting to compare the implemented model with those produced by the participants.

---

[159] Brin Thiedeman, National Solutions Director – Health with Oracle Corporation, Australia, with over 25 years data modeling experience, also provided his services on a pro bono basis.

The implemented model bore little relationship to any of the workable models produced by the participants[160], primarily because it did not implement a generalized solution to questionnaire ("survey") structure. Instead, it represented each questionnaire as a separate entity, and subsequently as a separate relational table. This was a considered choice over the more generalized option, based primarily on simplicity of programming. The substantial reduction in flexibility (defined as the ease with which the model can cope with business and / or regulatory change) was partially offset and subsumed by an application-wide assessment of flexibility. It was agreed that adding tables to the database and adapting existing programs was simpler than maintaining the data needed to drive the more generalized option. Understandability was also a key consideration; new users would be more able to understand and use data that was structured to mirror the questionnaires.

11.9. DISCUSSION

The problem presented to participants was simple by industry standards (Maier 1996). Nevertheless, all seven measures of diversity indicated substantial differences amongst the models, and further variations were noted. We now summarize the nature of the diversity, and investigate explanations both compatible and incompatible with the characterization of data modeling as design.

11.9.1. Nature of the diversity

In this section we first discuss the nature of the diversity amongst the models, using Verelst's (2004a) classification of variability (discussed in Section 4.4.1) as a reference. Having noted a diverse range of potentially workable models, we then ask whether some are significantly better than others, or conversely, whether some (or even most) are markedly inferior, to the extent of not being true "solutions" that would count towards diversity. Quality assessment now takes a central role in the argument, insofar as it provides a potential means of reducing the number of acceptable models – in the extreme, to a single "right" or "best" representation. We examine the results of the expert evaluation, and discuss the limitations of

---

[160] One model showed the rudiments of a structure similar to that of the real-life solution, but was not developed beyond that. A "show of hands" as to level of generalization (which included participants who did not submit models) also produced only one person (presumably the same one) who had modeled individual surveys.

existing quality frameworks in differentiating amongst solutions produced by experienced modelers.

Characterizing the variation

The diversity in models could not be attributed entirely or even substantially to simple modeling errors (as distinct from contestable judgments that some might classify as "errors"), although a substantial number (29%) of the models were judged as unsound. The focus of the assessment of diversity was on core elements of the models, with unsound models (or, as appropriate, unsound components) being excluded.

There was evidence of all three of Verelst's (2004a) categories of variability:

- *Construct variability* (use of different modeling constructs – in the case of the conventions used here, entities, relationships and attributes – to represent the same real-world concepts) was evident in the choices described in Section 11.7.3. Such variability has not been noted in previous empirical studies; on the contrary, they suggest that choice of construct is relatively straightforward (Batra and Davis 1992). The choice of construct is not merely one of alternative representations, although that may have been true in the case of the entity / relationship alternatives. For example, the models that represented *Question* as an entity rather than an attribute allowed common questions to be represented independent of particular questionnaires. In each of the examples identified in the present research, one option was clearly preferred.

- *Vertical abstraction variability* (different levels of generalization) was evident in the generalization choices described in Section 11.7.3. The possibility, and to some extent the implications, of representing a concept at different levels of generalization are recognized in the literature (Simsion 1989; Hoberman 2002 pp363-426). Different choices in this area were the principal source of variability raised in thought-leader discussions (Section 6.4.5).

- *Horizontal abstraction variability* (choice of alternative abstractions at the same or similar level of generalization) was less obvious: an example was the modeling of surveys as National Survey and State Survey in some models and Patient Survey and Health-Worker Survey in others. It was also apparent in the diversity of entity names across the models. In the absence of supporting descriptions it is difficult to distinguish between simple synonyms and (perhaps subtle) differences in definitions.

Verelst does not claim that the framework covers all variation. The variation across the ten sub-models (model components) evaluated by the experts was not easily characterized by the framework. Nor could the models be simply decomposed and compared component by component. Lawson's design property (Section 2.2) *Design solutions are often holistic responses* seems pertinent. In the next section, we look at a more holistic comparison of models, based on quality criteria that apply to the models as a whole rather than to individual components.

Data model quality – and quality frameworks

The quality assessment described in Section 11.7.3 showed that although the expert data modelers were consistent in their overall evaluation of models, as indicated by the high inter-rater reliability ratings, there was no consensus as to which of four superior – and distinctly different – models was best. This was an unusually well-qualified panel of experts[161]; regardless of whether one of these models is objectively better than the others, it seems clear that all four would be likely to be accepted if proposed in a practical setting. Every one of the ten models was rated as workable by at least one evaluator and above the benchmark level by at least two. One evaluator wrote that she had encountered a similar scenario in practice (questionnaire processing) and noted that the solution closely matched Model No. 7. It bears noting in this context that her selection of a single model implies a clear differentiation of at least that model from the other nine.

The expert evaluation highlighted the limitations of existing data model quality frameworks in discriminating amongst models produced by experienced data modelers in practical situations. The syntactic correctness criterion was not considered relevant to the present work, and indeed arguably belongs to a different category from the other criteria. Experienced modelers did not generally make mistakes with syntax – nor should we expect them to. The criterion seems more useful for assessing a modeler's ability than choosing amongst models in a

---

[161] In number, qualifications and industry reputation it appears to be considerably stronger than any previously assembled for a published empirical study.

practical situation. It is perhaps a legacy of the framework's roots in assessment of students' work.

The completeness criterion is from Kim and March (1995), and was designed to check whether semantics incorporated in a problem statement had been included in the model – again rather a test of modeler competence (the *Person* dimension of the 5Ps framework, perhaps) than of product quality. In applying the criterion to a practical example, the name *completeness* is misleading insofar as anything other than a perfect score suggests that something has been overlooked. Not including semantics in the structure of the model may (and should) reflect a considered decision to hold them elsewhere. Simsion's (1994; 2005a) quality framework includes separate dimensions for completeness and enforcement of business rules.

Moody and Shanks' (2003) *simplicity* measure is simply a count of entities and relationships. Their empirical research did not establish it a substantial contributor to overall model quality (partial correlation (beta) of 0.033[162] in regression analysis). The present research showed a clear *negative* correlation (beta = 0.40, sig < 0.0005) with overall model quality.

Flexibility ratings made a negligible contribution (beta=0.017) in Moody and Shanks' regression model; here they were the most important contributor. This is interesting: English (1999 pp87-89) describes (and cites in the interview reported in Chapter 4– Section 6.4.5) a three-criterion framework for data quality in which two of the criteria are more precise versions of *flexibility* – viz *flexibility* and *stability*. This distinction was important in the real-world choice of a model that offered good flexibility (ease of extension to meet new requirements) rather than stability (no change in the face of new requirements) (Section 11.8).

Finally, *understandability* was the strongest contributor to overall quality in Moody and Shanks study (beta=0.53) whereas here it was the smallest. A possible explanation is that Moody and Shanks' evaluators preferred models that they could readily understand themselves. It appears that they were required to evaluate 35 models (the models were from the study in Shanks 1997b) with a mean of 32 entities and relationships (experts) and 24 entities and relationships (novices), with a mean understandability rating (as assessed by the evaluators themselves) of below the midpoint of the Likert scale. In the present study, with ten models, "cleaned up" in terms of presentation and standardized entity names and

---

[162] Significance value was not reported.

definitions, and a mean of 11 entities and relationships, the expert evaluators still found the task challenging, as indicated by correspondence with the author. An alternative explanation, consistent with the ultimate real-life choice of an easy-to-understand structure over one that was more stable, is that expert practitioners underrate the importance of understandability to non-expert stakeholders. (The evaluators in Shanks' (1997b) study were academics specializing in conceptual data modeling.)

In the context of the description / design question and Lawson's design Property (Section 2.2) *there are no optimal solutions to design problems,* it is worth noting that of the four measures used, all but one (*complexity*) required subjective evaluation.

As noted earlier, the three factors (*flexibility, understandability, complexity*) accounted for only 44% of the variation in the overall quality rating, although one of the evaluators (David Hay) commented "Certainly your rating descriptions [overall quality as described, understandability, flexibility] represent absolutely appropriate goals for data modeling." Conversely, the consistency amongst evaluators suggests that further underlying factors, not currently included in the framework, may have played a role.

11.9.2. Diversity as a consequence of design

I drew on abstract models from Hay and Silverston[163]

– Participant No. 149

Works very like a genealogical database

– Participant No. 118

Having noted the diversity amongst the models, we reiterate that diversity of product is a central distinguishing feature of design. This theoretical view has been reinforced in this book by the thought-leader positions (Chapter 6), in which diversity of product was a major point of dissent, and the *Characteristics of Data Modeling* survey (Chapter 10) in which responses to the 'diversity of product' questions were strong predictors of a respondent's overall position on the description / design question. Within the design characterization, two important

---

[163] Authors of books of data model patterns.

(and associated) sources of difference are the use of patterns, and individual style. We discuss each below.

Eighty-three and a half percent of participants stated that they had drawn on data models which they had seen or used in the past. If the patterns that the data modelers are drawing upon are different, we have an immediate source of diversity. The figure of 83.5% is very high, considering that 32.6% of the sample claimed to have developed five models or less. In the *Characteristics of Data Modeling* survey (Chapter 7), a smaller percentage of respondents agreed or strongly agreed with the propositions:

- I frequently re-use patterns (structures) from other data models that I have developed myself. (76.3% agreed)

- I frequently re-use patterns (structures) that I have seen in models developed by others. (67.6% agreed)

The higher percentage here could be a result of reflecting on a specific and recent task, rather than responding in the abstract.

It is possible that individual data modelers prefer particular representations or structures independent of the specific modeling problem. "Style" is a well-recognized distinguishing characteristic of designers (Section 4.3.4). While there was no correlation found between the three "attribute or entity" construct decisions noted, there was a correlation between the generalization decisions. This is in line with David Hay's observation reported in Section 6.4.6 that modelers tend to choose a consistent level throughout a model. As the research task only entailed a single modeling exercise, it was not possible to determine whether the preferences would apply across more than one model.

11.9.3. Alternative explanations for the diversity

The purpose of this component of the research was to investigate diversity in data models because diversity is a distinguishing characteristic of design. The diversity of workable models observed is consistent with the design paradigm; however, the data collected allows some examination of alternative explanations that could be supported within the description paradigm.

It is possible that the diversity is a result of inadequate information and consequent different assumptions by the modelers, and that the different models would converge on a common solution if a more complete set of information was available. There is some subtlety in this argument, insofar as a sufficiently precise set of information would effectively describe the model (analogously to an architect's client specifying the exact dimensions of each room). As a practical matter, we can look at whether the modelers believed that they were provided with sufficient information: it is reasonable to assume that they would then regard any assumptions which they made as within their discretion.

As noted in Section 11.7.1, 79[164]% of respondents stated either that they did not make any guesses about the requirements or made only guesses which were "unimportant". Fifty eight percent of respondents stated that they understood the requirements "fairly well" or "very well". Nor can lack of time be cited as a major cause of diversity with 69% of participants stating that they did not expect that their model would be substantially different if they had more time for the exercise.

The argument that differences arose because modelers lacked the competence necessary to tackle the model has some substance; despite questionnaire responses indicating that the problem was well understood and the task not difficult, there was a substantial number of poor models. On the other hand, the group of ten models evaluated by the experts, and selected not primarily on quality but because the entity choices made them more easily comparable, were largely rated as workable. Models of poor quality will inevitably have contributed to the diversity, but diversity remains once they are discounted.

It is possible that the modeling problem was unusually amenable to diverse solutions, and hence not representative of problems that would be encountered in practice. As the problem was chosen by the author, there is the possibility of researcher bias. Against this argument is the fact that the problem was a "real-world" example (unlike most data modeling research examples, as noted in Section 5.3). Further, it reflected a scenario that we could expect to occur elsewhere, as confirmed by comments from one of the participants and one of the expert evaluators. Finally it was a very simple problem, at least as measured by the total number of entities and relationships in the solutions and the short time required to produce at least outlines of solutions.

---

[164] Percentages cited in this section refer to the percentage of *valid* responses.

11.9.4. Summary

In a relatively simple, constrained exercise, data modelers (most of them experienced) produced a wide range of different workable conceptual data models in response to a common scenario. A selected subset of these were evaluated by experts as providing a suitable basis of workable, acceptable and different database schemas, with no agreement as to which solution was best.

This is a strong result in support of the view that data modeling problems have multiple workable solutions that differ in non-trivial ways, and that selection amongst them is at least partly subjective. As such, it is a strong result in support of the design characterization.

Finally, we should note that the generalizability of the most important results here does not depend on the composition or representativeness of the sample. The key result is a *demonstration* that some practitioners will produce different viable solutions to the same problem.

CHAPTER 12
DIVERSITY IN LOGICAL DATA MODELING

The devil is in the detail.

– Anon

God is in the detail.

– Mies van der Rohe

12.1. OBJECTIVES AND APPROACH

Chapter 11 examined diversity of product in the conceptual data modeling stage of data modeling, and reported that practitioners faced with a common scenario produced a variety of different solutions. As the possibility of multiple solutions is one of the defining characteristics of design disciplines (Section 4.4), this result provided some support for characterizing that stage of data modeling as design. The research component described in this chapter looks at diversity of product in the *logical data modeling* stage of database design – after the initial identification of entities, relationships and attributes (*conceptual data modeling*), but before the introduction of performance goals and decisions (*physical data modeling / physical database design*). Diversity in physical data modeling is outside the scope of this project (Section 1.4.2).

Although there is no consensus amongst academics (Chapter 3) or practitioners (Chapter 8) as to the exact boundaries of logical data modeling, there is broad agreement that it takes into account the generic database architecture and includes table and column[165] definition prior to compromises needed to achieve performance goals. Normalization is included in this stage.

In many descriptions of data modeling, the logical data modeling stage is characterized as a mechanistic (and deterministic) transformation of a conceptual data model (Section 3.6). In contrast, the study of practitioners' perceptions of

---

[165] The term "column" suggests a relational database implementation. Given the dominance of DBMSs based on the Relational Model, and use of a relational example for the exercise described in this chapter, we use relational terminology throughout this chapter, and prefer the industry standard terms (ISO/IEC9075-1:2003 2003) *table, column* and *row* to *relation, attribute* and *tuple*.

data modeling *Scope and Stages* reported in Chapter 8 suggested that practitioners may make a number of decisions during this stage. Simsion and Witt's (2005 pp321-357)) discussion of the stage identifies some 20 decision types, within a scope that is narrower than that described by the *Scope and Stages* results. A middle position is taken by authors such as Halpin (2001 pp403-456) who provide a default transformation, but also guidance and heuristics as to when and how to deviate from it. Halpin's advice focuses on changes to meet performance or application programming requirements.

The practical question (the *Diversity in Logical Modeling* sub-question from Section 7.2) is: *Will different data modeling practitioners produce different logical data models from the same conceptual data model?* Designing a laboratory task[166] to investigate this is reasonably straightforward – more so than for the conceptual modeling stage described in Chapter 11, as we can reduce the potential ambiguities associated with human stakeholders' descriptions of the scenario by presenting participants with a detailed conceptual model as a starting point. With a well-controlled input, it is less easy to attribute differences in models to differences in perception of the problem.

An appropriately-designed task also allows, as did the conceptual modeling task (Chapter 11) a preliminary investigation of *style–* a distinguishing feature of design disciplines. We look for indications of consistency (or bias) in decision-making across each model that cannot be explained solely in terms of the data modeler's level of expertise or adherence to a particular convention. This issue is taken up in more depth in Chapter 13, where we look for evidence of consistency *across* models.

The remainder of this chapter follows the same sequence as other chapters that present empirical results. The initial sections cover the research design, measures, materials, and methods specific to this research component (aspects common to all empirical components are covered in Section 7.4). The next section describes the sample (participants), including response rates and demographics. Results are then presented as described in the *Method* section. The chapter concludes with a discussion of results and their implications for the description / design question.

---

[166] The word "experiment" has been avoided as the task does not comply with the definition as used strictly in social research. Our interest is in description and measurement rather than causality, and the task design reflects that.

12.2. RESEARCH DESIGN

This research component tested the contention that different data modelers will produce different models in response to a common set of requirements. It was designed around a data modeling task conducted in the field under controlled conditions, similar to the laboratory conditions used in other empirical work in data modeling (Chapter 5).

The task needed to meet a number of requirements:

1. The problem must be simple enough to allow most participants to complete it in the time that could reasonably be allowed (no more than 20 minutes within the one-day seminars that provided access to experienced modelers).

2. The problem should have face validity; it should be one which data modelers could expect to encounter in practice, allowing for some simplification. Ideally it should be based on a real problem to reduce the possibility and appearance that it was contrived to encourage (or restrict) variability in the models.

3. The domain should be familiar to modelers to avoid conflicting assumptions and reduce the need for explanation. There is an alternative argument that the problem should be designed to eliminate the imposition of assumptions derived from real-world experience; the extreme view of this would entail the use of "meaningless" data names. This approach was rejected as incompatible with objective (2) and probably with (1) as extra time would probably be required to gain understanding of an unfamiliar domain.

A data modeling problem which the author had encountered during a consulting assignment provided an excellent fit. It dealt with budgeted and actual expenditure – a scenario most practitioners might be expected to have encountered in a business or personal context if not as a modeling problem *per se*. The business stakeholders had provided an initial model in the form of a single table with columns based on their existing (manual) records. At the time, the author re-worked the model without explicit consideration of "modeling decisions" and would have described the process as essentially mechanistic and driven by the objective of producing a fully normalized model. Only some years later did he reflect on the implicit decisions which the model embodied (Simsion 1994 pp228-

232). The task put the same choices in front of participants to observe whether they would make the same decisions as the author – and each other.

The framework for classifying data model variability used in the study of conceptual modeling (Section 11.3.1) was used here with minor adaptations, and provided a starting point for a deeper analysis of differences than that of earlier studies. The demographic data allowed (in particular) comparison of novices and experts. A set of *process* questions addressing assumptions and level of difficulty (common to all modeling exercises used in this research project) was added to the standard demographics questionnaire.

A true experimental dimension was added to this research component to test whether additional information would influence modeling decisions – and hence whether assumptions of this kind could account for differences in the models. In particular, a common argument against using high levels of generalization is that non-expert users will find the structures difficult to understand and use (Simsion 1993; Moody 1996; Shanks 1996b; Hoberman 2002 p369). The hypothesis (supporting the contention, consistent with the descriptive characterization, that differences in models are due to differences in perceived requirements) was that participants who were advised that the users of the database would be accountants would produce less generalized models than participants who were advised that the users would be expert programmers. A two-group, post-test only design was used. There were two versions of the task statement, specifying different users, and allocation of participants to a particular version was random.

12.3. ASSESSMENT OF DIVERSITY

The assessment of diversity used five measures. The first four were drawn from those used for the study of conceptual modeling[167] (Section 11.3.1) and their provenance is not repeated here.

1. The perceived level of difference between pairs of models as reported on the questionnaires.

2. The number of tables in each model.

---

[167] The conceptual modeling study used two additional measures: *matching nouns* (not relevant here as the problem was not in the form of a text description) and horizontal variability which in this case is closely related to level of generalization.

3.   The variety of table names after consolidation of obvious synonyms.

4.   Whether particular concepts were represented as tables or as columns[168], and the level of generalization chosen for any such tables (*choice of construct*).

5.   Which columns were generalized or changed to improve consistency of representation (the latter being an implicit generalization insofar as the column is recognized as belonging to a common class of columns). A *Generalization Score* was calculated by scoring one point for each instance in which a generalized or consistent representation was chosen over the original representation. Generalization scores were tested for correlation with the problem variants (the alternative responses to the question "who's going to use this database"), the demographic groupings (Section 7.4.3), and the responses to the process questions.

A log of observations of individual models was kept, noting significant variations that fell outside those covered by the indicators above.

---

[168] If a concept was represented as a table, the column would usually appear also as the primary key of that table and as foreign key in other tables.

12.4. MATERIALS

The task, as presented to participants, is shown in Figure 12-1.

Budgeted and Actual Expenditure

Draw a data model (to serve as the specification for a relational database) for the following scenario. If you run out of time, just provide a list of entities or tables.

The user has given you a list of data items (below). "These are the things we need to report on", she says. "Each Department has an annual budget, covering expenditure on Labor, Material and Other (miscellaneous) items, broken down into four quarters. Later we record the actual expenditure, so that we can compare budgeted and actual expenditure. We want to produce a whole range of reports – for example comparing Labor expenditure across Departments, or within the same Department over several years.

Department Number (Primary key item)

Year (Primary key item)

Approved-By

Budget-First-Quarter-Material

Budget-Second-Quarter-Material

Budget-Third-Quarter-Material

Budget-Last-Quarter-Material

Actual-First-Quarter-Material

Actual-Second-Quarter-Material

Actual-Third-Quarter-Material

Actual-Total-Material

Budget-First-Quarter-Labor

Budget-Second-Quarter-Labor

Budget-Third-Quarter-Labor

Budget-Last-Quarter-Labor

Actual-First-Quarter-Labor

Actual-Second-Quarter-Labor

Actual-Third-Quarter-Labor

Actual-Total-Labor

Budget-Other

Actual-Other

Discretionary-Spending-Limit

Questions and Answers

What does the data item "Approved-By" mean?
It is the ID of the manager who approved the budget for that Department and that year.

What does the item "Discretionary-Spending-Limit" mean?
It is the maximum amount which that Department may spend on any single item without senior management approval. It may vary from year to year.

Why are Labor and Material amounts recorded by quarter, whereas Other amounts appear to be recorded only as totals for the entire year?
"Other" expenditure is generally small, and in the past we haven't seen a need to break it down into quarters. Doing so would not be difficult, though.

Who's going to use this database?

Version 1:

Mainly the accounting people. They have a team of expert programmers available to develop data entry and reporting programs and to respond to ad hoc reporting needs.

Version 2:

Mainly the accounting people who will want to produce various ad hoc reports. They have worked with the DBMS before and are confident that they can also build some simple data entry screens.

Figure 12-1: Annual Budget task

It bears noting that the model as presented is a workable specification for a database: a single table as per Figure 12-1 enables the users' data to be stored, and is fully normalized[169]. There is no need for the modeler to add further information about the Universe of Discourse.

The two versions of the answer to *who is going to use the database?* were to support the testing of the hypothesis that modelers who were told that accountants would use the model would be less likely to introduce new generalized concepts.

The reference to "data entry" programs or screens in both versions of the task characterizes the database as supporting transaction processing. Without this information it might be interpreted by some as a data warehouse or data mart application, which could influence the choice of data model structures (Kimball 2002 p11).

12.5. METHOD

Aspects of method common to several components of the research, including survey piloting, administration, ethical issues, coding of demographics and use of statistics are covered in Chapter 7.

12.5.1. Administration of laboratory task

The Logical Data Modeling task and associated questionnaire were administered to attendees at seminars on advanced data modeling conducted by the author at four locations. The administration followed the general procedure described in Section 7.4, with the following additions:

- The problem was piloted during data modeling training courses for experienced practitioners. It became apparent that almost any practical time-frame would be considered too short by some participants. This was consistent with observations that the design process is endless (Section 4.3.1) (Lawson 1997) and that data modelers have difficulty in judging when to stop (Moody 1995; Avison and Fitzgerald 2003 p180). On the basis of this experience, participants were told that they had ten

---

[169] The various quarterly items are not technically repeating groups as they stand – they are different items with different names and meanings. Viewing them as repeating groups requires generalization (a decision that in fact many of the participants took).

minutes for completion of the exercise, but were given a further two minutes at the end of that period to complete the exercise and a further five to complete the questionnaire[170].

- Participants at some locations[171] were asked to pair off with a person of their choice on the same side of the room (the two questionnaire variants were distributed to different sides) and assess the amount of difference between their partner's model and their own. To encourage participants to take the task seriously, they were informed in advance that they would be showing their model to another participant. This part of the exercise was voluntary. Seven minutes was provided for the comparison.

12.5.2. Initial review and coding

Demographic information was coded according to the procedure and coding schemes described in Section 7.4. As this was a simpler and considerably more constrained problem than the conceptual modeling task described in Chapter 11, it was not considered necessary to use external experts to validate the workability of the models. All models were reviewed by the author (and experienced data modeling consultant) and an assistant (working together) to establish:

1. Whether each model was syntactically sound – in particular whether it was normalized. This was a process of looking for errors (e.g. primary key not unique) rather than a review against a formal checklist. Some latitude was allowed here if the intent was clear – for example if the model showed a relationship but the foreign key had been incorrectly marked.

2. Whether each model was semantically adequate insofar as a database that implemented it would be able to hold any data that a direct implementation of the original model would be able to hold. There was no requirement that every business rule (constraint) implied by the original model be implemented in the new model, provided that the rule

---

[170] Times for this stage varied slightly when the participants had a second model to complete – see Section 13.5.1 for details.

[171] Pittsburgh and London. The decision was made on the basis of total time available for research tasks at each seminar.

could reasonably be implemented in some other part of the final application.

To support the measurement of diversity as described in Section 12.3:

1. The number of tables in each model was recorded.

2. All table names used in the models were noted, and their frequency of use across all models recorded. Obvious synonyms were consolidated.

3. Concepts that had been represented as tables in some models and (only) as columns in others were noted, as were differences in the level of generalization of the tables. A coding scheme was established to represent the options and the choices made in each model were recorded.

4   A list of differences in levels of generalization (including "consistency" decisions) across models was produced. A coding scheme was established to represent the options and the choices made in each model were recorded.

12.5.3. Analysis of diversity

The measures set out in Section 12.3 were calculated and checked for differences across the standard demographic splits (Section 7.4.3).

For Diversity Measure No. 4 (choice of construct), a table showing the frequency with which each *combination* of choices appeared was constructed. This provided a picture of overall variation due to these construct choices. Covariance of construct choices was measured to determine whether modelers showed consistency in preferring one construct over another.

Similarly, for Diversity Measure No. 5 (column generalization), a table showing the frequency with which each *combination* of choices appeared was constructed. This provided a picture of overall variation due to these generalization decisions. Covariance of decisions was measured to determine whether modelers showed consistency in preferring a higher or lower level of generalization.

Finally, to provide a picture of overall variation attributable to objective measures of difference, a table showing the frequency with which different combinations of number of tables, construct choices, and column generalization choices appeared was constructed.

12.6. SAMPLES

The logical data modeling task and associated questionnaire were administered to attendees at advanced data modeling seminars conducted by the author at the European Data Management Association / Metadata Annual Conference in London[172], UK and the Enterprise Data Forum[173] in Pittsburgh, USA, both in November 2002. Both conferences attracted predominantly practitioner audiences. The initial analysis of diversity was based on results from these conferences.

Later, the Annual Budget problem was incorporated into a laboratory task investigating data modeling style, described in Chapter 13, conducted in at an advanced data modeling workshop in Stockholm Sweden, in March 2004 and a commercial advanced data modeling class in Los Angeles (LA), USA, in November 2004. Because of time restrictions[174], the task component in which participants compared their model with that of another participant was not included at these locations.

The analysis of table names, perceptions of others' models, and number of tables used responses from London and Pittsburgh. The analysis of generalization decisions and their correlations with demographic measures used responses from all four locations.

---

[172] This seminar was conducted jointly with Graham Witt. Mr Witt did not participate in the seminar until after the completion of the research activities.

[173] The Enterprise Data Forum was a commercial conference run by Wilshire Conferences and attracting a predominantly North American audience.

[174] At these locations, time needed to be allocated for participants to develop a second model.

Sample sizes are shown in Table 12–1.

Location	Number of attendees	Number of responses which included a model	User Alternative 1 "Expert Programmers"	User Alternative 2 "Accountants"
London	20 (est.)	17	6	11
Pittsburgh	30 (est.)	22	12	10
Stockholm	40	27	11	16
Los Angeles	35	30	17	13
TOTALS	125	96 (77%)	46	50

Table 12–1: Participants in logical data modeling task

Two participants returned the questionnaire but did not submit a model.

12.7. RESULTS

12.7.1. Process: Perceptions of the task

Hard to get into the mood – then it's easy

– Stockholm Respondent No. 11

Twenty-five respondents provided responses stating that they understood the problem fairly well, did not find it "very difficult", made only unimportant guesses and did not think their models would be substantially different if more time was allowed i.e. they did not provide any reason that their model would be different in a practical setting. The time factor was the most significant contributor to the relatively small size of this group, consistent with experience in piloting the task (Section 12.5.1). If this factor is excluded, the size of the group increases to 41.

There was a moderate negative correlation (gamma = -0.42, p=0.003) between understanding of the problem and perceived difficulty. Perceived difficulty was also significantly higher for novice modelers (1 year or less experience, Gamma = 0.53, p=0.004; one model or less, Gamma = 0.51, p=0.05).

Pattern re-use was moderately (negatively) correlated with perceived difficulty (Gamma = -0.40, p= 0.008), and with the perception that the models would be different if more time was available (Gamma = -0.49, p=0.01). There was no significant correlation (p>0.28) between pattern re-use and any of the four standard experience groupings.

12.7.2. Accuracy and completeness of models

Ninety-three of the 96 solutions were presented as diagrams, using Information Engineering ("crow's foot") conventions. Two used relational notation, and the remaining model used the British Army standard of CBML (Department of Defence (UK) 2005).

Most models included lists of columns within or adjacent to the boxes on the diagram. Many were supplemented with explanations, coding schemes and / or commentary. A few models included only primary key columns or did not include columns at all. In these cases it was assumed that columns would be located in the correct tables with respect to the specification, as determined by the rules of normalization. Such assignment of columns was generally straightforward.

All but two of the submitted models were judged as being workable in that they were able to support the data specified by the original table. This is not the same as saying that the models were semantically complete: almost all solutions omitted some constraints that were present in the original model. In many cases provision had been made for such constraints to be represented as data values; in the remainder it was not difficult to envisage how they might be implemented in procedural logic.

For example, the original table included separate columns for each quarterly material budget. Some models generalized these into a single Quarterly Material Budget column and a Quarter Number column (as in Figure 12-9 that appears later in this chapter), losing the constraint that there could only be four quarterly amounts in each year. This constraint could readily be implemented in procedural code or (if the model provided for it) as a data value in a column Maximum Number of Quarters[175].

---

[175] In fact, no model provided such a column, though several provided reference ("look-up") tables with allowed values for categorical items such as "labor" and "material".

Some modelers included semantics that were not present in the original problem, presumably drawing on direct knowledge of the business domain or of models of similar domains.

The tables generally met Parsons and Wand's (1992; 1996) guidelines for choosing classes. As noted in Section 4.4.2, these guidelines reflect common modeling practice, and violations would have been obvious to the reviewers. More broadly, it was difficult to find violations of any widely promulgated guidelines; even optional columns which are sometimes advised against (Date 1998 pp575-577) were unusual.

With three exceptions (LA No. 31 contained a transitive dependency in one table and LA No. 34 and LA No. 35 carried derivable totals) all models were fully normalized[176]. There were some minor oversights (e.g. failure to correctly include a foreign key to support a relationship[177] or omission of a reasonably obvious column) and ambiguities largely arising from difficulty deciphering handwritten models. These were corrected to allow the models to be included in the analysis.

Thirteen of the models included subtype structures. Although these could be implemented directly using some (extended) relational DBMSs – in particular those complying with the SQL99 or later standard, (ISO/IEC9075-1:2003 2003)) – they were converted to pure relational form to allow comparison with other models. As discussed in Section 3.6, there is no consensus on the best mapping of subtypes to tables: we used the mapping at the supertype level recommended by Halpin (2001 p428) and implemented in, *inter alia*, the *Powerdesigner* and the *Visio for Enterprise Architects* (Halpin, Evans et al. 2003) modeling tools. The mapping was chosen because it was the most conservative approach in supporting an assessment of diversity, as it minimized the total number of tables, and did not treat alternative subtypings – or the use of subtypes in itself – as giving rise to difference.

---

[176] In the few cases in which the modeler did not provide for a full list of columns, some straightforward (and generally obvious) assumptions were made about the columns that would be allocated to each table. The imposition of such assumptions in a consistent manner by the author may have contributed to an underestimate of underlying model diversity.

[177] Most of the models used "Information Engineering" conventions for the diagrams, including relationships between tables. Some models consistently included the foreign keys required to support the relationship; others consistently excluded them. These differences were treated as differences in conventions rather than actual differences in the models for the purpose of this research. The "minor oversights" referred to here relate to inconsistency or inaccuracy in the use of the conventions.

12.7.3. Diversity measures

Diversity measures were calculated as per Section 12.3 and are presented here. For Measure 4 (choice of construct) and Measure 5 (choice of column generalization) we also show the frequency with which different combinations of choices appear in the models.

Diversity measure no. 1: Participants' perceptions of difference

I'd hate to say mine was the 'right' way, but let's just say, it, hopefully, was an acceptable version. I didn't have the time to fully analyze and critic [sic] the other model, but I had a 'sense' it was wrong, even though every piece of data had a home.

— Pittsburgh Respondent No. 61

Table 12–2 summarizes the responses to the question: "How similar were the two models?" for London and Pittsburgh (this part of the task was not included for the Stockholm and LA groups). Eight respondents did not answer this question (including two who did not submit models).

Location	London	Pittsburgh	Total	Percentage
Models were identical	0	0	0	0%
Models were identical except for naming / agreed errors	2	1	3	9.1%
Models were structurally different in minor ways	8	5	13	39.4%
Models were structurally different in important ways	7	10	17	51.5%
Total	17	16	33	100%

Table 12–2: Participants perceptions on "How similar were the two models?"

Diversity measure no. 2: Number of tables

Figure 12-2 shows the frequency distribution of the number of tables in the models from London and Pittsburgh. No participant submitted a model with only one table, even though the original one-table model represented a workable, if inelegant, solution. (Some of the inelegance could have been removed by redefinition of columns [e.g. replacing Last Quarter and Total columns with Fourth Quarter columns] within the single table.)

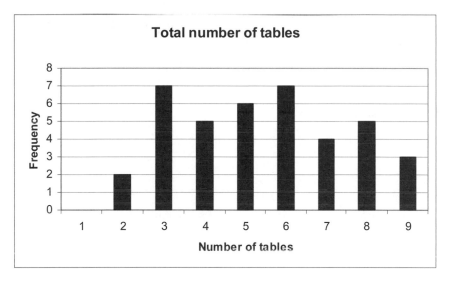

Figure 12-2: Total number of tables

Diversity measure no. 3: Variety of table names

The 39 models from London and Pittsburgh contained, in total, 73 different table names. Consolidation of reasonably obvious synonyms (e.g. Time Period with Time, Budget Item with Budget Line Item, and Expenditure with Expense) yielded a total of 66 names. This number provides only a preliminary indication of diversity. In addition to unrecognized synonyms, it contains some homonyms. In particular, tables named *Department* usually had a primary key of Department Number but some models used this name for a table with primary key of Department Number and Year (surely a poor choice in terms of communication [*understandability* in quality framework language], but not one that was judged to render the models unworkable).

Diversity measure no. 4: Construct variability – column or table?

Examination of the London and Pittsburgh models identified eight concepts that were represented in some models as tables and in others as columns. These are listed in the first column of Table 12–3.

Concept	Not Represented	Column	Literal Table	Generalized Table (in scope)	Generalized Table (beyond scope)	Total
Approved By	0	13	7	1	18	39
Department	0	4	34	1	0	39
Disc Spending Limit	0	27	12	0	0	39
Year	0	26	6	7	0	39
LMO-Type	14	7	18	0	0	39
Quarter	10	13	8	7	1	39
BA-Type	28	7	4	0	0	39

Table 12–3: Alternative representations of concepts

Where participants implemented tables rather than columns, they frequently added non-key items (e.g. Description) that did not appear in the original model.

The last three concepts in Table 12–3 above do not directly reflect columns in the original table. They were introduced by modelers to capture semantics lost as a result of generalizing some of the original columns. For example, if the modeler had generalized the columns Budget-First-Quarter-Material, Budget-Second-Quarter-Material, Budget-Third-Quarter-Material, and Budget-Last-Quarter-Material to produce a new column Quarterly-Material-Budget, then they would have needed to add a column Quarter to identify which quarter a particular Quarterly-Material-Budget referred to. This modeling decision is illustrated by the model of Figure 12-3[178] Stockholm Number 17 (the Expenditure Type and Expenditure tables are the relevant part of the model).

---

[178] For consistency, all models are presented using relational notation regardless of the conventions used by the participants.

```
DEPARTMENT (Department Number, Manager Id)

MANAGER (Manager Id)

BUDGET (Department Number, Year, Discretionary
Spending Limit)

YEAR (Year)

EXPENDITURE TYPE (Expenditure Type Code,
Expenditure Type)

EXPENDITURE (Department Number, Year,
Expenditure Type Code, First Quarter Budget,
Second Quarter Budget, Third Quarter Budget,
Fourth Quarter Budget, First Quarter Actual,
Second Quarter Actual, Third Quarter Actual,
Fourth Quarter Actual)
```

Figure 12-3: Example model: Stockholm no. 17

In Figure 12-4, generalization has resulted in two further columns:

Quarter Number arises from the generalization of quarterly amounts.

BA-Type (named, in this solution, "Budget Actual Type") arises from the generalization of Budget and Actual amounts.

```
PARTY (Party ID)

ROLE (Role ID)

PARTY ROLE (Party ID, Role ID)

SPEND LIMIT (Party ID, Year, Limit Amount)

EXPENDITURE TYPE (Expenditure Type Code,
Description)

BUDGET (Expenditure Type Code, Party ID,
Quarter Number, Year, Budget Actual Type,
Amount)
```

Figure 12-4: Example model: London no. 6

Models which did not include the LMO-Type, Quarter, and / or BA-Type concepts (because they did not generalize the relevant columns) are counted under "Not Represented" in the relevant rows of Table 12–3 above.

Some participants had, in implementing a table, generalized the concept which it represented, as indicated by the name of the table and its columns. In some cases the generalization allowed the table to represent two or more concepts already present in the problem description (i.e. Approver *and* Department or Year *and* Quarter). In others (primarily in the case of Approved By) the generalization allowed the table to represent concepts beyond the problem description (e.g. Employee [8 occurrences] Manager [3 occurrences], Person [3 occurrences]). One model (London No. 30) generalized the "quarter" concept by introducing a convention that the value *zero* represented a full year.

The representation of "Approved By" illustrates four different options:

- Column: An "Approved By" column as in the original table

- Literal Table: A table named "Approved By" or "Approver"

- Generalization Within Scope of Problem Description: A table named "Department /Approver"

- Generalization Beyond Scope of Problem Description: A table named "Party".

Table 12–3 shows the frequency with which these four options as well as the "not represented" option were employed across the seven concepts.

Table 12–4 shows how different combinations of these seven decisions resulted in different models. The "Not Represented" option has been combined with the "Column" option (value zero), as the distinction is covered later in this section under *Column Generalization Choices*.

Approved By	Department	DSL	Year	LMO Type	Qtr	BA Type	Frequency
0	0	0	0	0	0	0	5
0	1	0	0	0	0	0	3
0	1	0	1	0	0	0	1
0	1	0	2	0	2	0	2
0	1	1	0	1	0	0	1
0	1	1	2	1	2	0	1
1	0	0	0	0	0	0	1
1	1	0	0	0	0	0	1
1	1	0	1	1	1	1	1
1	1	0	2	1	2	1	1
1	1	1	0	0	0	0	1
1	1	1	1	0	1	0	1
1	1	1	1	1	1	0	1
2	2	1	0	1	0	0	1
3	0	0	0	0	0	0	2
3	0	0	0	1	1	0	1
3	1	0	0	0	0	0	2
3	1	0	0	1	0	0	2
3	1	0	0	1	1	0	1
3	1	0	0	1	3	0	1
3	1	0	1	1	1	1	1
3	1	0	2	1	2	0	2
3	1	1	0	0	0	0	1
3	1	1	0	1	0	0	1
3	1	1	0	1	0	1	1
3	1	1	0	1	1	0	1

0=column or not represented; 1 literal table, 2 generalized in scope, 3 generalized beyond scope

Table 12–4: Combinations of table and column decisions

Approved By	Department	DSL	Year	LMO Type	Qtr	BA Type	Frequency
3	1	1	1	0	1	0	1
3	1	1	2	1	2	0	1

0=column or not represented; 1 literal table, 2 generalized in scope, 3 generalized beyond scope

Table 12-4: (cont.)

The 28 rows in Table 12–4 above represent 28 model variants arising from this set of decisions. If differing levels of generalization are ignored and only the (binary) choices of representing each concept as either a column or table is considered, there are 19 variants attributable purely to different combinations of those choices.

Covariance amongst the eight decisions as to whether to code as a table or column, was 0.70 (KR20 coefficient) indicating some overall consistency in these decisions (0.70 is widely cited as the threshold value for good reliability when using this measure to measure covariance of questions on surveys – in this case decisions play the role of questions). The interpretation is that the underlying concept being measured was the preference for tables over simple column representations. Correlations between individual decisions (phi) ranged from negligible to strong, and were positive in all non-negligible cases.

Diversity measure no. 5: Column definition and generalization scores

Column generalization choices

Examination of the models revealed five common[179] situations in which modelers had made different decisions about the choice and definition of columns. To accommodate some minor variants, two of the decisions were framed in terms of the (business) rules which they supported rather than in terms of the exact implementation. The five situations together with the different options and coding for each are shown in Table 12–5. The option in the column headed "No" is the one used in the original conceptual model. The color coding is retained in later figures.

We refer to all these choices as *generalization decisions*, as they all require at least the recognition of commonality, but they are manifested in different ways:

Gen Qtr, Gen BA and Gen LMO are pure generalization decisions.

Other Qtr is a disaggregation of quarterly Other amounts presumably to achieve consistency with Labor and Material amounts.

Fourth Qtr LM is a consistency decision, bringing representation of fourth quarter amounts in line with other amounts.

Decision Name	Yes (1)	No (2)	Unclear (3)	Both (4)
Gen QTR (generalization decision)	Quarterly amount columns generalized – no columns specific to a particular quarter.	Columns for individual quarters		N/A
Gen LMO (generalization decision)	Labor, Material, Other generalized – no columns specific to a particular type	Specific columns for Labor, Material, Other amounts		N/A
Gen BA (generalization decision)	Budget and Actual columns generalized no columns specific to a particular type.	Specific Columns for Budget and Actual amounts		N/A
Other QTR (consistency / disaggregation decision)	Support for quarterly values[180] for "Other" amounts – no column for annual amount	Support only for annual values for Other amounts –		Both options supported
Fourth QTR LM (consistency decision)	Direct representation of Fourth Quarter Labor and Material Actual amounts	Annual totals held for Labor and Material Actual amounts		N/A

Table 12–5: Generalization choices in the logical data models

All but one of the twelve models that retained Budget-Last-Quarter Labor and Budget-Last-Quarter-Material columns rather than generalizing them replaced the word "Last" with "Fourth" in the names. This is noted as an example of implicit generalization but is not included in the assessment of generalization decisions as it did not affect the structure of the models.

Figure 12-5 shows the frequency distribution of the decisions. Results from all four locations are included.

---

[179] Each of the alternative decisions occurred in at least five models.

[180] The original model supported only annual values for Other amounts – Labor and Material amounts were recorded on a quarterly basis.

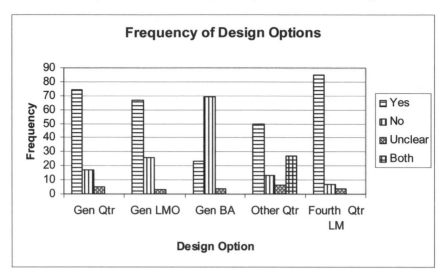

Figure 12-5: Frequency of design options

Combinations of column generalization choices

Table 12–6 shows how these decisions were combined in the models, and the number of occurrences of each combination.

Gen Qtr	Gen LMO	Gen BA	Other Qtr	Fourth Qtr LM	Frequency
1	1	1	1	2	13
1	1	1	2	2	1
1	1	1	4	1	6
1	1	2	1	1	20
1	1	2	1	2	1
1	1	2	3	1	1
1	1	2	4	1	15
1	1	3	1	1	1
1	1	3	4	1	2
1	2	1	1	1	1
1	2	2	1	1	5
1	2	2	2	1	3
1	2	2	2	2	2
1	2	2	4	1	1
1	3	1	4	1	1
1	3	3	1	1	1
2	1	1	1	1	1
2	1	2	1	1	3
2	1	2	4	1	1
2	2	2	1	1	3
2	2	2	2	1	4
2	2	2	2	2	2
2	2	2	3	1	1
2	2	2	3	2	1
2	2	2	4	1	1
3	1	2	3	3	2
3	2	2	1	1	1
3	2	2	2	3	1
3	3	2	3	3	1
					96

Table 12–6 Model variants arising from different column generalization decisions

287

The 18 rows in Table 12–6 that do not contain a '3' (i.e. for which all decisions were clear) represent 18 valid model variants which are attributable solely to these column definition decisions.

There are some interesting correlations amongst the decisions, as is evident from Figure 12-6, in which each column represents a model, and the shaded cells indicate which generalization decisions (codes 1 and 4 combined) were taken. Models with any unclear decisions (coded '3') have been excluded.

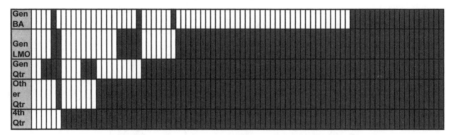

Figure 12-6: Generalization decisions in individual models

Figure 12-6 shows a hierarchy of decision making in which (for example), 19 of the 22 modelers who generalized Budget and Actual amounts (Gen BA) also made the other four generalizations. This graphic impression of covariance amongst the decisions is supported by a value for the KR20 statistic of 0.68. The interpretation is that there was an underlying concept of "propensity to generalize" on the part of the modeler. Correlations between individual decisions (phi) ranged from negligible to strong, and were positive in all cases.

Generalization scores

Generalization scores were calculated by scoring one point for each generalization decision taken (in the case of "Other Quarter" values '2' and '4' both scored one point, as they both represented a decision to generalize[181]). Results from all four locations were included.

Figure 12-7 shows the frequency distribution of the Generalization Scores

---

[181] Alternatives considered were to score 1 point for code 2 and 2 points for code 4 (which would have increased the weight of this component of the score) or to score 1 for code 4 and some lesser score (say ½) for code 2 – which would have reduced the weight of code 2 decisions.

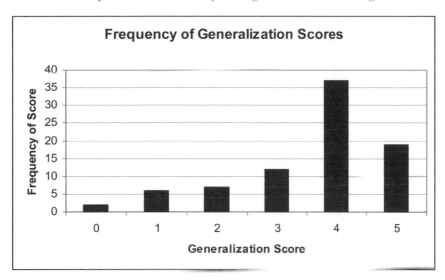

Figure 12-7: Frequency distribution of generalization scores

With one exception, generalization scores were not significantly correlated with the standard demographic groupings or with responses to the process questions. The sole significant correlation was that participants who had developed more than one model in practice had significantly higher generalization scores (Kendall's tau-b =0.34, p=0.002).

Table 12–7 shows the mean generalization totals for the models developed in response to the two alternative answers to the question "Who's going to use this database?"

Who's going to use this database?	N	Mean Gen. Score
Expert Programmers	35	3.69
Accountants	47	3.55

Table 12–7: Generalization scores for alternative scenarios

The difference in means, although in the expected direction, was not significant (t(80) = 0.46, p=0.64).

Overall diversity

Combining the measures

If we draw together the objective[182] indicators of structural difference in models: (number of tables, choice of representation as model or table and column generalization) for the 39 valid London and Pittsburgh responses, we can obtain an overview of the diversity in models resulting from different combinations of these decisions. The full list of decisions shows that only three pairs of models had matching values for the construct (table vs. column) and column choices and that only two models (Pittsburgh 35 and Pittsburgh 46) were the same in all three dimensions. (As a matter of interest, they were checked, and found to be different in other respects – hence no two models from Pittsburgh and London were structurally identical).

Other variation

The measures discussed in the preceding subsection do not account for all differences amongst the models. We noted "unique modeling decisions", falling outside those covered explicitly by the preceding analysis, against fifteen of the models from London and Pittsburgh. For example:

- LA Model No. 19 generalized Labor and Material amounts but did not include Other amounts in the generalization, presumably because the Other amounts were accounted for annually rather than quarterly.

- Pittsburgh Model No. 55 replaced the quarterly amounts with generic amounts plus start and end dates.

- London Model No. 22 changed the accounting periods to months rather than quarters and years – presumably based on some knowledge or experience[183].

Two models introduced a table (and associated new column) to represent valid combinations of LMO-Type (Labor / Material / Other indicator) and BA-Type (Budget / Actual indicator)[184] (Figure 12-8 shows one of these models).

---

[182] Participants' perceptions of partners' models are not included. Nor are differences in table names other than those to which meaning has been attributed through the analysis of modeling decisions.

[183] This was a marginal case when judging "workability", as there was no guarantee that the business would be able to provide amounts on a monthly basis.

```
DEPARTMENT BUDGET (Department, Year, Approved
By [Foreign Key to User ID], Discretionary
Spending Limit)

USER PROFILE (User ID, Name)

REC-TYPE (Rec-Type, Description)

DEPARTMENT BUDGET QUARTER (Department, Year,
Quarter, Rec-Type, Budget/Actual)

Rec-Type has values:

BM for Budget Material; BL for Budget Labor; BO
for Budget Other; AM for Actual Materials; AL
for Actual Labor, AO for Actual Other
```

Figure 12-8: Example model: Pittsburgh no. 26

These two models created "overloaded attributes", or non-scalar types (Date 1998 p115) that can have drawbacks (Fleming and von Halle 1989 pp-312-313; Rob and Coronel 2002 p184; Hoberman 2005 pp66-67; Simsion and Witt 2005 pp150-151) but in exchange supported the enforcement of business rules about allowable combinations of LMO-Type and BA-Type. In this case, the enforcement of the rules would seem to be of limited value (all combinations are possible), and the Description column in the Rec-Type table of questionable utility, prompting the speculation that the modelers may have been applying a familiar pattern. Both modelers responded "Yes" to the question *In developing the data model, did you draw on data models that you have seen or used in the past?*

In a few cases (as in Figure 12-9, below) modelers specified separate tables for budgeted and actual amounts despite them having the same primary key; this represents disaggregation beyond that needed to satisfy 5th Normal Form[185], but is not generally considered an error (Date 1998 p391).

---

[184] A minor correction has been made in reproducing this model; the modeler omitted one of the six combinations.

[185] Some writers discourage such further disaggregation in the interests of simplicity or efficiency without actually proscribing it (e.g. Nijssen and Halpin 1989 254).

```
DEPARTMENT (Department Number)

DEPARTMENT BUDGET YEAR (Department Number,
Year, Discretionary Spending Limit, Approved
By)

BUDGET (Department Number, Year, Quarter,
Budget Material, Budget Labor, Budget Other)

ACTUAL (Department Number, Year, Quarter,
Actual Material, Actual Labor, Actual Other)
```

Figure 12-9: Example model: Pittsburgh no. 20

12.8. DISCUSSION

The data modeling task that formed the focus of this research component entailed only a subset of the activities included in most descriptions of logical data modeling (Section 3.6), and might be better characterized as a model review than as a substantial step in model development. The problem was also very simple by industry standards (Maier 1996).

Nevertheless, each of the five indicators of diversity that were measured – participants' assessment of difference between pairs of models, number of tables, variety of table names, choice between table and column, and column generalization decisions – showed substantial differences amongst the models, and numerous further variations were noted. The last of these measures in particular was designed to be independent of differences in perceptions of scope by focusing on a few common decision areas, yet it accounted for 18 model variants.

12.8.1. Nature of the diversity

Characterizing the variation

The diversity in models could not be attributed to simple modeling errors (as distinct from contestable judgments). In contrast to the solutions to the conceptual modeling task (Chapter 8), almost all models were judged workable, and minor errors were corrected rather than allowing them to contribute to diversity. Given the relative simplicity of the problem and the experience of the participants, the high rates of errors that bedevil data modeling research using students (Chapter 5) would have been surprising. None of the structures that caused difficulties for experienced modelers in Hitchman's (1995) survey were required or used for this task.

Verelst (2004a) classifies variability in (sound) data models into three categories, and there was evidence of all three:

- *Construct variability* is the use of different modeling constructs (in the case of the Relational Model, columns and tables) to represent the same concepts. This was evident in the choices between tables and columns summarized in Table 12–3.

- *Vertical variability* arises from different levels of generalization, and was evident at both the table level (Table 12–3) and the column level (Table 12–5). Differences in level of generalization at the column level were an important contributor to variation, yet are little acknowledged in the literature. For example, Teorey Lightstone et al (2006 p235) *define* generalization only in terms of its applicability to entities. Verelst does include examples at the column / attribute level, and there is some discussion in Hoberman (2002 pp388-399) and Simsion and Witt (Simsion and Witt 2005 pp171-177).

- *Horizontal variability* alternative abstractions at the same or similar level of generalization were apparent in the "consistency" decisions applied to columns (Table 12–5). Replacement of quarter identifiers with start and end dates might also fall into this category. Horizontal variability was less common at the table level. Splitting of budgeted and actual amounts into separate tables with the same primary key was the most obvious example.

Different combinations of some selected decisions in these three categories accounted for 36 variants amongst 39 models.

Verelst does not claim that the framework covers all variation, and in Chapter 8 we noted that much of the difference between models could be best characterized as holistic. Some differences that did not fall obviously into the framework included:

1. Use of subtypes. These were excluded from our assessment of diversity rather than treated as construct variability (because it was assumed that some modelers were using a set of constructs – the pure Relational Model – that did not include subtypes). Including the subtypes and applying a widely-recommended transformation (each supertype and

subtype becomes a table – refer Section 3.6) would have created further differences amongst the models, perhaps best classified as a combination of vertical and horizontal variability.

2. Introduction of semantics not covered in the problem description. This was not a major factor in model variability: despite 48% percent of participants stating that they had deliberately added semantics that could not be deduced from the problem description. This was only obvious in three of the models[186] as evidenced by new concepts, and perhaps in those models that introduced four quarters for Other amounts (to match the rule for Labor and Material amounts) despite the statement in the description that "in the past we haven't seen the need to break it down into quarters" with the qualification that "doing so would not be difficult". It seems that these modelers gave a higher priority to consistency than to the client requirement as stated.

3. Differences in naming. Modelers frequently introduced new names for columns present in the original model, and differed in the names that they gave to new tables and columns. As Len Silverston observed in the thought-leader interviews (Section 6.4.5), variation in names may reflect subtle differences in the definition of a concept. Such differences might fall within the definition of horizontal variability.

Random or systematic?

Some of the diversity in the models arose from different combinations of a relatively small number of modeling decisions – in particular column generalization and choices between (literal or generalized) tables and columns to represent concepts. These decisions (and their measures) were not independent:

1. The very existence of certain constructs (e.g. LMO-Type), and hence the possibility of implementing them as tables was the result of generalization decisions. In turn, these tables contributed to the diversity of table names and affected the number of tables.

2. There was some correlation (from negligible to strong) and covariance amongst the decisions as to whether to implement a concept as a column,

---

[186] London No. 6, London No. 22, Stockholm No. 34

literal table, or generalized table. There appeared to be two factors in play here: the propensity of the modeler to choose a particular construct and the attractiveness of particular constructs to implement each concept (for example, Department was most commonly implemented as a table, Year as a column).

3.   There was similarly some correlation (from negligible to strong) and covariance amongst the column generalization decisions and some evidence of a hierarchy in the decisions.

The net effect of these correlations was that some combinations of decisions were much more common than others, and many did not appear at all.

Model quality – are some solutions better than others?

Having observed a variety of workable models, we need to ask whether some are significantly better than others, or conversely, whether some (or perhaps most) are markedly inferior, to the extent of not being true "solutions" that would count towards diversity. In the preceding chapter we used Moody and Shanks' (2003) quality framework as a basis for independent expert assessment, and noted that it relied heavily on the subjective assessments of the evaluators – who in turn were unable to agree on a clear "winner" amongst at least four of ten different models.

This was a simpler, more constrained task, where the differences in the models could be more easily reduced and described, in contrast to the "holistic" differences in the conceptual models of Chapter 11. It would seem a good candidate for the assessment method typically used for data modeling laboratory tasks – evaluation by the researcher(s) using a set of quality criteria. Unfortunately, as we move beyond the low quality models produced by students (Section 5.2), the ability of even the most well-developed quality framework support an objective comparison of models is severely diminished.

As noted in Section 11.3.2, Moody and Shanks's (2003) quality framework used five criteria used in its empirical validation: syntactic correctness, completeness, simplicity, understandability, flexibility. The syntactic correctness again is of little assistance in differentiating the models produced here. There were few syntactical errors, as would be expected from experienced modelers (and for the purposes of the present research, it makes more sense to rectify obvious errors of this kind as would presumably be done in practice). The *completeness* criterion was potentially misleading. Modelers very frequently removed semantics that were present in the initial model (e.g. limit of four quarters, only three varieties of expenditure, "other" amounts budgeted annually), presumably in the interests of flexibility, simplicity and consistency, and with the implication that they would be handled elsewhere in the application (as noted earlier, this was not difficult to envisage). The *simplicity* measure is simply a count of entities and relationships (tables and foreign keys are the equivalent here), and would therefore be expected to favor the more generic models, which would also be likely to score higher on the *flexibility* measure (Simsion 1989; Hoberman 2002 p367).

In the empirical application of Moody and Shanks's framework, *flexibility* and *understandability* were judged by expert modelers. None of the constructs used in these models were considered difficult to understand by the author's assistant, who had a basic knowledge of modeling, but minimal practical experience. An earlier paper (Moody 1998) suggested that *understandability* might be measured by other stakeholders. It seems likely that the end-users would have been more comfortable with the less-generic models, which contained familiar concepts that the end-users had specified themselves. All of the models could be thus be seen as representing different trade-offs amongst the criteria (excluding *correctness*). Any assessment of relative superiority would be entirely a function of the weightings given to each criterion – which the framework does not yet provide.

The limitations of the framework in assessing "good" models become apparent if we compare the original single-table model, which every modeler chose to "improve", with an archetypal solution embodying the most common combination of column generalization decisions (chosen by 20 of 96 modelers) and the most common (compatible) table vs. column decisions (Figure 12-10).

```
DEPARTMENT (Department ID)

DEPARTMENT BUDGET YEAR (Department ID, Year,
Discretionary Spending Limit, Approved By)

BUDGETED AMOUNT (Department ID, Year, Quarter,
LMO-Type ID, Budget Amount)

ACTUAL AMOUNT (Department ID, Year, Quarter,
LMO-Type ID, Actual Amount)

LMO-TYPE (LMO-Type ID, LMO-Type Name)
```

Figure 12-10: Model synthesized from most common choices

Table 12–8 shows how the archetypal model compares with the original, one-table model. The selection of the superior model according to each dimension of the quality framework is based on the author's application of the comments in the second and third columns of Table 12–8 and those in the discussion above. *Correctness* and *simplicity* are objective measures.

Quality Measure	Original Single-Table Model	Archetypal Solution	Superior model on this measure
Correctness	No syntax errors	No syntax errors	Neither
Completeness	Embodies detailed semantics per original spec.	Missing many semantics in the original spec.	Original
Simplicity	One table	Five tables	Original
Understandability	Uses terms chosen by users; expert can also understand	Uses generalization, introduces new concept (LMO-Type)	Original
Flexibility	Judged adequate by user	Accommodates additional quarters and amount types.	Archetype (but only if this flexibility has business value)

Table 12–8 Quality comparison of archetypal model with original one-table model

The above comparison of models shows the framework producing a verdict contrary to that of the participants in this exercise, unless very heavy weight is given to the ability to introduce additional quarters and amount types (flexibility). As such, it highlights some gaps in the framework. The *simplicity* measure does not capture the consistency that some modelers introduced, presumably in search of conceptual simplicity, though it might be reflected in greater *understandability*. In the same vein, the framework has nothing direct to say on a variety of factors, including choice of construct, that differentiated the solutions to this exercise.

In summary, quality frameworks of this kind, at this stage of their development, can help to articulate some of the ways in which the models differ and the nature of the trade-offs, but are of limited value in allowing a researcher (or practitioner) to objectively choose amongst models of the quality produced in this exercise – which in turn would seem to be a conservative estimate of the quality of models produced in practice, given the limited time allowed.

12.8.2. Source of the diversity

Having noted the diversity amongst the models, it is interesting to look at some possible sources, beyond random variation, consistent with the design characterization.

Fifty-three percent of participants stated that they had drawn on data models which they had seen or used in the past ("pattern re-use"), and 48% stated that they had added "entities, relationships etc that could not be deduced from the problem description alone". These figures may be conservative estimates of the actual use of patterns and external domain knowledge, as they do not take account of unconscious use. The "pattern re-use" figure is well below the 83.5% figure reported in the conceptual modeling task.

Although there was evidence that individual modelers favored certain constructs, this bias did not reach the level of a clear rule. For example, of the 39 models in the London–Pittsburgh sample, only two represented all four of the (observed) columns in the original model as tables, and only one model represented none of them as tables.

Preference for certain structures could be a result of modeler *style* – a propensity towards particular representations independent of the specific modeling problem. As this exercise only entailed a single modeling exercise, it was not possible to determine whether the preferences would apply across more than one model.

It is also interesting to note what the data modelers did *not* do. No modeler *introduced* different structures for labor and material amounts, nor for the different quarterly amounts, nor for budgeted and actual amounts. Given the fairly obvious symmetry in this problem, such differentiation would have been perverse – or at least difficult to explain – but could conceivably have arisen from the modeler's bringing external knowledge about accounting quarters or differences in accounting for labor and material. Some of the variety in the models arose from different levels of consistency being *added*; none arose from it being taken away from the original model.

In contrast to generalization, which was widespread, no modeler specialized any concept from the original model (nor were there any obvious opportunities to do so).

12.8.3. Alternative explanations for the diversity

The diversity of models ("product") is consistent with the design paradigm. The data collected also allows us to explore some examination of alternative explanations for this diversity that are consistent with the description paradigm.

Inadequate information

It is possible that the diversity was a result of inadequate information and consequent different assumptions by the modelers, and that the different models would have converged towards a common solution if a more complete set of information had been available. As noted in Section 11.9.3, there is some subtlety in this argument, insofar as a sufficiently precise set of information would effectively describe the model (analogously to an architect's client specifying the exact dimensions of each room). The information given to the modelers was consistent with that required to support a mechanical translation (e.g. Teorey, Lightstone et al. 2006 pp83-106)[187].

As noted in Section 12.7.1, 74[188]% of respondents stated either that they did not make any guesses about the requirements or made only guesses which were "unimportant". Fifty-eight percent of respondents stated that they understood the requirements "fairly well" or "very well".

The provision of different additional information – viz the nature and capabilities of the users of the model – had no significant effect on the generalization decisions. Academic and practitioner writers on data model quality regularly cite understandability as a key quality factor (Shanks and Darke 1997; Moody and Shanks 2003; Simsion 2005a), and higher levels of abstraction are seen as potentially difficult for end-users to understand (Hoberman 2002 p369). At the extremes, it would seem that "First Quarter Labor Budget" would be simpler for an accountant to understand than "Amount" qualified by LMO-Type, Budget-Actual Indicator, Period, and Period Type – yet modelers did not significantly alter their preference to suit the audience.

---

[187] In fact, it represented an intermediate stage in the transformation – and, as noted earlier, was a viable model as it stood.

[188] Percentages cited in this section refer to the percentage of *valid* responses.

Insufficient time / models incomplete

Two arguments suggest that the diversity was not a result of models being incomplete due to lack of sufficient time.

Firstly, 56.5% of respondents stated that they did not expect that their model would be substantially different if they had more time for the exercise. Although the percentage who *did* believe it would change is substantial (43.5%), this figure needs to be taken in the context of the observation (Section 12.5.1) that no practical amount of time was likely to be considered adequate by some. Even selective removal of this percentage from the sample would not substantially reduce the diversity (beyond reducing the absolute number of cases). As noted in Section 12.7.3, every model from the Pittsburgh and London responses was structurally different.

Secondly, much of the variation amongst the models arose from fundamentally different choices of tables and columns rather than minor differences in detail. It seems unlikely that modelers would have revised these decisions towards a common outcome if given more time – particularly (and perhaps paradoxically in the context of the description / design question) if they regarded the process of modeling as being essentially descriptive.

Insufficient expertise / problem too difficult

The argument that differences arose because modelers lacked the competence necessary to tackle the model – and hence produced a range of flawed or sub-optimal models – is hard to sustain. Sixty-eight percent of respondents stated that they found the task "very easy", "fairly easy" or "neither easy nor difficult", with only 5% selecting the option "very difficult". Thirty-two percent of respondents claimed more than 5 years of data modeling experience and 46% to have "played a leading role in developing" 10 or more data models. All respondents had chosen to attend an "Advanced Data Modeling" seminar.

We have previously noted the relative simplicity of the problem and the basic soundness of all but a few models.

The modeling problem was not representative

It is possible that the modeling problem was unusually amenable to diverse solutions, and hence not representative of problems that would be encountered in practice. As the problem was chosen by the author, there is the possibility of researcher bias.

Against this argument is the fact that the problem was a "real-world" example (unlike most data modeling research examples, as noted in Chapter 5). Further it reflected a very common business scenario that might be expected to appear in some form in many or most organizations' models, given the ubiquity of budgeting and financial reporting. Finally it was a very simple problem, at least as measured by the total number of columns and the time required to produce workable solutions.

12.8.4. Summary

In a relatively simple, constrained exercise, data modelers (most of them experienced) produced a wide range of different workable logical data models in response to a common "conceptual" data model. The differences resulted primarily, but not exclusively, from alternative choices of construct and of level of generalization for both columns and tables. There was some evidence of style – consistency in generalization and choice of construct by individual modelers.

Established quality criteria provided some assistance in clarifying the trade-offs that each model represented, but little in selecting or rejecting some solutions over others. Perhaps the most interesting result was the propensity of data modelers not to accept the constraints or business rules incorporated in the original model, but to produce something different and (arguably) better.

If this limited task produces substantially different workable models, we could reasonably expect an even greater variety in a less constrained and / or more complex situation. More broadly, the results are strongly at odds with characterizing logical data modeling / logical database design as a mechanistic translation.

Chapter 12 – Diversity in logical data modeling

CHAPTER 13
STYLE IN DATA MODELING

The higher up you go, the more mistakes you are allowed. Right at the top, if you make enough of them, it's considered to be your style.

— Fred Astaire

13.1. OBJECTIVES AND APPROACH

In the preceding two chapters, we saw that different people may develop different but workable data models in response to the same set of requirements. It is difficult to completely eliminate the possibility that these differences are the result of random differences in understanding of the requirements, and that the models would converge if more detail or time was available. This explanation would be consistent with a characterization of data modeling as description.

Conversely, design theory recognizes the role of individual contribution and *style* (Section 4.3.4). Designers bring something of themselves to the process, and an individual designer's product may be distinguished (and even recognizable) by particular features or biases. Evidence that some of the non-trivial differences amongst data models are due to individual modeler style would support the design characterization in general, and counter the argument that diversity in the preceding research tasks was entirely due to inadequate understanding.

In examining the data models produced in the conceptual and logical data modeling tasks described in Chapter 11 and Chapter 12 respectively, we noted correlation amongst modeling decisions *within* models, in particular, choice of construct and level of generalization. Thought-leader David Hay's observation (Section 6.4.6) that generalization decisions tend to be at a similar level across a model suggests that modeler style is not the only explanation for consistency within a model. Such consistency could be a goal in its own right, albeit not one recognized directly in current quality frameworks (*elegance* (Simsion and Witt 2005 pp13-14) which includes *consistency* in its definition, probably comes closest).

This component of the research therefore examines whether data modelers exhibit personal preferences[189] in their modeling, independent of the specific problem, and across more than one stage of the data modeling process. It addresses the research sub-question (Section 7.2): *Do data modeling practitioners exhibit personal styles that influence the data models that they create?* Our interest is in preferences, and resulting choices, that have a substantial impact on the structure of the resulting databases, and thus the design of the applications that use them.

The research design, described in the next section, required participants to develop conceptual and logical data models in much the same manner as for the investigations of diversity in conceptual data modeling (Chapter 11) and logical data modeling (Chapter 12). The resulting models were reviewed for diversity to supplement the earlier results. The logical data models were included in the analysis in Chapter 12, as noted there, as they used the same modeling problem. Diversity in the conceptual data models (responses to data modeling problems not used elsewhere in the research) is discussed in this chapter.

13.2. RESEARCH DESIGN: AN INDICATOR OF STYLE

The principal challenge in seeking evidence of data modeling style was to identify a generic preference that could be measured, and that was likely to be present in solutions to laboratory tasks. The most obvious candidates were qualities that involved "trade-offs" with other qualities, e.g. *stability* vs *enforcement of business rules*, *scope* vs. *ease of programming*, *nonredundancy* vs. *performance*, *integration* vs. *elegance* (Simsion 2005a). A propensity to regularly choose (for example) stability ahead of enforcement of business rules would meet our description of *style*. Unfortunately, most of these quality factors are difficult to measure objectively, as noted in the discussions in Chapter 11 and Chapter 12 (Sections 11.9.1 and 12.8.1), and some (such as *integration*) would be difficult to incorporate in a laboratory task.

Consideration of quality factors suggested another property – *level of generalization,* which is not a quality factor in its own right, but is closely

---

[189] The word *bias* could also be used, and might be preferred by subscribers to the descriptive paradigm who could see such imposition as interfering with objectivity. The choice of *preference* is based on the observation in Chapters 8 and 9 that good quality models can arise from different choices.

associated with stability, simplicity, understandability, ease of programming and enforcement of business rules (Simsion 1993; Hoberman 2002 p367).

Level of generalization has a number of useful attributes as an indicator of style:

1. Several of the thought-leaders observed that some modelers preferred higher or lower levels of generalization (Section 6.4.6). The resulting differences in models were seen as important and indeed controversial.

2. It is strongly associated with data model variability; in Verelst's (2004a) framework it is (as *vertical variability*) one of three types of variability, along with construct variability and horizontal variability.

3. It is easy to observe, being associated with individual concepts rather than requiring a holistic view.

4. It is straightforward to quantify (or at least code) at the level of individual concepts, and an aggregate figure for a model can be produced as in Chapter 8 and Chapter 9.

5. Variability in this dimension was common in both of the earlier laboratory tasks, whereas construct variability was uncommon in the conceptual modeling task (Chapter 8) and horizontal variability less common in the logical data modeling task (Chapter 9). This experience suggested that it would not be necessary to contrive an example (and thus compromise face validity) in order to have a reasonable expectation of obtaining vertical variability in the solutions.

6. There are few published guidelines on choosing the level of generalization. Conversely there are guidelines for construct selection. Differences amongst modelers in construct selection might simply reflect application of different rules (although the analysis of the logical data modeling task, where there was some variation in construct choice, did not find any evidence of such consistency).

7. The level of generalization significantly affects the quality of the data model, or, more exactly, the factors that contribute to the quality of the model, typically improving some factors at the expense of others, and may have a major impact on the application as a whole (Simsion 1993; Hoberman 2002 p367).

Given this choice of indicator, the research question for this component can be framed as: *do some modelers consistently exhibit higher levels of generalization in their models than others?* To answer this, participants were asked to develop models for two different scenarios. Correlation between the levels of generalization in the two models produced by each modeler was then measured.

Three different modeling problems were used in this research component, with each participant being assigned two. Two of the tasks required the development of a data model from a text description (for convenience we refer to these as *conceptual data modeling* problems, but note the ambiguity of that term given the results of the Scope and Stages component – Chapter 8) and one required the development of a logical data model from a conceptual data model and associated explanatory material.

The logical data modeling problem was the same task as was used to investigate diversity in logical modeling (Chapter 11); its prior use served as a pilot and established the nature of variation to be expected. The conceptual data modeling problems were devised specifically for this research component[190]. One was adapted from a common example in the literature, the other from practice. The only measure taken to encourage variation amongst the models was to consciously write the two conceptual modeling problems as descriptions of the business scenario rather than of a pre-defined solution.

13.3. MEASURES

The measurement of generalization broadly followed the approaches used in Chapter 11 and Chapter 12, with some refinement to the approach to dealing with subtypes, which reflect generalization decisions. In the review of the solutions to the conceptual modeling problem described in Chapter 11, it was noted that the majority of models that used subtype constructs attached relationships only to one level; typically, but not always, the supertype level. This was likely a result of the overall simplicity of the problems, rather than application of a rule[191], but it did suggest a focus on that level by the modeler. Indeed, subtypes at the level below

---

[190] The problem used in the research component described in Chapter 8 was too complex (hence time-consuming) to be used here.

[191] The author is unaware of any such rule in the academic or practitioner literature, modeling tools, or practice.

were sometimes incomplete (and annotated to that effect), seeming to serve primarily as examples to clarify the meaning of the supertype. On this basis, when models employed subtypes, the level at which the relationships were predominantly attached was used in determining the level of generalization.

Initial examination of the models identified common constructs subject to different levels of generalization. Levels of generalization were coded as 0-lowest, 1-next-lowest, etc. A total *generalization score* was calculated for each model as the total of the coded generalization decisions. Models which omitted one of more of the relevant constructs were not allocated a score and were excluded from associated analysis.

13.4. MATERIALS

Three data modeling problems were used in this research component.

1. The *Annual Budget* problem, described in Section 12.4. In this problem, participants were presented with a conceptual model and some supporting information, and asked to produce a logical data model.

2. A *Bank Loans* problem, a simplified version of a real example, presented as a short plain-language description written by the author (Figure 13-1).

3. A *Family Tree* problem, including the concept of *marriage*, a classic textbook example (e.g. Kent 1978 pp111-114; Hawryszkiewycz 1991 p162; Date 1998 p427; McFadden, Hoffer et al. 1999 p107; Thalheim 2000 p48; Simsion and Witt 2005 pp111-122), presented as short plain-language description written by the author (Figure 13-2).

Bank Loans

To support the business of a bank, we need to record details of personal loans, housing loans and motor vehicle finance loans. Against each loan, we need to record the details of the borrower(s), the Loan Officer who approved the loan, and (in some cases) a guarantor. We also need to record payments, drawings (initial and further borrowings) and interest transactions against each loan.

Figure 13-1: Bank Loans data modeling problem

Family Tree

We are developing a database to record details of a family tree. For each person of interest to us, we need to be able to record details (where known) of their mother, father, children, and marriages, and their date of birth, death and marriages.

Figure 13-2: Family Tree data modeling problem

Each participant was given two of the three problems with instructions to "draw a data model for each of the following scenarios". The sequence of the two problems on the page was reversed in half of the cases to compensate for order effects.

A set of "process" questions addressing assumptions, level of difficulty and use of patterns for each of the two problems (common to all modeling exercises used in this research project) was added to the standard demographics questionnaire.

13.5. METHOD

Aspects of method common to several components of the research, including survey piloting, administration, ethical issues, coding of demographics and use of statistics are covered in Chapter 7. Here we cover aspects of administration specific to this task, review and coding of the models, and analysis of the results.

13.5.1. Administration

The data modeling tasks and associated questionnaires (as described in the previous section), were administered to attendees at seminars on advanced data modeling conducted by the author. The version of the task involving two conceptual modeling problems was administered at one location only[192]; the other two combinations were assigned randomly at two locations. The sequence of the two problems was assigned randomly (from pre-prepared alternatives) at all locations.

The administration followed the general procedure described in Section 7.4, and comprised the following steps.

1. Participants were told that they had 20 minutes to complete both problems, or, if time was insufficient, to provide a list of entities or (for the logical data modeling problem) tables.

---

[192] This research component was originally designed only to compare style across two conceptual models. It was later extended to include logical modeling.

2. At the end of 10 minutes they were advised (but not instructed) to move on to the second problem. A further five minutes "extension[193]" was provided at the end of the twenty minutes, with participants being reminded at that point of the option to provide only an entity or table list.

3. Ten minutes were then allocated to complete the associated questionnaire. Submission of the questionnaires and the models (numbered by the participants to match the pre-numbered questionnaire) was voluntary.

13.5.2. Initial review and coding

Demographic information and responses to the process questions were coded according to the procedure and coding schemes described in Section 7.4.

All models were reviewed by the author (an experienced data modeling consultant) to establish:

1. Use of conventions, in particular subtyping which is a factor in the measurement of generalization.

2. Whether each model was workable. The test here was *not* whether all of the semantics included in the inputs had been represented in the model, but whether a database specified by the model could hold the data needed to support an application that met the requirements. This left open the possibility of some semantics being represented as program logic, data values, or external to the application as discussed in Section 4.4.1. Syntax or other minor errors were corrected where the intention seemed clear from context as the goal was not to assess modeler competence (the assumption is that in a practical setting such errors would be rectified without disturbing the structure).

3. The names of the entities (or alternative abstractions, such as tables or objects) used in each model. Obvious synonyms (singular and plural, spelling differences, etc) were consolidated. This step was not required

---

[193] In piloting, subjects spent more than half of the time on the first problem, even when the total time was longer than 20 minutes. The extension was an attempt to compensate, and encourage participants who had run out to time to provide at least an entity list.

for the assessment of style, but provided an indication of conceptual modeling diversity to supplement the findings reported in Chapter 11.

4.   A list of concepts that had been represented at different levels of generalization across the models for each problem. This was effectively an open coding process; it had already been performed for the initial set of Annual Budget models (refer Section 12.7.3), and the code set produced from that exercise was re-used for the new solutions[194].

All models were coded using the above lists and a number to reflect level of generalization for each concept as it appeared in the model, as per Section 13.3, and a *generalization score* was calculated for all models in which all of the listed concepts appeared.

13.5.3.Analysis

Generalization scores for the Bank Loans and Family Tree models were checked for correlation with the standard demographic splits as described in Section 7.4.3 (Annual Budget generalization score correlations, including the models developed for the present research component, were covered in Section 12.7.3).

Generalization decisions were cross-tabulated within models, and correlations and overall covariance noted. This was to measure "internal style" (consistency of generalization *within* models), which had already been observed in the conceptual and logical data models described in the two preceding chapters.

Generalization scores were checked for correlation across models. Where significant correlations with demographics had been noted, correlation of generalization scores *within* those demographic categories was also measured.

13.6. SAMPLES

The three modeling problems and associated questionnaire were given to attendees at advanced data modeling seminars in the USA (two seminars) and in Stockholm, Sweden in 2003 and 2004 (Section 7.6). The seminars attracted predominantly practitioner audiences.

---

[194] The possibility of isolated new structures emerging and requiring coding was not relevant; the coded features needed to be common to most or all models.

Tasks and response rates for the three locations are summarized in Table 13–1.

Location	Modeling Problems	Number of Attendees	Number of Solutions (both models) Submitted	Response rate (%)
Orlando, FL, USA	Bank Loans Family Tree	53	41	77%
Stockholm, Sweden	Annual Budget PLUS Bank Loans OR Family Tree	40	25 (plus 2 that only did 1 model)	63%
Los Angeles, CA, USA	Annual Budget PLUS Bank Loans OR Family Tree	35	25 (plus 5 that only did 1 model)	71%
Total		128	91	71%

Table 13–1: Responses at each location

Five participants submitted models but did not submit the demographics questionnaire. Their models were included in the parts of the analysis in which demographic measures were not used.

13.7. RESULTS

13.7.1. The Annual Budget model

The solutions for the Annual Budget exercise produced for this research component were incorporated in the analysis that appears in Chapter 12. Detailed results for that task are not repeated here. The key findings of relevance to this component of the research were that correlations between generalization decisions within the model ranged from negligible to strong (all positive), and co-variance as measured by the Kuder-Richardson 20 (KR20) coefficient was 0.68. This indicated some consistency in level of generalization within the models.

13.7.2. Perceptions of the task and models: questionnaire responses

Responses to the process questions indicated that the majority of participants understood the problem at least "fairly well" and did not find it "very difficult."

These figures also need to be seen in the light of the high percentage of workable models (next section).

13.7.3. Initial review and coding

This section covers the initial review of the models, including a preliminary assessment of diversity, as described in Section 13.5. As noted earlier, the assessment of diversity is not necessary for the measurement of style, but it provides some confirmation of results on conceptual model diversity reported in Chapter 11.

All but one of the 64 Bank Loans models and all but eight of the 68 Family Tree models submitted were judged as being workable in that they were able to support the data required for the application as described. Although some of these models were deficient in some areas, they were considered to provide sufficient information of the modeler's intent to be included in the analysis.

Conventions

Figure 13-3 summarizes the modeling conventions used. Eighty-eight percent of the responses to the Bank Loans and 87% of solutions to the Family Tree problems used some variant of the "crow's foot" notation (Section 3.4) in which the key constructs are entities, relationships and (optionally) attributes. These terms have therefore been used in discussing these models, whereas relational terminology has been used in discussing the responses to the Annual Budget problem, in keeping with the analysis in Chapter 12.

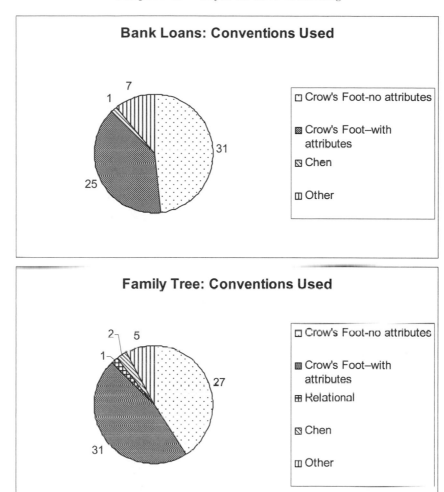

Figure 13-3: Conventions used in Bank Loans and Family Tree data modeling problems

Twenty-seven of the bank loans models and six of the Family Tree models included subtype structures.

Number of entities

Figure 13-4 is a frequency distribution of the number of entities in the Bank Loans and Family Tree models, including subtypes, providing an initial indication of the diversity in the solutions.

Bank Loans

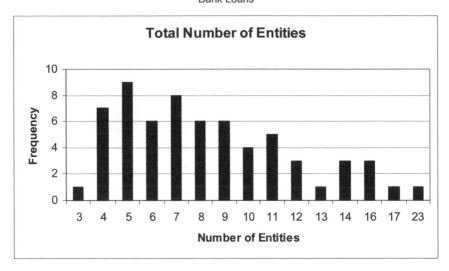

Family Tree

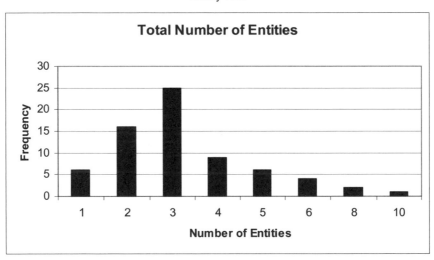

Figure 13-4: Number of entities used in Bank Loans and Family Tree data modeling problems

Variety of entity names

After consolidation of reasonably obvious synonyms, the 64 Bank Loans models contained, in total, 118 different entity names, and the 69 Family Tree models, in total, 59 different entity names. Again, this provided some overall indication of diversity amongst the models.

Concepts subject to variation in generalization

Review of the models identified four concepts[195] in the Bank Loans solutions and three concepts in the Family Tree solutions as being subject to different levels of generalization. In each case, only two different levels were noted (Table 13–2). With one exception, the decisions were logically independent i.e. any one could be taken without a requirement that any of the others were taken. The exception, in the Bank Loans model, was the generalization of Loan Officer which was hard to envisage (and did not occur) without the inclusion of Borrower and Guarantor within the generalized entity (i.e. the *Customer* generalization decision).

Generalization Decision	Abbreviation
Borrower and guarantor generalized	Customer
Loan officer generalized with other parties	Party
Relationships to all involved parties generalized	Party Relationship
Payments, drawings and interest generalized	Transaction

Table 13–2: Bank Loans concepts subject to different levels of generalization

Figure 13-5 and Figure 13-6 show the frequency with which each level of generalization was used.

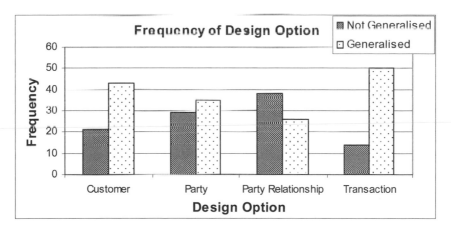

Figure 13-5: Bank Loans generalization decisions

---

[195] This excludes generalization of different types of loan to a single loan entity and generalization of initial and further borrowings to a single borrowing entity – decisions taken by all but one modeler.

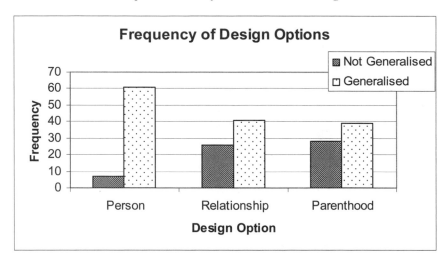

Figure 13-6: Family Tree generalization decisions

Different combinations of these decisions gave rise to ten different versions of the Bank Loans model and five different versions of the Family Tree model, the most popular choice in each case accounting for 50% of the models.

Figure 13-7 and Figure 13-8 show the frequency distributions of generalization scores (calculated by counting[196] the individual decisions) for the Bank Loans and Family Tree models.

---

[196] As all decisions were binary, the calculation of the generalization scores, as described under *Method*, is reduced to a simple count.

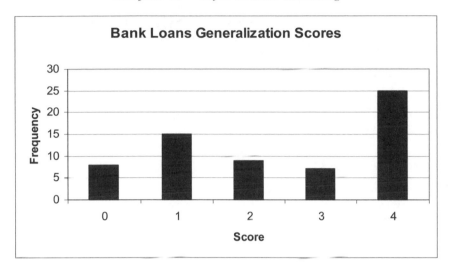

Figure 13-7: Generalization scores for Bank Loans modeling problem

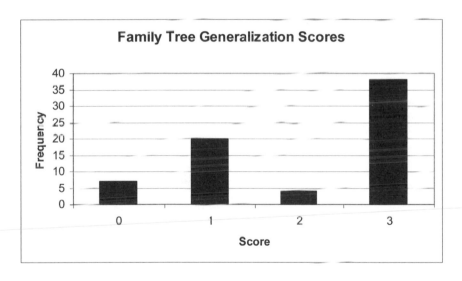

Figure 13-8: Generalization scores for Family Tree modeling problem

13.7.4. Analysis

The analysis covers correlations between generalization scores and demographic categories, correlation and co-variance of design decisions within models, and finally the key result of correlation of generalization decisions between models.

Correlation between generalization scores and demographic category

Table 13–3 and Table 13–4 show the correlations between the generalization scores and binary demographic categories for experience and job role. A positive correlation indicates that scores were higher for the *second* of the two demographic categories listed in that row.

Bank Loans Generalized Score Correlation	Kendall's tau-b Value	p value
Other Occupations vs. Data Modelers	0.31	<0.0005
0-5 years experience vs. >6 years experience	0.24	0.03
0-1 years vs. >1 years experience	0.15	0.17
0-10 models developed vs. >11 models developed	0.31	<0.0005
0-1 models developed vs. >1 model developed	0.11	0.22

Table 13–3: Bank Loans generalized score correlation

Family Tree Generalized Score Correlation	Kendall's tau-b Value	p value
Other Occupations vs. Data Modelers	0.10	0.41
0-5 years experience vs. >6 years experience	0.17	0.13
0-1 years vs. >1 years experience	-0.01	0.94
0-10 models developed vs. >11 models developed	0.30	0.01
0-1 models developed vs. >1 model developed	-0.15	0.15

Table 13–4: Family Tree generalized score correlation

The results for the Bank Loans model show a significantly higher level of generalization in models produced by the more experienced modelers and those whose principal occupation was data modeler. The difference is less pronounced in the Family Tree models but the sole significant result is again with a higher experience group.

Correlation between generalization decisions within models

Correlations between generalization decisions within Annual Budget models were covered in Section 12.7.3. Table 13–5 and Table 13–6 show the correlation (phi statistic) between each pair of generalization decisions *within* the Bank Loans and Family Tree models.

	Party	Party Relationship	Transaction
Customer	0.77 (p<0.0005)	0.58 (p<0.0005)	0.27 (p=0.03)
Party		0.75 (p<0.0005)	0.28 (p=0.03)
Party Relationship			0.36 (p<0.0005)

Table 13–5: Bank Loans generalization decisions

	Relationship	Parenthood
Person	0.39 (p<0.0005)	0.37 (p<0.0005)
Relationship		0.88 (p<0.0005)

Table 13–6: Family Tree generalization decisions

Covariance as measured by the Kuder-Richardson 20 (KR20) coefficient was 0.80 for the Family Tree decisions and 0.73 (excluding the *customer* decision[197]) for the Bank Loans decisions. These results are consistent with those for the earlier conceptual and logical data modeling tasks, which showed some correlation amongst the generalization decisions *within* individual models.

Correlation between generalization scores across the conceptual models

We now turn to the key question addressed by this research component – the propensity of individual modelers to generalize, as indicated by correlation in generalization scores between different models that they develop.

Generalization scores for the Family Tree and Bank Loans models were moderately positively correlated (Kendall's tau-b=0.51, p<0.0005). As this is the key result for the research we also note the less conservative gamma statistic (gamma=0.69, p<0.0005), which would be interpreted as a strong correlation. In order to test whether this correlation could be attributed to the correlation with demographic categories noted in the preceding section, the analysis was repeated for each of the relevant demographic categories. Table 13–7 shows that the correlation remained moderate and significant (p<0.005) within all but one group.

---

[197] As noted earlier, the customer decision and party decision co-vary as a result of the coding scheme. The KR20 value with the customer decision included was 0.75.

Demographic Group	Kendall's tau-b	Approx. Sig.
> 10 models produced	0.54	<0.0005
<= 10 models produced	0.27	0.32
Occupation = Data Modelers	0.52	<0.0005
Occupation = Non Data Modelers	0.62	0.001
> 6 Years Experience	0.56	0.001
< 6 Years Experience	0.49	0.003
Total Sample	0.51	<0.0005

Table 13–7: Correlation between generalization scores across the conceptual models

Correlation between generalization scores for logical and conceptual models

No significant correlation was found between the generalization scores for the Annual Budget (logical) model and either the Family Tree or Bank Loans conceptual model (Family Tree: gamma = 0.26, p=0.46; Bank Loans; gamma = -0.53, p=0.86).

13.8. DISCUSSION

The research component reported in this chapter asked, essentially, whether some data modelers were more inclined to generalize than others. For the participants who performed the two conceptual modeling tasks, this was clearly true, supporting the thought-leaders' contention (Section 6.4.6) that different modelers preferred different levels of generalization. But a propensity to generalize in a conceptual modeling task did not correlate with a propensity to generalize in the logical data modeling task.

We therefore have some evidence to suggest an element of style in conceptual modeling, but not one that influences logical data modeling. A possible explanation for the lack of correlation is that the preference does not apply to generalization *per se*, but to generalization of *entities*. Generalization at the column level might be a distinct preference, or not subject to preference at all.

Another possible explanation for the correlation between the two conceptual models is the interaction with the use of patterns and a goal of consistency of generalization within models[198]. Both models include people, a feature common to most data models (Hay 1996a p23; Silverston 2001 p21). If a modeler's "pattern" for dealing with people is at a particular level of generalization, and if that level is adopted for the rest of the model, then we would expect the two models to reflect that level overall.

This explanation does not dispose of the idea of style, any more than do the correlations noted with occupation or experience. They simply suggest some possible reasons for data modeler style. For the present, the important result is the evidence that individual data modelers do appear to bring something beyond the description of the problem to conceptual data modeling tasks, resulting in important differences in the solutions that they produce. This is clearly in line with the concept of style and, more broadly, with the characterization of data modeling as design.

This appears to be the first study of data modeling style. In the context of the present research it provided evidence that diversity in data models was not solely a result of random differences in interpretation, and that data modelers exhibited a trait characteristic of designers. The results surely have wider implications, if the choice of data modeler (beyond simple experience and qualifications) pre-determines at least something of the result.

In developing a fuller picture, it would be useful to know whether modelers show consistency across two *logical* data modeling tasks, and whether style is manifest in factors other than generalization (e.g. preference for particular patterns). Further research, which could be based on the current research design, would be required to answer this question.

---

[198] This goal was suggested by David Hay in interview (Section 6.4.6).

Chapter 13 – Style in data modeling

PART IV – SYNTHESIS AND CONCLUSIONS

CHAPTER 14
SYNTHESIS AND CONCLUSIONS

14.1. INTRODUCTION

This book began with a question – *Is data modeling better characterized as description or design?* – prompted by a suspicion that its widespread characterization as description did not reflect data modeling practice.

In the body of the book we addressed the question from five perspectives – *Environment, Problem, Process, Product,* and *Person.* Using this *5Ps*[199] framework, we reviewed the data modeling literature in some detail and formulated eleven research sub-questions. These were addressed through seventeen interviews with practitioner thought-leaders, three surveys, and three laboratory studies. The research involved a total of 489 participants, predominantly data modeling practitioners from North America, the United Kingdom, Scandinavia, and Australia, ranging in experience from novices to internationally recognized thought-leaders in the profession. This number is substantially larger than the total number of practitioner participants in data modeling research covered by surveys of the literature (Chapter 5), and enabled the use of statistical techniques, which was not possible with the smaller samples used in previous studies.

The chapters that report the results of each research component include an analysis of results in terms of the description / design question and the literature, and hence of the contribution that they make in their own right. As discussed in Section 7.3.2, the research design allowed for most sub-questions to be addressed by more than one research component. We begin this final chapter by drawing together the results from the various research components to synthesize a response to each of the sub-questions and, in turn, to the description / design question from each of the five perspectives. In Section 14.3, we review the results from the alternative perspective of theory versus practice and, more specifically, *espoused theory* versus *theory-in-use* following Argyris and Schon (1974 pp6-7).

---

[199] The *P* for *environment* is from the synonym *press.*

In Section 14.4, we comment on the design and limitations of the research, insofar as they determine the extent to which the findings can be generalized. With these caveats in mind, we return to the *raison d'être* for the research – the argument that the answer to the description / design question is of fundamental importance to data modeling research, teaching, and practice. This argument was outlined in the Introduction (Chapter 1) and explored further in Part II through the review of the literature and interviews with thought-leaders. We identify areas that warrant review – or re-thinking – in the light of the research findings, and suggest some directions for further research.

14.2. ANSWERING THE SUB-QUESTIONS

In this section, we draw together the results relevant to each of the sub-questions, within the 5Ps framework. Before proceeding, however, we note the broad answer that they provided to the description / design question: consistently, the research results supported the characterization of data modeling as *design*. The exception was in *espoused* positions, where views were divided, or, in the case of positions implicit in definitions of data modeling, favored the descriptive characterization.

The discussion that follows generally does not repeat detailed findings from individual research components (presented in the dedicated chapters), but focuses on drawing together the broader picture.

14.2.1. Environment

Three sub-questions addressed the *environment* in which data modeling takes place. The first two addressed the cultural environment – beliefs about the characterization of data modeling in terms of the description / design dichotomy. The third addressed the technical environment – the database design process and the role of data modeling within it.

Is the description / design question considered important by data modeling practitioners?

We considered the perceived importance of the description / design question from three perspectives: the literature (including the practitioner literature), the explicit views of thought-leaders, and the extent to which a position was embodied in practitioners' definitions of data modeling.

The lack of attention given to the issue in the academic literature – beyond a few papers in the late 1980s that examined alternative views of data modeling from a philosophical perspective (Sections 3.2 and 3.4) – was one of the motivations for the present research. Some of the earlier practice-oriented texts[200] explored the nature of data modeling, but current texts seldom even acknowledge alternative views[201].

In contrast to the relative silence in the literature, the thought-leader interviews revealed strong and even passionate positions. Presented with the question directly, all considered the correct characterization of data modeling to be of fundamental importance – but almost without exception, they considered themselves to be in possession of the right answer. It is perhaps drawing a fine distinction to say that it was not the *question* that they saw as important, but the articulation of their own positions, but this may partly explain the lack of exploration of alternatives in the practitioner literature. Evidence of the importance of the question lay not only in the fact that there was support for both characterizations, but that four of the interviewees reported changing their position (two in each direction) and saw the change as having had a major impact on their approaches to data modeling.

Practitioners' definitions of data modeling (Chapter 9) followed the literature in embodying, in most cases, a position on the description / design question, evidence of its pervasiveness if not its explicit recognition. It is worth reiterating that definitions of data modeling consistent with both academic and practitioner perceptions of its scope and purpose do not need to embody such a characterization. *Specification of a conceptual schema to meet business data requirements* is an example of a reasonably neutral alternative[202]. But it seems that the characterization of data modeling as description or (less commonly) design is so fundamental that it is routinely included in definitions. If the characterization was settled, there might be no real problem in incorporating it in definitions, but, as was apparent from the thought-leader interviews and the espoused positions survey (see next sub-question, following), this is not the case.

---

[200] Notably Kent's (1978) *Data and Reality*

[201] A notable exception is Hay's (2003 pp xxxii-xxxiii) recognition of description ("analysis") and design perspectives, and declaration of his own (description) position.

[202] This response would have been coded as not embodying a position.

What are the (espoused) beliefs of data modeling practitioners on the description / design question?

Espoused beliefs were identified from:

1. *Definitions* of data modeling in the academic and practitioner literature and in responses to the *Espoused Positions* survey question *what is data modeling?*

2. *Explicit positions* on the definition / design question from the literature, interviews with thought-leaders, and responses to the forced-choice (closed-ended) presentation of the description / design question in the *Espoused Positions* survey.

Definitions from all sources overwhelmingly embodied a characterization of data modeling as description. The picture changed dramatically when the description / design issue was addressed explicitly. Presented with the two options, both practitioners and thought-leaders were approximately evenly divided as to which characterization was more appropriate. Similarly, neither characterization emerges as having clear majority support from the few occasions in the literature in which alternatives are acknowledged.

What do data modeling practitioners believe is the scope and role of data modeling within the database design process?

The *Scope and Stages* survey described in Chapter 8 directly addressed the place of data modeling within the overall process of database design. Despite differences in the database design processes and data modeling stages nominated by respondents, a core set of activities was consistently classified (by at least 80% of respondents) as data modeling and as primarily the responsibility of data modelers. This set of activities included all of those associated with conceptual schema specification, following the identification of business requirements, except for changes made for performance reasons. With the important caveat that the sample was dominated by data modelers, but noting that the classification held for all of the demographic subgroups (as defined in Section 7.4.3), this supported a practitioner definition of data modeling as *at least*:

the specification of the initial conceptual schema, to meet agreed business requirements, prior to any performance tuning.

The primary purpose of this sub-question was to provide a basis for interpreting answers to other survey questions about data modeling. However, the definition of scope that emerged has direct relevance to the description / design question, which could be restated as: *Is (pre-performance) conceptual schema specification better characterized as description or design?* This view of data modeling does not allow for some later "conceptual schema design" stage; if data modeling is descriptive, then the resulting description must be a complete, workable (pre-performance tuning) conceptual schema.

14.2.2. Problem

A single research sub-question addressed the *Problem* dimension.

Are data modeling problems perceived as design problems by data modeling practitioners?

One distinguishing feature of design is that it is a response to a problem – a set of requirements to be met. Description does not require a problem as such. The *Scope and Stages* survey was important in providing evidence that data modelers do work from a problem statement rather than solely from observations of the Universe of Discourse. Most respondents (80%) to the survey specified a *Business Requirements Analysis* stage, almost always preceding the identification of entities, relationships, and attributes. Primary responsibility for this stage was most commonly assigned to business analysts.

The *Characteristics of Data Modeling* survey described in Chapter 10 indicated that participants saw data modeling problems as having the characteristics of design problems. Data modelers scored significantly higher on the design index for this dimension than the sample of architects, whereas their scores were similar to those of the architects in the *process* and *product* dimensions. Data modelers offered only weak support for the design characteristic "business requirements are often negotiable," but strongly supported the statement that "the most difficult part of data modeling is understanding the business requirements". The two responses are consistent with a scenario in which data modelers *believe* that they are describing when in reality they are designing. Seeking an objective understanding of something that is subjective, volatile, and emergent from the modeling process (all characteristics supported by respondents) is indeed likely to be difficult.

The thought-leader interviews identified contrasting views on the negotiability of requirements, consistent with interviewees' positions on the description / design issue. For some, the negotiability of data modeling requirements was the primary reason for their characterization of data modeling as design – they were less sure of the level of choice available once requirements were finalized. Supporters of the descriptive characterization regarded business requirements as virtually inviolable; none even raised the idea of suggesting that a change to the business might allow the production of a better database and associated application. By contrast, supporters of the design paradigm saw themselves as helping to design a better business.

14.2.3. Process

The two sub-questions on the data modeling process addressed methods used in practice, and data modelers' perceptions of the task of data modeling.

Do database design methods used in practice support a descriptive or design characterization of data modeling?

The *Scope and Stages* survey (Chapter 8) asked participants to describe the high-level stages in the database design process (of which data modeling is a part) and to identify the stages in which some key activities took place. The responses were compared with methods described in the literature, and analyzed in terms of the assumptions that they embodied about the characterization of data modeling. Six areas were investigated and all but one provided support for the design characterization over the descriptive characterization. The exception was that physical database design, which is generally characterized as a design activity, was not included within the scope of data modeling. (Had it been included, the effect would in fact have been to *weaken* other results that supported the characterization of data modeling as design, insofar as the characterization might have been entirely due to the contribution of the physical database design activity).

Findings from the survey were supplemented by the thought-leader interviews, and observations from the laboratory tasks.

The most important findings were:

330

1. The consolidation of most data modeling activities into a single *logical data modeling* stage, in contrast to their separation in the academic (and some practitioner) literature into conceptual and logical data modeling stages. As described in the survey responses, the conceptual modeling stage delivered a high-level entity-relationship model that might best be described as a "sketch plan" rather than a detailed model suitable for mechanical transformation into a conceptual schema. The focus on the logical data modeling stage was also evident in the thought-leader interviews, with most interviewees using *logical data modeling* as a synonym for *data modeling* and one stating simply: "we model the tables". All of the laboratory tasks asked modelers to "draw a data model" to serve as the basis of a database design; on no occasion was the author, in administering the tasks, asked "what type of model?" Inputs ranged from recorded interviews with business stakeholders to a detailed conceptual model[203], but almost all of the models produced in response used the same set of conventions – the "crow's foot" notation which is little more than a diagrammatic version of the Relational Model. No participant provided separate conceptual and logical data models[204], nor showed any work that would indicate a two-stage process.

2. The specification of a *Business Requirements Analysis* stage by 80% of respondents (noted above under *Problem*), and a consensus that this stage was performed prior to the identification of entities, relationships, and attributes (hence prior to the entity-relationship "sketch plan" of conceptual modeling). The existence of this stage is clearly at odds with the common representation of data modeling as directly describing the Universe of Discourse.

3. The (complete) absence of support for the "view-definition – view-integration –view-reconstruction" approach that dominated the early data modeling literature and continues to be cited and advocated. This approach reflected a descriptive characterization of modeling, albeit one in which different but reconcilable views were acknowledged.

---

[203] The usage of *conceptual model* here follows the literature rather than the practitioner descriptions.

[204] A single possible exception was one participant in the Diversity in Logical Modeling task who produced two models labeled *analysis* and *design*.

We also note the importance of *diagrams* in the approaches described and used by participants. Graphical representation was a common theme in definitions of data modeling (Section 9.5.3). Data models from the laboratory tasks overwhelmingly used diagrams; the use of the word *draw*[205] in the instructions doubtless influenced this, but even for the logical data modeling exercise, when the input was presented as a list of attributes rather than as a diagram, all but two of the 96 respondents introduced diagrams to present their solutions. The use of diagrams is a common feature of design disciplines (Porter and Goodman 1988; Lawson 1997 pp241-259).

Are data modeling processes perceived as design processes by data modeling practitioners?

Perceptions of data modeling processes came from two sources: interviews with thought-leaders (Chapter 6) and the *Characteristics of Data Modeling* surveys (Chapter 10).

The thought-leader interviews focused on the role of creativity in data modeling, and provided some context for interpreting answers to the survey question: *Data modeling requires a high level of creative thinking.* All of the thought-leaders who viewed data modeling as design believed that creativity played an important role – but so did some from the description camp. The difference was that the latter saw creativity as relevant not to developing the *content* of the model but to more peripheral activities, in particular communication of the model. This suggests caution in interpreting creativity as an indicator of design. Indeed, even the accountants scored above "neutral" on this question, though significantly lower than the data modelers and architects.

Respondents to the *Characteristics of Data Modeling* survey saw data modeling processes as having characteristics consistent with the design paradigm – with scores similar to those of architects.

---

[205] Chosen to avoid words that strongly implied description or design. This was obviously a poor choice if observation of propensity to use diagrams had been an explicit goal of the research.

14.2.4. Product

The research design emphasized the *Product* dimension, in particular the "one right answer" issue captured by two of Lawson's (1997 pp121-127) design properties:

1. There is an inexhaustible number of different solutions

2. There are no optimal solutions to design problems

Several factors motivated this emphasis:

1. The thought-leader interviews indicated that diversity of product was a central point of difference between "describers" and "designers".

2. The "one right answer" assumption (or weaker forms that recognize only trivial alternatives) is probably the most common and clearest manifestation of the description assumption in research, notably in the form of a *gold standard* model in empirical work and the *reality mapping* paradigm that underlies the proposal and evaluation of formalisms.

3. The issue is critical to work on data model quality, in terms of whether the problem is to decide whether a model is *right* (description paradigm) or adequate / better than alternatives (design paradigm). This issue is of particular importance in software package evaluation (Section 1.3.3).

The research indicated that data modelers *perceive* data models as having the characteristics of design products, and that experienced modelers claim to use patterns (another of Lawson's design properties). But the most dramatic finding was the diversity in models produced by experienced modelers in response to common scenarios. The finding was surprising not for the diversity *per se* (which, given the results of the *Characteristics* survey, was not unexpected) but for the *amount* of diversity, epitomized by the 39 structurally-different models produced by 39 modelers in response to a highly-constrained logical data modeling problem.

We now look at the individual research sub-questions in the *product* dimension.

Are data modeling products perceived as design products by data modeling practitioners?

Responses to the *Characteristics of Data Modeling* survey supported a perception of data modeling products as design products, with an overall score significantly greater than the neutral value, and not significantly different from that of the architects. The question *In most practical business situations, there is a wide range of possible (and workable) data models* was strongly correlated[206] with the total design score (across all three dimensions), lending support to the view that the "one right answer" issue is central to the description / design characterization.

Will different data modeling practitioners produce different conceptual data models for the same scenario?

Given the merging of the conceptual and logical data modeling phases in practice (noted under *Process* above), we need to differentiate this sub-question from the logical data modeling one that follows. The relevant research components were designed in terms of the academic model in which conceptual modeling proceeds from the business requirements or knowledge of the Universe of Discourse to deliver a platform-independent model, and logical data modeling (or logical database design) translates that model into a DBMS-specific model. Accordingly the tasks investigating conceptual data modeling used plain language business descriptions as the primary input, whereas the single task that investigated logical data modeling used a conceptual data model as input.

The thought-leader interviews revealed a range of views on diversity in conceptual modeling, from an absolute position that expert modelers should produce identical models ("one version of the truth") to the contention that models produced by different experts would be "absolutely different". There was significant and well-argued support for both extremes.

Three laboratory tasks contributed to the investigation of the question. The research component described in Chapter 11 was specifically designed to address this sub-question, and involved the development of a model from interview transcripts and supporting materials. Participants were also asked to develop models from plain language scenario descriptions (two different tasks) as part of the investigation of style described in Chapter 13.

A range of measures was used to assess and classify differences in models. For each task, all of the measures showed substantial diversity amongst models. In the case of the task described in Chapter 8, the measures included differences in

---

[206] It had the second-highest Corrected Item-Total Correlation value of any question: 0.44.

choice of construct and level of generalization, and subjective (overall) assessments by other participants. Much of the variation could only be classified as "holistic" rather than reduced to individual mappings. Of ten holistically-different models sent for evaluation to nineteen data modeling experts, five were rated by a majority of the experts as equal to or better than typical models produced in current practice (a remarkable result, considering the limited time given for the task), and four different models had support from at least three of the experts as the "best" solution. The most well-developed of the published quality frameworks (Moody and Shanks 2003) was employed in the evaluation, but was of limited value in differentiating amongst workable models.

Will different data modeling practitioners produce different logical data models from the same conceptual model?

The thought-leaders were less inclined to countenance diversity in the latter stages of data modeling than in the earlier stages, where the negotiability of the problem was seen as an important contributor. A single laboratory task, used in both the *Diversity in Logical Modeling* and *Style* research components, but described in full in Chapter 12, addressed the question. It produced the most compelling evidence of diversity in modeling, because the variety of different models was in response to a more tightly-specified input – a single entity with twenty-two attributes – than could be provided for the conceptual modeling tasks. Differences in the models could not be so readily attributed to differences in perception of the problem.

Different choices of construct (by far most commonly cited reason in the literature for differences in models) were one source of diversity, but another major contributor was difference in generalization at the attribute / column level. The impact of the latter was frequently quite complex: for example, generalization of a set of columns might prompt the inclusion of a reference table of column meanings, which might itself then be generalized. Nineteen different combinations of six construct decisions and 18 combinations of five column generalization decisions were observed. The various combinations of these decisions alone created 36 variants amongst 39 models. The variants were non-trivial, and would be clearly assessed as different using (for example) Moody and Shanks' (2003) quality framework. Virtually all were workable in the sense that they could support the data and processes specified by the users, albeit with different program logic.

These results are inconsistent with the common characterization of the logical data modeling / logical database design stage as well-defined and deterministic. Whatever might be desirable or possible, experienced practitioners appear to make important – and different – decisions when "transforming" even simple real-world conceptual models.

Do data modeling practitioners use patterns when developing models?

The use of patterns is one of Lawson's Properties of design. Participants' use of patterns was investigated through four questions.

The *Characteristics of Data Modeling* survey (Chapter 10) asked participants whether they frequently re-used patterns / structures (a) from models that they had developed themselves and (b) from models developed by others (two questions).

These were two of only four questions in which the data modelers scored significantly higher than the architects, with more experienced modelers scoring significantly higher than less experienced modelers, presumably because they had wider "libraries" to draw upon.

Each of the four data modeling tasks used in the laboratory studies was accompanied by a questionnaire that included the questions:

In developing the data model, did you draw on data models that you have seen or used in the past?

Did you deliberately add entities, relationships etc that could not be deduced from the problem description alone?

The responses are summarized in Table 14–1 and Table 14–2.

Task	No	Yes	Not Reported	Total
PND Study (Chapter 11)	15	76	2	93
Annual Budget (Chapter 12)	32	24	1	57
Bank Loans (Chapter 13)	24	41	2	67
Family Tree (Chapter 13)	29	41	2	72
Total	100	182	7	289

Table 14–1: Responses to "drawing on data models used in the past"

Task	No	Yes	Not Reported	Total
PND Study (Chapter 11)	53	30	2	93
Annual Budget (Chapter 12)	28	24	5	57
Bank Loans (Chapter 13)	34	28	5	67
Family Tree (Chapter 13)	45	22	5	72
Total	160	112	17	289

Table 14–2: Responses to "deliberately adding entities, relationships etc"

These results strongly suggest that a significant proportion of data modelers consciously use patterns, sometimes to the extent of introducing concepts that can not be deduced from the problem description, despite the fact that data modelers are generally taught to work from "first principles" (Batra and Wishart 2004). The value of the finding in supporting the design characterization needs to be qualified by the views of thought-leaders (Chapter 6). Some proponents of the *descriptive* characterization (notably David Hay, author of two books of data model patterns) saw patterns as relevant; in terms of that characterization, they provide the correct model or sub-model for a business problem.

14.2.5. Person

Although only one of the research sub-questions (*Style*) was classified under the *Person* dimension, all seven research components would qualify as studies of human factors in data modeling[207]. In Chapter 5 we noted some limitations of previous empirical studies of human factors in providing answers to the description / design question. Before addressing the *style* sub-question, we briefly review the extent to which the present study addressed some of those limitations.

The present research targeted experienced practitioners rather than using students (who comprised 95% of participants in the earlier human factors studies listed in the Appendix), but included 44 participants who had developed zero or one models only and 102 who had one year or less experience. The numbers of such "novices" were still small in most research components, and only a few statistically-significant results were noted. Novices were more likely to find the modeling problems difficult and to produce unworkable solutions. In the *Characteristics of Data Modeling* Survey, novices scored lower (i.e. favored the design characterization less) on several individual questions, but not significantly lower overall, and in the conceptual modeling task, experienced modelers were more likely to generalize than novices.

The investigation of diversity in modeling required that the tasks be formulated without a "gold standard" solution in mind. Accordingly, the common practice of reverse-engineering "business requirements" from pre-defined models was eschewed. In the *Diversity in Conceptual Data Modeling* and *Diversity in Logical Data Modeling* tasks in particular, the goal was to achieve mundane realism by presenting real-world examples in a form that a modeler might encounter in practice. Videos, transcripts and supporting materials (conceptual data modeling) and a conceptual model with answers to frequently-asked questions[208] (logical data modeling) were used. The result was the diversity of workable solutions noted above under *Product*.

The use of experienced participants allowed greater task complexity than has been possible with students, but the conceptual data modeling problem appeared to be close to the limit of difficulty practical in a laboratory setting, with 27 of 93

---

[207] If published in an appropriate journal / forum, they would clearly have qualified for inclusion in Topi and Ramesh's (2002) *Human Factors in Data Modeling* survey.

[208] As determined by extensive piloting in industry training courses.

models being judged unworkable, and almost half of participants reporting some problem with understanding, difficulty, completeness of specification, or available time.

We now address the final research sub-question.

Do data modeling practitioners exhibit personal styles that influence the data models that they create?

Four of the thought-leader interviewees (Section 6.4.6) observed that data modelers exhibit personal styles, an attribute associated with design rather than description. The common example was a preference for a higher or lower level of generalization.

The *Diversity in Conceptual Data Modeling* and *Diversity in Logical Data Modeling* components provided evidence of correlation within models in choice of construct and level of generalization (i.e. modelers showed a propensity to choose one construct over another or to choose a higher or lower level of generalization *within a particular model*). This behavior could be evidence of personal style. Alternatively, modelers might simply be seeking consistency within each individual model.

The *Style in Data Modeling* research component showed a statistically significant correlation between the levels of generalization of entities not only within models but across models developed by the same modeler from plain language requirements. (No significant correlation was found between such entity generalization and column generalization in a separate logical data modeling task.) This result suggests that modeler characteristics, beyond the competence required to produce a workable model, contribute to the nature of the data models that they produce.

14.3. AN ALTERNATIVE PERSPECTIVE

The preceding section summarized the research results by sub-question within the 5Ps framework. This organization of the results hides an important trend: as we move from theory to practitioner perceptions and finally towards observations of practice, the characterization of data modeling moves from description to design. The research can be seen as addressing five points on that continuum:

1. Theory – as espoused or assumed in research and teaching publications directed at both the academic and practitioner communities. This was covered by the literature review, which noted the strong dominance of the description characterization.

2. The positions embodied in practitioners' definitions of data modeling. These were solicited using the survey question *what is data modeling?* in order to ascertain their positions prior to any reflection that might be prompted by the description / design question itself. The descriptive characterization was dominant, but there was some clearly identifiable support for the design characterization.

3. Practitioners' espoused positions on the description / design characterization obtained by presenting survey participants and thought-leaders directly with the description / design question. The two characterizations now received approximately equal support within both groups. As the survey participants also answered the *what is data modeling?* question, it was possible to observe individuals moving from a definition that embodied description to a "design" response to the description / design question.

4. Practitioners' perceptions of individual properties of data modeling, from the *Characteristics of Data Modeling* survey. The intent of this research component was to encourage reflection independent of views held on the overall characterization. Mean scores strongly supported the design characterization. Covariance of responses to individual questions suggested that there was variation amongst modelers in terms of their position on the description / design continuum.

5. Observations of simulated practice, in the three laboratory studies. In the observations of diversity, there was little opportunity for individual modelers' beliefs to influence the outcome, insofar as the measures applied to the models in aggregate[209]. In the study of style, it would seem unlikely that modelers' beliefs about the nature of modeling would have materially influenced their models. The results from these components very strongly supported the design characterization.

---

[209] The single exception was the peer evaluation of diversity, in which participants judged the level of difference between their model and that of another participant.

The most obvious interpretation of the above is that data modeling in practice is best characterized as design, in conflict with the dominant body of theory that supports the descriptive characterization. The progressive change in positions would reflect a shift from espoused theory to theory-in-use (Argyris and Schön 1974 pp6-7), as received positions (e.g. from textbooks, industry courses or other practitioners) gave way to reflections on experience and observations of practitioner behavior.

14.4. GENERALIZING THE FINDINGS

Having synthesized responses to the research sub-question, we now consider the extent to which the findings can be generalized to the broader population of data modeling practitioners. This discussion qualifies the next section, which assesses the implications of the research.

The research design described in Chapter 7 provided for generalization based on both statistical inference and replication of results (*analytic generalization*), and aimed to support a "reasoned argument" (Robson 1993) for generalizing findings to data modeling practitioners working in Western countries at least. The factors listed below would support such a generalization of the broad answer to the research question: viz *that data modeling is better characterized as design rather than description*, and, to a varying extent, generalization of individual findings that contributed to that answer. At a minimum, they support recognition of the data as providing the best available empirical basis for answering the description / design question and each of the eleven sub-questions.

1. The size of the practitioner samples used for each of the surveys or tasks. The smallest number of practitioner participants in any survey or laboratory task was 55. This (lowest) figure exceeds the number of practitioner participants in all but one of the previous studies of human factors in data modeling listed in 0. Numbers in all cases were sufficient to support the use of inferential statistics.

2. The approach to sampling. The recruitment of participants from seminars fell short of the ideal of random sampling of data modelers (which would seem impractical), but removed the author from direct involvement in selection. Most previous studies of practitioners or "experts" have used researchers' contacts and have frequently been dominated by individuals from a single organization. Some participants

may have been influenced to attend the seminars by knowledge of the author's views; this seems most likely for the one "stand alone" commercial seminar and least likely for the three regular DAMA chapter meetings in US cities in which apparently attract a regular cohort of attendees, and the Stockholm seminar in which the author's presentation was scheduled as a plenary session rather than requiring a choice to attend (Section 7.6).

3. Reliability: Three of the four laboratory tasks and two of the three surveys were administered in at least two different countries, with no significant material[210] differences in the results. Similarly, there were few differences amongst participants with different job titles (*data modeler* vs. *other*). In particular, the *Characteristics of Data Modeling* survey, which provided strong evidence for the design characterization, was administered to 266 participants in seven groups (minimum size 20) covering all settings (conferences, DAMA chapter presentations, and private classes) and geographic areas (UK, USA, Scandinavia, Australia) and did not produce significantly different results across the samples (Section 10.7.2).

4. Replicability: Table 7–2 in Chapter 7 shows how the research was designed to test the replicability of results. Aside from the differences between theory and practice (or espoused and observed behavior) discussed in Section 14.3 above, results across the research provided a consistent answer to the description / design question and to individual sub-questions. Three results with particularly important implications, discussed in the next section, were supported by multiple research components:

(a) The importance of and diversity of espoused positions on the description / design question was evident from thought-leader interviews and the *Espoused Positions* survey (as well as the literature).

---

[210] There were occasional significant differences – for example on individual questions in the *Characteristics of Data Modeling* survey – but not in overall scores nor in their support for the response to the relevant sub-question.

(b) The characterization of data modeling processes as design processes was supported by the *Scope and Stages* survey and the *Characteristics of Data Modeling* survey.

(c) Diversity of product (data models) was evident in four different laboratory tasks using inputs ranging from interview transcripts to a detailed conceptual model, and in responses to the *Characteristics of Data Modeling* survey.

The principal qualification to the above positive picture of the generalizability of results is that the sampling approach targeted practitioners who were investing (or whose employers were investing) in improving their data modeling knowledge and skills – implicitly those who recognized data modeling as a relevant activity. There is evidence (MacDonell 1994; Hitchman 1995; Maier 1996; Simsion 2005b) that many organizations do not recognize a formal role for data modeling or modelers, even though they may need to specify conceptual schemas and thus perform the broad process of data modeling, if under another name. Considerable caution would be required if results were to be applied to understanding data modeling in such organizations.

14.5. IMPLICATIONS

In introducing the description / design question in Chapter 1, we stated that the answer had important implications for data modeling research, teaching, and practice. In the three subsections that follow, we look at the key issues that the findings raise in each of these three areas, with emphasis on research. We conclude the section with a broader question: how should these results influence our view of data modeling as a whole? Specifically, we suggest that the results challenge the *integrity* of data modeling – its existence as a separate, definable activity with clear boundaries.

14.5.1. Implications for data modeling research

In this subsection, we summarize some important assumptions in the data modeling literature, and the challenges that the present research findings provide to them, or at least to their relevance to data modeling practice. The assumptions were discussed in Part II (the relevant sections are referenced below), and the discussions are not repeated here. It is, however, worth emphasizing that although these assumptions are long-established and have been frequently re-stated, most lack significant empirical support. Together, they represent a substantial part of the foundation upon which data modeling research has been built. They have in common a view of data modeling as descriptive; we should not be surprised that, by challenging this underlying premise, the present research calls them all into question.

Reality mapping

The view of data modeling as *reality mapping* was strongly contradicted by the research results. Reality mapping epitomizes the descriptive paradigm, which was explicitly treated as the antithesis of design in this research – and the numerous results that supported design are thus in direct conflict with it.

Reality mapping has been a central goal in work on data modeling languages, which in turn has been a dominant (probably *the* dominant) topic in data modeling research. Recent research that uses ontology as a basis for comparing languages also focuses on how well they map reality (Section 3.4). To re-iterate: the research indicated that data modeling practitioners do not map reality (at least not in any simple way) but create data structures to address business scenarios.

Conceptual data modeling

The common characterization of data modeling as including a conceptual modeling phase that delivers a detailed platform-independent model (Section 3.4) was not reflected in participants' descriptions of the database design process. The "conceptual modeling" phase included in most participants' descriptions appeared to be a high-level preliminary task, with most conceptual schema specification activities (including attribute identification) taking place in the "logical data modeling" phase. Much data modeling research focuses on the conceptual data modeling phase (as defined in the literature), allowing a range of "database design" decisions to be excluded from consideration. This convenient separation does not appear to reflect practice.

Mechanistic transformation to database tables

Logical data modeling (sometimes called logical database design) is frequently characterized as a mechanistic transformation from conceptual model to a (usually) relational "design" (Section 3.6). The assumption is important in assessing the value of work that addresses only conceptual data modeling (previous subsection), since it implies that once conceptual modeling is complete, the remaining work is relatively trivial. This view was strongly contradicted by the results of the *Diversity in Logical Data Modeling* research component.

Suitability for automation

A body of research has addressed automation of data modeling, usually as part of automation of the full database design process (Section 4.3.2). A key motivation has been the desire to obtain "consistent and reliable results" (Storey, Thompson et al. 1995) and it has been suggested – though not demonstrated – that conceptual "design" can be automated to the level of an intermediate performer (ibid). The characterization of data modeling as design would suggest that (for example) support and product improvement may be more appropriate goals than automation and consistency.

Data modeling languages – and the Entity-Relationship Model

As noted earlier, the search for better conceptual data modeling languages has been a constant theme in data modeling research. The Entity-Relationship (E-R) Model (Chen 1976) and Extended Entity-Relationship (EER) Model (Teorey, Yang et al. 1986) are frequently used as benchmarks for theoretical and empirical evaluation, on the basis that are the most widely used formalisms in practice.

Some researchers have challenged the belief that the E-R and EER Models are widely used by practitioners (Section 3.4); the present research provided very strong support for that challenge with only two participants across all of the laboratory tasks using these Models. Participants overwhelmingly used the "crow's foot" notation that is little more than a diagrammatic view of the Relational Model, and indeed very similar to the early Data Structure Diagrams (Bachman 1969). (Some of the models included subtypes, but these have for some time been supported by the relational (SQL) standard (Melton and Mattos 1995; ISO/IEC9075-1:2003 2003)). The impact of the very substantial amount of academic work on modeling languages appears to be minimal, with modelers apparently preferring to work directly with the DBMS language. This is not an incidental finding, but one consistent with the design characterization and Willem's (1991) statement that design solutions occur in terms of media.

Reductionist approach to differences in models

A common assumption in the literature is that differences in data models can be reduced to a set of relatively simple mappings that can be classified and resolved individually. View integration approaches (Section 3.5) – and particularly work on automating them – rely on this assumption. Even some recent work sympathetic to the design characterization (Verelst 2004a) seeks to classify differences in models in this reductionist way.

The *Diversity in Conceptual Modeling* research component found that many of the differences between workable models could best be described as holistic, as would be expected in the case of design products (Lawson's design property: *Design solutions are often holistic responses*). We have previously noted the absence of support for view integration approaches, perhaps reflecting the difficulty of applying such approaches to models that differ holistically.

Gold standard in research design

Much empirical research that has required participants to develop a data model has used the *gold standard* (predefined correct model) approach (Section 5.1), embodying the "single right answer" assumption. This approach has only occasionally been challenged (Atkins and Patrick 1996). The diversity of models produced from more realistic presentations of data modeling problems must seriously call the technique into question, or at least require researchers employing it to state exactly what part of the data modeling process is being investigated or simulated. Experiments based on the gold standard using student participants – a common combination – would thus appear to lack realism on two counts.

Objective measurement of data model quality

The assumption that data model quality can be measured objectively is implicit in much work on the subject over the last decade (Section 4.4.2). Most data quality frameworks have been developed and evaluated in the context of measuring student models against a "gold standard". Moody and Shanks' (2003) framework is unusual in drawing on practice, and incorporating some holistic measures that require subjective judgment, but it retains the goal of quantifying data model quality.

The Moody and Shanks framework was used formally in assessing models from the *Diversity in Conceptual Data Modeling* component, and was also used to characterize differences in models from the *Diversity in Logical Data Modeling* component. It was found to be of little value in differentiating amongst workable models developed by experienced practitioners, with the objective measures either irrelevant to sound models (syntactic *correctness*), simplistic (semantic *completeness*), or strongly and significantly correlated with overall assessment of quality in the *opposite* direction to that predicted (*simplicity*). The subjective measures (*understandability, flexibility*) scored by experts on a Likert scale were correlated with their scores for overall quality but the framework did not address a number of other important dimensions of difference noted in the models (and in qualitative practitioner frameworks for data quality), in particular the trade-off between representation of business rules and stability. This assessment was supported by regression analysis, in which the predictive power[211] (r-square measure) of the framework was much lower for the practitioner models than for Moody and Shanks' sample which included student models.

14.5.2. Teaching data modeling

The research results have two sets of implications for the teaching of data modeling, viz: *what* is taught and *how* it is taught.

Content

We have noted that espoused positions on the definition and (to some extent) characterization of data modeling are inconsistent with the design characterization derived from reflection and observation. Teaching of data modeling (in academe and industry) would seem to be one potential source of such positions. Teaching texts overwhelmingly support the descriptive characterization through definitions, limiting the discussion of model differences to choice of construct, and through exercises and examples with a single correct answer (Section 4.4.1). But once the description / design issue is considered explicitly (Chapter 6 and Chapter 9), practitioners frequently agree with the design characterization, and the present research has provided substantial evidence in support of it.

In short, teaching, if it reflects the assumptions in research and textbooks, is contributing to the disjunction between espoused theory and theory in use. At a minimum, the results of the present research suggest that the design

---

[211] The dependent variable was Overall Quality, also assessed subjectively by the expert reviewers.

characterization be recognized as an alternative to the descriptive characterization, and that statements in the literature be balanced with observations from practice.

Approach to teaching

Data modeling, as noted in Chapter 1, is notoriously difficult to teach – at least in the context of tertiary education. We commented there that if data modeling was design, but was taught as description, we would expect such difficulties. The present research supports that view, as do practitioner observations that data modelers learn by doing. Only $13^{212}\%$ of participants nominated tertiary education as a primary method of learning data modeling, compared with 51% who nominated "on the job" learning (experience) and 42% who nominated industry education (Section 7.6).

If the design characterization is accepted, then teachers of data modeling should logically seek to learn from approaches to teaching design, perhaps drawing on experience from both within and outside the information systems field. At a minimum, teaching should recognize that the process of data modeling involves more than "finding the nouns" and that different data models may be produced in response to common scenarios.

14.5.3. Data modeling practice

The key issue for data modeling practice that emerged from the research results was a disjunction between what practitioners *say* they do and what they *actually* do – between (arguably) received knowledge and knowledge acquired from experience. This is a well-established phenomenon in the professions (Argyris and Schön 1974 pp6-7). In this scenario, we would expect problems to be manifested not so much in performing the task, but in communication with other stakeholders, the design and use of methods, and more, subtly, in practitioners' 'making sense' of their experience. For example, we might expect:

1. Data modelers to present data modeling as a more straightforward process than it actually is – potentially reducing their own perceived value and raising expectations of performance that they fail to meet.

---

[212] Percentage of participants who provided a response to this demographics question. Multiple responses were allowed.

2. Business stakeholders to expect to see their understanding of the business reflected in the model – but be confounded by structures created by the modeler.

3. Data modelers to be unwilling to consider alternative models or to compromise their "correct description".

4. Confusion in the communication amongst modeling professionals, which could be expected to impede the advance of the discipline.

These issues are consistent with those identified in the practitioner literature (Section 4.3.6) and by thought-leaders (Chapter 6). The lack of a common process and terminology was evident in the responses to the *Scope and Stages* survey.

In Section 1.3.3 we noted that the "one right answer" issue was relevant to approaches to software package selection. The research results provide a clear demonstration that quite different models can achieve similar ends. Accordingly, a "gold standard" approach to evaluating the data models of candidate software packages could result in the rejection of sound solutions.

The research did not directly address data modeling as a tool for information systems planning and integration, but *prima facie*, the research results would suggest that there is no "single right answer" in this context either. Clashes between "enterprise architects" seeking to impose structures from an enterprise model and project-level modelers who have developed a different local model are legion (Goodhue, Kirsch et al. 1992; Shanks 1997a; Simsion and Witt 2005 p516, see also thought-leader interviews), and may be more understandable in the context of a paradigm that seeks a correct description rather than evaluating alternative designs in terms of relative strengths and weaknesses.

14.5.4. The integrity of data modeling

The emergence of data modeling as a task in its own right, separate from conceptual schema design, can be traced to Chen's (1976) publication of the Entity-Relationship approach. Chen's approach introduced the two-stage description-transformation process, embodying reality mapping, a modeling language distinct from the implementation languages, and mechanical transformation from platform-independent conceptual model to language-dependent conceptual schema specification. Within this scenario, data modeling (specifically *conceptual* data modeling) has a clear and distinct role.

As discussed in the preceding subsections (drawing particularly on the findings from the *Scope and Stages* research component), database design as performed in practice does not appear to incorporate any of these principles. Data modeling as a whole delivers (at least) a pre-performance-tuning conceptual schema. With the current diversity in the Data Models (languages, constructs) supported by commercial DBMSs, the data modeler must be aware of the DBMS Data Model in order to perform this task. There is no evidence of a preceding (detailed) DBMS-independent model. *Conceptual* data modeling delivers only a high-level version of the schema.

It is difficult to see how this scenario differs materially from that which existed prior to the publication of the E-R approach, or how "data modeling" as practiced is distinct from "logical database design" or "conceptual schema design". Indeed, with data modeling delivering a conceptual schema, there is no room for a separate logical database design phase, and responses to the *Scope and Stages* survey reflected this.

In summary, the academic view of data modeling as an activity distinct from logical database design is not reflected in practice, where the former term has (at least in some organizations) simply displaced the latter. This puts an interesting perspective on organizations that claim not to do data modeling at all (MacDonell 1994; Hitchman 1995; Maier 1996); are they simply using the term *database design* to embrace what others would call *data modeling*?

The issue is not merely one of different terms for the same set of activities (although the inclusion of the word *design* in one term but not the other is interesting in the context of the description / design question) but rather whether it makes sense to separate these activities into two groups for independent investigation. The research results suggest that, whilst we may retain the term *data modeling,* the concept of a descriptive, implementation-language-independent discipline may not be sustainable.

14.6. RESEARCH DIRECTIONS

The preceding section supports Hitchman's (1999) contention that assumptions made by researchers are divorced from current data modeling practice, and suggests that the academic view, as manifested in teaching, may in fact contribute to confusion in practice. Wand and Weber's (2002) conceptual modeling research agenda, whilst advocating stronger links with practice, embodies many of the assumptions challenged by the results of the present research.

It would appear that if future data modeling research is to be relevant to practice, one of three directions needs to be taken:

1. Refute the conclusions drawn from the present research, and retain the established characterization of data modeling, *as performed in practice*, as descriptive. Refutation of the conclusions would address the risk of undertaking research on unsound assumptions about the nature of data modeling.

2. Pursue the descriptive paradigm in research, with a view to developing approaches superior to those now used in practice. This approach would be justified by the belief that the need for design is a result of limitations in these established approaches.

3. Accept the characterization of data modeling as design, and direct research towards better understanding and supporting the design process. This would represent a substantial change to the current data modeling research agenda.

The first option relies on finding a significant fault in the research reported here. Since the results that conflict with current research assumptions come from a rigorous, multi-method empirical study, involving significant numbers of data modeling practitioners from diverse backgrounds, the most likely basis for disputing the conclusions would be a re-interpretation of these results. The framework for re-interpretation could come from theory or from the responses of researchers or practitioners (particularly those with a belief in the descriptive paradigm) to the results and conclusions. In that context, the present research could have benefited from deeper discussions with "ordinary" practitioners. The thought-leader interviews were of considerable value not only in designing the research but in interpreting the findings. Extending the interaction with other practitioner participants beyond surveys and laboratory tasks might have provided further insights.

The second option, of continued commitment to the description paradigm as an alternative to current practice, relies on researchers eventually being able to ultimately demonstrate the superiority of their approach, and convince the practitioner community to adopt it. This would seem to be a very difficult task. Practitioners already appear to have "heard the message" insofar as it is reflected in espoused positions, but have apparently not been able to make it work in practice. Further pursuit of the descriptive approach would surely benefit from an analysis of the reasons that it has not been implemented.

The third option, of adopting a research agenda based on the design paradigm, offers some interesting possibilities. A logical starting point would be an examination of practice, where the design approach appears to be well entrenched, if not universally acknowledged. By beginning with an analysis of data modeling as performed in industry, researchers would have at least the possibility of linking ongoing research to practice. Areas for investigation might include:

1. *Environment*: An agreed description of the place and role of data modeling – in particular *conceptual* data modeling – in the overall database design process is fundamental to the design and interpretation of research. The present research has indicated that the established separation of conceptual and logical data modeling in the literature is not reflected in practice, and may not be workable within the design paradigm. More broadly, the evidence that there are many workable data models for a given business scenario suggests some investigation as to how much this matters; how important is the choice of data model to the overall quality of the applications that use it?

2. *Problems*: If data modelers do not work directly or solely from perceptions of the Universe of Discourse, but rather from a problem statement, what should this problem statement comprise? What, formally, are the inputs to data modeling?

3. *Process*: Design theory acknowledges different generic design processes (Lloyd and Scott 1994). Which of these are most appropriate / effective for data modeling? How can the data modeling process be made more effective? At the individual level, how do data modelers arrive at the different models noted in the examination of *Product*? Recognizing data modeling as design does not preclude rigor, but the approaches used to achieve it need to be appropriate to design (Hevner, March et al. 2004).

4. *Product*: The present research has highlighted the need for more sophisticated frameworks for data model evaluation, in particular to compare alternative solutions to the same problem. Such quality frameworks could also serve as a basis for evaluating alternative

solutions to generic data modeling problems, to improve the repertoire of patterns available to the profession.

5. *People:* Research on people has focused on basic competence within a narrow subset of the activities required to produce a data model. We know relatively little about the skills and personal characteristics needed to produce superior or innovative designs.

Regardless of the direction, or directions, that data modeling research takes, the research reported here has demonstrated that there are insights to be gained by viewing data modeling problems as design problems, data modeling processes as design processes, data models as design products and data modelers as designers. In looking at data modeling through a design lens, researchers gain not only an alternative interpretation of results, but one that is likely to provide a better understanding of their relevance to practice.

Chapter 14 – Synthesis and conclusions

REFERENCES, APPENDIX
& INDEX

REFERENCES

Adelman, S., L. Moss and M. Abai (2005). Data Strategy. Addison Wesley.

Agerfalk, P. J. and O. Eriksson (2004). "Action-Oriented conceptual modelling." European Journal of Information Systems 13(1): 80.

Aiken, P. (1995). Data Reverse Engineering: Slaying the Legacy Dragon. McGraw Hill.

Aiken, P., A. Muntz and R. Richards (1994). "Reverse Engineering Data Requirements: DOD Department of Defense legacy systems." Communications of the ACM 37(5): 26-41.

Akin (1991). "Architects' reasoning with structures and functions." Environment and Planning is Planning and Design 20: 273-294.

Akin, O. (1990). "Necessary conditions for design expertise and creativity." Design Studies 11(2): 107-113.

Alexander, C. (1979). The Timeless Way of Building. Oxford University Press.

Alexander, C., S. Ishikawa and M. Silverstein (1977). A Pattern Language: Towns, Buildings, Construction (Center for Environmental Structure Series). Oxford University Press.

Alford, R. (1998). The craft of inquiry: Theories, method, evidence. New York, Oxford University Press.

Alur, D., D. Malks and J. Crupi (2003). Core J2EE Patterns: Best Practices and Design Strategies, Second Edition. 2nd, Prentice Hall PTR.

Ambler, S. (2002). Agile Modeling: Effective Practices for Extreme Programming and the Unified Process. Wiley.

Ambler, S. (2003). Database Techniques: Effective Strategies for the Agile Software Developer. Wiley.

Amer, T. S. (1993). "Entity-relationship and relational database modeling representations for the Audit Review of Accounting Applications: An experimental examination of effectiveness." Journal of Information Systems 7(1): 1-15.

Anderson, J. R. (1982). "Acquisition of Cognitive Skill." Psychological Review 89(4): 369-406.

Andersson, M. (1994). Extracting an Entity Relationship Schema from a Relational Database through Reverse Engineering. ER'94 Entity-Relationship Approach 1994 LNCS881, Springer Verlag.

Angeles, P. A. (1981). Dictionary of Philosophy. New York, NY, Harper Collins Publishers.

ANSI/X3/SPARC, S. (1975). "Study Group on Data Base Management Systems: Interim Report." ACM-SIGMOD Newsletter 7(2).

Antony, S. and D. Batra (1999). Empirical validation of knowledge-based systems for conceptual database design. Americas Conference on Information Systems, Milwaukee.

Antony, S., D. Batra and R. Santhanam (1997). Design and evaluation of a database design consulting system for novices.

Archer, B. (1979). "Design as a discipline." Design Studies 1(1): 17-20.

Archer, L. B. (1965). "Systematic method for designers."

Argyris, C. and D. Schön (1974). Theory in practice: Increasing professional effectiveness. California, Jossey Bass.

Atkins, C. (1996). Prescription or description: Some observations on the conceptual modelling process. ICSE'96 18th International Conference Software Engineering, IEEE, Dunedin, New Zealand.

Atkins, C. (2003). When Analysts Design and Designers Analyse: Data Modeling in Crisis (working paper - personal communication). Nelson, New Zealand.

Atkins, C. and J. Patrick (1996). Evaluating conceptual data models: An investigation of frameworks, methods, and measurements. Palmerston North, New Zealand, Massey University.

Atkins, C. F. (1997). INTECoMM: An integrated conceptual data modelling method using Entity-Relationship and NIAM-CSDP techniques. Palmerston North, New Zealand, Massey University.

Avison, D. and C. Cuthbertson (2002). A Management Approach to Database Applications. McGraw Hill.

Avison, D. and G. Fitzgerald (2003). Information Systems Development: Methodologies, Techniques and Tools. 3rd Edition, Berkshire, McGraw Hill.

Babbie, E. (1998). The Practice of Social Research. Belmont CA, Wadsworth.

Bachman, C. W. (1969). "The Data Structure Diagrams." Database 1(2): 4-10.

Bachman, C. W. and M. Daya (1977). The Role Concept in Data Models. Proc. 3rd Intl. Conf. on Very Large Data Bases, New York, IEEE.

Barclay, P., A. Crerar and K. Davidson (1994). Interfaces to data models: taking a step backwards. 2nd International workshop on user interfaces to databases, London, Springer-Verlag.

Barker, R. (1990). CASE*Method Entity Relationship Modelling. Wokingham, UK, Addison-Wesley Publishing Company.

Barker, R. (1996). Foreword. Data Model Patterns Conventions of Thought. D. C. Hay. New York, New York, Dorset House Publishing: xvii-xviii.

Barkin-Goodwin, M. (2005). Handling of Subtypes in ERWIN. P. C. t. G. Simsion. Boulder, Colorado.

Barsalou, L. W. (1983). "Ad-hoc categories." Memory & Cognition(11): 211-227.

Barsalou, L. W. (1984). Determinants of Graded Structure in Categories. Psychology Department. Atlanta, Emory University.

Batini, C., S. Ceri and S. B. Navathe (1992). Conceptual Database Design: An Entity-Relationship Approach. Redwood City, California, Benjamin/Cummings.

Batini, C. W., M. Lenzerini and S. Navathe (1986). "A Comparative Analysis of Methodologies for Database Schema Integration." ACM Computing Surveys 18(4): 323-364.

Batra, D. (1996). Human error behaviour in conceptual and logical database design. New York, Marcel Kekker Inc.

Batra, D. (2005). "Conceptual Data Modeling Patterns: Representation and Validation." Journal of Database Management 16(2): 84-106.

Batra, D. and S. R. Antony (1994a). "Effects of data model and task characteristics on designer performance: a laboratory study." International Journal of Human - Computer Studies 41: 481-508.

Batra, D. and S. R. Antony (1994b). "Novice errors in conceptual database design." European Journal of Information Systems 3(1): 57-69.

References

Batra, D. and S. R. Antony (2001). "Consulting support during conceptual database design in the presence of redundancy in requirements specifications: an empirical study." International Journal of Human - Computer Studies **54**(1): 25-51.

Batra, D. and J. G. Davis (1992). "Conceptual data modelling in database design: Similarities and differences between expert and novice designers." International Journal of Man-Machine Studies **37**(1): 83-101.

Batra, D., J. A. Hoffer and R. P. Bostrom (1990). "Comparing representations with relational and EER models." Communications of the ACM **33**(2): 126-139.

Batra, D. and P. Kirs (1993). "The quality of data representations developed by novice (nonexpert) designers: An experimental study." Journal of Database Management **4**(4): 17-29.

Batra, D. and G. M. Marakas (1995). "Conceptual data modelling in theory and practice." European Journal of Information Systems **4**: 185-193.

Batra, D. and M. K. Sein (1994). "Improving conceptual database design through feedback." International Journal of Human-Computer Studies **40**(4): 653-676.

Batra, D. and A. Srinivasan (1992). "A review and analysis of the usability of data management environments." International Journal of Man-Machine Studies **36**(3): 395-417.

Batra, D. and N. A. Wishart (2004). "Comparing a rule-based approach with a pattern-based approach at different levels of complexity of conceptual data modelling tasks." International Journal of Human - Computer Studies **61**: 397-419.

Batra, D. and S. H. Zanakis (1994). "A conceptual database design approach based on rules and heuristics." European Journal of Information Systems **3**(3): 228-39.

Benyon, D. (1997). Information and Data Modelling. 2nd Edition, London, McGraw-Hill.

Berczuk, S. P. and B. Appleton (2002). Software Configuration Management Patterns: Effective Teamwork, Practical Integration. Addison-Wesley Professional.

Berger, P. and T. Luckmann (1967). The Social Construction of Reality. Middlesex, Penguin University Books.

Berkowitz, L. and E. Donnerstein (1982). "External Validity is More Than Skin Deep: Some Answers to Criticisms of Laboratory Experiments." American Psychologist(March): 245-257.

Berlin, B. and P. Kay (1969). Basic Color Terms: Their Universality and Evolution. Berkeley CA, University of California Press.

Bernstein, P. A. (1976). "Synthesizing Third Normal Form Relations from Functional Dependencies." ACM Transactions on Database Systems **1**(1): 277-298.

Beynon-Davies, P. (1992). "The realities of database design: an essay on the sociology, semiology and pedagogy of database work." Journal of Information Systems **2**: 207-220.

Beynon-Davies, P. (1994). "Information Management in the British National Health Service: The Pragmatics of Strategic Data Planning." International Journal of Information Management **14**: 84-94.

Bhagwat, A. (2003). "Data Modeling and Enterprise Project Management Part 1: Estimation." The Data Administration Newsletter(October).

Blaha, M. and W. Premerlani (1998). Object-Oriented Modeling and Design for Database Applications. Englewood Cliffs, NJ, Prentice Hall.

Blaikie, N. (2003). Analysing Quantitative Data: From Description to Explanation. London, Sage.

Bock, D. B. and T. F. Ryan (1993). "Accuracy in Modeling with Extended Entity Relationship and Object Oriented data models." Journal of Database Management 4(4): 30-39.

Bodart, F., A. Patel, M. Sim and R. Weber (2001). "Should Optional Properties Be Used in Conceptual Modelling? A Theory and Three Empirical Tests." Information Systems Research 12(4): 384-405.

Bodart, F. and R. Weber (1996). Optional properties versus subtyping in conceptual modelling: A theory and empirical test. 17th International Conference of Information Systems, Cleveland, Ohio, ACM.

Boehm, B. W. (1981). Software engineering economics. Englewood Cliffs, N.J, Prentice-Hall.

Borrie, H. (2004). The Firebird Book: A Reference for Database Developers. Apress.

Boulding, K. E. (1956). The Image: Knowledge in Life and Society. Ann Abor, University of Michigan Press.

Bouzeghoub, M. (1992). Using expert systems in schema design. Conceptual Modeling, Databases, and Case. P. Loucopoulos and R. Zicari, Wiley: 465-487.

Brackett, M. H. (2000). Data Resource Quality. New Jersey, Addison-Wesley.

Brancheau, J. C. and J. C. Wetherbe (1986). "Information Architectures: Method and Practice." Information Processing and Management 22(6): 453-463.

Brodie, M. L., J. Mylopoulos and J. W. Schmidt (1984). On Conceptual Modelling. New York, Springer-Verlag.

Brooks, F. P. (1995). The Mythical Man Month: Essays on Software Engineering. 20th Anniversary Edition, Addison Wesley.

Brosey, M. and B. Shneiderman (1978). "Two experimental comparisons of relational and hierarchical database models." International Journal of Man-Machine Studies 10(6): 625-637.

Bruce, T. A. (1992). Designing Quality Databases with IDEF1X Information Models. New York, Dorset House.

Bubenko, J. A. (1986). Information Systems Methodologies: A research view. Information Systems Design Methodologies: Improving the Practice. T. W. Olle, H. G. Sol and A. A. Verrijn-Stuart. North-Holland, Amsterdam.

Bubenko, J. A. (1995). "Challenges in Requirements Engineering." IEEE Software.

Buchanan, R. (1990). "Myth and maturity: toward a new order in the decade of design." Design Issues 6(2): 70-80.

Buist, A. E., B. Barnett, J. Milgrom, S. Pope, J. Condon, D. Ellwood, P. M. Boyce, M.-P. Austin and B. Hayes (2002). "To screen or not to screen - that is the question in perinatal depression." Medical Journal of Australia 177(7).

Bunge, M. A. (1977). Treatise on Basic Philosophy. Boston, Reidel.

Burrell, G. and G. Morgan (1979). Sociological Paradigms and Organizational Analysis. London, Heinemann.

Burton-Jones, A. and R. Weber (1999). Understanding relationships with attributes in entity-relationship diagrams. International Conference of Information Systems, Charlotte, North Carolina, United States, Association for Information Systems.

Campbell, D. (1992). "Entity Relationship Modeling: one style fits all?" Data Base 23(3): 12-18.

Caplan, R. D., R. K. Naidu and R. C. Tripathi (1984). "Coping and defense: constellations vs components." Journal of Health and Social Behavior 25: 303-320.

References

Carlis, J. and J. Maguire (2001). Mastering Data Modeling - A User-Driven Approach. New Jersey, Addison Wesley.

Catledge, L. and C. Potts (1996). Collaboration during conceptual design. Proceedings of ICRE: Second International Conference on Requirements Engineering, Los Alamitos, IEEE Computer Society Press.

Cerpa, N. (1995). "Pre-Physical data base design heuristics." Information & Management 28(6): 351-359.

Chaiyasut, P. and G. G. Shanks (1994). Conceptual data modelling process: A study of novice and expert data modellers. 1st International Conference on Object-Role Modelling, Magnetic Island, Australia, University of Queensland.

Chan, C.-S. (1999). "Can style be measured?" Design Studies 21(3): 277-291.

Chan, C.-S. (2001). "An examination of the forces that generate a style." Design Studies 22(4): 319-346.

Chan, H., K. Siau and K.-K. Wei (1998). "The effect of data model, system and task characteristics on user query performance - an empirical study." The DATA BASE for Advances in Information Systems 29(1): 31 49.

Chen, P. P. (1983). "English sentence structure and entity relationship diagrams." Information Sciences 29: 127-149.

Chen, P. P. S. (1977). The Entity-Relationship Model: a Basis for the Enterprise View of Data. Proceedings of 1977 National Computer Conference, Dallas, Texas.

Chen, P. P.-S. (1976). "The entity-relationship model - Toward a unified view of data." ACM Transactions on Database Systems 1(1): 9-36.

Chiang, R. H. L., T. M. Barron and V. C. Storey (1997). "Framework for the design and evaluation of Reverse Engineering methods for relational databases." Data & Knowledge Engineering 21: 57-77.

Chikofsky, E. J. and J. H. I. Cross (1990). "Reverse Engineering and design recovery: a taxonomy." IEEE Software: 13-17.

Chisholm, R. (1996). A Realistic Theory of Categories - An Essay on Ontology. Cambridge University Press.

Claxton, J. C. and P. A. McDougall (2001). "Measuring the Quality of Models." The Data Administration Newsletter(January).

Coad, P. (1997). Object Models:Strategies, patterns and applications. New Jersey, Prentice Hall.

Coad, P. and E. Yourdon (1990). Object-Oriented Analysis. Englewood Cliffs, NJ, Prentice Hall.

CODASYL (1971). "Data base task group report." ACM.

Codd, E. F. (1970). "A Relational Model of Data for Large Shared Data Banks." Communications of the ACM 13(6): 377-387.

Codd, E. F. (1979). "Extending the Database Relational Model to Capture More Meaning." ACM TODS 4(4): 397-434.

Codd, E. F. (1990). The Relational Model for Database Management: Version 2. Reading, MA, Addison-Wesley.

Cohen, J. (1988). Statistical Power Analysis for the Behavioral Sciences. 2nd Edition, Hillsdale NJ, Lawrence Erlbaum Associates.

Colaizzi, P. (1978). Psychological research as the phenomenologist views it. Existential Phenomenological Alternative for Psychology. R. Valle and M. King. New York, Oxford University Press: 48-71.

361

Connolly, T. and C. Begg (2005). Database Systems: A Practical Approach to Design, Implementation, and Management. 4th, Harlow, England, Addison-Wesley.

Coplien, J. O. and D. C. Schmidt (1995). Pattern Languages of Program Design. Addison-Wesley Professional.

Couger, J. D. (1988). "Key Human Resource Issues in IS in the 1990's." Information & management 14: 161-174.

Couger, J. D. (1996). A Framework for Research on Creativity/Innovation in IS Organizations. 29th Annual Hawaii International Conference on Systems Sciences, Maui, Hawaii.

Couger, J. D. and G. Dengate (1992). Measurement of Creativity for I.S. Products. Proceedings of the 29th Annual Hawaii International Conference on System Sciences.

Crawford, W. and J. Kaplan (2003). J2EE Design Patterns. O'Reilly.

Crerar, A., P. J. Barclay and R. Watt (1996). TOTEM: an interactive tool for creative data modelling. 3rd International Workshop on Interfaces to Databases, Napier University, Edinburgh, British Computer Society.

Crockett, H. D., J. Guynes and C. W. Slinkman (1991). "Framework for development of conceptual data modelling techniques." Information and Software Technology 33(2): 134-142.

Cross, N. and K. Dorst (1999). Co-evolution of problem and solution spaces in creative design. Computational Models of Creative Design IV, Key Centre of Design Computing and Cognition. J. S. Gero and M. L. Maher. Sydney, Australia, University of Sydney: 243-262.

DAMA-International (2002). Guidelines to Implementing Data Resource Management. 4, Washington, DAMA International.

Danoch, R., P. Shoval and M. Balabaan (2005). Comprehension of Hierarchical ER Diagrams Compared to Flat ER Diagrams. Information Modeling Methods and Methodologies. J. Krogstie, T. Halpin and K. Siau. Hershey, PA, Idea Group Inc.: 241-257.

Darke, P. and G. G. Shanks (1995). "Defining system requirements: A critical assessment of the NIAM conceptual design procedure." Australian Journal of Information Systems 2(2): 50-62.

Date, C. J. (1998). An Introduction to Database Systems. 8, Addison-Wesley.

Davis, A. M. (1993). Software Requirements: Object, Functions and States. 2nd, New Jersey, Prentice Hall.

Davydov, M. M. (1994). "From model to database." Database Programming & Design March: 46-52.

de Carteret, C. and R. Vidgen (1995). Data Modelling for Information Systems. London UK, Pitman Publishing.

de Vaus, D. A. (1995). Surveys in Social Research. Sydney, Allen and Unwin.

DeAngelis, M. C. (2000). Data Modeling with ERwin. Indiana, Sams Publishing.

DeMarco, T. (1978). Structured Analysis and System Specification. New York, Yourdon Press Computing Series.

Deming, W. E. (1986). Out of the crisis. Cambridge, Mass, Massachusetts Institute of Technology, Center for Advanced Engineering Study.

Department of Defence (UK) (2005). Corporate Business Modelling Language (CBML).

References

Dexter, L. A. (1970). Elite and Specialized Interviewing. Evanston, IL, Northwestern University Press.

Dey, D., V. C. Storey and T. M. Barron (1999). "Improving Database Design through the Analysis of Relationships." ACM Transactions on Database Systems **24**(4): 453-474.

D'Orazio, R. and G. Happel (1996). Practical Data Modelling for Database Design. Queensland, John Wiley & Sons.

Douglass, B. P. (2002). Real-Time Design Patterns: Robust Scalable Architecture for Real-Time Systems. Addison-Wesley Professional.

Duffy, R. J. (2000). "Modeling Realities: Communicating Consensus." The Data Administration Newsletter(May).

Dunn, C. L. and G. J. Gerard (2001). "Auditor efficiency and effectiveness with diagrammatic and linguistic conceptual model representations." International Journal of Accounting Information Systems **2**(4): 223-248.

Durding, B. M., C. A. Becker and J. D. Gould (1977). "Data organization." Human Factors **19**: 1-14.

Duyne, D. K. v., J. A. Landay and J. I. Hong (2002). The Design of Sites: Patterns, Principles, and Processes for Crafting a Customer-Centered Web Experience. Addison-Wesley Professional.

Earl, M. J. (1993). "Experiences in Strategic Information Systems Planning." MIS Quarterly **17**(1): 1-24.

Eden, P. (1996). A step by step method for conceptual data analysis. 1996 International Conference Software Engineering: Education & Practice, Dunedin, New Zealand, IEEE Computer Society Press.

Ellis, H. and P. Nell (2005). Removing Technical Bias from Semantic Conceptual Modeling of Business Information. Semantic Technology Conference, San Francisco.

Elmasri, R. and S. B. Navathe (1994). Fundamentals of Database Systems. Redwood City, CA, Benjamin/Cummings.

English, L. (1999). Improving Data Warehouse and Business Information Quality: Methods for Reducing Costs and Increasing Profits. New York, Wiley.

Everest, G. C. (1986). Database Management Objectives, System Functions, and Administration. New York, McGraw-Hill Book Company.

Everest, G. C. (1988). ER modeling versus binary modeling. 16th International Conference on E-R Approach, North-Holland, Amsterdam.

Falkenberg, E. D. (1993). DETERM: Deterministic Event-Tuned Entity-Relationship Modeling. 12th International Conference on the ER Approach, Arlington, Texas, USA.

Fellers, J. and R. P. Bostrom (1993). Application of Group Support Systems to Promote Creativity in Information Systems Organizations. Proceedings of 26th Annual Hawaii International Conference on Systems Science.

Fenton, N., S. L. Pfleeger and R. L. Glass (1994). "Science and substance: a challenge to software engineers." IEEE Software **11**(4): 86-95.

Ferg, S. (1991). Cardinality Concepts in Entity-Relationship Modeling. 10th Conference on the Entity Relationship Approach, San Mateo, CA, USA.

Finkelstein, C. (1989). An Introduction to Information Engineering: From Strategy Planning to Information Systems. Addison Wesley, Sydney.

References

Finkelstein, C. and P. Aiken (1999). Building Corporate Portals with XML. McGraw Hill.

Finkelstein, C. and J. Martin (1981). Information Engineering. Karnforth, Lancs, UK, Savant Institute.

Fitts, M. P. and M. I. Posner (1967). Human Performance. Monteray, California, Brooks/Cole.

Fleming, C. C. and B. von Halle (1989). Handbook of Relational Database Design. MA, Addison Wesley.

Flynn, D. J. and O. F. Diaz (1996). Information Modelling; An international perspective. Prentice Hall,.

Fowler, M. (1997). Analysis Patterns:Reusable object models. Massachusetts, Addison-Wesley.

Fowler, M. (1999). Is there such thing as Object Oriented Analysis". Distributed Computing.

Friedlander, B. J. (1985). "Planning for Information Resource Management." Journal of Systems Management(June): pp45-52.

Frost, R., J. Day and C. V. Slyke (2006). Database Design and Development: A Visual Approach. Upper Saddle River, New Jersey, Prentice Hall.

Galambos, G., G. Vasudeva, J. Adams and S. Koushik (2001). Patterns for e-Business : A Strategy for Reuse. Mc Press.

Gane, C. P. and T. Sarson (1979). Structured System Analysis: Tools and Techniques. Englewood Cliffs, NJ, Prentice Hall.

Gasson, S. (1998). Framing design: a social process view of information systems development. Proceedings of the 19th International Conference on Information Systems, Helsinki.

Gat, D. and A. Gonen (1981). "Orientation map for planning and design methods." Design Studies 2(3): 171-175.

Gemino, A. (1998). To be or may to be: An empirical comparison of mandatory and optional properties in conceptual modeling. Administrative Sciences Association of Canada - Annual Conference, Canada, ASAC.

George, J. F., D. Batra, J. S. Valacich and J. A. Hoffer (2004). Object-Oriented Systems Analysis and Design. International Edition, New Jersey, Pearson Education, Inc.

Gero, J. S. and M. L. Maher (1993). Preface. Modeling Creativity and Knowledge-Based Creative Design. J. S. Gero and M. L. Maher. New Jersey, Lawrence Erlbaum Associates, Inc.

Gjersvik, R. (1993). The Reconstruction of Management Reality: A case study of how the construction of a computer-based information system produced organizational closure. 11th EGOS Colloquium, ECSP, Paris, France.

Glass, R. L. and I. Vessey (1994). Sortware Tasks: Intellectual, Clerical ... or Creative? 27th Annual Hawaii International Conference on System Science, Wailea, HI.

Goguen, J. A. and C. Linde (1993). Techniques for Requirements Elicitation. Proceedings Re'93 IEEE International Symposium on Requirements Engineering 1993, San Diego, CA, USA.

Goldfine, A. (1986). "Database Directions: IRM Making It Work"." Bulletin of the IEEE Computer Society Technical Committee on Data Engineering.

Goldschmidt, G. (1991). "The Dialectics of Sketching." Creativity Research Journal 4(2): 123-143.

References

Goldstein, R. C. and V. C. Storey (1990). Some findings on the intuitiveness of entity-relationship constructs. Entity-Relationship Approach to Database Design and Querying. F. H. Lochovsky. Amsterdam, Elsevier Science.

Goodhue, D. L., L. J. Kirsch, J. A. Quillard and M. D. Wybo (1992). "Strategic Data Planning: Lessons From the Field." MIS Quarterly 16(1): 11-35.

Goodhue, D. L., J. A. Quillard and J. F. Rockart (1988). "Managing the data resource: a contingency perspective." MIS Quarterly 12.

Gorman, M. (2000). "Data Model Evaluation Workplan." The Data Administration Newsletter(May).

Gray, D. E. (2004). Doing Research in the Real World. London, Sage Publications.

Groves, R. M. (1996). How do we know what we think they think is really what they think. Answering Questions. N. Schwarz and S. Sudman. San Francisco, Jossey-Bass: 389-402.

Gruber, T. (1993). "A Translation Approach to Portable Ontologies." Knowledge Acquisition 2: 199-220.

Hall, P. A. V. (1992). "Overview of Reverse engineering and reuse research." Information and Software Technology 34(4): 239-249.

Halpin, T. (2001). Information Modeling and Relational Databases. From Conceptual Analysis to Logical Design. California, Morgan Kaufmann Publishers.

Halpin, T., Evans, P. Hallock and M. B (2003). Database Modeling with Microsoft Visio for Enterprise Architects. San Francisco, Morgan Kaufmann.

Halpin, T. and M. Orlowska (1992). "Fact-oriented modelling for data analysis." Journal of Information Systems 2: 97-119.

Hammer, M. (1990). "Reengineering Work: Don't Automate, Obliterate." Harvard Business Review(July-August): 70-91.

Hammer, M. and J. Champy (1993). Reengineering the Corporation - A Manifesto for Business Revolution. HarperCollins.

Hammer, M. and D. McLeod (1981). "Database description with SDM: A semantic database model." ACM Transactions on Database Systems 6(3): 351-386.

Hampton, J. A. (1979). "Polymorphous Concepts in Semantic Memory." Journal of Verbal Learning and Verbal Behavior(18): 441-461.

Hanscome, B. (1998). Process Patterns : Building Large Scale Systems Using Object Technology (SIGS: Managing Object Technology). Cambridge University Press.

Hardgrave, B. and N. P. Dalal (1995). "Comparing Object-Oriented and Extended-Entity-Relationship Data Models." Journal of Database Management 6(3): 15-21.

Hawryszkiewycz, I. T. (1991). Database Analysis and Design. 2nd, New York, Macmillan Publishing Company.

Hawryszkiewycz, I. T. (1997). Introduction to Systems Analysis and Design (4th edition). Sydney, Prentice Hall.

Hay, D. (2005). "Data Model Quality: Where New Data Begin." The Data Administration Newsletter(January).

Hay, D. C. (1996a). Data model patterns: Conventions of Thought. New York, Dorset House Publishing.

Hay, D. C. (1996b). Letter: Data modeling is design? I don't think so. Database Programming & Design. 9: 10.

Hay, D. C. (2003). Requirements Analysis From Business Views to Architecture. Upper Saddle River, NJ, Prentice Hall.

Hay, D. C. (2006). <u>Data Model Patterns: A metadata map - in press</u>. San Francisco, Morgan Kaufmann.

Hedrick, T. E., L. Bickman and D. J. Rog (1993). <u>Applied Research Design: A Practical Guide</u>. Newbury Park, CA, Sage.

Henderson, D. (2002). Data Modeling Fundamentals. <u>Guidelines to Implementing Data Resource Management</u>. 4, D. International. Washington, Data Management Association: 115-129.

Hevner, A. R., S. T. March, J. Park and S. Ram (2004). "Design Science in Information Systems Research." <u>MIS Quarterly</u> **28**(1): 75-105.

Hirschheim, R., H. K. Klein and K. Lyytinen (1995). <u>Information Systems Development and Data Modeling - Conceptual and Philosophical Foundations</u>. Cambridge, Cambridge University Press.

Hitchman, S. (1995). "Practitioner perceptions on the use of some semantic concepts in the entity-relationship model." <u>European Journal of Information Systems</u> **4**(1): 31-40.

Hitchman, S. (1997). "Using DEKAF to understand data modelling in the practitioner domain." <u>European Journal of Information Systems</u>.

Hitchman, S. (1999). "Ternary relationships - to three or not to three, is there a question?" <u>European Journal of Information Systems</u> **8**(3): 224-231.

Hoberman, S. (2002). <u>The Data Modeler's Workbench. Tools and Techniques for Analysis and Design</u>. New York, John Wiley & Sons, Inc.

Hoberman, S. (2005). <u>Data Modeling Made Simple: A Practical Guide for Business & Information Technology Professionals</u>. Technics Publications, LLC.

Hoffer, J. A. (1982). <u>An empirical investigation into individual differences in database models</u>. Third International Conference on Information Systems.

Hohpe, G. and B. Woolf (2003). <u>Enterprise Integration Patterns : Designing, Building, and Deploying Messaging Solutions</u>. Addison-Wesley Professional.

Howard, G. S., T. Bodnovich, T. Janicki, J. Liegle, S. Klein, P. Albert and D. Cannon (1999). "The efficacy of matching information systems development methodologies with application characteristics - an empirical study." <u>The Journal of Systems and Software</u> **45**(3): 177-195.

Howe, D. (2001). <u>Data Analysis for Database Design</u>. Butterworth Heinemann.

Hull, R. and R. King (1987). "Semantic Database Modeling: survey, applications, and research issues." <u>ACM Computing Surveys</u> **19**(3): 201-260.

Hutchins, E. L., J. D. Hollan and D. A. Norman (1985). "Direct manipulation interfaces." <u>Human Computer Interaction</u>(1): 311-338.

Inmon, W. H. (1992). <u>Building the Data Warehouse</u>. Somerset, NJ, Wiley-QED Publishing Group.

ISO/IEC9075-1:2003 (2003). Information Technology - Database languages SQL Part 2: Foundation (SQL/Foundation).

ISO/TC97/SC/WG3-N695 (1982). Concepts and Terminology for the Conceptual Schema and the Information Base. J. van Griethuysen. New York.

ISO/TR9007:1987(E) (1987). Information processing systems - Concepts and terminology for the conceptual schema and information base.

Jackson, M. A. (1975). <u>Principles of Program Design</u>. Academic Press.

Jackson, M. A. (1995). <u>Software Requirements & Specifications. A Lexicon of practice and prejudices</u>. ACM Press.

Jajodia, S. and P. Ng (1984). "Translation of Entity-Relationship Diagrams into Relational Structures." Journal of Systems and Software 4(2-3): 123-133.

Jardine, D. A. (1984). "Concepts and Terminology for the Conceptual Schema and the Information Base." Computers and Standards 3(17).

Jarvenpaa, S. L. and J. J. Machesky (1989). "Data analysis and learning: An experimental study of data modelling tools." International Journal of Man-Machine Studies 31(4): 367-391.

Jones, J. C. (1970). Design Methods: Seeds of Human Futures. New York, Wiley Interscience.

Jones, T. H. and I.-Y. Song (1996). "Analysis of binary/ternary cardinality combinations in entity-relationship modeling." Data & Knowledge Engineering 19: 39-64.

Juhn, S. H. and J. D. Naumann (1985). The effectiveness of data representation Characteristics on user validation. Sixth International Conference on Information Systems, Indianapolis.

Juran, J. and A. B. Godfrey (1999). Juran's Quality Handbook. Fifth Edition, McGraw Hill.

Kahn, D. K. (1983). "Some Realities of Data Administration." Communications of the ACM 26(10): 794-799.

Kalman, K. (1991). "Implementation and critique of an algorithm which maps a Relational Database to a Conceptual Model." Advanced Information Systems Engineering: 393-415.

Kao, D. and N. P. Archer (1997). "Abstraction in conceptual model design." International Journal of Human - Computer Studies(46): 125-150.

Kaposi, A. and B. Kitchenham (1987). "The Architecture of System Quality." Software Engineering Journal 2(8).

Kent, W. (1978). Data and Reality: Basic Assumptions in Data Processing Reconsidered. Amsterdam, New York, North-Holland Pub. Co.

Kent, W. (1983). "A simple guide to five normal forms in relational database theory." Communications of the ACM 26(2): 120-125.

Kent, W. (1984). "Fact-based data analysis and design." Journal of Systems and Software 4(2-3): 99-121.

Kepner, C. H. (1996). "Calling all thinkers." H R Focus 73(10): 3.

Kesh, S. (1995). "Evaluating the quality of entity relationship models." Information and Software Technology 37(12): 681-689.

Keuffel, W. (1996). "Battle of the modeling techniques." DBMS(August): 83-97.

Kim, H. (2002). "Predicting how ontologies for the semantic web will evolve." Communications of the ACM 45(2): 48-54.

Kim, W., I. Choi, S. Gala and M. Scheevel (1995). On resolving schematic heterogeneity in mulitdatabase systems. Modern Database Systems: The Object Model, Interoperability, and Beyond. W. Kim. New York, NY, ACM Press/Addison-Wesley Publ Co: 521-550.

Kim, Y. and G. C. Everest (1994). "Building an IS Architecture: Collective Wisdom from the Field." Information & management(26): 1-10.

Kim, Y.-G. and S. T. March (1995). "Comparing data modeling formalisms." Communications of the ACM 38(6): 103-115.

Kimball, R. (2002). The Data Warehouse Toolkit. 2nd Edition, John Wiley & Sons, Inc.

Kimball, R. and J. Caserta (2004). The Data Warehouse ETL Toolkit. John Wiley & Sons.

Klein, H. K. and R. A. Hirschheim (1987). "A comparative framework of data modelling paradigms and approaches." The Computer Journal **30**(1): 8-15.

Kroenke, D. M. (2005). Database Processing: Fundamentals, Design, and Implementation. New Jersey, Pearson Prentice Hall.

Krogstie, J., O. I. Lindland and G. Sindre (1995). Towards a deeper understanding of quality in requirements engineering. 7th International Conference of Advanced Information Systems Engineering (CAiSE), Springer-Verlag.

Kung, C. H. and A. Solvberg (1986). Activity modeling and behaviour modeling. Information Systems Design Methodologies: Improving the Practice. T. W. Olle, H. G. Sol and A. A. Verrijn-Stuart. Amsterdam, Netherlands, North-Holland: 145-171.

Lakoff, G. (1987). Women, Fire and Dangerous Things - What Categories Reveal about the Mind. Chicago, The University of Chicago Press.

Langefors, B. (1963). "Some Approaches to the Theory of Information Systems." BIT **3**: 229-254.

Langefors, B. and B. Sundgren (1975). Information Systems Architecture. New York, Van Nostrand Reinhold.

Larman, C. (1998). Applying UML and Patterns: An Introduction to Object-Oriented Analysis and Design. Upper Saddle River, New Jersey, Prentice Hall.

Lawson, B. (1997). How Designers Think: The Design Process Demystified. Oxford, Architectural Press.

Lawson, B. R. (1994). Design in Mind. Oxford, Butterworth Architecture.

Lederer, A. L. and V. Sethi (1988). "The implementation of strategic information systems planning methodologies." MIS Quarterly **12**(3): 445-461.

Lee, A. S. (1991a). "Architecture as a reference discipline for MIS." Information Systems Research: 573-592.

Lee, A. S. (1991b). "Integrating Positivist and Interpretive Approaches to Organizational Research." Organization Science **2**(4).

Lee, H. and B. G. Choi (1998). "A comparative study of conceptual data modeling techniques." Journal of Database Management **9**(2): 26-35.

Lewis, P. J. (1993). "Linking soft systems methodology with data-focused information systems development." Journal of Information Systems **3**: 169-186.

Liao, C. and P. C. Palvia (2000). "The impact of data models and task complexity on end-user performance: an experimental investigation." International Journal of Human - Computer Studies **52**(5): 831-845.

Lindland, O. I., G. Sindre and A. Sølvberg (1994). "Understanding quality in conceptual modelling." IEEE Software **11**(2): 42-49.

Lloyd, P. and P. Scott (1994). "Discovering the design problem." Design Studies **15**(2): 125-140.

Lofland, J. and L. H. Lofland (1995). Analyzing social settings. 3, Belmont CA, Wadsworth.

Loosely, C. and C. Gane (1990). "Information Systems Modeling Part 1: The object of processing is data." InfoDB **4**(4).

Lubars, M., C. Potts and C. Richter (1993). A review of the state of the practice in requirements modeling. RE=93: Proceedings of the IEEE International Symposium on Requirements Engineering, Los Alamitos, CA, IEEE Computer Society Press.

Lyytinen, K. (1987). "Two views of information modeling." Information & management **12**: 9-19.

MacDonell (1994). "Software Development, CASE tools and 4GLs - A Survey of New Zealand Usage. Part 1: 750 New Zealand Organisations." New Zealand Journal of Computing **5**(1): 23-33.

Magyari-Beck, I. (1990). "An Introduction to the Framework of Creatology." The Journal of Creative Behaviour **24**(3): 151-161.

Maher, M. L., J. Poon and S. Boulanger (1996). Formalising design exploration as co-evolution: a combined gene approach. Advances in formal design methods for CAD. J. S. Gero and F. Sudweeks. London, UK, Chapman and Hall.

Maiden, N. and A. Gizikis (2001). "Where do Requirements Come From?" IEEE Software(September/October).

Maier, R. (1996). Benefits and quality of data modelling - Results of an empirical analysis. International conference on Conceptual modeling, Germany, Springer.

Mannino, M. V. (2001). Database Application Development & Design. New York, McGraw-Hill.

Mantha, R. W. (1987). "Data flow and data structure modelling for database requirements determination: A comparative study." MIS Quarterly **11**(4): 531-545.

March, S. T. (1992). "Information resource management: integrating the pieces." Database **Summer 1992**: 27-38.

Marche, S. (1991). "On what a building might not be - a case study." 55-66.

Marche, S. (1993). "Measuring the stability of data models." European Journal of Information Systems **2**(1): 37-47.

Marcos, E. and A. Marcos (2001). "A Philosophical Approach to the Concept of Data Model: Is a Data Model, in Fact, a Model?" Information Systems Frontiers **3**(2): 267-274.

Marinescu, F. (2002). EJB Design Patterns: Advanced Patterns, Processes, and Idioms. Wiley.

Martin, J. (1982). Strategic Data-Planning Methodologies. Englewood Cliffs, NJ, Prentice Hall.

Martin, J. (1987). Recommended Diagramming Standards for Analysts and Programmers. Englewood Cliffs, New Jersey, Prentice Hall.

Martin, J. (1989). Strategic Data Planning Methodologies. Prentice Hall.

Martin, J. (1991). Information Engineering: Introduction. Prentice Hall.

Martin, J. and J. Odell (1992). Object-Oriented Analysis and Design. Englewood Cliffs, Prentice-Hall.

Mattos, N. M. (1989). "Abstraction concepts: The basis for data and knowledge modeling." 473-492.

McComb, D. (2004). Sematics in Business Systems. California, Elsevier.

McDermid, J. A. (1991). "In praise of architects." Information and Software Technology **33**(8): 566-575.

McFadden, F. R., J. A. Hoffer and M. Prescott (1999). Modern Database Management. Reading, MA, Addison-Wesley.

McQuade, J. (2005). "Loving to Hate the Data Administrator." The Data Administration Newsletter(October).

Melton, J. and N. M. Mattos (1995). An Overview of the Emerging Third-Generation of the SQL Standard. Proc. ACM SIGMOD Intl. Conf. on Mgt. of Data.

Meyer, B. (1988). Object Oriented Software Construction. First Edition, Prentice Hall.

Miles, M. B. and A. M. Huberman (1994). Qualitative Data Analysis. 2nd Edition, Thousand Oaks, CA, Sage.

Milton, S. K. (2004). Top-Level Ontology: The Problem with Naturalism. Formal Ontology in Information Systems. IOS Press Amsterdam. **114:** 85-94.

Milton, S. K. (2005). Observations of expert data modelers. P. C. t. G. Simsion. Melbourne Australia.

Milton, S. K. and E. Kazmierczak (2004). "An Ontology for Data Modelling
Languages: A Study Using a Common-Sense Realistic Ontology." Journal of Database Management **15**(2): 19-38.

Moody, D. L. (1995). The Seven Habits of highly effective Data Modellers (and Object Modellers?). ER'95 Entity-Relationship Approach 1995 LNCS 1021, Springer Verlag.

Moody, D. L. (1996). Graphical Entity Relationship Models: Towards a more user understandable representation of data. 15th International Conference on Conceptual Modelling, Cottbus, Germany.

Moody, D. L. (1998). Metrics for evaluating the quality of entity relationship models. Seventeenth International Conference on Conceptual Modelling.

Moody, D. L. (2000). Strategies for improving the quality of entity relationship models: a "toolkit" for practitioners. Information Resource Management Association Conference (IRMA), Anchorage, Alaska, Idea Group Publishing.

Moody, D. L. (2001). Dealing with complexity:a practical method for representing large entity-relationship models. Department of Information Systems. Melbourne, Australia, University of Melbourne.

Moody, D. L. (2002). Complexity effects on end user understanding of data models: an experimental comparison of large data model representation. European Conference on Information Systems, Gdansk, Poland.

Moody, D. L. and G. G. Shanks (1994). What makes a good data model? Evaluating the quality of entity-relationship models. 13th International Conference on the Entity-Relationship Approach, Manchester.

Moody, D. L. and G. G. Shanks (1998). "Improving the quality of entity-relationship models: An action research programme." The Australian Computer Journal **30**(4): 129-138.

Moody, D. L. and G. G. Shanks (2003). "Improving the quality of data models: empirical validation of a quality management framework." Information Systems Journal.

Moody, D. L. and G. C. Simsion (1995). "Justifying Investment in Information Resource Management." Australian Journal of Information Systems: 25-37.

Moody, D. L., G. C. Simsion, G. G. Shanks, N. Olson and J. Venable (1995). Stakeholder Perspectives in Conceptual Modelling. 6th Australiasian Conference on Information Systems, Perth, Australia.

Moody, D. L., G. Sindre, T. Brasethvik and A. Solvberg (2003). "Evaluating the quality of information models: Empirical testing of a conceptual model quality framework." IEEE Software: 295-305.

Muller, R. J. (1999). Database Design for Smarties: Using UML for Data Modeling. San Francisco, CA, USA, Morgan Kaufmann.

Murphy, G. L. (2002). The Big Book of Concepts. Cambridge MA, MIT Press.

Myers, I. B. and M. H. McCaulley (1985). MBTI Manual: A Guide to the Development and use of the Myers-Briggs Type Indicator. 2nd Edition, Palo Alto CA, Consulting Psychologists Press Inc.

Myers, I. B., M. H. McCaulley, N. L. Quenk and A. L. Hammer (1998). MBTI Manual (A guide to the development and use of the Myers Briggs type indicator). 3rd Edition, Consulting Psychologists Press.

Myrdal, G. (1973). The beam in our eyes. Comparative Research Methods. D. Warwick and S. Osherson. Englewood Cliffs, NJ, Prentice Hall: pp89-99.

Narayan, S. and J. A. Krosnick (1996). "Education moderates some response effects in attitude measurement." Public Opinion Quarterly(60): 58-88.

Navathe, S., R. Elmasri and J. Larson (1986). "Integrating User Views in Database Design." IEEE Computer 19(1): 50-62.

Navathe, S. and S. Gadgil (1982). A Methodology for View Integration in Logical Database Design, Eighth Very Large Data Base Conference.

Navathe, S. B. (1992). "Evolution of data modeling for databases." Communications of the ACM 35(9): 112-123.

Neuman, W. L. (1999). Social Research Methods: Qualitative and Quantitative Approaches. Needham Heights MA, Allyn & Bacon.

Newell, A., J. Shaw and H. A. Simon (1962). The Process of Creative Thinking. Contemporary Approaches to Creative Thinking. H. Gruber, G. Terrell and M. Wertheimer, Atherton Press.

Newell, A. and H. A. Simon (1972). Human Problem Solving. Englewood Cliffs, N.J., Prentice-Hall.

Nijssen, G. M. and T. A. Halpin (1989). Conceptual Schema and Relational Database Design. Prentice Hall Australia.

Nisbett, R. E. and T. D. Wilson (1977). "Telling more than we can know: Verbal reports on mental processes." Psychological Review 84: 231-259.

Nordbotten, J. C. and M. E. Crosby (1999). "The effect of graphic style on data model interpretation." Information Systems Journal 9(2): 139-155.

Nunally, J. (1978). Psychometric Theory. New York, McGraw Hill.

Oei, J. L. H., L. J. G. T. van Hemen, E. Falkenberg and S. Brinkkemper (1992). The meta model hierarchy: A framework for information systems concepts and techniques. Netherlands, Department of Information Systems, University of Nijmegen, The Netherlands.

Olle, T. W. (1993). "Data modelling and conceptual modelling: A comparative analysis of functionality and roles." Australian Journal of Information Systems 1(1, September): 46-57.

Olle, T. W., J. Hagelstein, MacDonald, Rolland, Sol, V. Assche and Verrijn-Stuart (1991). Information Systems Methodologies - A Framework for Understanding. Addison-Wesley.

O'Rourke, C., N. Fishman and W. Selkow (2003). Enterprise Architecture using the Zachman Framework. Thomson Course Technology.

Ostrander, S. (1993). "Surely you're not in this just to be helpful: Access, rapport and interview in three studies of elites." Journal of Contemporary Ethnography 22: 7-27.

Owen, C. L. (1992). "Context for creativity." Design Studies 13(3): 216-228.

Oxborrow, E. (1986). Database and Database Systems: Concepts and Issues. Lund, Chartwell-Bratt.

Oxford (2005). Oxford Dictionary of Accounting. 3rd Edition, New York, Oxford University Press.

Palvia, P. (1991). "On end-user computing productivity: Results of controlled experiments." Information & Management 21(4): 217-224.

Palvia, P. C., C. Liao and P.-L. To (1992). "The impact of conceptual data models on end-user performance: an experimental investigation." Journal of Database Management 3(4): 4-15.

Parent, A. (1997). "Analysing design-oriented dialogues: a case study in conceptual data modelling." Design Studies 18(1): 43-66.

Parsons, J. (1996). "An Information model based on classification theory." Management Science 42(10): 1437-1449.

Parsons, J. and L. Cole (2004). An experimental examination of property precedence in conceptual modelling. First Asia-Pacific Conference on Conceptual Modelling (APCCM 2004), Dunedin, New Zealand.

Parsons, J. and Y. Wand (1992). Guidelines for Evaluating Classes in Data Modeling. International Conference on Information Systems (ICIS), Dallas, Texas, USA.

Parsons, J. and Y. Wand (1996). "Choosing Classes in Conceptual Modeling." Communications of the ACM 40(6): 63-69.

Parsons, J. and Y. Wand (2000). "Emancipating instances from the Tyranny of Classes in information modeling." ACM Transactions on Database Systems 25(2): 228.

Pascal, F. (2000). Practical Issues in Database Management: A Reference for the Thinking Practitioner. New Jersey, Addison-Wesley.

Pascal, F. (2004). ""Universal Data Models": Levels of Representation and the Importance of Thinking Precisely." The Data Administration Newsletter(March).

Peckham, J. and F. Maryanski (1988). "Semantic data models." ACM Computing Surveys 20(3): 153-189.

Penker, M., M. Penker and H.-E. Eriksson (2000). Business Modeling With UML: Business Patterns at Work. Wiley.

Persson, A. and J. Stirna (2001). Why Enterprise Modelling? An explorative study into current practice. CAiSE'01 Advanced Information Systems Engineering LNCS 2068, Springer Verlag.

Pervan, G. P. and D. J. Klass (1992). The Use and Misuse of Statistical Methods in Information Systems Research. Information Systems Research: Issues, Methods and Practical Guidelines. R. D. Galliers. Oxford, Blackwell: 208-229.

Piscione, R. (2003). "Measures of Data Model Value." The Data Administration Newsletter(Jan).

Pletch, A. (1989). "Conceptual Modelling in the Classroom." SIGMOD record 18(1): 74-80.

Porter, T. and S. Goodman (1988). Designer Primer for Architects, Graphic Designers and Artists. London, Butterworth Architecture.

Portillo, M. and J. H. Dohr (1994). "Bridging Process and Structure through Criteria." Design Studies 15(4): 403-416.

Post, G. (1999). Database Management Systems: Designing and Building Business Applications. Irwin/McGraw Hill.

References

Premerlani, W. J. and M. R. Blaha (1994). "An Approach for Reverse Engineering of Relational Databases." Communications of the ACM **37**(5): 42-49.

Prietula, M. J. and S. T. March (1991). "Form and substance in physical database design: An empirical study." Information Systems Research **2**(4): 287-314.

Ramesh, V. and G. J. Browne (1999). "Expressing causal relationships in conceptual database schemas." The Journal of Systems and Software **45**(3): 225-232.

Reiner, D. (1991). "Research areas related to Practical Problems in Automated Database Design." SIGMOD record **20**(3): 79-82.

Reiner, D. (1992). Database design tools. Conceptual Database Design: An Entity-Relationship Approach. C. Batini, S. Ceri and S. B. Navathe. Redwood City, CA, Benjamin/Cummings.

Rhodes, M. (1961). "An Analysis of Creativity." Phi Delta Kappan(42): 305-310.

Ridjanovic, D. (1986). Comparing quality of data representations produced by non-experts using logical data structures and relational data models. Brisbane, University of Queensland.

Rob, P. and C. Coronel (2002). Database Systems Design, Implementation, and Management. Massachusetts, Course Technology.

Robson, C. (1993). Real World Research. Oxford, Blackwell.

Rolland, C., C. Souveyet and M. Moreno (1995). "An approach for defining ways of working." Information Systems **20**(4): 337-359.

Roman, G. C. (1985). "A Taxonomy of Current Issues in Requirements Engineering." IEEE Computer **18**(4): 14-22.

Roozenburg, N. F. M. and N. G. Cross (1991). "Models of the design process: Integrating across the disciplines." Design Studies **12**(4): 215-220.

Rosch, E. (1978). Principles of Categorisation. Cognition and Categorisation. E. Rosch and B. B. Lloyd. Hillsdale, New Jersey, Lawrence Erlbaum Associates: 27-48.

Ross, R. G. (2003). Principles of the Business Rule Approach. Boston MA, Addison-Wesley.

Rueping, A. (2003). Agile Documentation : A Pattern Guide to Producing Lightweight Documents for Software Projects. John Wiley & Sons.

Rumbaugh, J. (1993). "On the horns of the modeling dilemma." Journal of Object Oriented Programming: 8-17.

Rumbaugh, J., I. Jacobson and G. Booch (1999). The Unified Modeling Language Reference Manual. Reading, Masachuttsess, Addison-Wesley.

Ryan, S. D., B. Bordoloi and D. A. Harrison (2000). "Acquiring Conceptual Data Modeling Skills: The Effect of Cooperative Learning and Self-Efficacy on Learning Outcomes." The DATA BASE for Advances in Information Systems **31**(4): 9-24.

Sager, M. T. (1988). "Data Centred Enterprise Modelling Methodologies - A study of Practice and Potential." The Australian Computer Journal **20**(3): 145-150.

Sampson, J. (2002). Understanding Categorisation: An Experientialist Perspective. Xth European Conference on Information Systems (ECIS), Gdansk, Poland.

Sapir, E. (1931). "Conceptual Categories in Primitive Languages." Science **74**: 578.

Saunders, M., P. Lewis and A. Thornhill (2000). Research Methods for Business Students. London, Prentice Hall.

Sayer, A. (1992). Method in Social Science: A Realist Approach. 2nd Edition, New York, Routledge.

References

Scheer, A.-W. and A. Hars (1992). "Extending data modeling to cover the whole enterprise." Communications of the ACM **35**(35): 9.

Schenck, D. A. and P. R. Wilson (1994). Information Modeling: The EXPRESS Way. New York, Oxford University Press.

Schmidt, B. (1996). Letter: Data modeling is design? I don't think so. Database Programming & Design. **9:** 10.

Schmidt, D., M. Stal, H. Rohnert and F. Buschmann (2000). Pattern-Oriented Software Architecture, Volume 2, Patterns for Concurrent and Networked Objects. West Sussex, UK, John Wiley & Sons Ltd.

Schouten, H. (1993). A Comparison of Conceptual Graphs with NIAM. NIAM-ISDM Conference, Utrecht, The Netherlands.

Schwartz, R. B. and M. C. Russo (2004). "How to Quickly Find Articles in the top IS Journals." Communications of the ACM **47**(2): 98-101.

Searle, J. R. (1997). The Construction of Social Reality. Free Press.

Seiner, R. S. (2001). "Importance of the data and knowledge management specialist." The Data Administration Newsletter(October).

Senko, M. E., E. B. Altman, M. M. Astrahan and P. L. Feiider (1973). "Data Structures and accessing in data-base systems." IBM Systems Journal **12**(1): 30-93.

Shanks, G. G. (1996a). Building and Using Corporate Data Models. Department of Information Systems. Melbourne, Australia, Monash University.

Shanks, G. G. (1996b). Enterprise Data Architectures: An Empirical Study. Melbourne, Australia, Monash University.

Shanks, G. G. (1997a). "The challenges of strategic data planning in practice: An interpretive case study." Journal of Strategic Information Systems **6**(1): 69-90.

Shanks, G. G. (1997b). "Conceptual data modelling: An empirical study of expert and novice data modellers." Australian Journal of Information Systems **4**(2): 63-73.

Shanks, G. G. and P. Darke (1997). Quality in conceptual modelling: Linking theory and practice. Pacific Asia Conference on Information Systems, Brisbane, Queensland University of Technology.

Shanks, G. G. and P. Darke (1999). "Understanding corporate data models." Information & management **35**(1): 19-30.

Shanks, G. G., J. Nuredini, D. Tobin, D. Moody and R. Weber (2002a). "Representing Things and Properties in Conceptual Modelling: an Empirical Evaluation."

Shanks, G. G., J. Nuredini, D. Tobin, E. Tansley and R. Weber (2002b). "An Empirical Evaluation of Conceptual Modelling Practices."

Shanks, G. G., J. Nuredini, D. Tobin and R. Weber (2002c). "Representing Things and Properties in Conceptual Modelling: Understanding the Impact of Task Type."

Shanks, G. G., A. Rouse and D. Arnott (1993). "A Review of Approaches to Research and Scholarship in Information Systems."

Shanks, G. G. and G. C. Simsion (1992). Automated support for creative database design. Research and Practical Issues in Databases. B. Srinivasan and J. Zeleznikov, World Scientific Publishing**:** 293-305.

Shanks, G. G., G. C. Simsion and M. Rembach (1993). The Role of Experience in Conceptual Schema Design. Proc. 4th Australian Conference on Information Systems, Brisbane, Australia.

Shanks, G. G. and P. A. Swatman (1997). Building and using corporate data models: A case study of four Australian Banks. Proc. Pacific Asia Conference on Information Systems, Brisbane, Queensland University of Technology.

Shanks, G. G., E. Tansley, J. Nuredini, D. Tobin and R. Weber (2002). Representing Part-Whole Relationships in Conceptual Modeling: An Empirical Evaluation. Twenty-Third International Conference on Information Systems.

Shanks, G. G., E. Tansley and R. Weber (2003). "Using Ontology to Validate Conceptual Models." Communications of the ACM 46(10): 85-89.

Shanks, G. G., E. Tansley and R. Weber (2004). "Representing Composites in Conceptual Modeling." Communications of the ACM 47(7): 77-80.

Sharp, A. and P. McDermott (2001). Workflow Modeling: Tools for Process Improvement and Application Development. MA, ARTECH HOUSE INC.

Sharp, J. K. (1993). A Comparison of IDEF1X and NIAM-ISDM. Proceedings of the NIAM-ISDM Conference, Utrecht, The Netherlands.

Shasha, D. and P. Bonnet (2003). Database Tuning. California, Morgan Kaufmann.

Shave, M. J. R. (1981). "Entities, functions and binary relations: steps to a conceptual schema." The Computer Journal 24(1): 42-46.

Sheth, A. P. and J. A. Larson (1990). "Federated database systems for managing distributed, heterogeneous, and autonomous databases." ACM Computing Surveys 22(3): 183-236.

Shoval, P. (1997). "Experimental comparisons of Entity-Relationship and Object-Oriented Data models." Australian Journal of Information Systems 4(2).

Shoval, P. and M. Even-Chaime (1987). "Data base schema design: An experimental comparison between normalization and information analysis." Database 18(3): 30-39.

Shoval, P. and I. Frumermann (1994). "OO and EER Conceptual Schemas: A Comparison of User Comprehension." Journal of Database Management 5(4): 28-38.

Shoval, P. and S. Shiran (1997). "Entity-relationship and object-oriented data modeling - experimental comparison of design quality." Data & Knowledge Engineering 21(3): 297-315.

Siau, K., Y. Wand and I. Benbasat (1996). When Parents Need Not Have Children. Cognitive Biases in Information Modeling. International Conference in Advanced Systems Enginering (CAiSE '96).

Siau, K., Y. Wand and I. Benbasati (1995). A Psychological Study on the Use of Relationship Concept - Some Preliminary Findings. Lecture Notes in Computer Science. J. Ilvari, K. Lyytinen and M. Rossi, Springer. 932: 341-354.

Silverston, L. (2001). The Data Model Resource Book. John Wiley & Sons, Inc.

Silverston, L., W. H. Inmon and K. Graziano (1997). The Data Model Resource Book. New York, John Wiley & Sons, Inc.

Simon, H. A. (1973). "The structure of ill structured problems." Artificial Intelligence 4: 181-202.

Simsion, G. C. (1989). "A structured approach to data modelling." The Australian Computer Journal 21(2): 108-117.

Simsion, G. C. (1991). Creative data modelling - encouraging innovation in data design. Bridging the gap: 10th International Conference on Entity Relationship Approach, San Mateo, California, USA.

Simsion, G. C. (1993). Implementation of very generalised data structures. Fourth Australian Database Conference, Brisbane, Australia.

Simsion, G. C. (1994). Data Modeling Essentials: Analysis, Design, and Innovation. New York, Van Nostrand Reinhold.

Simsion, G. C. (1996). "Data Modeling: Testing the Foundations." Database Programming & Design(February).

Simsion, G. C. (2005a). Better Data Models - Today: Understanding Data Model Quality. The Data Administration Newsletter.

Simsion, G. C. (2005b). "Tackling Data Modelers' Toughest Challenge." The Data Administration Newsletter(2nd Quarter).

Simsion, G. C. (2005c). You're making it up! Data Modeling - Analysis or Design. The Data Administration Newsletter.

Simsion, G. C. and G. G. Shanks (1993). "Choosing Entity Types - A Study of 51 Data Modellers." Monash University Working Paper Series 17/93 Dept of Information Systems, Melbourne, Australia.

Simsion, G. C. and G. C. Witt (2005). Data Modeling Essentials. Third Edition, San Francisco, Morgan Kaufmann Publishers.

Singleton, R. and B. C. Straits (1999). Approaches to Social Research. 3rd Edition, Oxford University Press, USA.

Sinha, A. P. and I. Vessey (1999). An Empirical Investigation of Entity-Based and Object-Oriented Data Modeling: A Development Life Cycle Approach. International Conference on Information Systems, Charlotte, North Carolina, United States.

Smith, J. M. and D. C. P. Smith (1977). "Database Abstractions: Aggregation and Generalization." Communications of the ACM 20(6): 405-413.

Smith, J. M. and D. C. P. Smith (1978). Principles of database conceptual design. Proceedings of the NYU Symposium on Data Base Design Techniques in Requirements and Logical Structures, London, UK, Springer Verlag.

Soanes, C. and S. Hawker (2005). Compact Oxford English Dictionary of Current English. 3, Oxford, UK, Oxford University Press.

Sommerville, I. and P. Sawyer (1997). Requirements Engineering - a Good Practice Guide. New York, John Wiley & Sons.

Song, I.-Y., K. Yano, J. Trujillo and S. Lujan-Mora (2005). A Taxonomic Class Modeling Methodology for Object-Oriented Analysis. Information Modeling Methods and Methodologies. Hershey, Idea Group Publishing.

Sowa, J. F. and J. A. Zachman (1992). "Extending and formalizing the framework for information systems architecture." IBM Systems Journal 31(3): 590-616.

Srinivasan, A. and D. Te'eni (1990). Abstraction based modeling: an empirical study of the process. International Conference on Information Systems 1990.

Srinivasan, A. and D. Te'eni (1995). "Modeling as constrained problem solving: An empirical study of the data modeling process." Management Science 41(3): 419-435.

Stamper, R., K. Althans and J. Backhouse (1988). "Measur: Method for Eliciting, Analysing and Specifying User Requirements." Computerized Assistance During the Information Systems Life Cycle: 67-115.

Steinberg, G., R. Faley and S. Chinn (1994). "Automatic database generation by novice end-users using English sentences." Journal of Systems Management 45(3): 10-15.

References

Stephens, R. K. and R. R. Plew (2001). Database Design. Indiana, Sams Publishing.

Stodder, D. B. (1996). Editorial: Data modeling is design? I don't think so. Database Programming & Design. **9**: 9.

Storey, V. C., D. Dey, H. Ullrich and S. Sundaresan (1998). "An ontology-based expert system for database design." Data & Knowledge Engineering **28**(1): 31-46.

Storey, V. C. and R. C. Goldstein (1988). "A methodology for creating user views in database design." ACM Transactions on Database Systems **13**(3): 305-338.

Storey, V. C., R. C. Goldstein and J. Ding (2002). "Common Sense Reasoning in Automated Database Design: An Empirical Test." Journal of Database Management **Winter**: 3-14.

Storey, V. C., C. B. Thompson and S. Ram (1995). "Understanding database design expertise." Data & Knowledge Engineering **16**: 97-124.

Strauss, A. (1987). Qualitiative analysis for social scientists. New York, Cambridge University Press.

Sutcliffe, A. G. and N. A. M. Maiden (1992). "Analysing the Novice Analyst: Cognitive Models in Software Engineering." International Journal Man-Machine Studies **36**(5): 719-740.

Tansley, E. (2003). Quality in Data Modelling: Creating and Understanding Data Models. Faculty of Informatics and Computing. Rockhampton, Australia, Central Queensland University.

Tauzovich, B. (1990). An Expert system for Conceptual Data Modelling. ER'90 Entity-Relationship Approach 1990, North-Holland, Elsevier Science Publishing.

Teorey, T. J. (1999). Database Modeling and Design. Third Edition, San Francisco, CA, Morgan Kaufmann Publishers.

Teorey, T. J., S. Lightstone and T. Nadeau (2006). Database Modeling and Design. 4th Edition, San Francisco, Morgan Kaufmann.

Teorey, T. J., D. Yang and J. P. Fry (1986). "A Logical Design Methodology for Relational Databases Using the Extended Entity-Relationship Model." ACM Computing Surveys **18**(2): 197-222.

Thalheim, B. (2000). Entity-Relationship Modelling: Foundations of Database Technology. Berlin Heidelberg, Springer Verlag.

Thomasson, A. L. (2003). "Foundations for a Social Ontology." Proto-Sociology **18**(19): 269-290.

Tolis, C. (1996). Working with models in development work: Differences that hinder or facilitate. Proceedings of the 7th Australian Conference on Information Systems, (ACIS'96), University of Tasmania, Hobart, Tasmania.

Topi, H. and V. Ramesh (2002). "Human factors research on data modeling: a review of prior research, an extended framework and future research directions." Journal of Database Management **13**(2): 3-19.

Toumin, S. (1972). Human Understanding - the Collective Use and Evolution of Concepts. Princeton, NJ, Princeton University Press.

Tsichritzis, D. C. and F. H. Lochovsky (1982). Data Models. Englewood Cliffs, New Jersey, Prentice-Hall.

Venable, J. R. (1999). "Commentary on 'the effect of graphic style on data model interpretation'." Information Systems Journal(9): 157-160.

Verelst, J. (2004a). Variability in Conceptual Modeling. University of Antwerp.

Verelst, P. d. J. (2004b). The influence of the level of abstraction on the evolvability of conceptual models of information systems. 2004 International Symposium on Empirical Software Engineering (ISESE'04), Redondo Beach, California.

Verheijen, G. M. A. and J. van Bekkum (1982). NIAM: An Information Analysis Method. Information System Design Methodologies: A Comparative Review. T. W. Olle, H. G. Sol and A. A. V. Stuart, North-Holland, Amsterdam: 537--590.

Veryard, R. (1984). Pragmatic Data Analysis. Oxford, Blackwell Scientific Publications.

Veryard, R. (1992). Information Modelling: Practical Guidance. Englewood Cliffs, New Jersey, Prentice-Hall.

Vitalari, N. and G. Dickson (1983). "Problem solving for effective systems analysis: an experimental exploration." Communications of the ACM 26(11): 948-956.

von Halle, B. (1991). "Data: Asset or Liability." Database Programming & Design 4(7).

Wade, S. (1991). "A New Course in Systems Analysis and Design." International Journal of Information Management 11: 238-247.

Wand, Y., D. E. Monarchi, J. Parsons and C. C. Woo (1995). "Theoretical foundations for conceptual modelling in information systems development." Decision Support Systems 15(4): 285-305.

Wand, Y., V. C. Storey and R. Weber (1999). "An ontological analysis of the relationship construct in conceptual modeling." ACM Transactions on Database Systems 24(4): 494-528.

Wand, Y. and R. Weber (1989). An ontological evaluation of systems analysis and design methods. Information Systems Concepts: An In-depth Analysis. E. D. Falkenberg and P. Lindgreen, North-Holland: 79-107.

Wand, Y. and R. Weber (1990). "An ontological model of an information system." IEEE Transactions on Software Engineering 16(11): 1282-1292.

Wand, Y. and R. Weber (1993). "On the ontological expressiveness of information systems analysis and design grammars." Journal of Information Systems 3(4): 217-237.

Wand, Y. and R. Weber (2002). "Research Commentary: Information systems and conceptual modeling - a research agenda." Information Systems Research 13(4): 363-376.

Warner, R. (1996). Letter: Data modeling is design? I don't think so. Database Programming & Design. 9: 10.

Weber, R. (1996). "Are Attributes Entities? A Study of Database Designers' Memory Structures." Information Systems Research 7(2): 137-161.

Weber, R. (1997a). The link between data modeling approaches and philosophical assumptions: A critique. Americas Conference on Information Systems, Indianapolis.

Weber, R. (1997b). Ontological Foundations of Information Systems. Melbourne, Australia, Coopers & Lybrand and the Accounting Association of Australia and New Zealand.

Weber, R. (1997c). "Optional properties versus subtyping in conceptual modeling: Further evidence." Unpublished.

Weber, R. and Y. Zhang (1991). An ontological evaluation of NIAM's grammar for conceptual schema diagrams. 12th International Conference on Information Systems, New York.

Wedemeijer, L. (2002). Exploring Conceptual Schema Evolution. Technische Universiteit Delft.

References

Willem, R. A. (1991). "Varieties of design." Design Studies **12**(3): 132-136.

Wimmer, K. and N. Wimmer (1992). "Conceptual modeling based on ontological principles." Knowledge Acquisition **4**: 387-406.

Winter, K. (1986). Entity Multityping. The Practitioners Blueprint for Logical and Physical Database Design. New Jersey, Prentice-Hall: 235-239.

Witt, G. C. (1997). "Is Data Modeling Standing Still?" Database Programming & Design **10**(8).

Witt, G. C. (1998). "The Role of Meta Data in Data Quality." Journal of Data Warehousing(Winter).

Witt, G. C. (2002a). Assertion-based Modeling. DAMA International Conference, San Antonio, Texas, USA.

Witt, G. C. (2002b). Developing an Enterprise Object Class Hierarchy. DAMA European Conference, London, UK.

Wittgenstein, L. (1953). Philosophical Investigations. New York, Macmillan.

Wood-Harper, A. T. and G. Fitzgerald (1982). "A taxonomy of current approaches to systems analysis." The Computer Journal **25**: 12-16.

Yacoub, S. M. and H. H. Ammar (2003). Pattern-Oriented Analysis and Design: Composing Patterns to Design Software Systems. Addison-Wesley Professional.

Yang, H.-L. (2003). "Comparing relational database designing approaches: some managerial implications for database training." Industrial Management & Data Systems **103**(3): 150-167.

Yao, S. B., S. B. Navathe and J. L. Weldon (1978). "A integrated approach to logical database design." NYU Symp. Database Design: 1-14.

Yin, R. K. (1994). Case Study Research: Design and Methods. 2nd Edition, Thousand Oaks CA, Sage.

Yourdon, E. (1989). Modern Structured Analysis. Englewood Cliffs, New Jersey, Yourdon Press Prentice Hall.

Yunker, K. (1993). The Dependency between Representation and Procedure. Proceedings of the NIAM-ISDM Conference, Utrecht, The Netherlands.

Zachman, J. A. (1987). "A framework for information systems architecture." IBM Systems Journal **26**(3): 275-291.

Zeleny, M. (1987). "Management support systems: Towards integrated knowledge management." Human Systems Management **7**: 59-70.

References

APPENDIX – STUDIES OF HUMAN FACTORS IN DATA MODELING

The papers listed below were located by the literature search described in Chapter 5. The information provided about each paper follows Topi and Ramesh ((2002).

Reference	Nature of investigation	Independent Variable	Dependent Variable
Amer, T. S. (1993)	Audit review of conceptual data models using 67 subjects.	Relational representation / (Chen) E-R representation	Data model characteristics (number of mistakes found)
Antony, S. and D. Batra (1999)	Use of knowledge based system as aid to modeling using 89 subjects.	Knowledge-based support system (2 versions – "restrictive" and "guidance) + control	Model accuracy, perceived ease of use, modeler satisfaction
Barclay, Crerar, and Davidson, (1994)	Comparing software tools using 3 subjects.	In-house software vs flip-chart	Subject interactions with modeling media
Batra, D., J. A. Hoffer, et al. (1990).	EER vs Relational modeling using 42 subjects.	Formalism	Correctness / accuracy of model. Perceived ease of use.
Batra, D. and J. G. Davis (1992)	Protocols of novices vs experts using 9 subjects.	Novice / Expert	Model quality, verbal protocol
Batra, D. and S. Antony (1994a).	Errors made by novices in conceptual and logical modeling using 31 (experiment 1), and 29 (experiment 2) subjects.	N/A ('experiment' is actually observation)	Verbal protocols, errors
Batra, D. and S. R. Antony (1994b).	Relational model vs ER in modeling user views using 32 subjects	Relational vs E-R conventions	Model quality
Batra, D. and S.R. Antony (2001)	Efficacy of consulting system in reducing data modeling errors using 72 subjects.	Use of tool	Model correctness
Batra, D. and Kirs (1993)	Comparison of approaches to Relational DB design: DA vs LRDM using 72 subjects.	Approach	Model correctness
Batra, D. and Sein (1994)	Improving conceptual modeling through feedback using 30 subjects.	Feedback	Accuracy of models
Batra, Wishart (2004)	Comparison of rule based and pattern based approaches to modeling using 27 subjects.	Training method (rule based or pattern based)	Quality of model

Research Task	Size of Model	Results
Laboratory experiment – identify errors in model vs narrative.	5 models, example has 8 entities	Subjects identified errors more readily in models documented using E-R conventions
Laboratory experiment – develop data model from description (not included in paper)	5 entities	Users of KB systems outperformed Control group
Create & label entity, relationships, attributes etc	~ 5 entities	Medium effected behaviour.
Develop model from description	8 entities including 2 subtypes, 5 relationships, 19 attributes	EER model scored higher on all constructs on unary relationships. No significant difference in ease of use
Develop a data model from given description.	Not stated	Experts used different protocols, focused on holistic understanding and recognition of patterns. Novices less competent and more literal.
Laboratory experiment: 8 different tasks – descriptions in a variety of formats	8 models. 4-5 entities in cases described	Novices made numerous errors. Bias was the result of anchoring. Protocol analysis showed other heuristics also leading to errors.
Create model of 'user view'	ranged from 1 to 3 entities, 3 to 13 attributes, 0 to 2 relationships	Novices performed better with ER model. Degree of nesting had a significant effect on performance
Develop a data model from given description.	5 entities, 4 entities	Consulting system reduced errors
Develop a data model from given description.	9 tables	No significant dif in relational solutions, but difficulty translating ER to relational
Develop model from text description	5 entities, 4 relationships, 14 attributes	Feedback improved models in 62.5% of cases
Develop model from description and forms	task 1: 3 entities 2 relationships, Task2: 5 entities 4 relationships, Task 3: 6 entities 4 relationships	Rule base superior in low complexity and high complexity cases. No significant difference in medium complexity case.

Reference	Nature of investigation	Independent Variable	Dependent Variable
Bock, D. B. and T. F. Ryan (1993)	Comparison of EER and Kroenke's OO model using 38 subjects.	EER vs OO	Model quality
Bodart, F., A. Patel, et al. (2001).	Should optional properties be used – 3 experiments using 52, 52 and 96 subjects.	Optional properties vs subtypes	Recall, comprehension, problem solving
Brosey, M. and B. Shneiderman (1978).	Relational model vs Hierarchical model using 38 subjects.	Relational vs Hierarchical, beginners vs advanced	Comprehension
Burton-Jones, A. and R. Weber (1999).	Relationships with attributes using 76 subjects.	Ontological clarity (relationships with and without attributes)	Problem solving performance, ease of understanding
Chaiyasut, P. and G. G. Shanks (1994).	Investigates cognitive behaviour using protocol analysis using 8 subjects.	Novice / Expert	Data model characteristics
Crerar, Barclay & Watt (1996)	Use of an interactive tool to support "creative" data modeling using 4 subjects.	N/A	N/A
Danoch, Shoval & Balabaan (2005)	Comprehension of hierarchical ER diagrams vs flat ER diagrams using 42 subjects.	Representation – flat or hierarchic	Comprehension, subject satisfaction, time to complete
Dunn & Gerard (2001)	Comparing understanding of ER vs Backus-Naur Form (BNF) using 46 subjects.	Formalism	Time, accuracy, perceived ease of use
Durding, Becker, Gould (1977)	How people organise data using 56 subjects.	Data semantics	Data organisation
Gemino, A. (1998).	Mandatory vs Optional Properties (attributes) using 64 subjects	Format of model, optional properties	Model comprehension
Hardgrave and Dalal (1995)	Database designers' comprehension of OO vs EER models using 56 subjects.	Formalism OO vs EER	Model comprehension, time to comprehend, perceived ease of use

Research Task	Size of Model	Results
Develop a data model from given description.	Not stated omitted	EER provided better results in 3 of eight facets of correctness
Recall, comprehension, problem solving	6 entities, 12 entities	Models using subtypes rather than optional properties were better understood at the deep level
Comprehension and memory – answer questions	Experiment 1: 7 tables, Experiment 2: 3 tables	Hierarchical model performed better
Problem solving	7 entities, 13 entities	Models in unfamiliar domain were better understood if attributes on relationships were avoided.
Verbal protocol exercise with small narrative problem	Not stated	Experts & novices spent much time in understanding, searching for solutions and representing information. Experts had holistic understanding of problem and reused generic models from previous experience.
Develop model from description	Not stated	"Experts" showed typical expert design behaviour – re-use, holistic approach
Answer questionnaire	21 entities, 49 attributes, 20 relationships	No significant difference in comprehension or time. Subjects preferred hierarchical model
Interpret models – answer questions from model	Model 1: 8 entities, 13 relationships 49 attributes Model 2: 8 entities, 13 relationships, 47 attributes	ER outperformed Backus-Naur Form (BNF)
Organise words into structures	N/A	Subjects organised most word sets on the basis of inherent sematic relations
Comprehension, problem solving	Model :19 entities, 10 relationships, 38 attributes, Model 2: 9 entities, 10 relationships, 32 attributes	Comprehension scores higher on models with subtypes
Answer multiple choice questions about models	Not stated	No significant differences

Reference	Nature of investigation	Independent Variable	Dependent Variable
Hitchman, S. (1995).	How well do practitioners understand ER constructs using 80 subjects.	N/A	N/A
Hoffer, J. A. (1982).	Differences in database models using 48 subjects.	Learning Style (Kolb LSI, experience, task)	Number of files, confidence, db architecture, formalism choice etc
Howard, Bodnovich, Janicki, Liegle, Klein, Albert, Cannon (1999)	Data-driven vs Process driven approaches using 30 subjects.	Sequence of E-R and DFD	Quality of designs judged by experts
Jarvenpaa, S. L. and J. J. Machesky (1989).	LDS vs Relational – ease of learning using 36 subjects.	Formalism, amount of practice	Accuracy, understanding, etc
Juhn, S. H. and J. D. Naumann (1985).	ER vs Relational vs Data Access Diagram, vs LDS using 30 subjects.	Formalism	Comprehension, model
Kim, Y.-G. and S. T. March (1995).	EER vs NIAM using 28 subjects.	Formalism	Task performance, perceived usefulness
Lee, H. and B. G. Choi (1998).	EER vs SOM vs ORM vs OMT using 100 subjects.	Formalism	Performance
Liao and Palvia (2000)	EER vs Relational vs OO using 66 subjects.	Formalism	model correctness, time, perceived ease of use
Mantha, R. W. (1987).	Differences in data and process models (only data covered here) using 10 subjects.	DSD vs DFD	model comprehensiveness
Moody (2002)	Comparison of approaches to data model leveling using 60 subjects.	Representation method (levelling approach)	Comprehension performance, verification performance

Research Task	Size of Model	Results
Create models for simple scenarios	Simple models of recursion, subtypes orthogonal subtypes, exclusivity	Many modelers did not show facility with basic ER constructs
Create model for a scenario	Not stated	Poor quality models incorporating process
Create DFD and ERD	Authors' solution was 8 entities and 8 relationships	No significant difference in performance
Develop a data model from given description.	5 entities	LDS gave superior results
Comprehension and creation of a model	10 entities	Graphical notations better understood. Modeling more systematic with these notations.
Modelling and validation	Comprehension model 12 entities, 12 relationships, 33 attributes. Discrepancy checking and Modeling task 12 entities, 13 relationships, 27 attributes	EER analysts did better than or equal to NIAM.
Modelling and validation	Not stated	Significant differences in performance across methodologies
Develop a model from text description	Not stated	Mixed
Create a model from text description and reports	22 entities	DSD analysts performed better
Answer questions (comprehension, verify against requirements)	98 entities + 11 including subtypes 480 attributes	Levelled model performed best, all performed poorly.

Reference	Nature of investigation	Independent Variable	Dependent Variable
Moody, D. L. and G. G. Shanks (2003).	Quality assessment of data models. Assess models developed in Shanks (1997) other empirical research reported in Shanks & Darke (1997)	Novice vs Expert	Model quality
Moody, D. L., G. Sindre, et al. (2003).	Quality assessment of data models using 192 subjects.	20 models?	Performance of evaluation task; Perception of framework
Nordbotten, J. C. and M. E. Crosby (1999).	Effect of "graphic style" on model comprehension – NIAM, SSM OODM using 35 subjects.	Formalism	Comprehension
Palvia (1991)	Compare hierarchical, network, relational, object formalisms using 149 subjects.	Formalism	Understanding of database and time taken.
Palvia, P. C., C. Liao, et al. (1992).	Effect of formalism on (a) comprehension / user productivity (b) perceptions using (a)121 (b) 30 subjects.	Formalism	(a) Comprehension, efficiency (b) perceptions
Parent (1997) Analysing Design	Analysing exchanges between novice modeler and domain expert using 7 subjects.	N/A	N/A
Parsons, J. and L. Cole (2004).	Effect of precedence extension on comprehension using 29 subjects.	Formalism, semantics	Comprehension
Prietula, M. J. and S. T. March (1991).	Experts vs novices in physical database design using 13 subjects.	Experience	Verbal protocols, Design quality
Ramesh and Browne (1999)	Use of causal relationships in modeling using 78 subjects.	Training in data modeling	Correct use of causal relationship
Ryan, S. D., B. Bordoloi, et al. (2000).	Training of data modelers individual work vs cooperative learning using 109 subjects.	Method of learning	Model quality etc

Research Task	Size of Model	Results
See Shanks 97 evaluate quality of models	Variable – Shanks 97	(a) Experts produced higher quality models
Develop a data model from given description. Evaluate another data model	Not stated	Framework easy to use, partially reliable
Interpret models	2 (primary) entity types + subtypes	Significant differences in comprehension – IDEF1X, SSM, OODM, NIAM (poorest)
Answer questions about model; make modifications	3 entities, 2 relationships	Object and network model performed better than relational and hierarchical
(a) Interpret models (b) Perceptions survey	3 entities	Significant differences in efficiency ranked OO, DSD, ER. Perceptions ranked OO, ER, DSD overall.
Develop model from description	16 entities, 20relationships, 40 attributes.	12 question types identified
Interpret models	4 objects	Extension helps verify precedence but not cardinality. ALSO informal semantics inferred from words in diagram may interfere with interpretation.
Develop physical design	2 models. More complex one had 6? (some ambiguity in text)	Significant differences in protocols and quality of designs
Develop model from text description	6 'critical' entities	Untrained modeler modeled causal relationships better. Both groups did poorly.
Develop model from text description	refer Kroenke 92 (heavy equip manufacture product adverts)	No significant difference in DM quality for different learning methods

Reference	Nature of investigation	Independent Variable	Dependent Variable
Shanks, G., G. Simsion, M Rembach. (1993). "The Role of Experience in Conceptual Schema Design."	Experts vs novices in conceptual schema design using 17 subjects.	Experience	Quality of model – completeness, innovation, stability
Shanks, G. G. (1997b)	Experts vs novices in preparing a conceptual model using 39 subjects.	Experience	Quality of model – correctness, completeness, innovation, flexibility, understandability, overall quality
Shanks, G. G. and P. Darke (1997)	Opinion of tool for evaluating quality of conceptual models using 20 subjects.	N/A	N/A
Shanks, Tansley, Nuredini, Tobin, Weber (2002 Representing Part whole relationships in conceptual (23rd conf on IS)	Testing part whole (ternary) relationships using ontology with 20 subjects.	Model type (representation)	Score (answer, tacit knowledge, explanation, Interpretation)
Shanks, G., J. Nuredini, Tobin, Moody, Weber. (2002)	Testing the understanding of Things & Properties using 2 different representations (prelim version) using 12 subjects.	Model type (representation)	score of understanding
Shanks, G., J. Nuredini, Tobin, Tansley Weber. (2002). Empirical Evaluation of conceptual modeling practices	Summary / Progress Report on previous 3 studies (Part whole relations, things & properties, cognitive process tracing)		
Shanks, G., J. Nuredini, Tobin, Weber. (2002).	Testing the understanding of Things & Properties using 3 different representations (full version) with 33 subjects.	Model type (representation)	Score of understanding
Shoval, P. and M. Even-Chaime (1987).	Normalization vs "Information Analysis" (NIAM) as database schema design techniques using 26 subjects.	Technique NIAM vs Normalization	Quality (correctness), time, preference

Research Task	Size of Model	Results
Develop model from text description	Expert sample solution contains 23 entities, novice sample contains 12 entities	Expert modelers produced more complete models, less matching nouns (65% vs 82%), more generic entities, more use of subtypes.
Develop model from text description	Not stated	Expert data modellers models are more correct, complete, innovative, flexible, and better understood than those built by novices.
Use tool and respond to survey	N/A	Subjects found the tool useful
Use model to answer questions	Sound has 15 entities, 2 subtypes. Unsound has 11 entities, 2 subtypes. Each has 4 ternary relationships	Ontologically sound model was easier to understand (4/11 questions had significantly higher scores for the sound model)
Use model to answer questions	Not stated	The ontologically sound model was easiest to identify model segment, but took longer to articulate – in comparison to the normalised model.
Use model to answer questions	Not stated	Ontologically sound model is easier to understand & takes less time to use – in comparison to the practice model, and the entity only model.
Develop model from DFDs	Simple	Normalization better in all 3 dimensions

Reference	Nature of investigation	Independent Variable	Dependent Variable
Shoval, P. (1997). Experiment Comparisons: refers to same studies as Shovel & Frumermann & Shoval & Shiran	Comprehension (reported in Shoval and Frumermann (1994)), ease of use (Shoval and Shiran (1996), perceptions of EER vs OO data models		
Shoval, P. and Frumermann (1994)	EER vs OO using 78 subjects.	Formalism	Comprehension
Shoval, P. and Shiran (1997)	Comparison of EER and OO models for design quality using 44 subjects.	EER vs OO	Correctness, time to complete, designer preference
Siau, Wand, Benbasat (1996)	Investigate use of syntactic and semantic information using 24 subjects.	Conflicting model vs non-conflicting model	Choice of interpretation, confidence level, perceived familiarity with model
Sinha, A. P. and I. Vessey (1999)	EER, OOD, RDM, OOT comparison using 19 subjects.	Formalism, type of data model used, type of modeling construct	Accuracy
Srinivasan, A. and D. Te'eni (1995).	The data modeling process using 6, 4 subjects.	Use of heuristics	Quality of model, levels of abstraction, error patterns
Verelst (2004)	Effect of abstraction on ease of change to model using 136 subjects.	Level of absraction, complexity / magnitude of change	Time, Correctness
Weber, R. (1996) Are Attributes Entities?	Do binary modelers differentiate mentally between attributes and entities? 60 subjects.	Experience, diagram complexity	Items recalled
Yang, H. L. (2003)	Top down vs Bottom up modeling approaches – 2 experiments, 101 & 98 subjects.	Modeling Method, demographics, cognitive style	Model correctness, time, perceived ease of use, preference

Research Task	Size of Model	Results
User comprehension questionnaire	12 entities (including 4 subtypes), 9 relationships 28 attributes	EER better for ternary relationships, OO better for 'other facts', overall no significant difference.
Develop model from description	13 entities, 12 entities	EER modelers did better with unary and ternary relationships
Interpretation (mandatory or optional) of information models	8 conflicting or non-conflicting models	Modelers focus on syntactic aspects of information and Ignore the sematic information
Develop model for description	15 entities (including 9 subtypes), 8 relationships, 27 attributes.	OOD superior to EER for representation; OOT superior to RDM for generalisation; OOD-OOT superior for mapping from conceptual to logical
Develop models (a) without heuristics, (b) with heuristics	5 entities?	Certain heuristics improved performance
Change model	7-8 /15 entities	Subjects generally perform better on changes to concrete model
Recall NIAM model	7 (simple) and 20 (complex) objects	Respondents tended to recall 'entities' first.
Develop model from text / tabular form	8 entities, 3 entities, 4 entities	Semantic better in descriptive, logical better in tabular form.

Appendix – Studies of human factors in data modeling

INDEX